Shojo Beat

BABY & Me

Vol. 16

Story & Art by **Marimo Ragawa**

BABY & ME

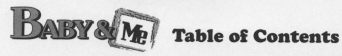

Table of Contents

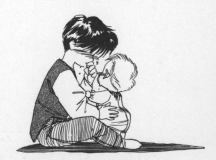

BABY & ME, Vol. 16
The Shojo Beat Manga Edition

Story & Art by
MARIMO RAGAWA

English Adaptation/Lance Caselman
Translation/JN Productions
Touch-up Art & Lettering/HudsonYards
Design/Yuki Ameda
Editor/Shaenon K. Garrity

VP, Production/Alvin Lu
VP, Publishing Licensing/Rika Inouye
VP, Sales & Product Marketing/Gonzalo Ferreyra
VP, Creative/Linda Espinosa
Publisher/Hyoe Narita

Akachan to Boku by Marimo Ragawa © Marimo Ragawa 1997. All rights reserved.
First published in Japan in 1997 by HAKUSENSHA, Inc., Tokyo. English language
translation rights arranged with HAKUSENSHA, Inc., Tokyo. The stories,
characters and incidents mentioned in this publication are entirely fictional.

Printed in Canada

Published by VIZ Media, LLC
P.O. Box 77010
San Francisco, CA 94107

Shojo Beat Manga Edition
10 9 8 7 6 5 4 3 2 1
First printing, October 2009

PARENTAL ADVISORY
BABY & ME is rated T for Teen and is
recommended for ages 13 and up. This
volume contains adult situations.
ratings.viz.com

store.viz.com

BABY & Me

Creator: Marimo Ragawa

SBM Title: *Baby & Me*

Date of Birth: September 21

Blood Type: B

Major Works: *Time Limit, Baby & Me, N.Y. N.Y.,* and *Shanimuni—Go* (Desperately—Go)

M arimo Ragawa first started submitting manga to a comic magazine when she was 12 years old. She kept up her submissions for four years, but to no avail. She decided to submit her work to the magazine *Hana to Yume*, where she received Top Prize in the Monthly Manga Contest as well as an honorable mention (Kasaku) in the magazine's Big Challenge contest. Her first manga was titled *Time Limit*. *Baby & Me* was honored with a Shogakukan Manga Award in 1995 and was spun off into an anime.

Ragawa's work showcases some very cute and expressive line work along with an incredible ability to depict complex emotions and relationships. Some of her other works include *N.Y. N.Y.* and the tennis manga *Shanimuni—Go*.

Ragawa has two brothers and two sisters.

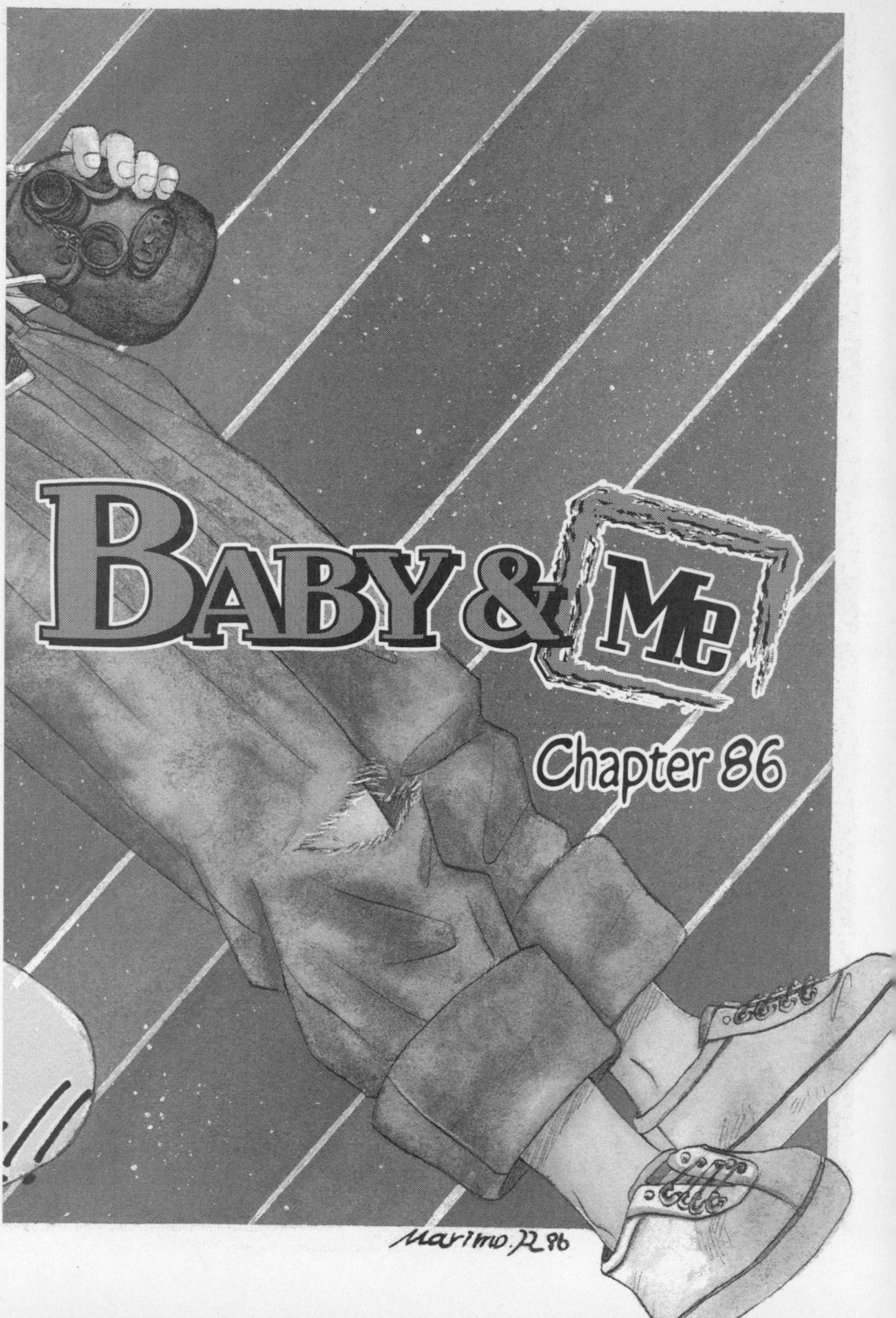
BABY & ME
Chapter 86
Marimo.R 96

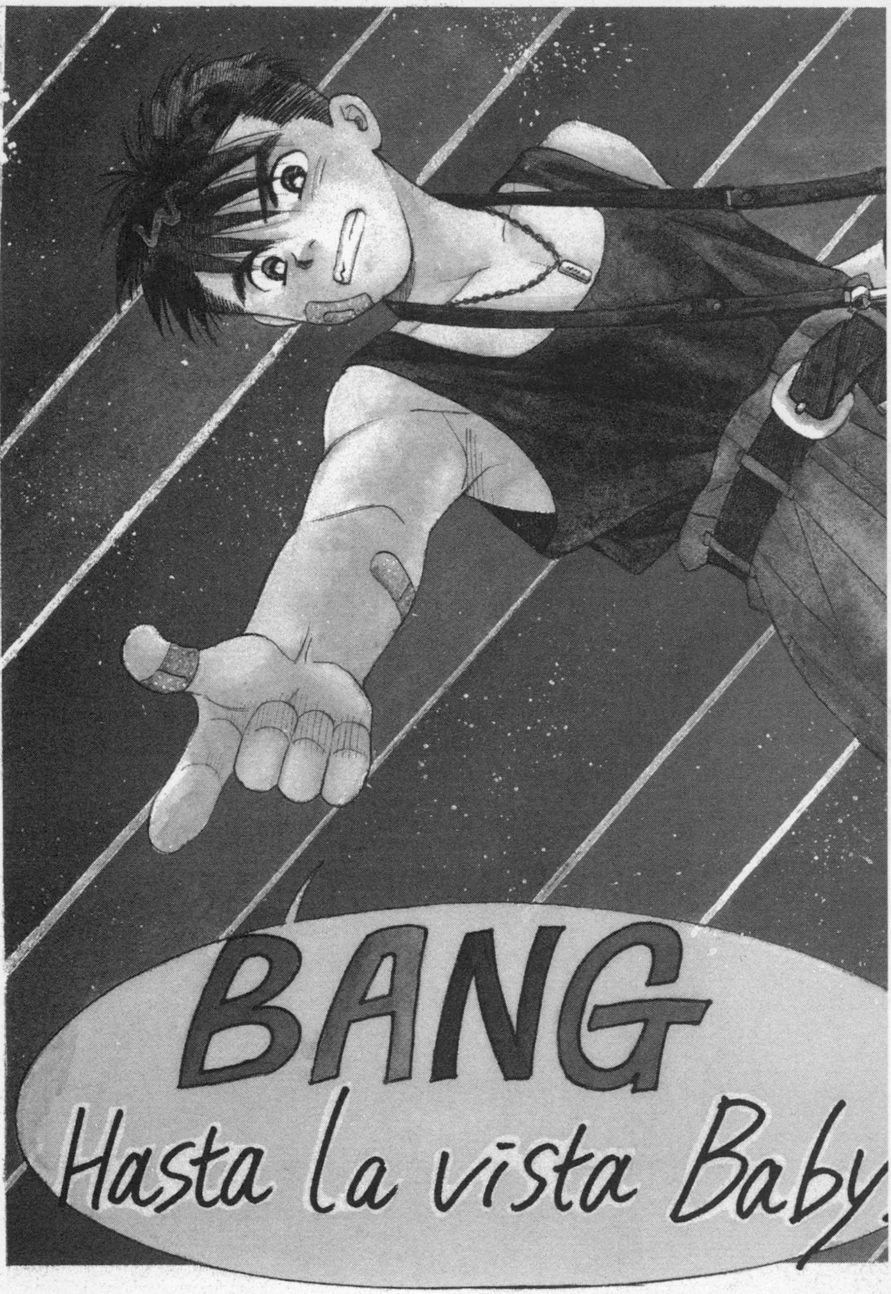
BANG
Hasta la vista Baby.

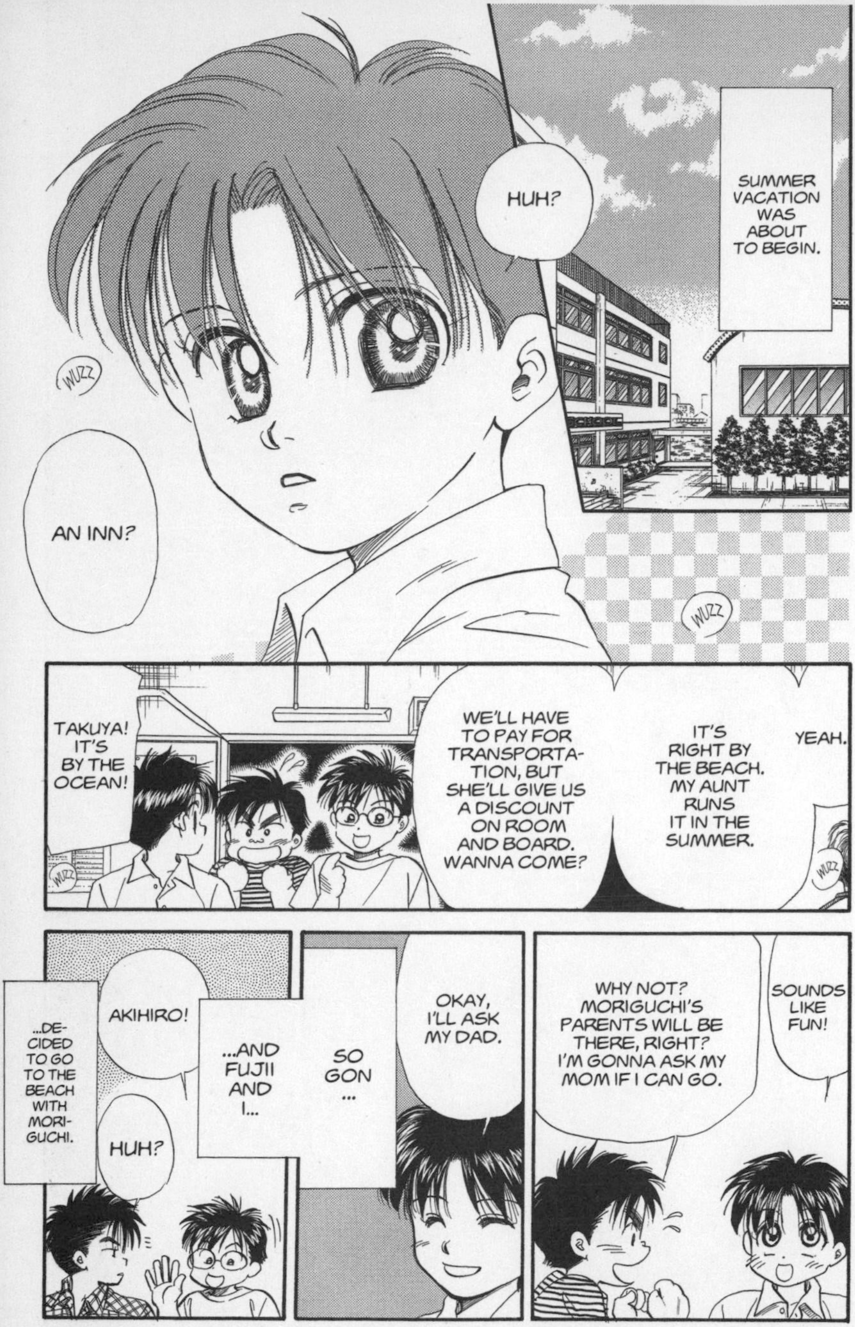
SUMMER VACATION WAS ABOUT TO BEGIN.
HUH?
WUZZ
AN INN?
WUZZ
YEAH.
IT'S RIGHT BY THE BEACH. MY AUNT RUNS IT IN THE SUMMER.
WUZZ
WE'LL HAVE TO PAY FOR TRANSPORTATION, BUT SHE'LL GIVE US A DISCOUNT ON ROOM AND BOARD. WANNA COME?
TAKUYA! IT'S BY THE OCEAN!
WUZZ
SOUNDS LIKE FUN!
WHY NOT? MORIGUCHI'S PARENTS WILL BE THERE, RIGHT? I'M GONNA ASK MY MOM IF I CAN GO.
OKAY, I'LL ASK MY DAD.
SO GON ...
...AND FUJII AND I...
AKIHIRO!
HUH?
...DECIDED TO GO TO THE BEACH WITH MORIGUCHI.

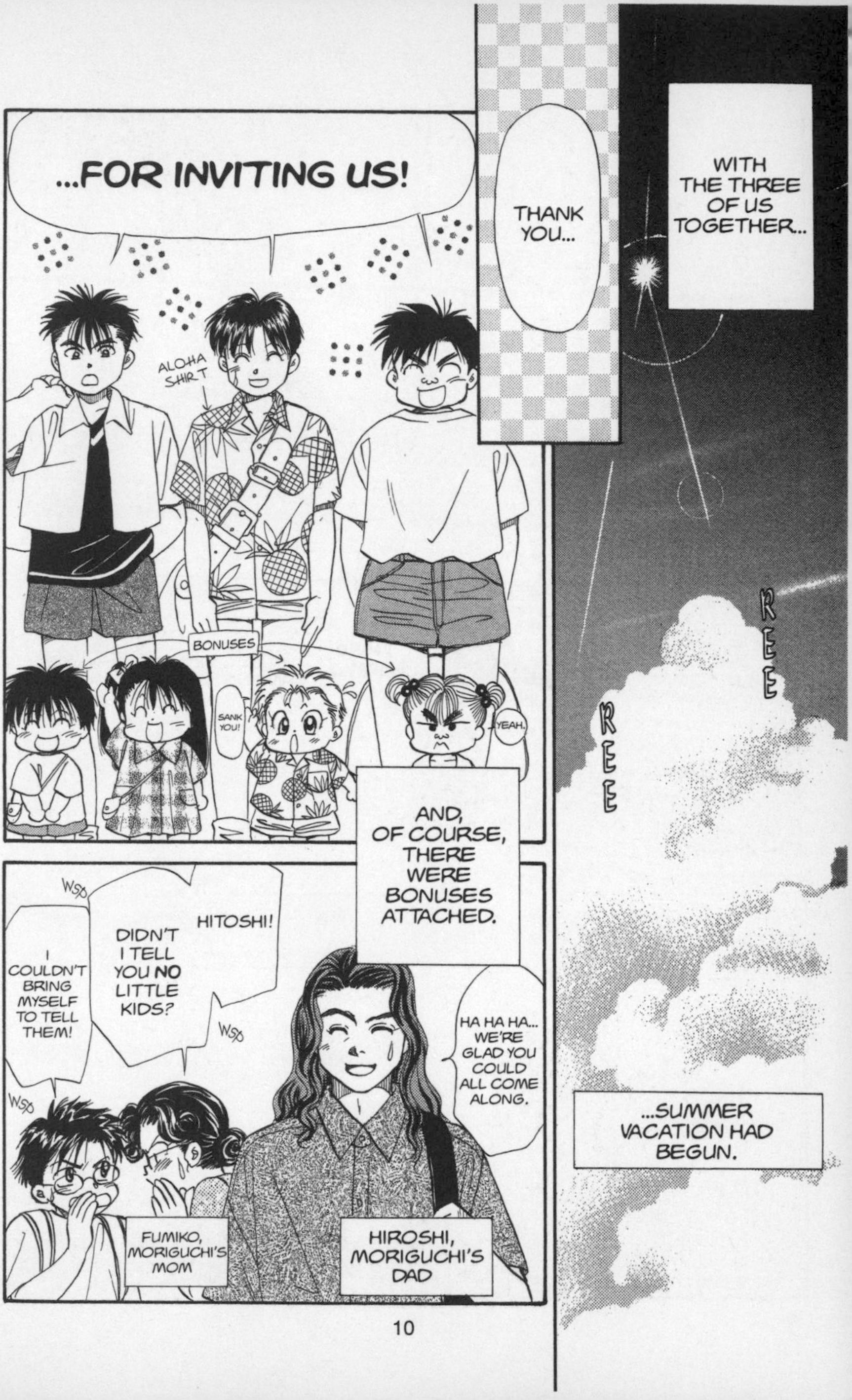
WITH THE THREE OF US TOGETHER...
REE REE
REE REE
...SUMMER VACATION HAD BEGUN.
THANK YOU...
...FOR INVITING US!
ALOHA SHIRT
BONUSES
YEAH.
SANK YOU!
AND, OF COURSE, THERE WERE BONUSES ATTACHED.
HA HA HA... WE'RE GLAD YOU COULD ALL COME ALONG.
HITOSHI!
DIDN'T I TELL YOU NO LITTLE KIDS?
I COULDN'T BRING MYSELF TO TELL THEM!
HIROSHI, MORIGUCHI'S DAD
FUMIKO, MORIGUCHI'S MOM

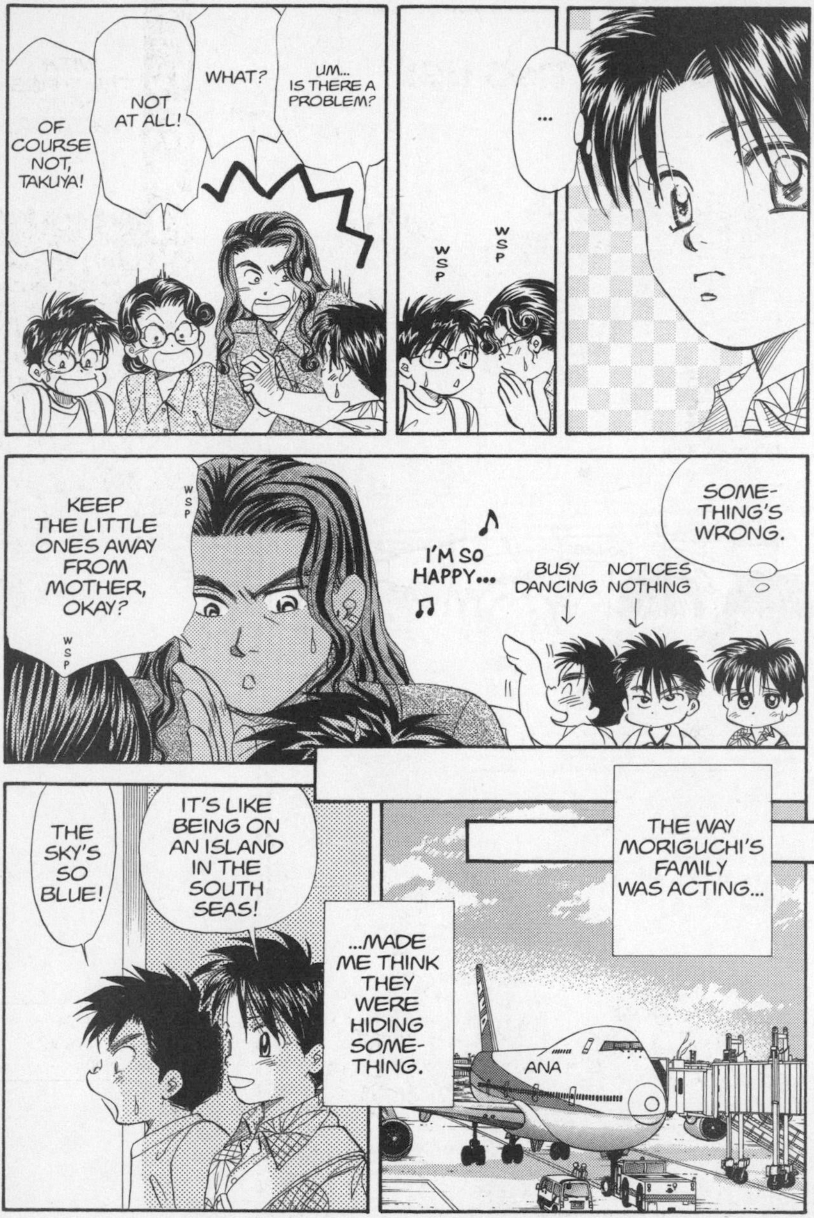
...
WSP
WSP
UM... IS THERE A PROBLEM?
WHAT?
NOT AT ALL!
OF COURSE NOT, TAKUYA!
SOME-THING'S WRONG.
NOTICES NOTHING
BUSY DANCING
I'M SO HAPPY...
WSP
KEEP THE LITTLE ONES AWAY FROM MOTHER, OKAY?
WSP
THE WAY MORIGUCHI'S FAMILY WAS ACTING...
...MADE ME THINK THEY WERE HIDING SOME-THING.
ANA
IT'S LIKE BEING ON AN ISLAND IN THE SOUTH SEAS!
THE SKY'S SO BLUE!

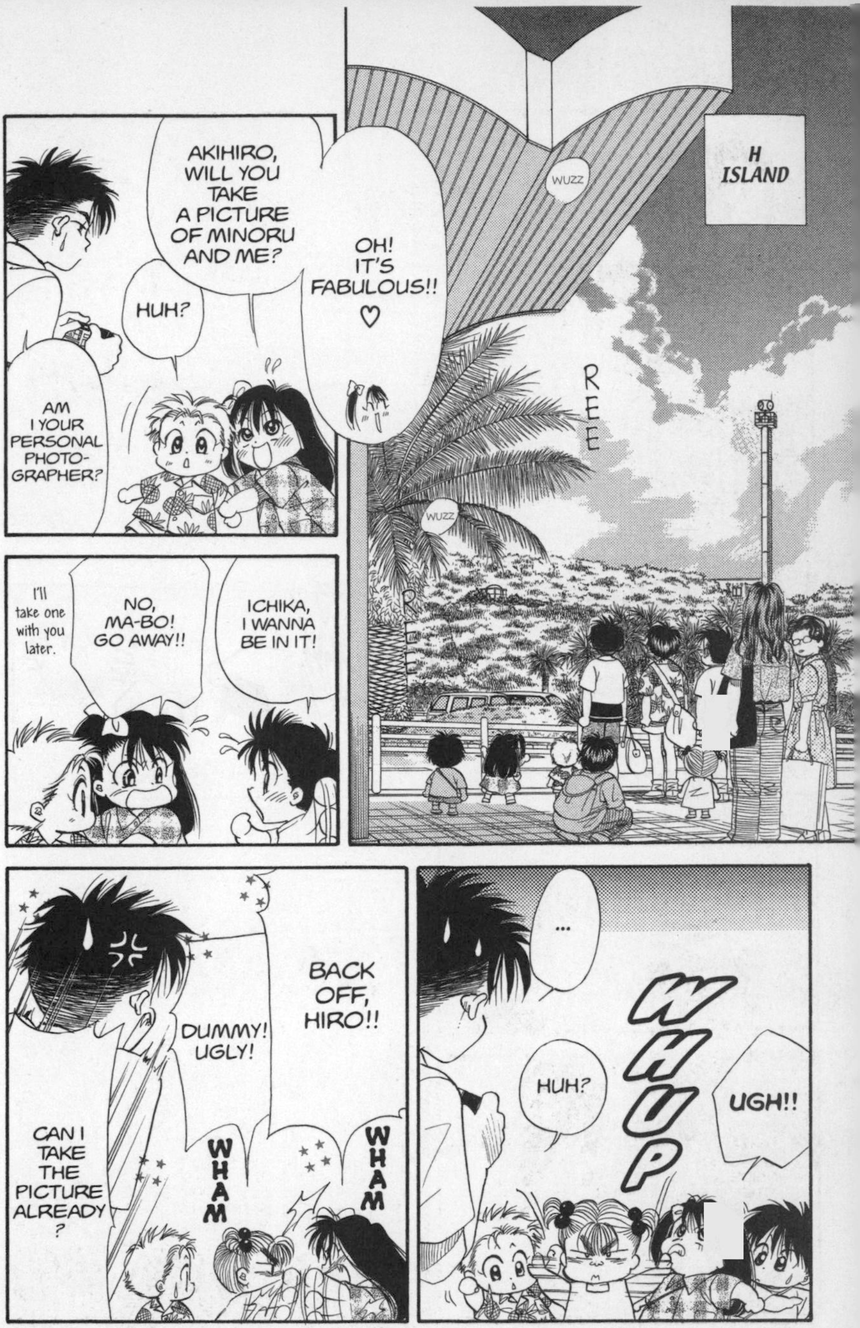
H ISLAND
WUZZ
OH! IT'S FABULOUS!! ♡
REE
WUZZ
REE
AKIHIRO, WILL YOU TAKE A PICTURE OF MINORU AND ME?
HUH?
AM I YOUR PERSONAL PHOTO-GRAPHER?
ICHIKA, I WANNA BE IN IT!
NO, MA-BO! GO AWAY!!
I'll take one with you later.
...
WHUP
UGH!!
HUH?
BACK OFF, HIRO!!
WHAM
DUMMY! UGLY!
WHAM
CAN I TAKE THE PICTURE ALREADY?

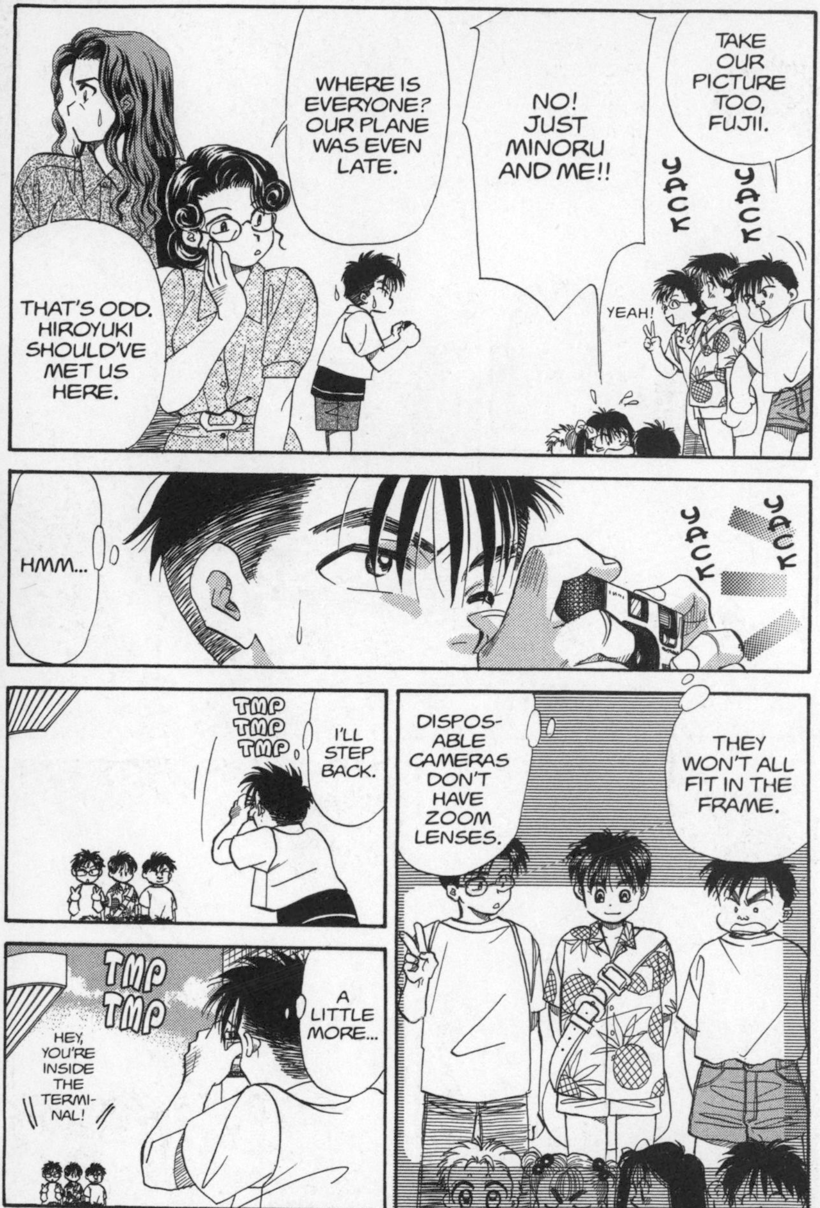
TAKE OUR PICTURE TOO, FUJII.
YACK YACK
NO! JUST MINORU AND ME!!
YEAH!
WHERE IS EVERYONE? OUR PLANE WAS EVEN LATE.
THAT'S ODD. HIROYUKI SHOULD'VE MET US HERE.
YACK YACK
HMM...
THEY WON'T ALL FIT IN THE FRAME.
DISPOS-ABLE CAMERAS DON'T HAVE ZOOM LENSES.
I'LL STEP BACK.
TMP TMP TMP
A LITTLE MORE...
TMP TMP
HEY, YOU'RE INSIDE THE TERMI-NAL!

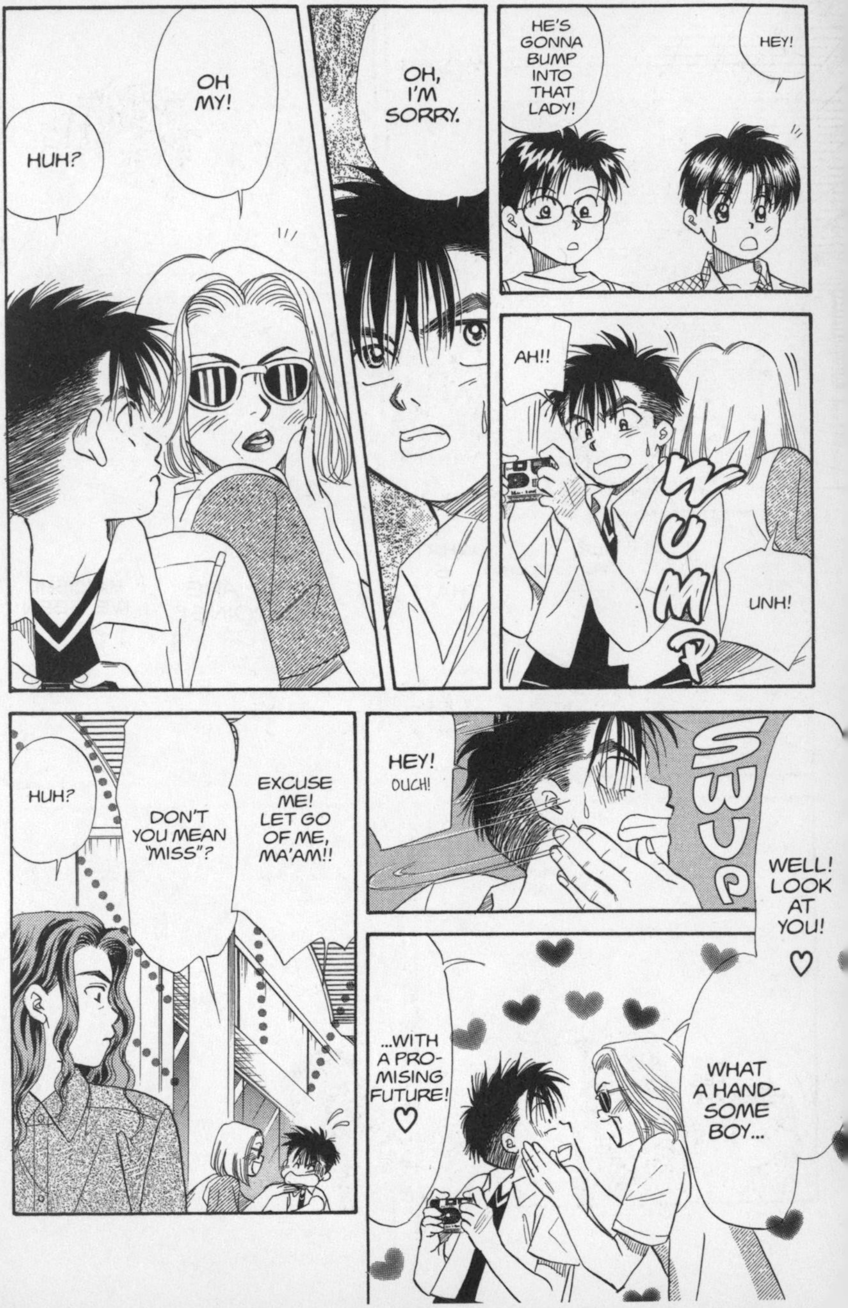
HEY!
HE'S GONNA BUMP INTO THAT LADY!
AH!!
WUMP
UNH!
OH, I'M SORRY.
OH MY!
HUH?
SWUP
HEY! OUCH!
WELL! LOOK AT YOU! ♡
WHAT A HAND-SOME BOY...
...WITH A PRO-MISING FUTURE! ♡
EXCUSE ME! LET GO OF ME, MA'AM!!
DON'T YOU MEAN "MISS"?
HUH?

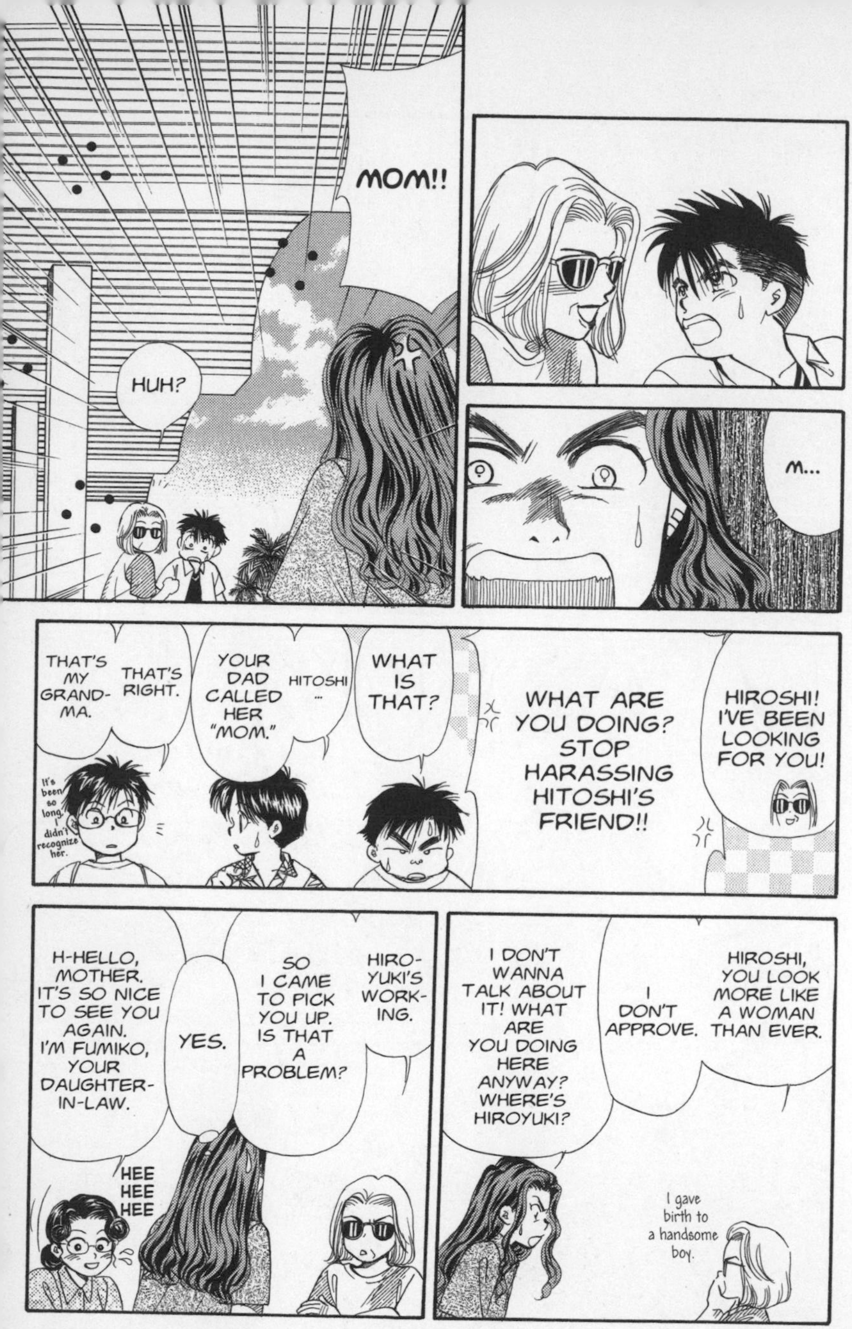
M...
MOM!!
HUH?
HIROSHI! I'VE BEEN LOOKING FOR YOU!
WHAT ARE YOU DOING? STOP HARASSING HITOSHI'S FRIEND!!
WHAT IS THAT?
HITOSHI ...
YOUR DAD CALLED HER "MOM."
THAT'S RIGHT.
THAT'S MY GRANDMA.
It's been so long, I didn't recognize her.
HIROSHI, YOU LOOK MORE LIKE A WOMAN THAN EVER.
I DON'T APPROVE.
I DON'T WANNA TALK ABOUT IT! WHAT ARE YOU DOING HERE ANYWAY? WHERE'S HIROYUKI?
I gave birth to a handsome boy.
HIROYUKI'S WORKING.
SO I CAME TO PICK YOU UP. IS THAT A PROBLEM?
YES.
H-HELLO, MOTHER. IT'S SO NICE TO SEE YOU AGAIN. I'M FUMIKO, YOUR DAUGHTER-IN-LAW.
HEE HEE HEE

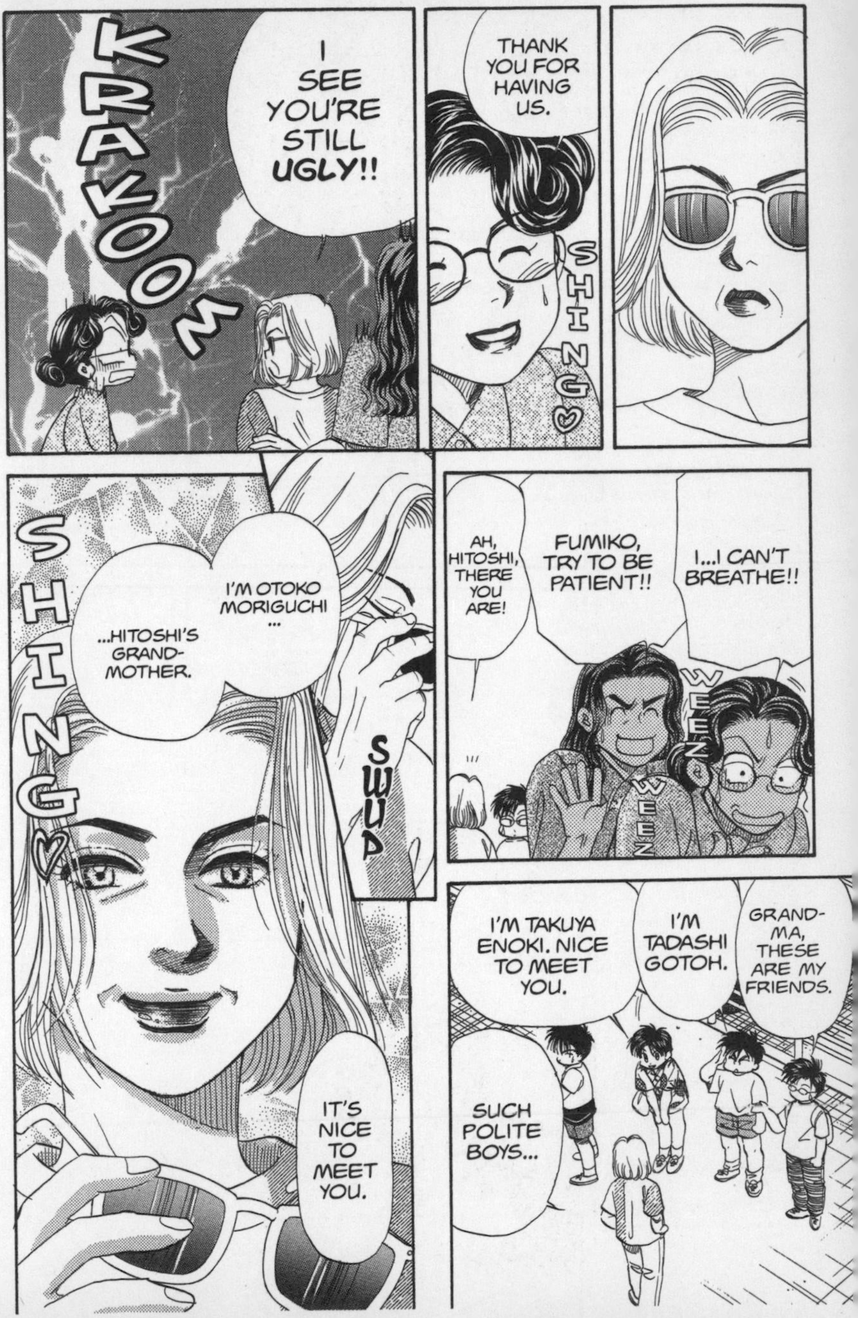
THANK YOU FOR HAVING US.
SHING
I SEE YOU'RE STILL UGLY!!
KRAKOOM
I...I CAN'T BREATHE!!
FUMIKO, TRY TO BE PATIENT!!
AH, HITOSHI, THERE YOU ARE!
WEEZ
WEEZ
GRAND-MA, THESE ARE MY FRIENDS.
I'M TADASHI GOTOH.
I'M TAKUYA ENOKI. NICE TO MEET YOU.
SUCH POLITE BOYS...
SWUP
I'M OTOKO MORIGUCHI ...
...HITOSHI'S GRAND-MOTHER.
SHING
IT'S NICE TO MEET YOU.

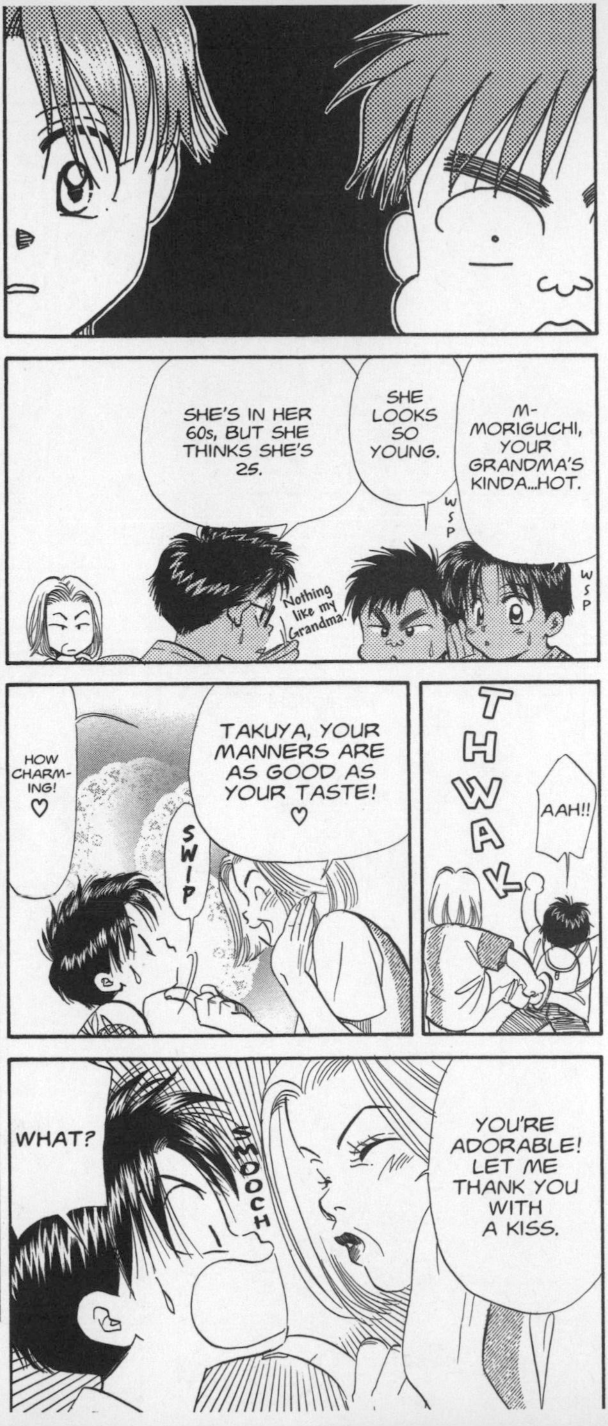
M-MORIGUCHI, YOUR GRANDMA'S KINDA...HOT.
WSP
SHE LOOKS SO YOUNG.
WSP
SHE'S IN HER 60s, BUT SHE THINKS SHE'S 25.
Nothing like my Grandma.
THWAK
AAH!!
TAKUYA, YOUR MANNERS ARE AS GOOD AS YOUR TASTE! ♡
SWIP
HOW CHARMING! ♡
YOU'RE ADORABLE! LET ME THANK YOU WITH A KISS.
SMOOCH
WHAT?

Author's Note Part 1

Ciao! Marimo Ragawa here. This is volume 16 of Baby & Me. Time really does fly. It seems like just yesterday we were working on volume 10. Unbelievable. As a manga artist, sometimes I feel like I'm stuck in a time warp. I often find myself writing the wrong year when I sign autographs and illustrations. The people around me change, but Iseem to stay the same. I haven't changed my makeup or clothing style for years. When I realized that, I was embarrassed. That's it! It's time for me to become a grown woman!

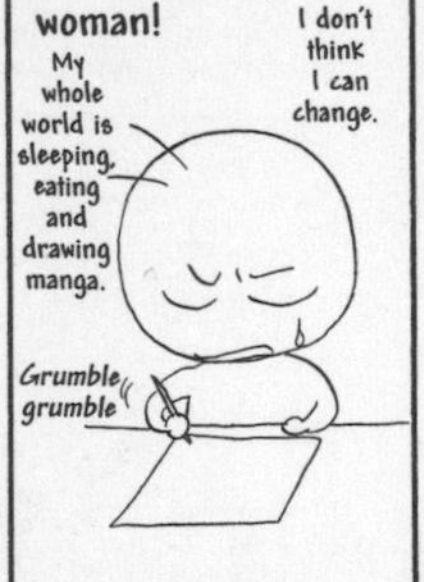
I don't think I can change.
My whole world is sleeping, eating and drawing manga.
Grumble grumble

The complaint of someone in her 20s... I haven't matured much either.

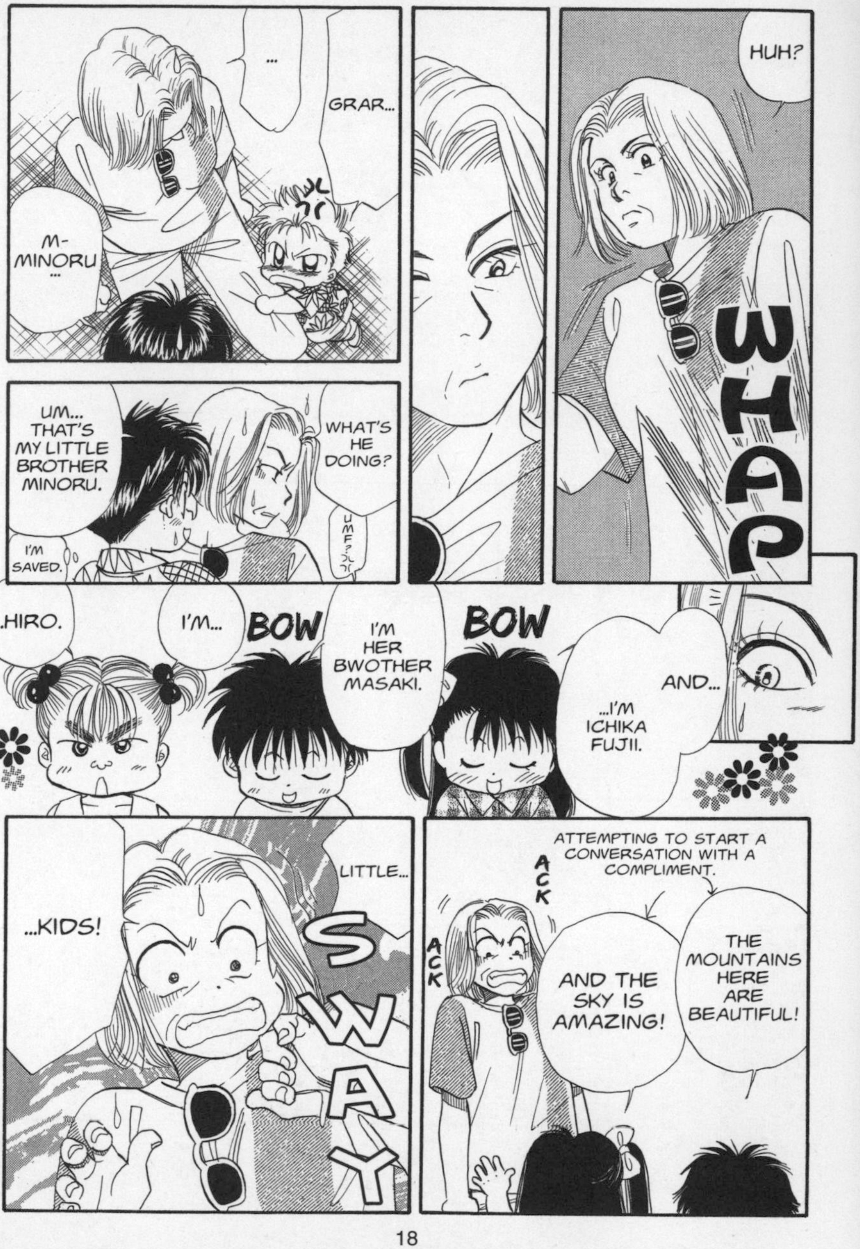
HUH?
WHAP
...
GRAR...
M-MINORU...
WHAT'S HE DOING?
UM... THAT'S MY LITTLE BROTHER MINORU.
UMF?
I'M SAVED.
AND...
...I'M ICHIKA FUJII.
BOW
I'M HER BWOTHER MASAKI.
BOW
I'M...
...HIRO.
ATTEMPTING TO START A CONVERSATION WITH A COMPLIMENT.
THE MOUNTAINS HERE ARE BEAUTIFUL!
AND THE SKY IS AMAZING!
ACK
ACK
LITTLE...
...KIDS!
SWAY

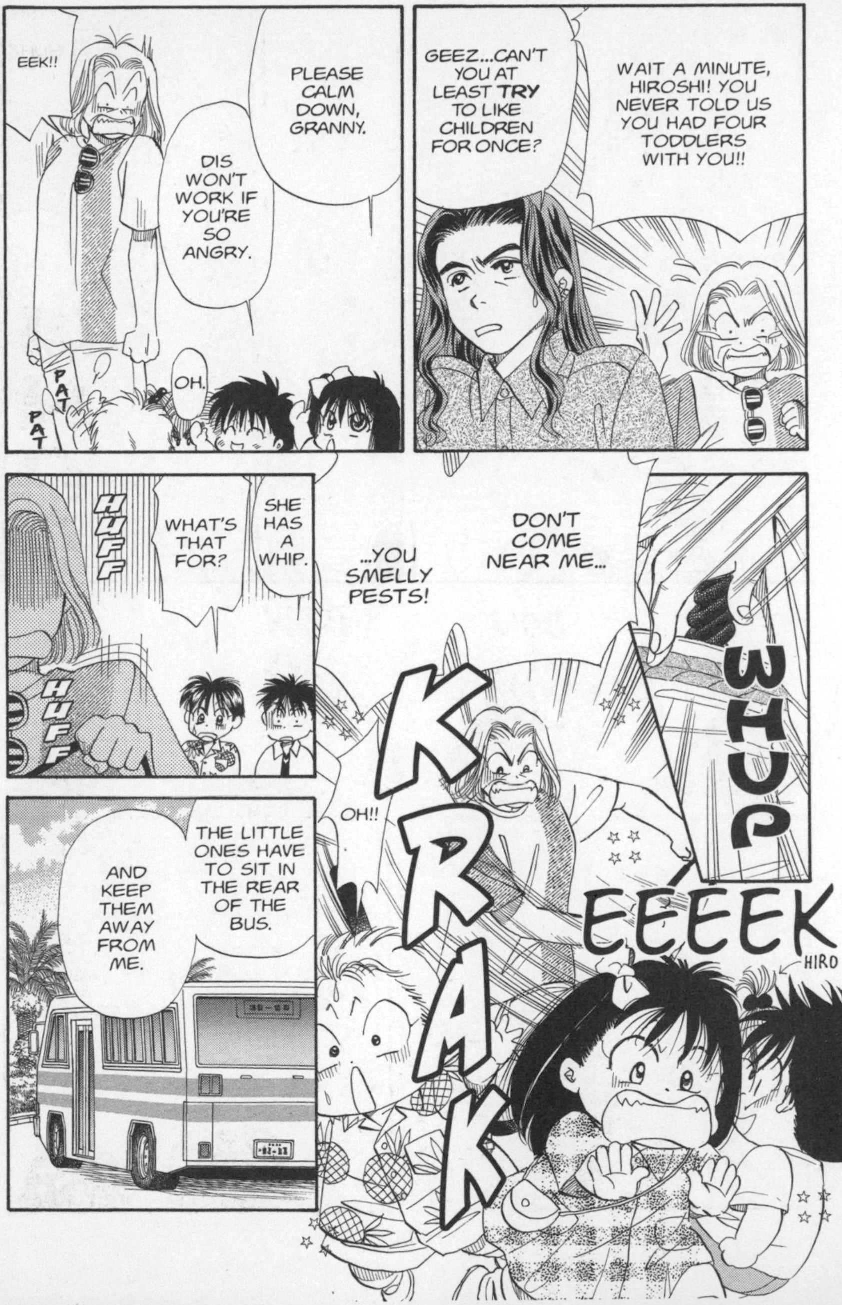
WAIT A MINUTE, HIROSHI! YOU NEVER TOLD US YOU HAD FOUR TODDLERS WITH YOU!!
GEEZ...CAN'T YOU AT LEAST **TRY** TO LIKE CHILDREN FOR ONCE?
PLEASE CALM DOWN, GRANNY.
EEK!!
DIS WON'T WORK IF YOU'RE SO ANGRY.
OH.
PAT
PAT
DON'T COME NEAR ME...
...YOU SMELLY PESTS!
WHUP
KRAK
OH!!
EEEEK
HIRO
SHE HAS A WHIP.
WHAT'S THAT FOR?
HUFF
HUFF
THE LITTLE ONES HAVE TO SIT IN THE REAR OF THE BUS.
AND KEEP THEM AWAY FROM ME.

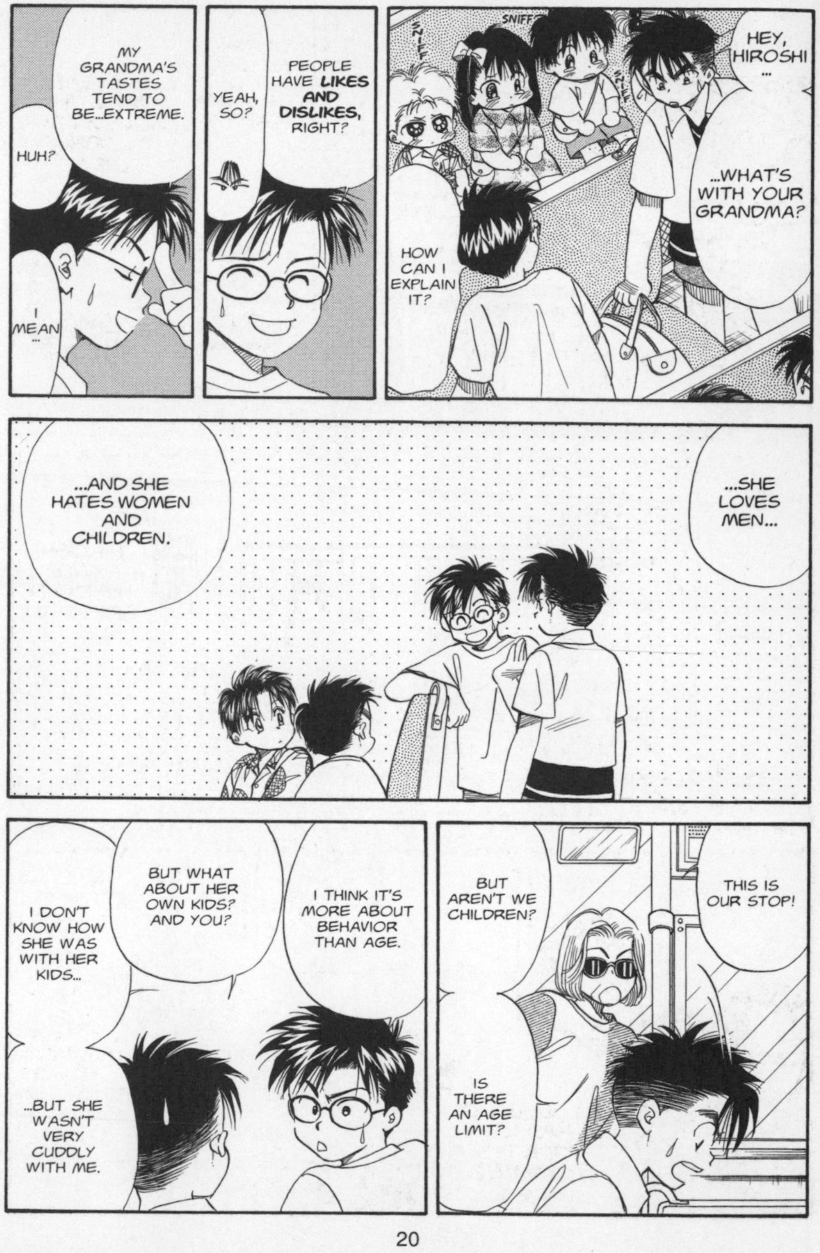
HEY, HIROSHI ...
SNIFF
SNIFF
SNIFF
...WHAT'S WITH YOUR GRANDMA?
HOW CAN I EXPLAIN IT?
PEOPLE HAVE LIKES AND DISLIKES, RIGHT?
YEAH, SO?
MY GRANDMA'S TASTES TEND TO BE...EXTREME.
HUH?
I MEAN ...
...SHE LOVES MEN...
...AND SHE HATES WOMEN AND CHILDREN.
THIS IS OUR STOP!
BUT AREN'T WE CHILDREN?
IS THERE AN AGE LIMIT?
I THINK IT'S MORE ABOUT BEHAVIOR THAN AGE.
BUT WHAT ABOUT HER OWN KIDS? AND YOU?
I DON'T KNOW HOW SHE WAS WITH HER KIDS...
...BUT SHE WASN'T VERY CUDDLY WITH ME.

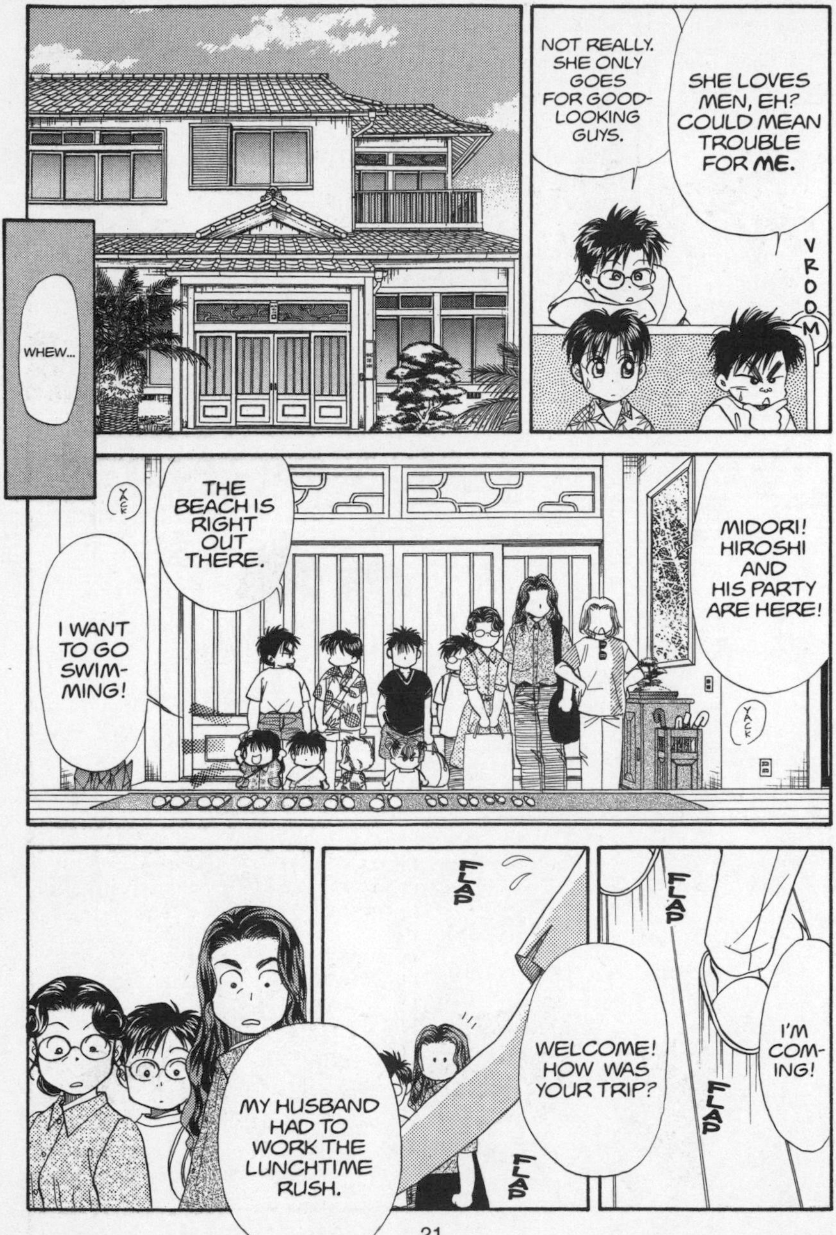

SHE LOVES MEN, EH? COULD MEAN TROUBLE FOR **ME**.
NOT REALLY. SHE ONLY GOES FOR GOOD-LOOKING GUYS.
VROOM
WHEW...
MIDORI! HIROSHI AND HIS PARTY ARE HERE!
YACK
THE BEACH IS RIGHT OUT THERE.
I WANT TO GO SWIM-MING!
YACK
FLAP
I'M COM-ING!
FLAP
FLAP
WELCOME! HOW WAS YOUR TRIP?
FLAP
MY HUSBAND HAD TO WORK THE LUNCHTIME RUSH.

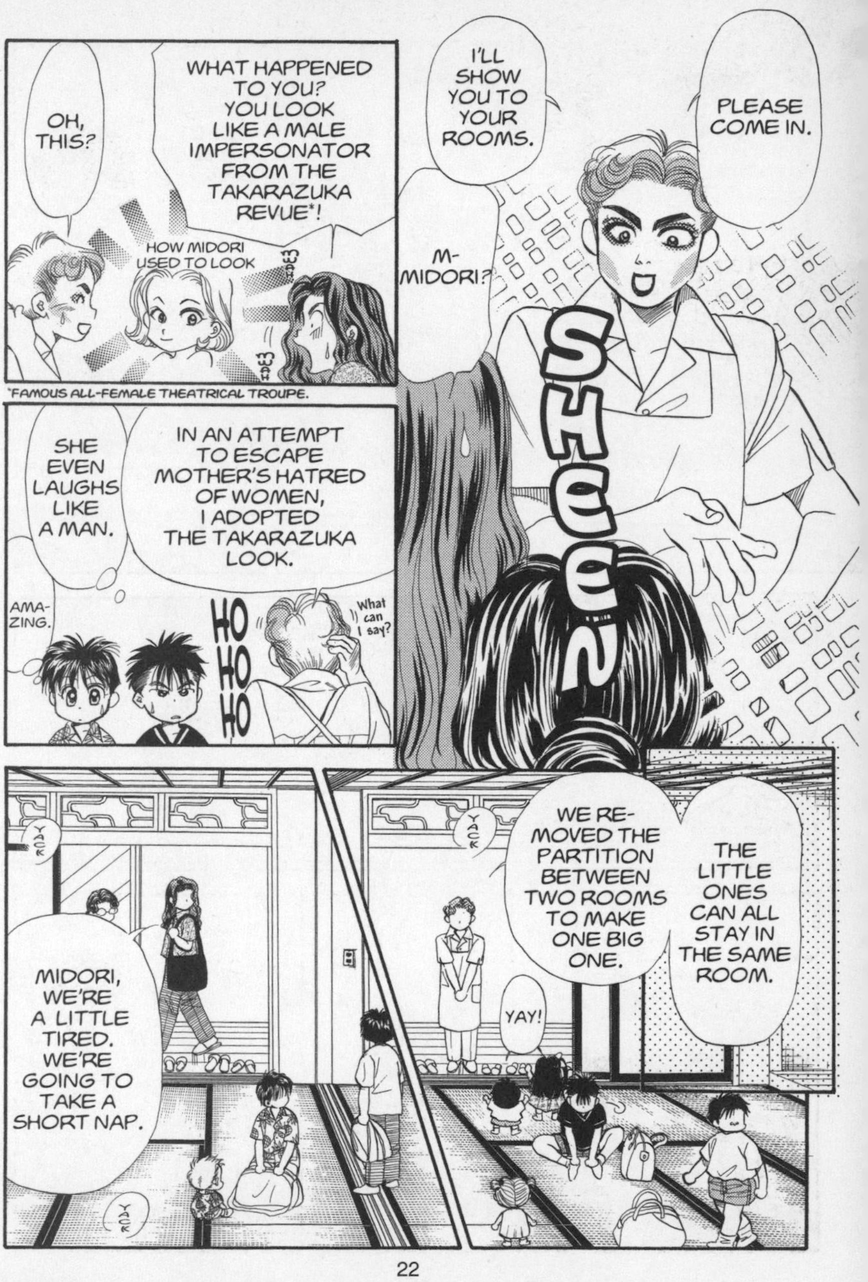
PLEASE COME IN.
I'LL SHOW YOU TO YOUR ROOMS.
M-MIDORI?
SHEEN
WHAT HAPPENED TO YOU? YOU LOOK LIKE A MALE IMPERSONATOR FROM THE TAKARAZUKA REVUE*!
OH, THIS?
HOW MIDORI USED TO LOOK
IN AN ATTEMPT TO ESCAPE MOTHER'S HATRED OF WOMEN, I ADOPTED THE TAKARAZUKA LOOK.
SHE EVEN LAUGHS LIKE A MAN.
What can I say?
HO HO HO
AMA-ZING.
THE LITTLE ONES CAN ALL STAY IN THE SAME ROOM.
WE RE-MOVED THE PARTITION BETWEEN TWO ROOMS TO MAKE ONE BIG ONE.
YACK
YAY!
YACK
MIDORI, WE'RE A LITTLE TIRED. WE'RE GOING TO TAKE A SHORT NAP.
YACK

*FAMOUS ALL-FEMALE THEATRICAL TROUPE.

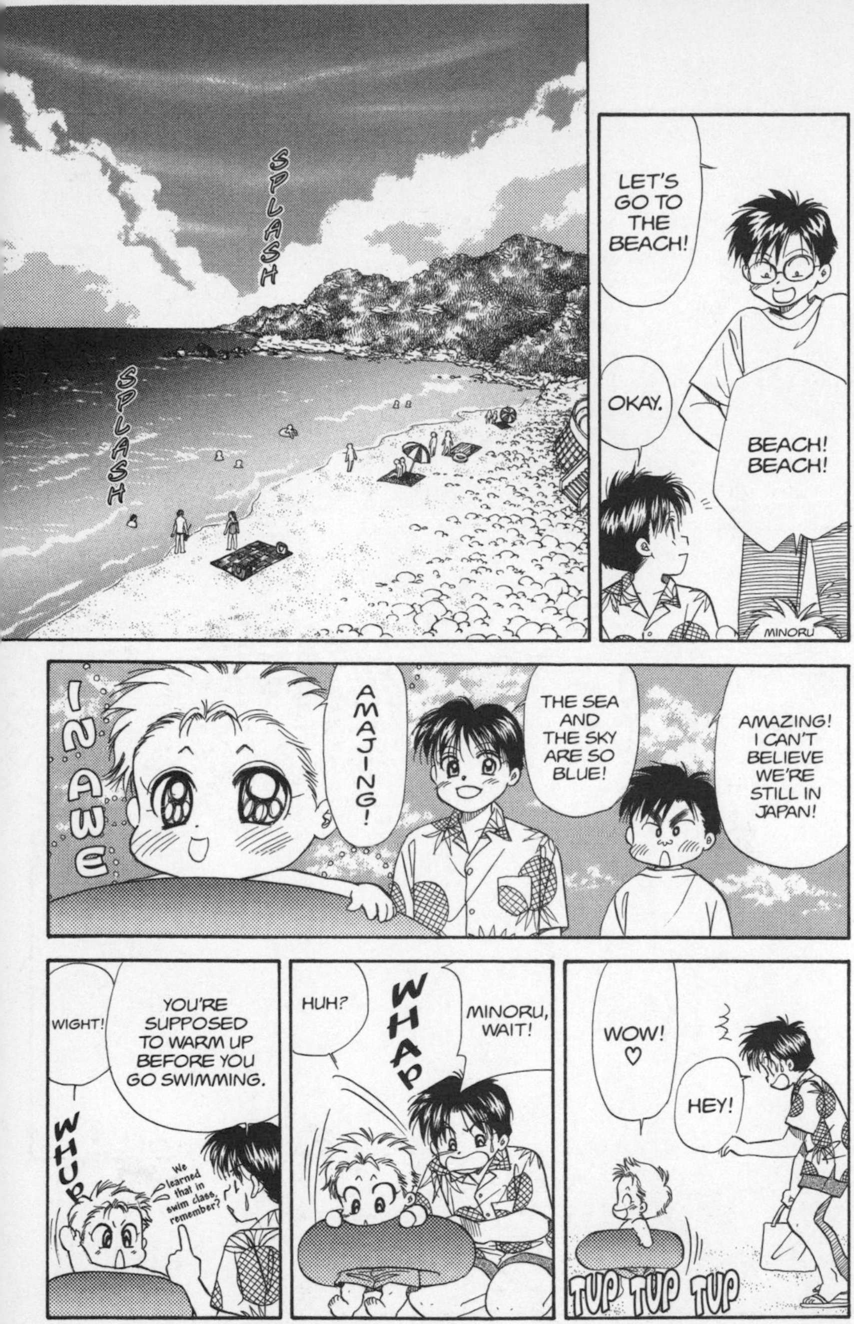
LET'S GO TO THE BEACH!
BEACH! BEACH!
OKAY.
MINORU
SPLASH
SPLASH
AMAZING! I CAN'T BELIEVE WE'RE STILL IN JAPAN!
THE SEA AND THE SKY ARE SO BLUE!
AMAJING!
IN AWE
WOW! ♡
HEY!
TUP TUP TUP
MINORU, WAIT!
WHAP
HUH?
YOU'RE SUPPOSED TO WARM UP BEFORE YOU GO SWIMMING.
WIGHT!
WHUP
We learned that in swim class, remember?

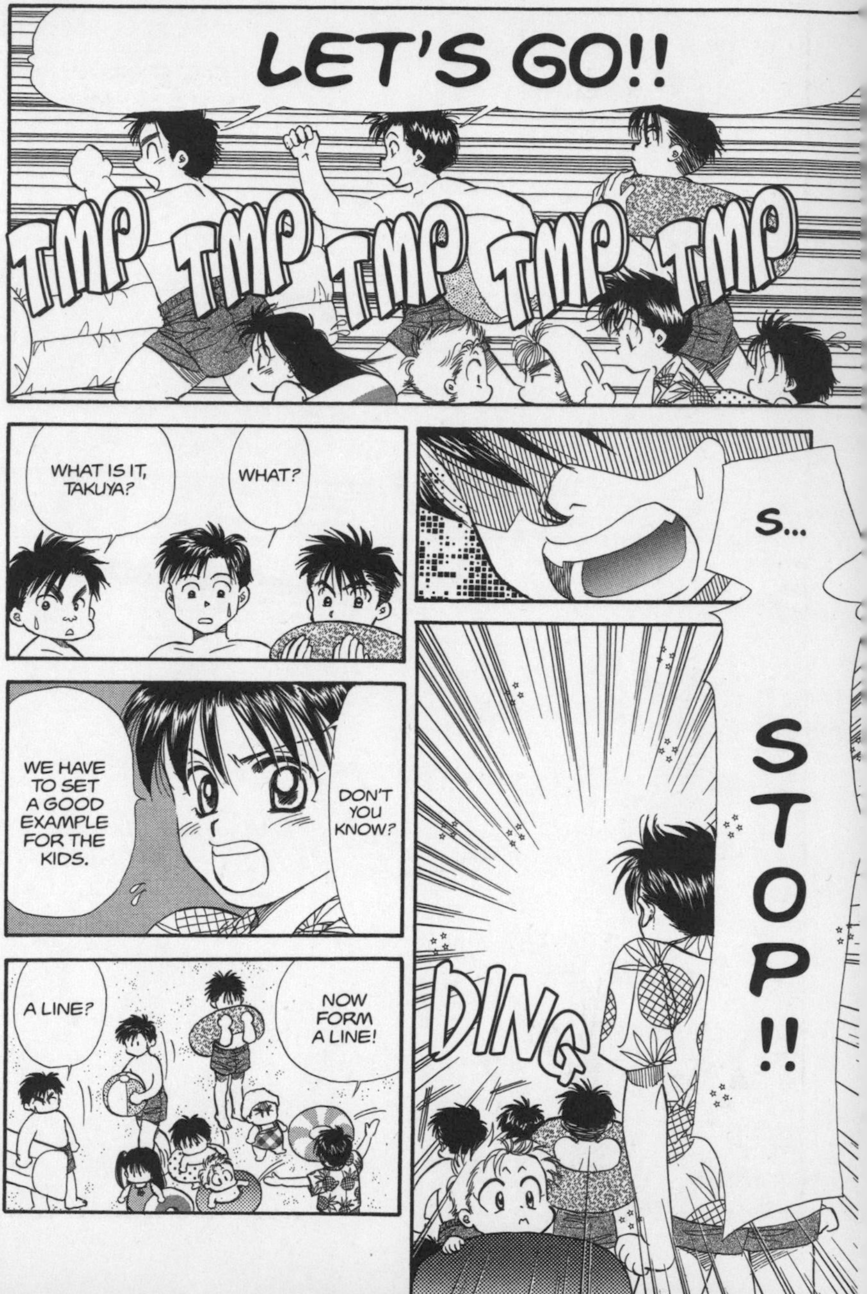
LET'S GO!!
TMP TMP TMP TMP TMP
S...
STOP!!
DING
WHAT?
WHAT IS IT, TAKUYA?
DON'T YOU KNOW?
WE HAVE TO SET A GOOD EXAMPLE FOR THE KIDS.
NOW FORM A LINE!
A LINE?

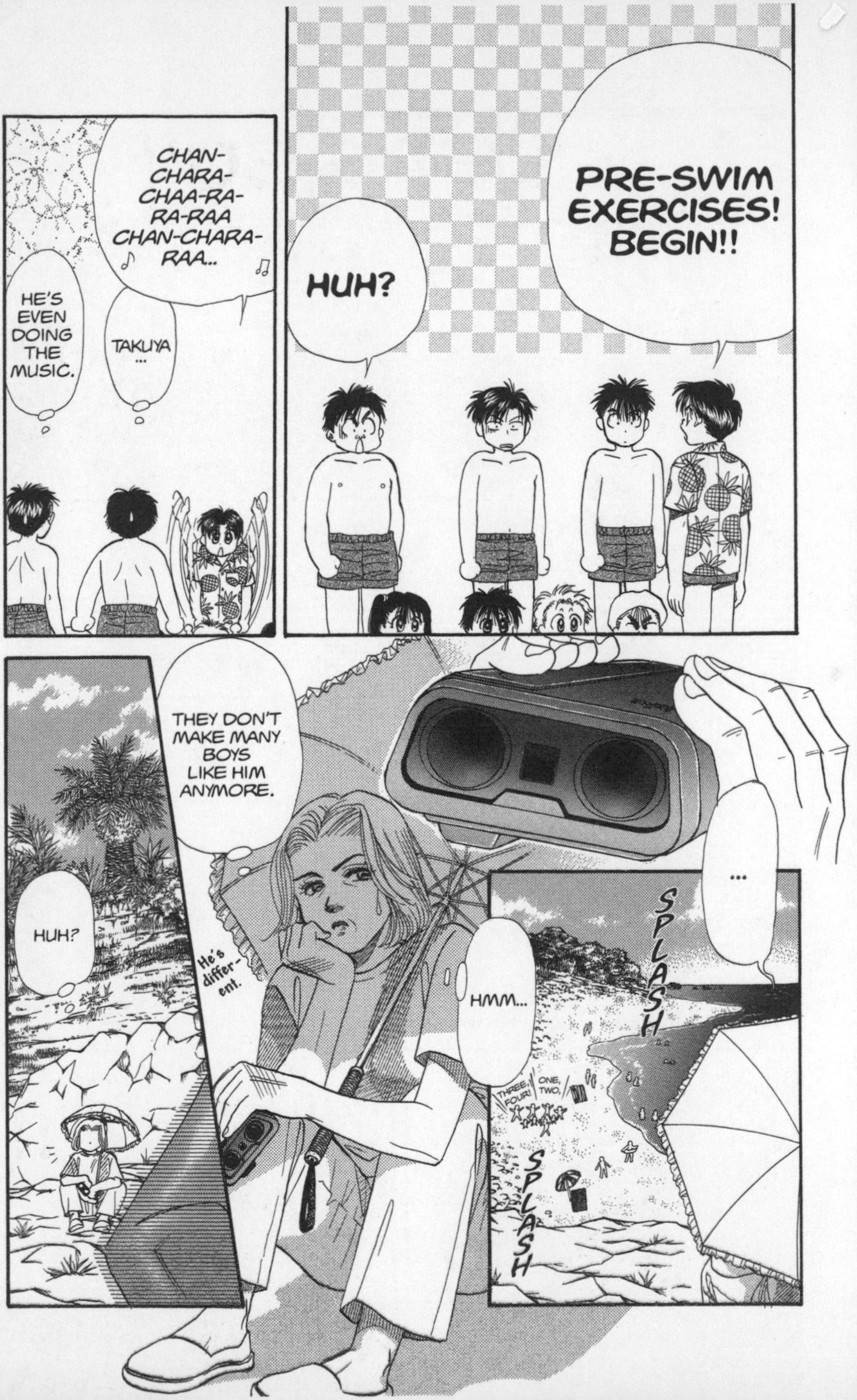
PRE-SWIM EXERCISES! BEGIN!!
HUH?
CHAN-CHARA-CHAA-RA-RA-RAA CHAN-CHARA-RAA...
TAKUYA...
HE'S EVEN DOING THE MUSIC.
...
SPLASH
HMM...
ONE, TWO,
THREE, FOUR!
SPLASH
THEY DON'T MAKE MANY BOYS LIKE HIM ANYMORE.
He's different.
HUH?

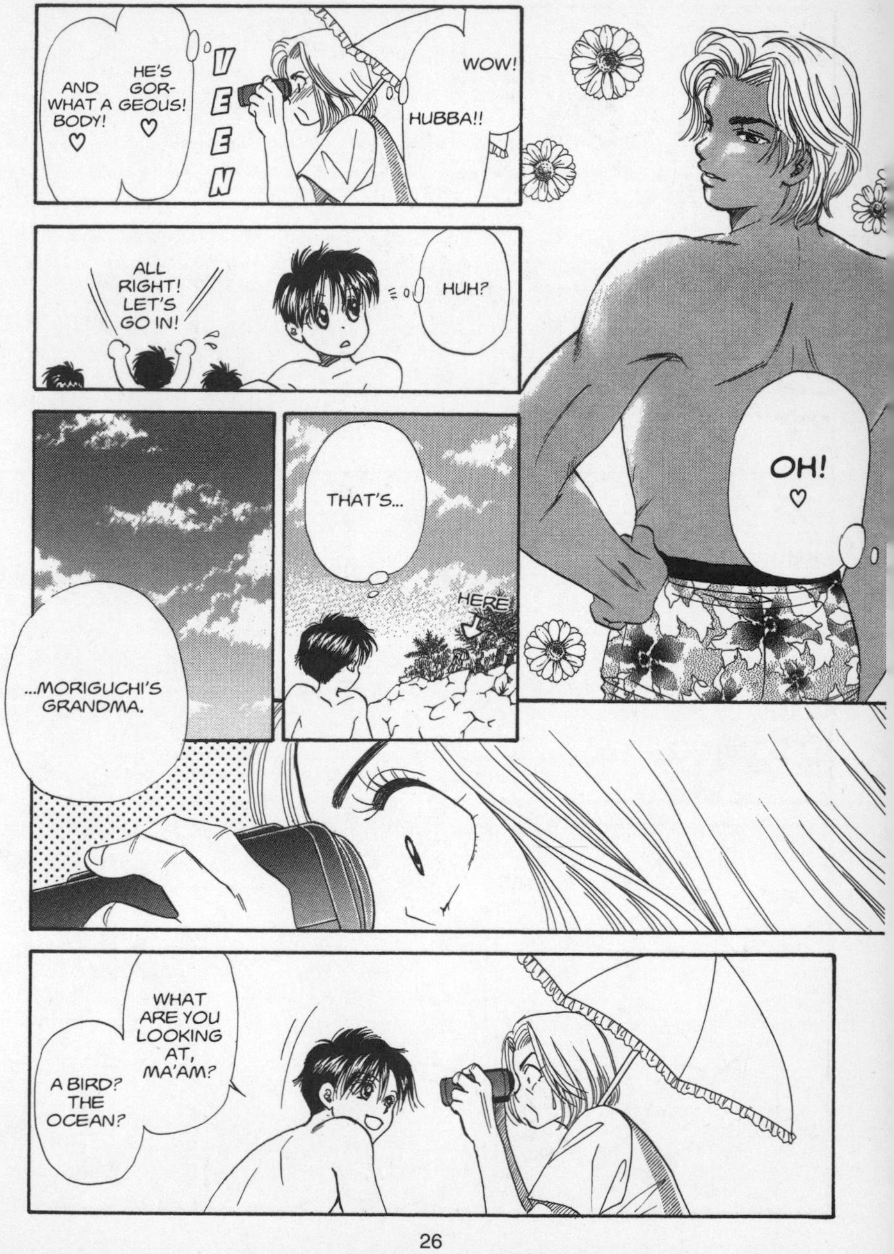
OH! ♡
WOW!
HUBBA!!
HE'S GOR-GEOUS! ♡
AND WHAT A BODY! ♡
VEEN
HUH?
ALL RIGHT! LET'S GO IN!
THAT'S...
HERE
...MORIGUCHI'S GRANDMA.
WHAT ARE YOU LOOKING AT, MA'AM?
A BIRD? THE OCEAN?

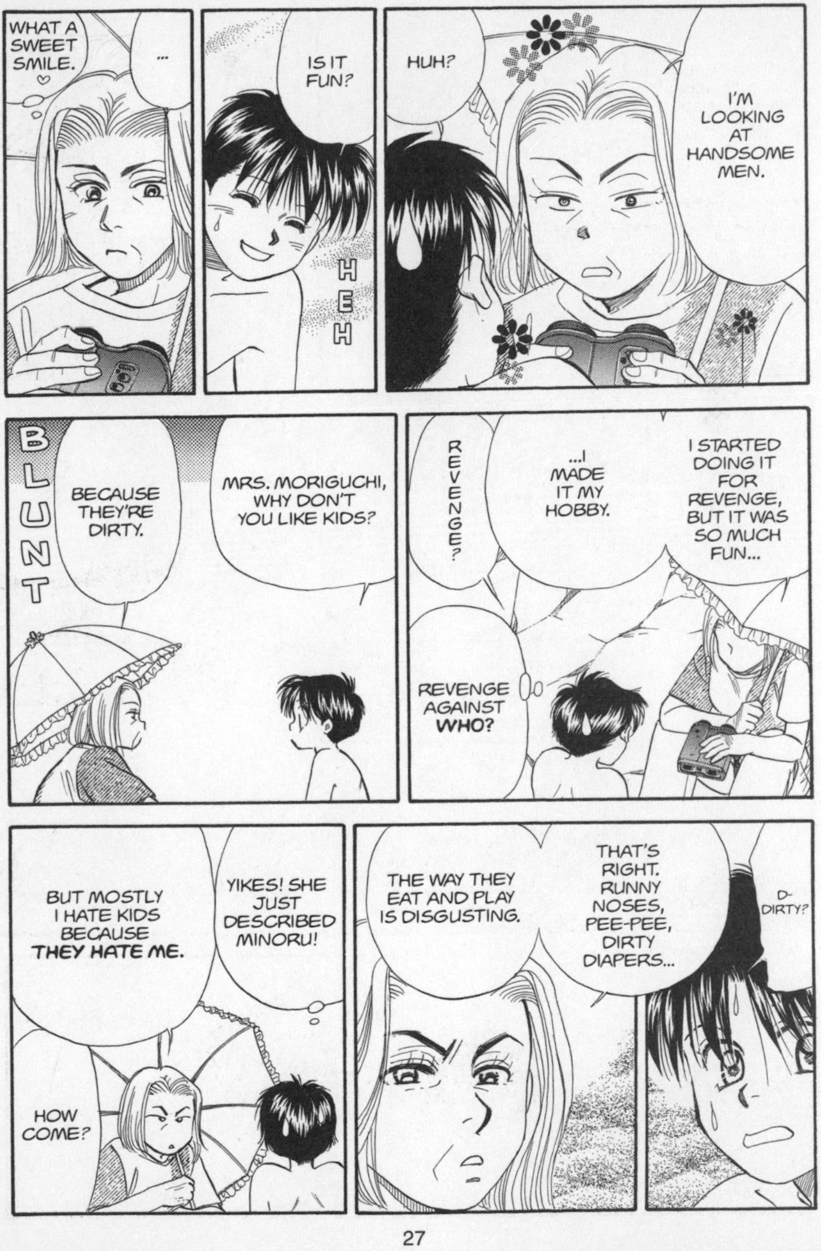
HUH?
I'M LOOKING AT HANDSOME MEN.
IS IT FUN?
HEH
...
WHAT A SWEET SMILE. ♡
I STARTED DOING IT FOR REVENGE, BUT IT WAS SO MUCH FUN...
...I MADE IT MY HOBBY.
REVENGE?
REVENGE AGAINST **WHO?**
MRS. MORIGUCHI, WHY DON'T YOU LIKE KIDS?
BECAUSE THEY'RE DIRTY.
BLUNT
D-DIRTY?
THAT'S RIGHT. RUNNY NOSES, PEE-PEE, DIRTY DIAPERS...
THE WAY THEY EAT AND PLAY IS DISGUSTING.
YIKES! SHE JUST DESCRIBED MINORU!
BUT MOSTLY I HATE KIDS BECAUSE **THEY HATE ME.**
HOW COME?

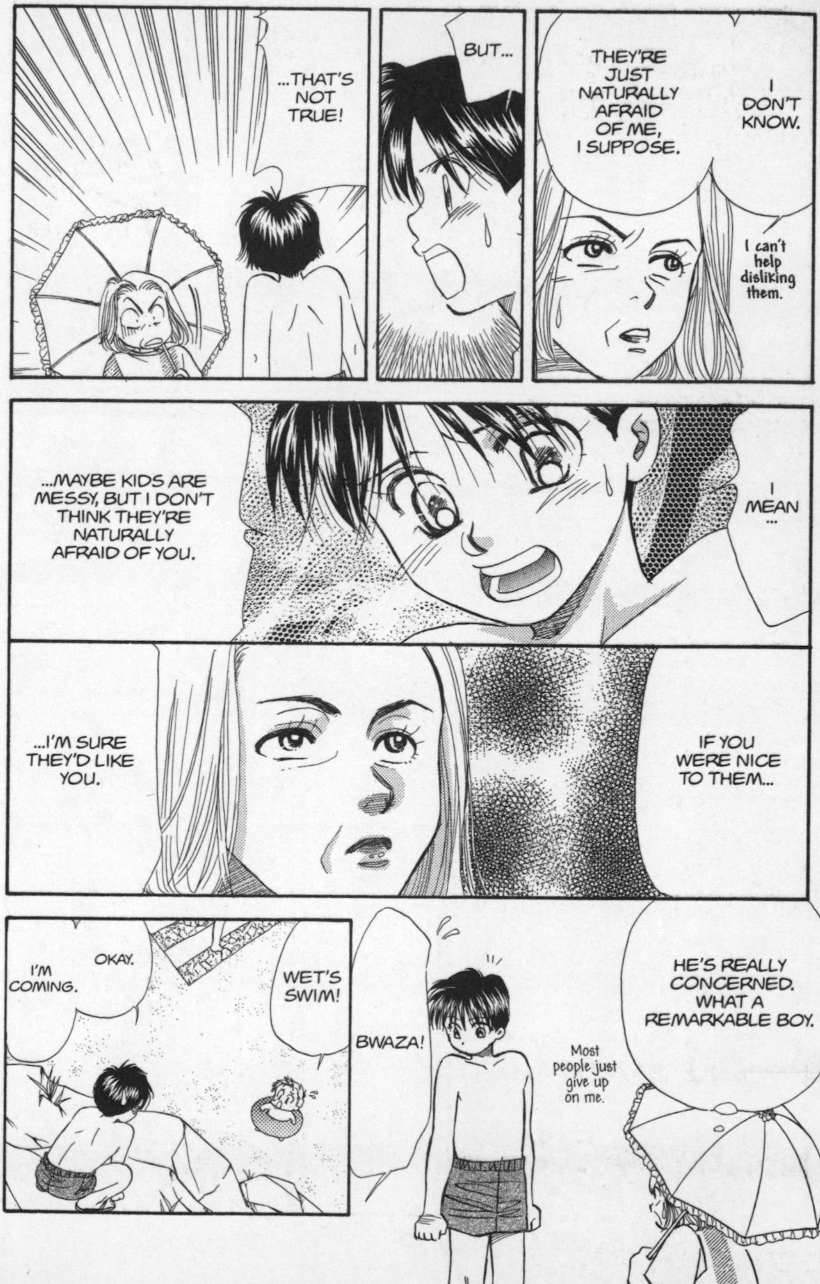
I DON'T KNOW.
THEY'RE JUST NATURALLY AFRAID OF ME, I SUPPOSE.
I can't help disliking them.
BUT...
...THAT'S NOT TRUE!
I MEAN...
...MAYBE KIDS ARE MESSY, BUT I DON'T THINK THEY'RE NATURALLY AFRAID OF YOU.
IF YOU WERE NICE TO THEM...
...I'M SURE THEY'D LIKE YOU.
HE'S REALLY CONCERNED. WHAT A REMARKABLE BOY.
Most people just give up on me.
BWAZA!
WET'S SWIM!
OKAY.
I'M COMING.

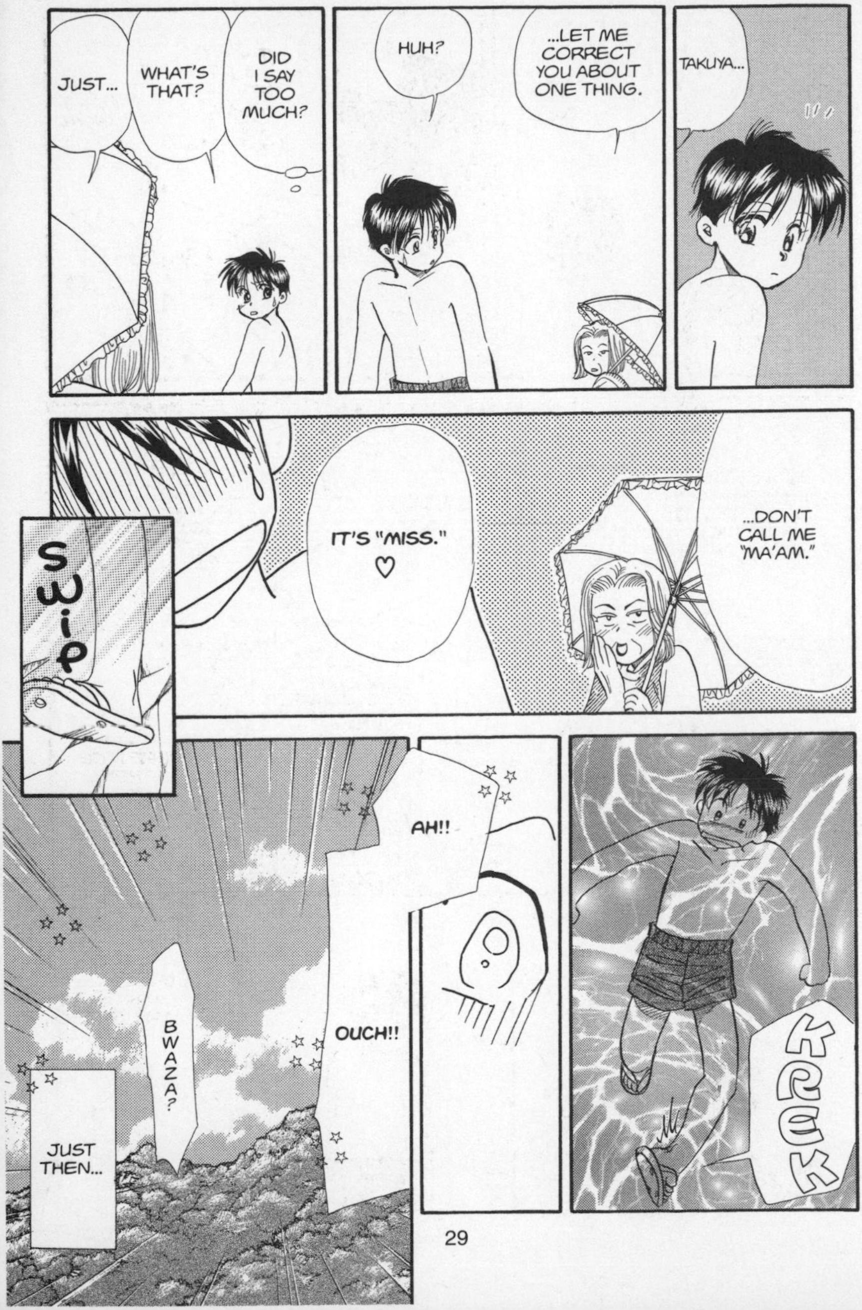
TAKUYA...
...LET ME CORRECT YOU ABOUT ONE THING.
HUH?
DID I SAY TOO MUCH?
WHAT'S THAT?
JUST...
...DON'T CALL ME "MA'AM."
IT'S "MISS." ♡
SWIP
KREK
AH!!
OUCH!!
BWAZA?
JUST THEN...

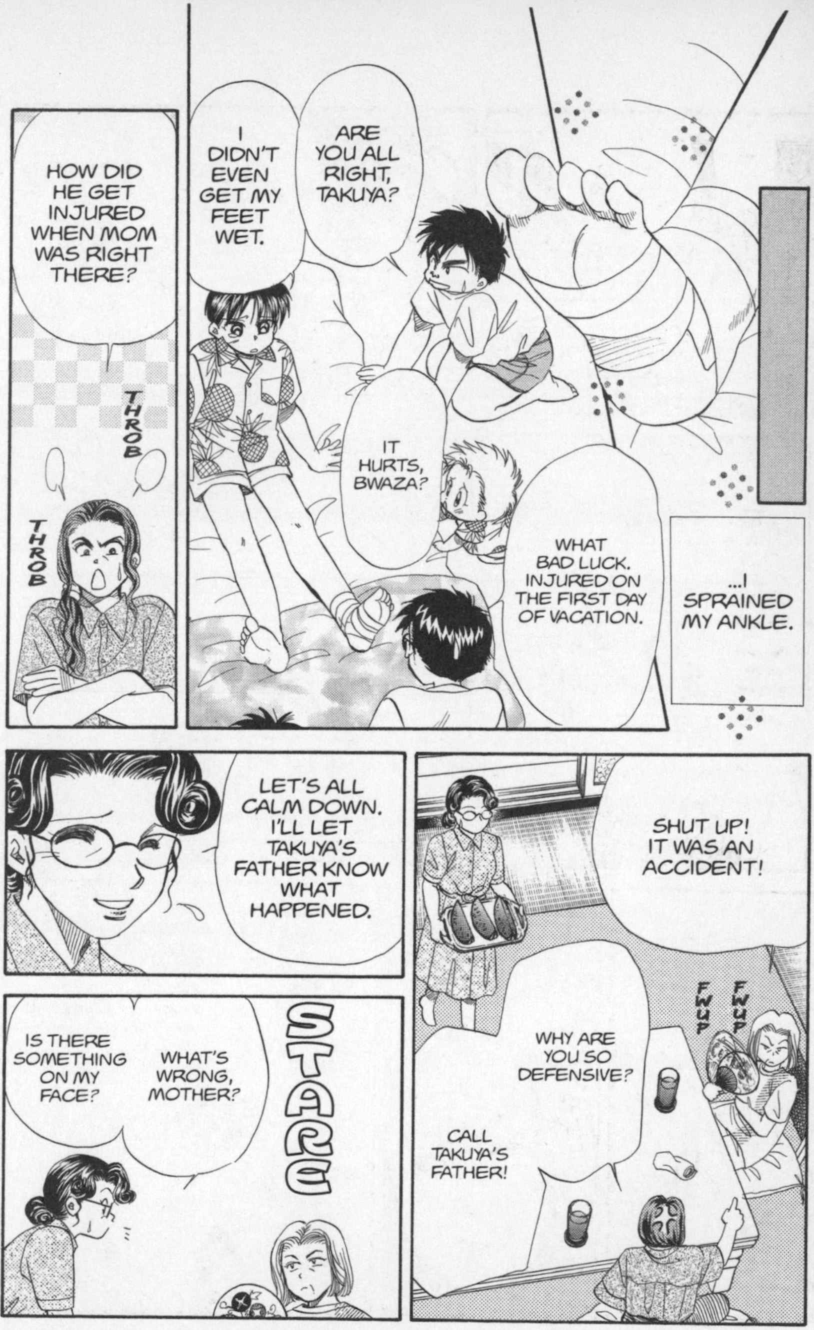
...I SPRAINED MY ANKLE.
WHAT BAD LUCK. INJURED ON THE FIRST DAY OF VACATION.
IT HURTS, BWAZA?
ARE YOU ALL RIGHT, TAKUYA?
I DIDN'T EVEN GET MY FEET WET.
HOW DID HE GET INJURED WHEN MOM WAS RIGHT THERE?
THROB
THROB
SHUT UP! IT WAS AN ACCIDENT!
FWUP FWUP
WHY ARE YOU SO DEFENSIVE?
CALL TAKUYA'S FATHER!
LET'S ALL CALM DOWN. I'LL LET TAKUYA'S FATHER KNOW WHAT HAPPENED.
STARE
WHAT'S WRONG, MOTHER?
IS THERE SOMETHING ON MY FACE?

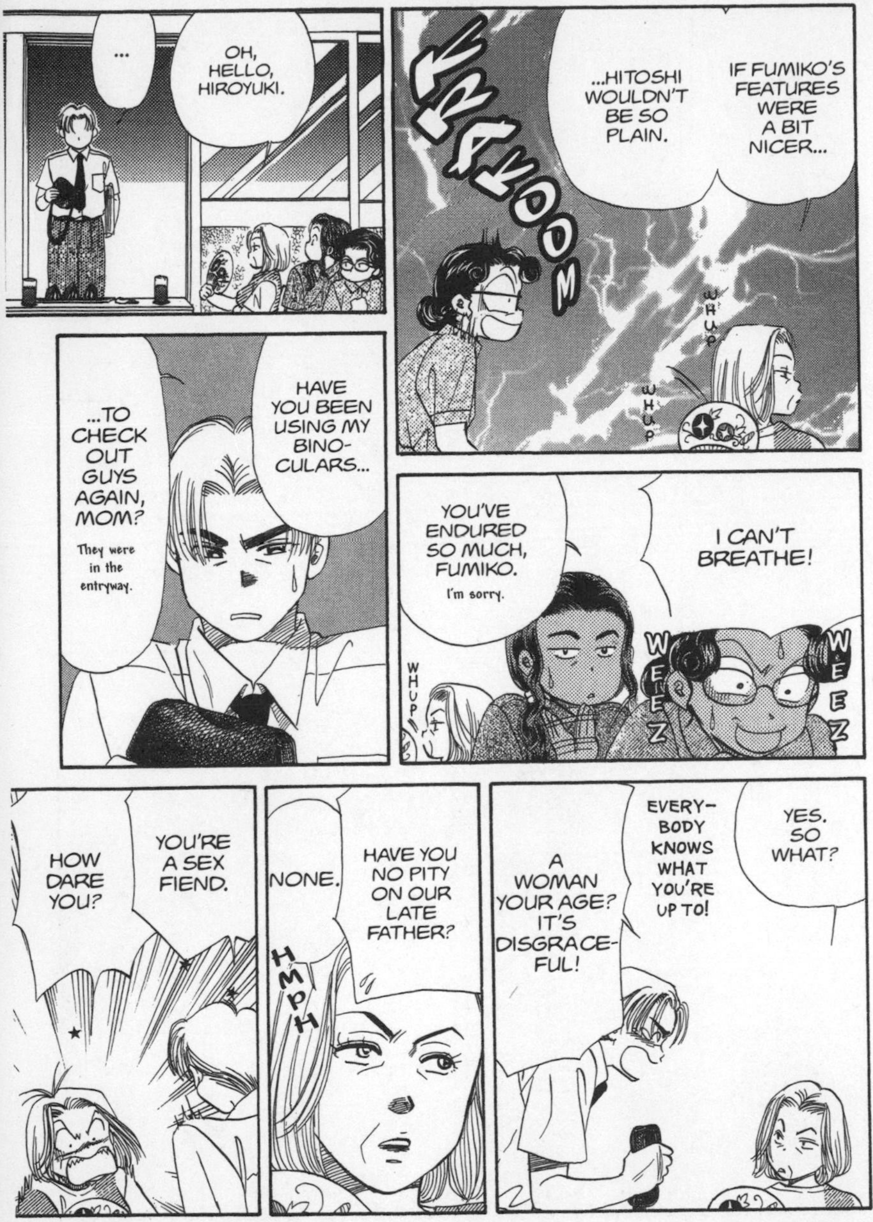
IF FUMIKO'S FEATURES WERE A BIT NICER...
...HITOSHI WOULDN'T BE SO PLAIN.
KRAKOOM
WHUP
WHUP
OH, HELLO, HIROYUKI.
...
I CAN'T BREATHE!
YOU'VE ENDURED SO MUCH, FUMIKO.
I'm sorry.
WEEZ
WEEZ
WHUP
HAVE YOU BEEN USING MY BINOCULARS...
...TO CHECK OUT GUYS AGAIN, MOM?
They were in the entryway.
YES. SO WHAT?
EVERYBODY KNOWS WHAT YOU'RE UP TO!
A WOMAN YOUR AGE? IT'S DISGRACEFUL!
HAVE YOU NO PITY ON OUR LATE FATHER?
NONE.
HMPH
YOU'RE A SEX FIEND.
HOW DARE YOU?

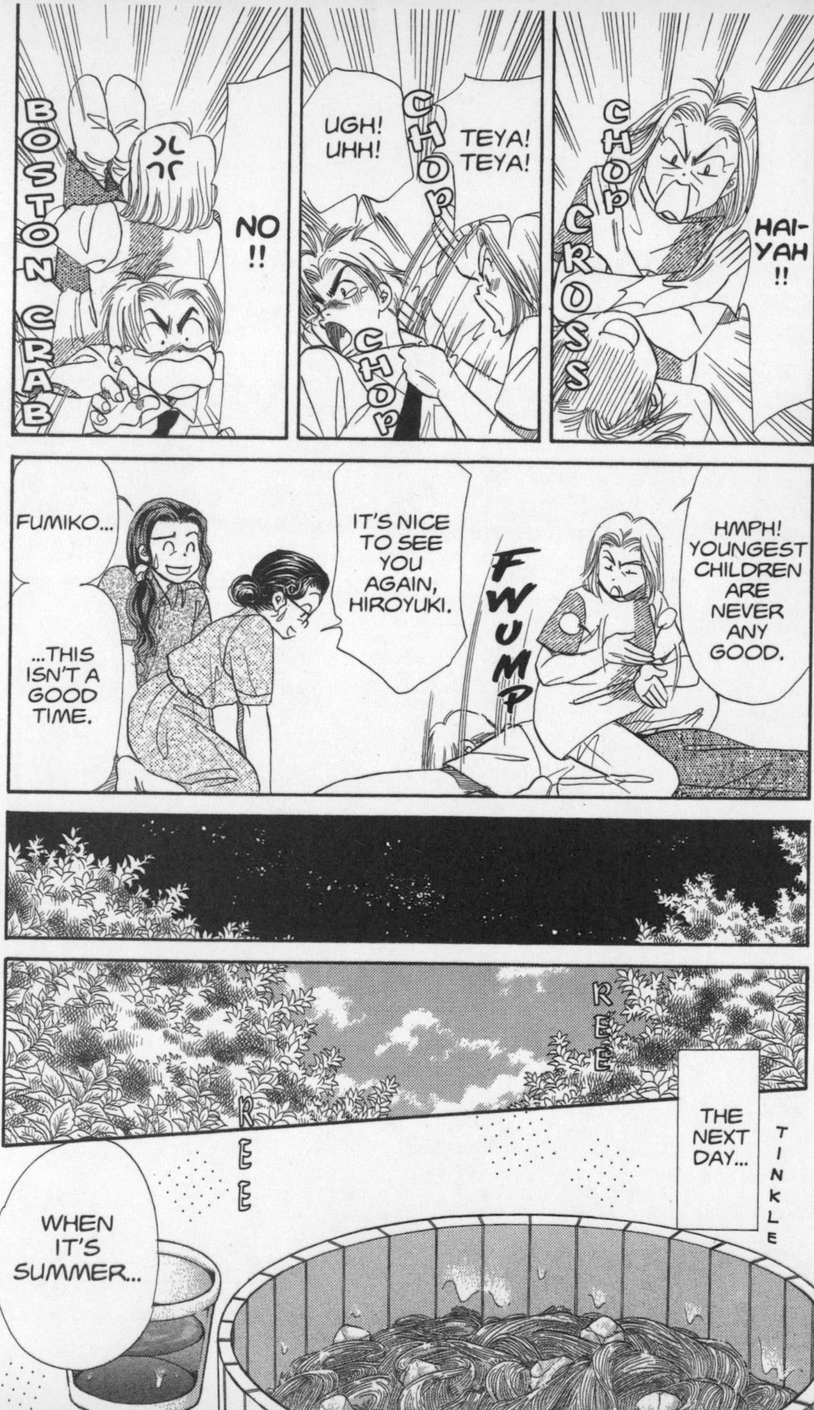

CHOP CROSS
HAI-YAH!!
TEYA! TEYA!
CHOP
UGH! UHH!
CHOP
NO!!
BOSTON CRAB
HMPH! YOUNGEST CHILDREN ARE NEVER ANY GOOD.
FWUMP
IT'S NICE TO SEE YOU AGAIN, HIROYUKI.
FUMIKO...
...THIS ISN'T A GOOD TIME.
REE
THE NEXT DAY...
TINKLE
REE
WHEN IT'S SUMMER...

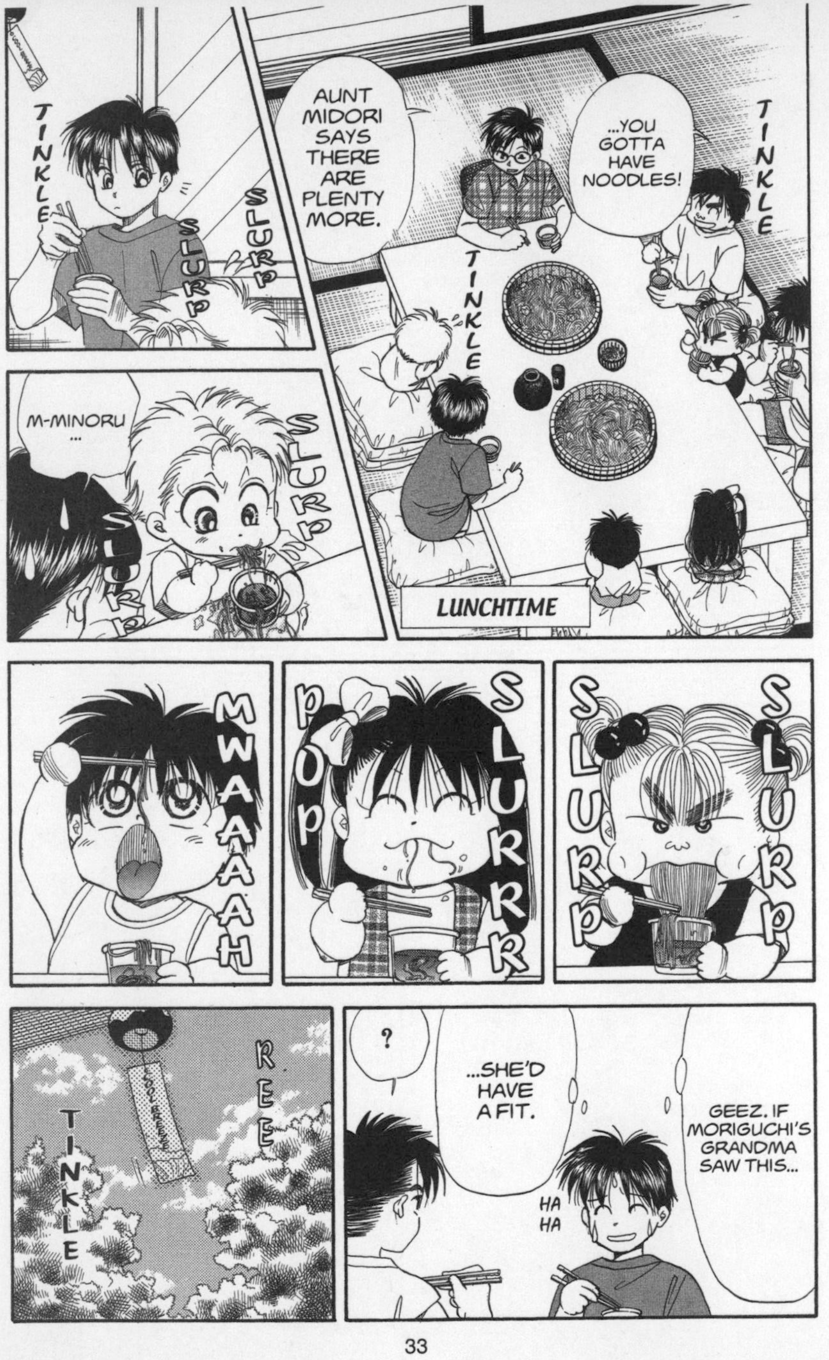
...YOU GOTTA HAVE NOODLES!
TINKLE
AUNT MIDORI SAYS THERE ARE PLENTY MORE.
TINKLE
LUNCHTIME
TINKLE
SLURp
SLURp
M-MINORU ...
SLURp
SLURp
SLURp
SLURp
SLURRR
pop
MWAAAAH
GEEZ. IF MORIGUCHI'S GRANDMA SAW THIS...
...SHE'D HAVE A FIT.
?
HA HA
REE
TINKLE
COOL BREEZE

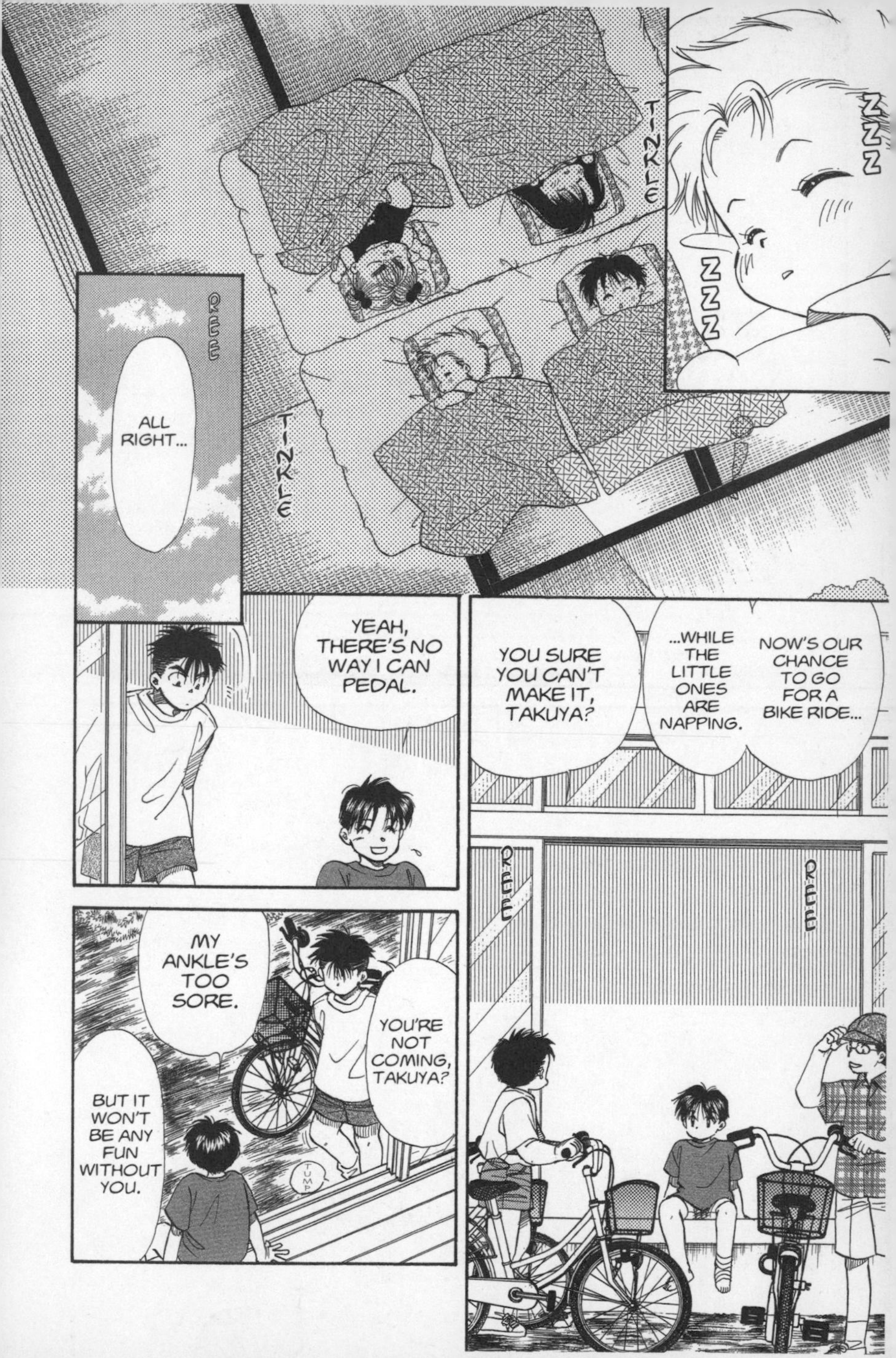
ZZZ
ZZZ
TINKLE
TINKLE
REE
ALL RIGHT...
NOW'S OUR CHANCE TO GO FOR A BIKE RIDE...
...WHILE THE LITTLE ONES ARE NAPPING.
YOU SURE YOU CAN'T MAKE IT, TAKUYA?
REE
REE
YEAH, THERE'S NO WAY I CAN PEDAL.
MY ANKLE'S TOO SORE.
YOU'RE NOT COMING, TAKUYA?
TUMP
BUT IT WON'T BE ANY FUN WITHOUT YOU.

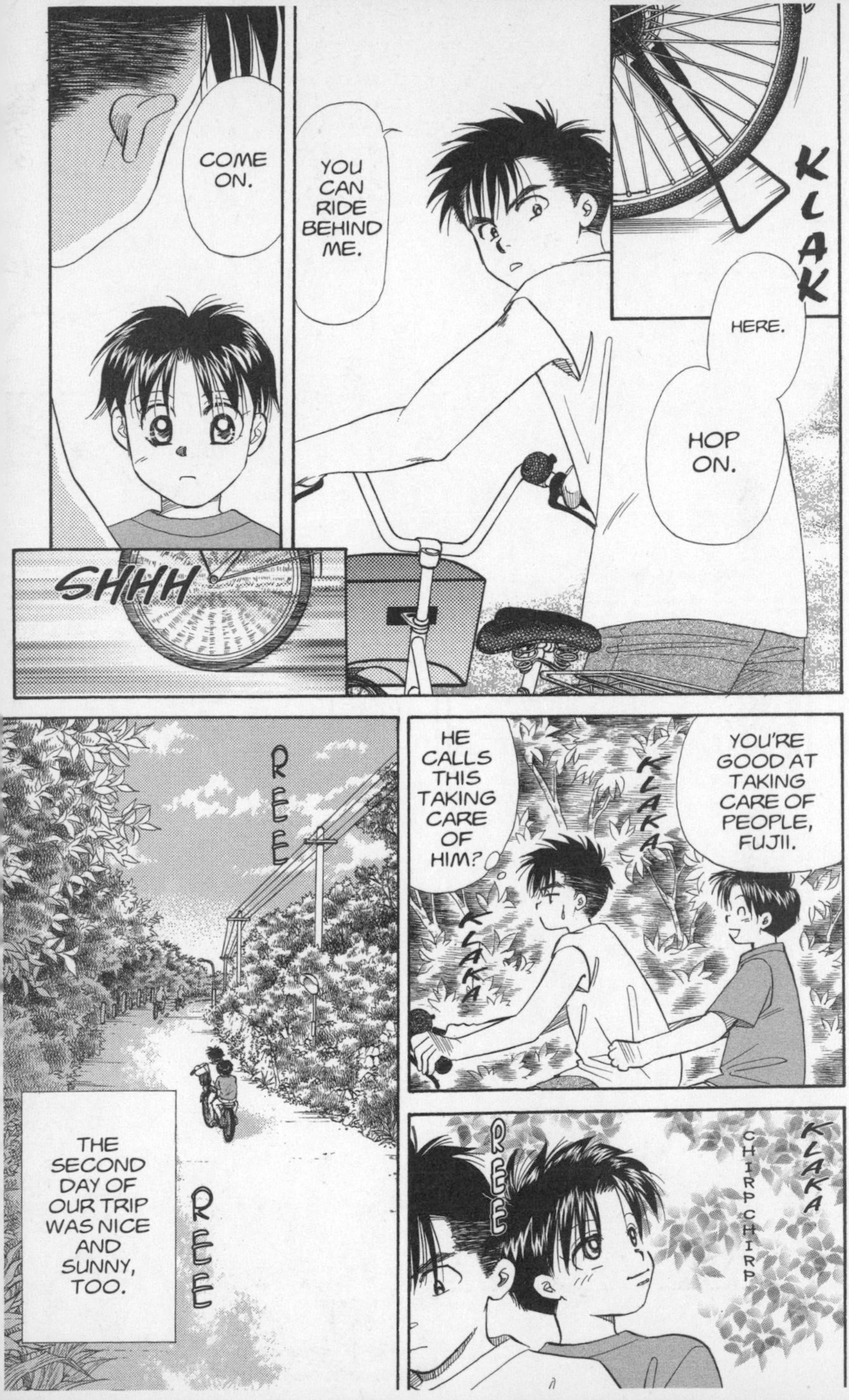
KLAK
HERE.
HOP ON.
YOU CAN RIDE BEHIND ME.
COME ON.
SHHH
YOU'RE GOOD AT TAKING CARE OF PEOPLE, FUJII.
KLAKA
HE CALLS THIS TAKING CARE OF HIM?
KLAKA
KLAKA
CHIRP CHIRP
REE
REE
REE
THE SECOND DAY OF OUR TRIP WAS NICE AND SUNNY, TOO.

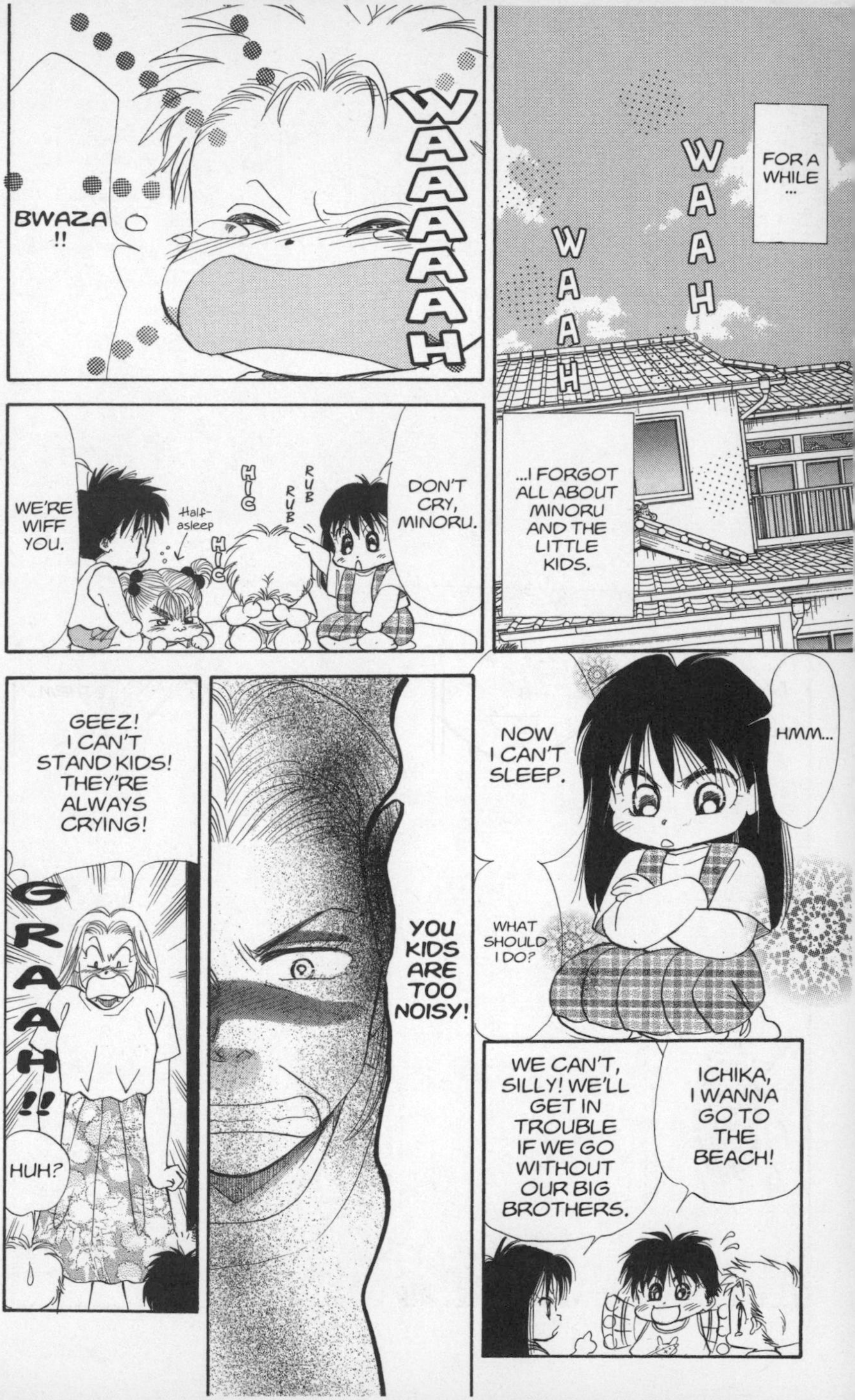

FOR A WHILE ...
WAAH
WAAH
...I FORGOT ALL ABOUT MINORU AND THE LITTLE KIDS.
WAAAAAH
BWAZA!!
DON'T CRY, MINORU.
RUB RUB
HIC HIC
Half-asleep
WE'RE WIFF YOU.
HMM...
NOW I CAN'T SLEEP.
WHAT SHOULD I DO?
ICHIKA, I WANNA GO TO THE BEACH!
WE CAN'T, SILLY! WE'LL GET IN TROUBLE IF WE GO WITHOUT OUR BIG BROTHERS.
YOU KIDS ARE TOO NOISY!
GEEZ! I CAN'T STAND KIDS! THEY'RE ALWAYS CRYING!
GRAAAH!!
HUH?

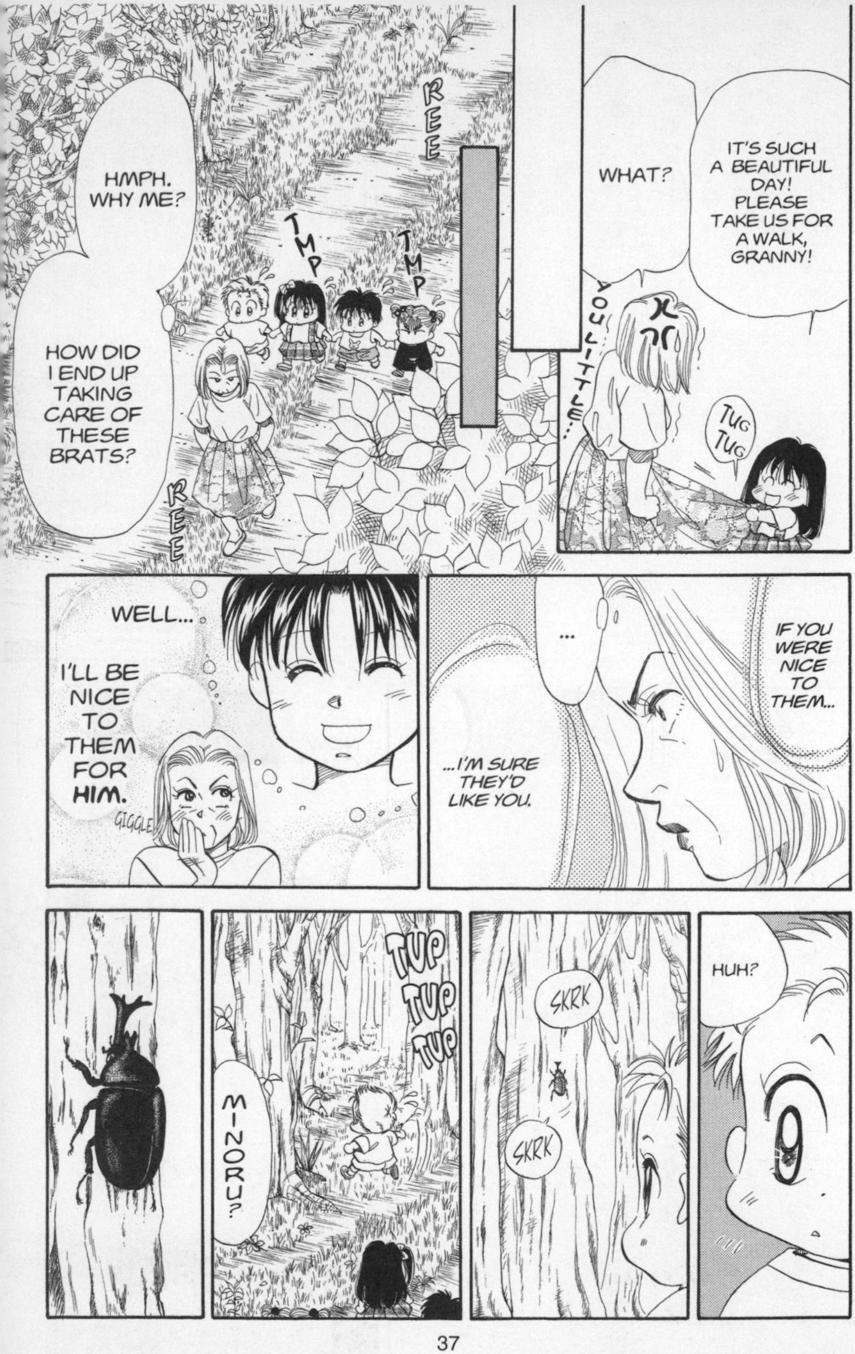
IT'S SUCH A BEAUTIFUL DAY! PLEASE TAKE US FOR A WALK, GRANNY!
WHAT?
TUG TUG
YOU LITTLE...
REE
TMP
TMP
HMPH. WHY ME?
HOW DID I END UP TAKING CARE OF THESE BRATS?
REE
IF YOU WERE NICE TO THEM...
...
...I'M SURE THEY'D LIKE YOU.
WELL...
I'LL BE NICE TO THEM FOR **HIM.**
GIGGLE
HUH?
SKRK
SKRK
TUP TUP TUP TUP
MINORU?

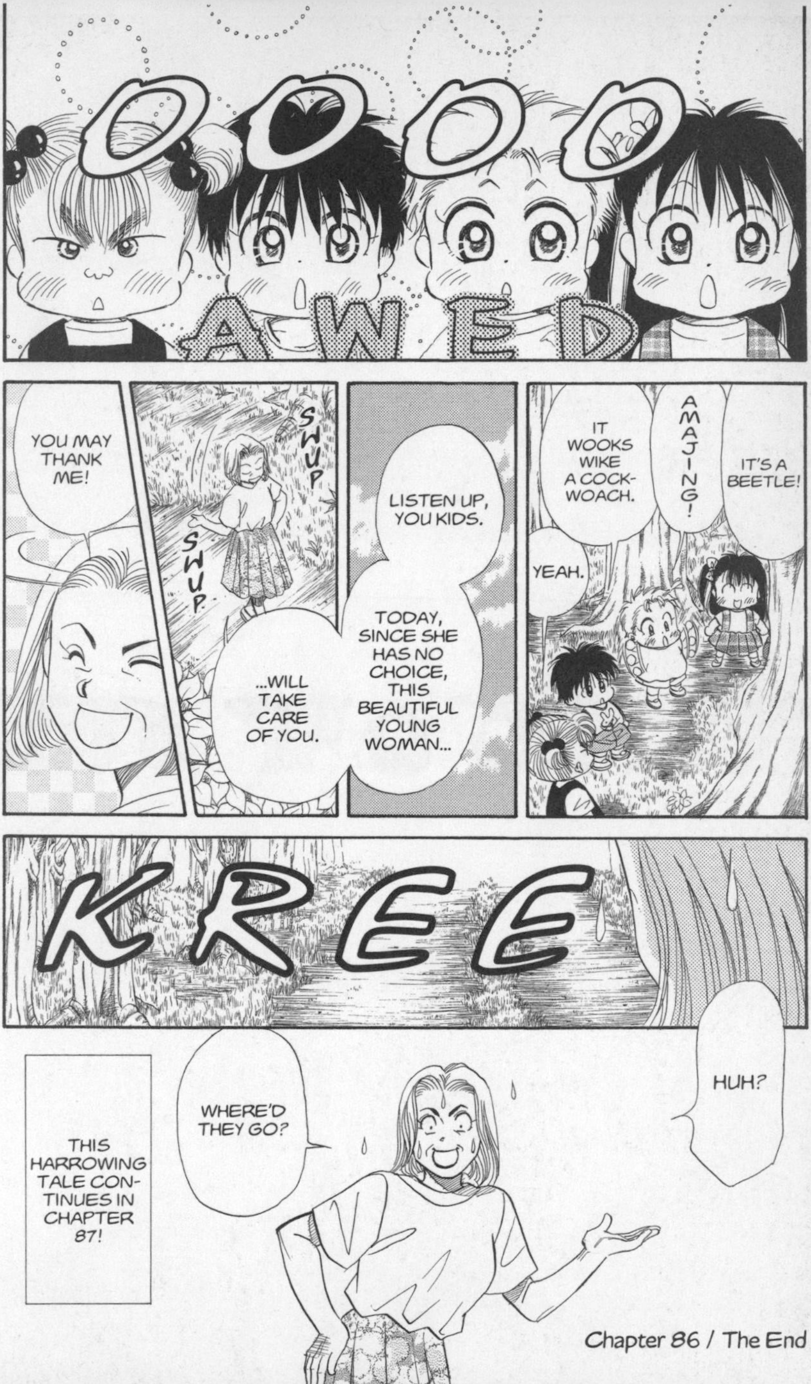
OOOO
AWED
IT'S A BEETLE!
AMAJING!
IT WOOKS WIKE A COCK-WOACH.
YEAH.
LISTEN UP, YOU KIDS.
TODAY, SINCE SHE HAS NO CHOICE, THIS BEAUTIFUL YOUNG WOMAN...
...WILL TAKE CARE OF YOU.
SWUP
SWUP
YOU MAY THANK ME!
KREEE
HUH?
WHERE'D THEY GO?
THIS HARROWING TALE CONTINUES IN CHAPTER 87!

Chapter 86 / The End

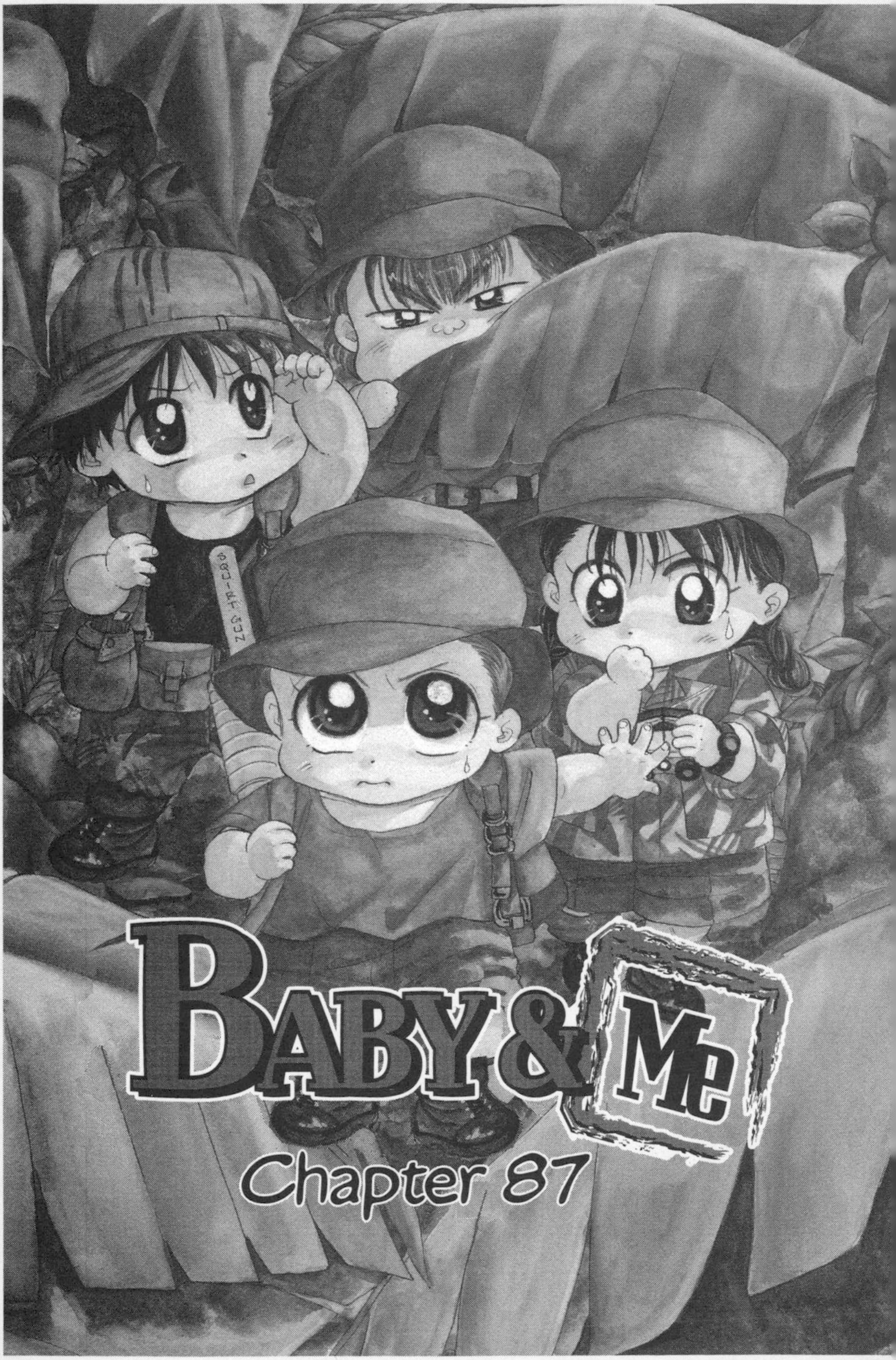
SQUIRT GUN
BABY & Me
Chapter 87

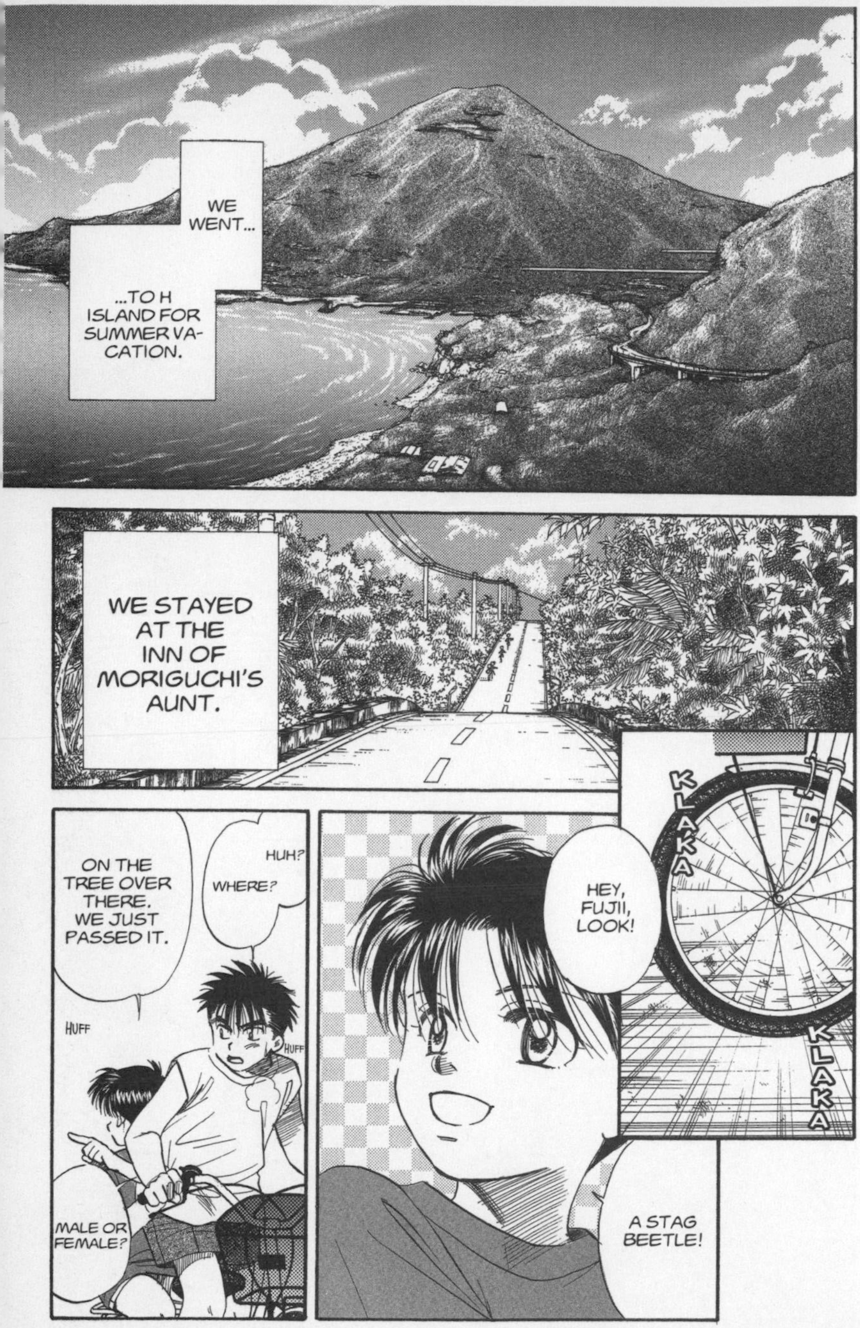
WE WENT...
...TO H ISLAND FOR SUMMER VA-CATION.
WE STAYED AT THE INN OF MORIGUCHI'S AUNT.
KLAKA
KLAKA
HEY, FUJII, LOOK!
A STAG BEETLE!
HUH?
WHERE?
ON THE TREE OVER THERE. WE JUST PASSED IT.
HUFF
HUFF
MALE OR FEMALE?

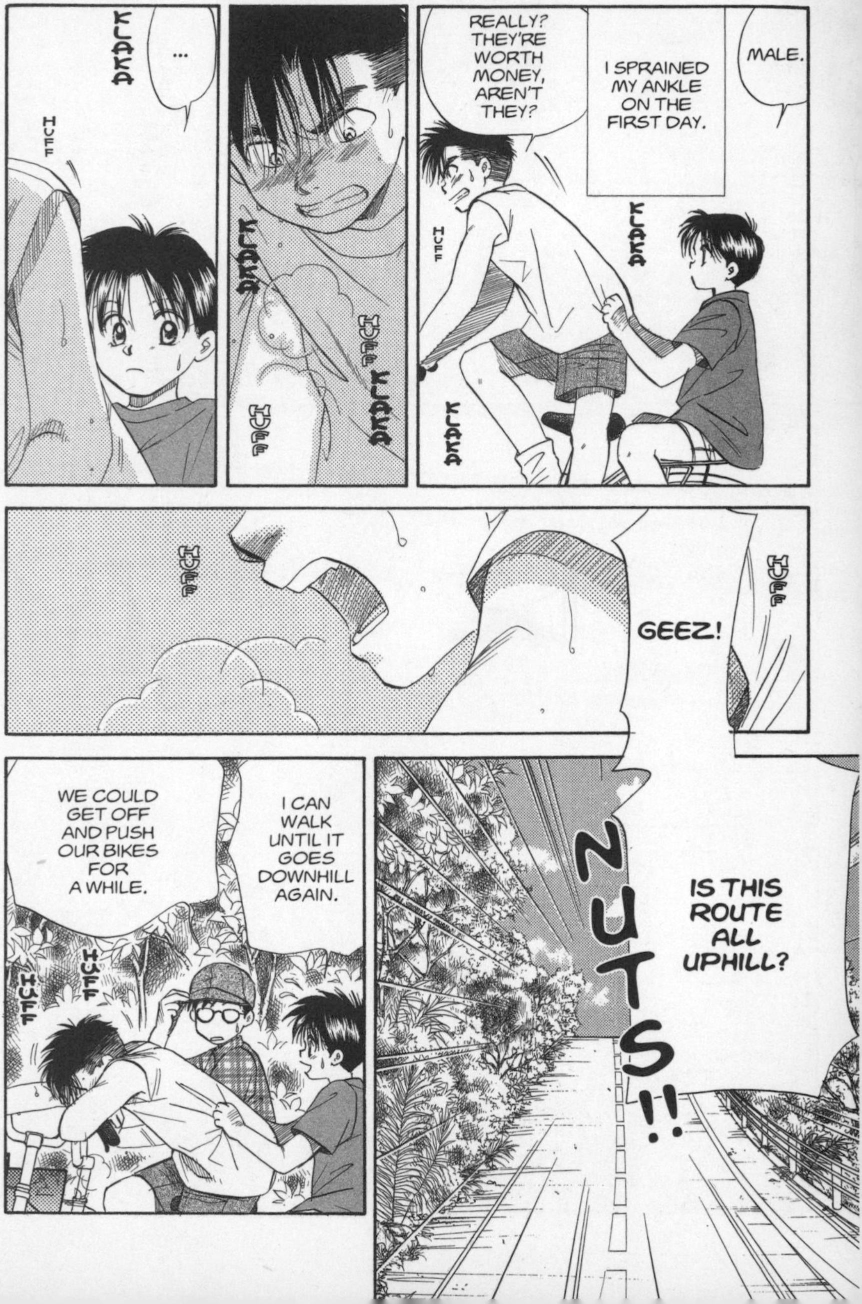
MALE.
I SPRAINED MY ANKLE ON THE FIRST DAY.
REALLY? THEY'RE WORTH MONEY, AREN'T THEY?
KLAKA
HUFF
KLAKA
KLAKA
HUFF
KLAKA
HUFF
KLAKA
...
HUFF
HUFF
GEEZ!
HUFF
IS THIS ROUTE ALL UPHILL?
NUTS!!
I CAN WALK UNTIL IT GOES DOWNHILL AGAIN.
WE COULD GET OFF AND PUSH OUR BIKES FOR A WHILE.
HUFF
HUFF

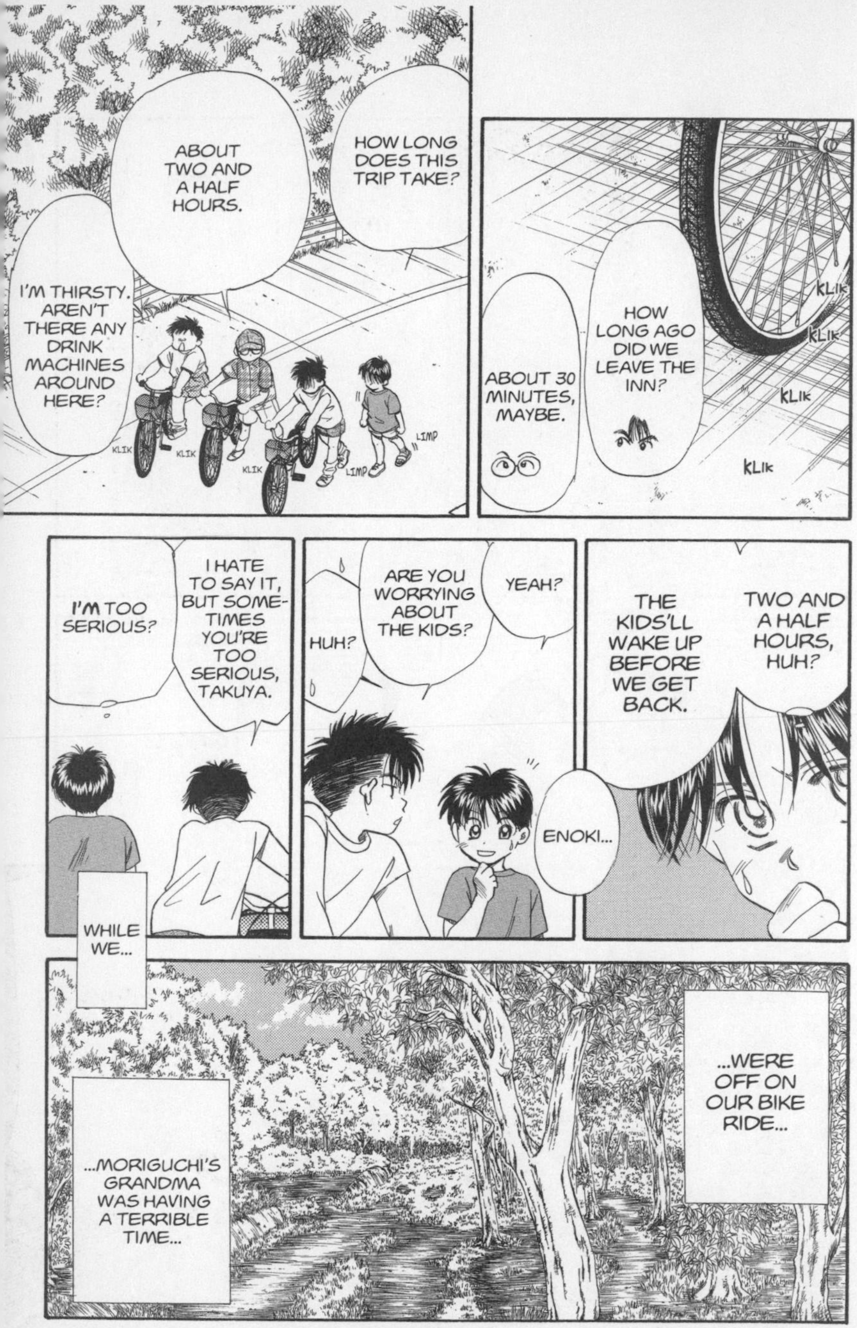
KLIK
KLIK
KLIK
KLIK
HOW LONG AGO DID WE LEAVE THE INN?
ABOUT 30 MINUTES, MAYBE.
HOW LONG DOES THIS TRIP TAKE?
ABOUT TWO AND A HALF HOURS.
I'M THIRSTY. AREN'T THERE ANY DRINK MACHINES AROUND HERE?
KLIK
KLIK
KLIK
LIMP
LIMP
TWO AND A HALF HOURS, HUH?
THE KIDS'LL WAKE UP BEFORE WE GET BACK.
ENOKI...
YEAH?
ARE YOU WORRYING ABOUT THE KIDS?
HUH?
I HATE TO SAY IT, BUT SOMETIMES YOU'RE TOO SERIOUS, TAKUYA.
I'M TOO SERIOUS?
WHILE WE...
...WERE OFF ON OUR BIKE RIDE...
...MORIGUCHI'S GRANDMA WAS HAVING A TERRIBLE TIME...

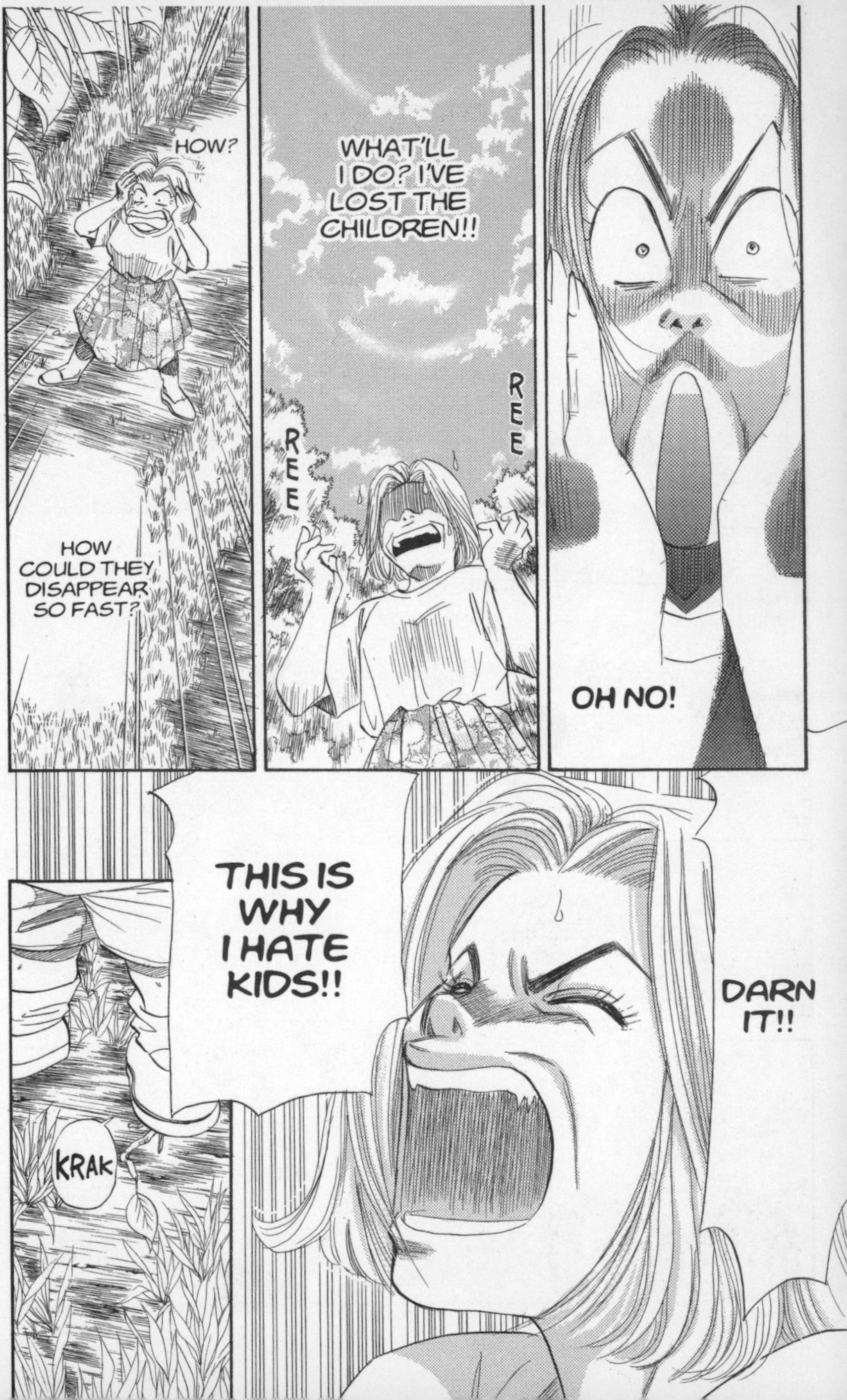
OH NO!
WHAT'LL I DO? I'VE LOST THE CHILDREN!!
REE
REE
HOW?
HOW COULD THEY DISAPPEAR SO FAST?
THIS IS WHY I HATE KIDS!!
DARN IT!!
KRAK

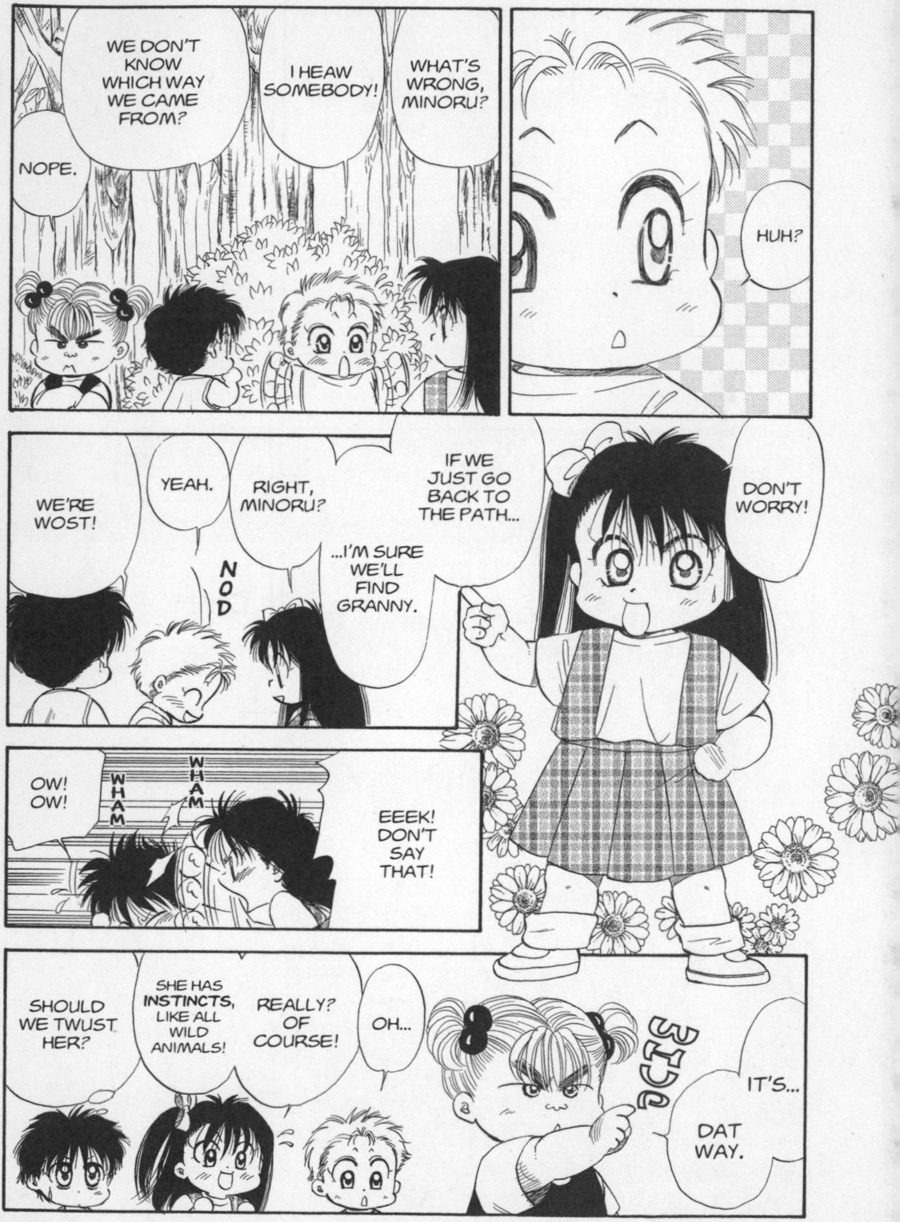
HUH?
WHAT'S WRONG, MINORU?
I HEAW SOMEBODY!
WE DON'T KNOW WHICH WAY WE CAME FROM?
NOPE.
DON'T WORRY!
IF WE JUST GO BACK TO THE PATH...
...I'M SURE WE'LL FIND GRANNY.
RIGHT, MINORU?
YEAH.
NOD
WE'RE WOST!
EEEK! DON'T SAY THAT!
WHAM
WHAM
OW! OW!
IT'S...
DAT WAY.
OH...
REALLY? OF COURSE!
SHE HAS **INSTINCTS**, LIKE ALL WILD ANIMALS!
SHOULD WE TWUST HER?

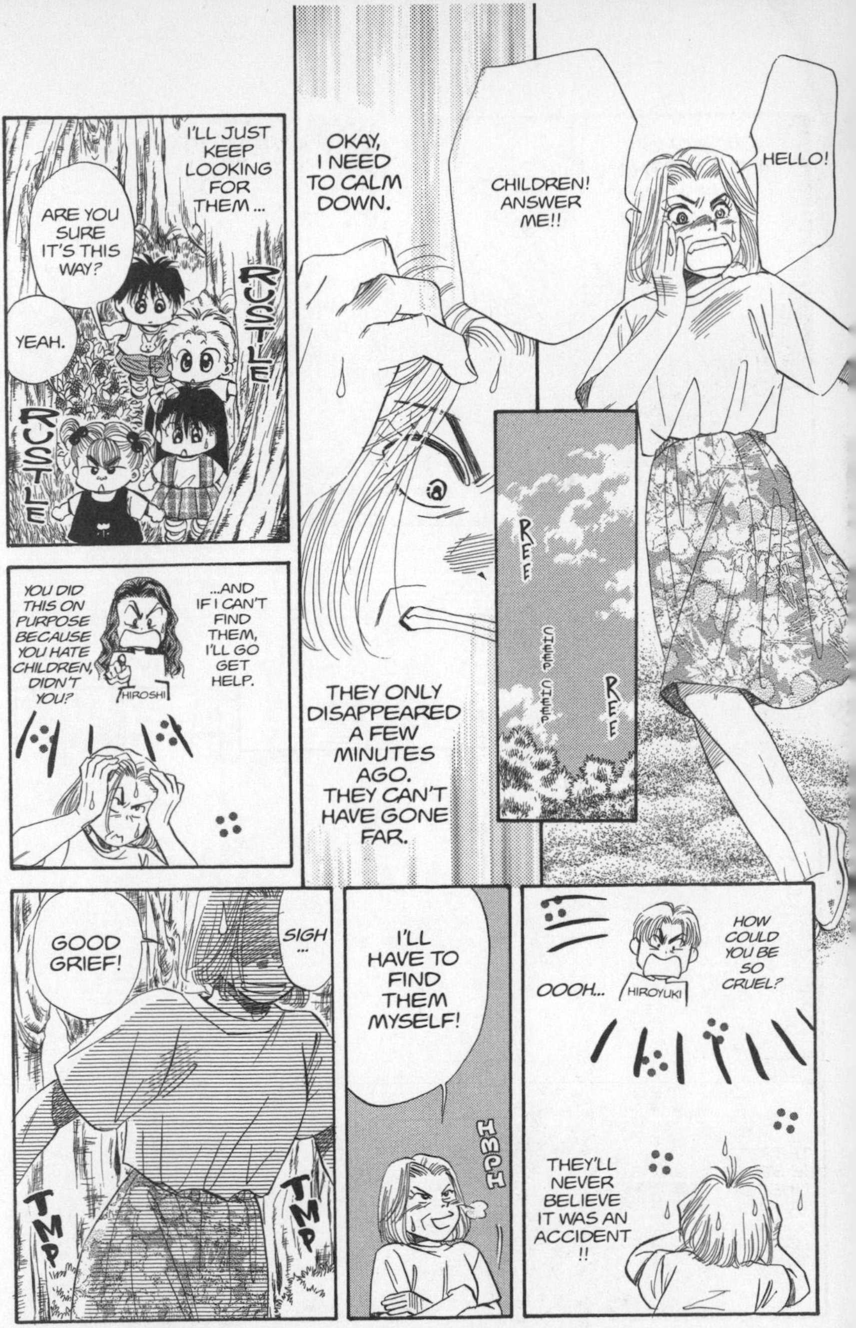
HELLO!
CHILDREN! ANSWER ME!!
OKAY, I NEED TO CALM DOWN.
THEY ONLY DISAPPEARED A FEW MINUTES AGO. THEY CAN'T HAVE GONE FAR.
REE
CHEEP CHEEP
REE
I'LL JUST KEEP LOOKING FOR THEM ...
ARE YOU SURE IT'S THIS WAY?
RUSTLE
YEAH.
RUSTLE
...AND IF I CAN'T FIND THEM, I'LL GO GET HELP.
YOU DID THIS ON PURPOSE BECAUSE YOU HATE CHILDREN, DIDN'T YOU?
HIROSHI
HOW COULD YOU BE SO CRUEL?
HIROYUKI
OOOH...
THEY'LL NEVER BELIEVE IT WAS AN ACCIDENT !!
I'LL HAVE TO FIND THEM MYSELF!
HMPH
SIGH ...
GOOD GRIEF!
TMP
TMP

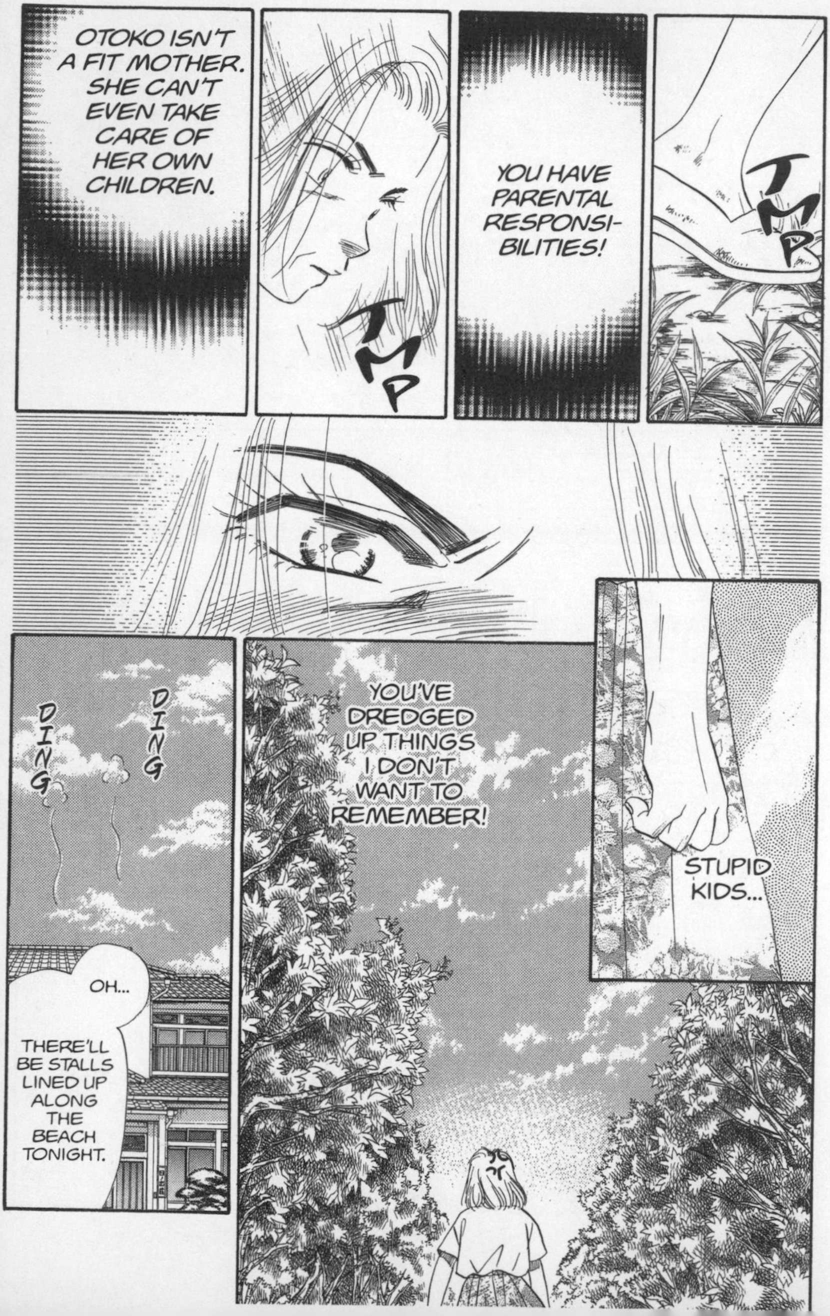
TMP
TMP
YOU HAVE PARENTAL RESPONSI-BILITIES!
TMP
OTOKO ISN'T A FIT MOTHER. SHE CAN'T EVEN TAKE CARE OF HER OWN CHILDREN.
STUPID KIDS...
YOU'VE DREDGED UP THINGS I DON'T WANT TO REMEMBER!
DING
DING
OH...
THERE'LL BE STALLS LINED UP ALONG THE BEACH TONIGHT.

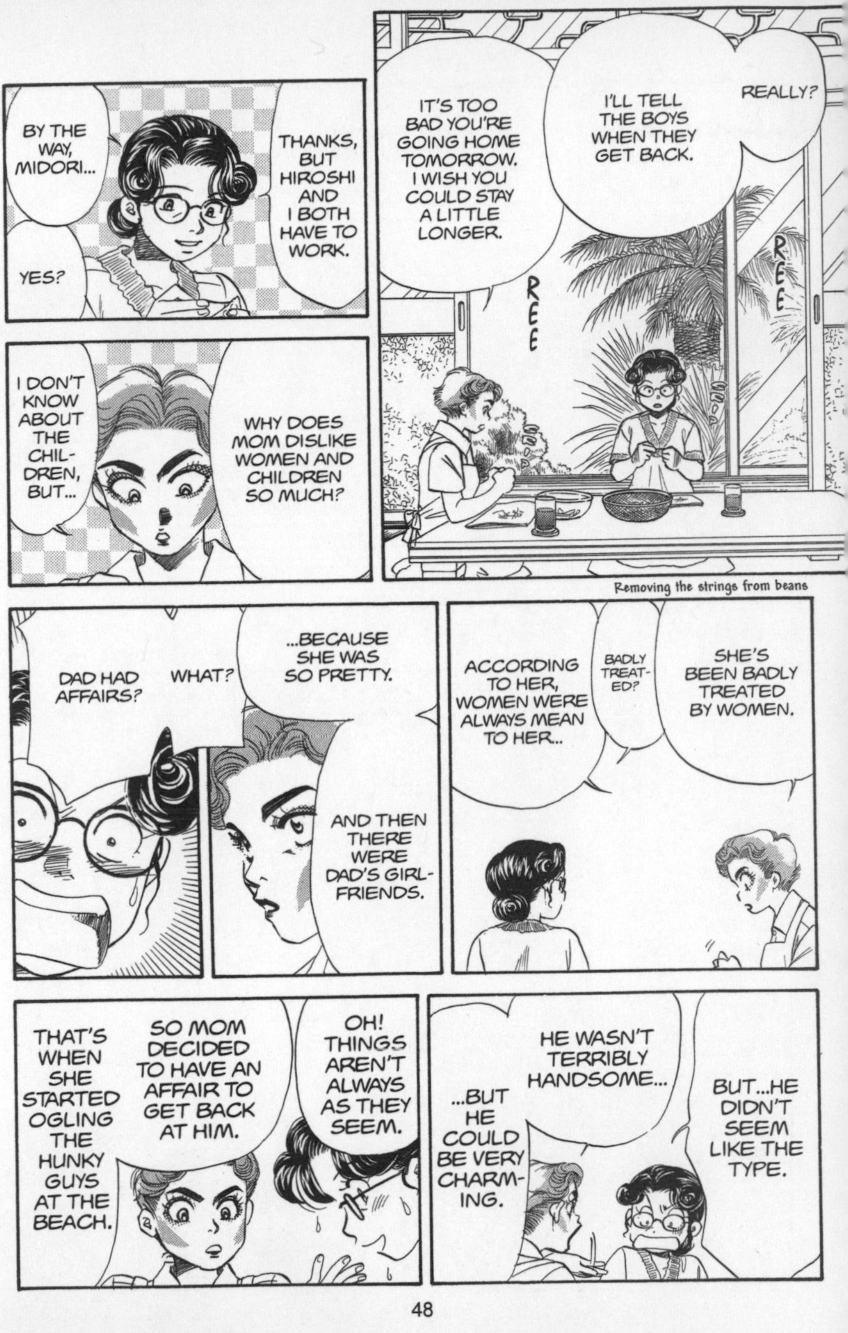
REALLY?
I'LL TELL THE BOYS WHEN THEY GET BACK.
IT'S TOO BAD YOU'RE GOING HOME TOMORROW. I WISH YOU COULD STAY A LITTLE LONGER.
REE
REE
Removing the strings from beans
THANKS, BUT HIROSHI AND I BOTH HAVE TO WORK.
BY THE WAY, MIDORI...
YES?
WHY DOES MOM DISLIKE WOMEN AND CHILDREN SO MUCH?
I DON'T KNOW ABOUT THE CHIL-DREN, BUT...
SHE'S BEEN BADLY TREATED BY WOMEN.
BADLY TREAT-ED?
ACCORDING TO HER, WOMEN WERE ALWAYS MEAN TO HER...
...BECAUSE SHE WAS SO PRETTY.
AND THEN THERE WERE DAD'S GIRL-FRIENDS.
WHAT?
DAD HAD AFFAIRS?
BUT...HE DIDN'T SEEM LIKE THE TYPE.
HE WASN'T TERRIBLY HANDSOME...
...BUT HE COULD BE VERY CHARM-ING.
OH! THINGS AREN'T ALWAYS AS THEY SEEM.
SO MOM DECIDED TO HAVE AN AFFAIR TO GET BACK AT HIM.
THAT'S WHEN SHE STARTED OGLING THE HUNKY GUYS AT THE BEACH.

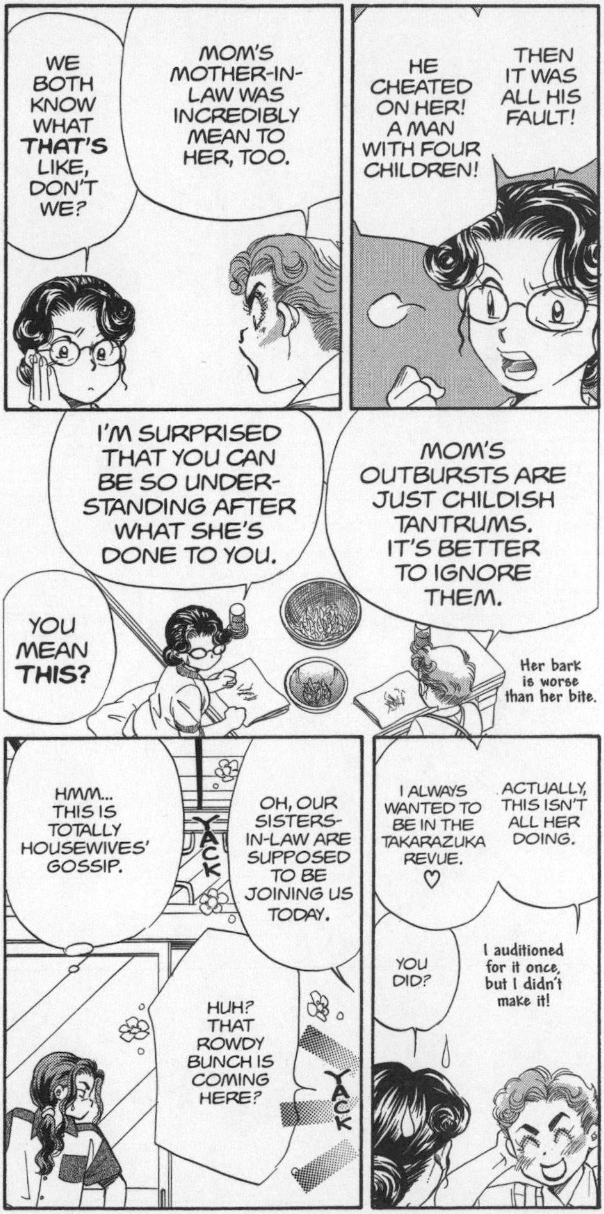
THEN IT WAS ALL HIS FAULT!
HE CHEATED ON HER! A MAN WITH FOUR CHILDREN!
MOM'S MOTHER-IN-LAW WAS INCREDIBLY MEAN TO HER, TOO.
WE BOTH KNOW WHAT THAT'S LIKE, DON'T WE?
MOM'S OUTBURSTS ARE JUST CHILDISH TANTRUMS. IT'S BETTER TO IGNORE THEM.
I'M SURPRISED THAT YOU CAN BE SO UNDERSTANDING AFTER WHAT SHE'S DONE TO YOU.
Her bark is worse than her bite.
YOU MEAN THIS?
ACTUALLY, THIS ISN'T ALL HER DOING.
I ALWAYS WANTED TO BE IN THE TAKARAZUKA REVUE. ♡
I auditioned for it once, but I didn't make it!
YOU DID?
OH, OUR SISTERS-IN-LAW ARE SUPPOSED TO BE JOINING US TODAY.
YACK
HMM... THIS IS TOTALLY HOUSEWIVES' GOSSIP.
HUH? THAT ROWDY BUNCH IS COMING HERE?
YACK

Author's Note Part 2

I visited Orlando, Florida in February. Hooray!
We went to Walt Disney World!
I was so tired I slept all the way there, so I didn't suffer from jet lag at all.

Our Schedule
Day 1: Epcot
↓
Day 2: Disney-MGM Studios
↓
Day 3: Universal Studios
↓
Day 4: The Magic Kingdom

It wasn't terribly crowded, maybe because we went in the middle of the week. (We still had to wait 60 minutes for the Twilight Zone Tower of Terror at Disney-MGM Studios.)

I'll tell you what I thought of the rides and attractions in upcoming Author's Notes.

Yes!!

Continued in Part 3

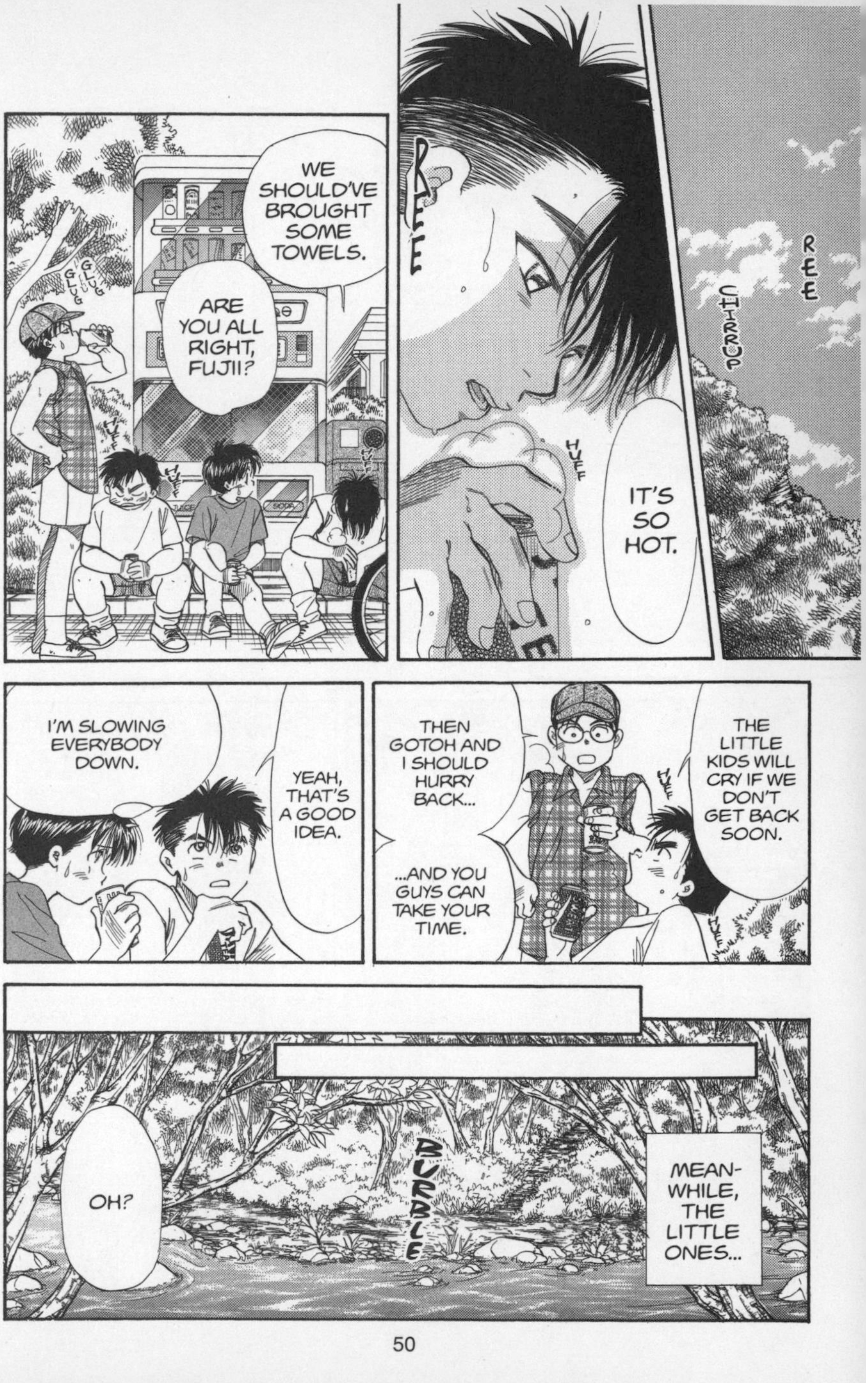
REE
CHIRRUP
REE
HUFF
IT'S SO HOT.
WE SHOULD'VE BROUGHT SOME TOWELS.
ARE YOU ALL RIGHT, FUJII?
GLUG GLUG
HUFF
HUFF
HUFF
THE LITTLE KIDS WILL CRY IF WE DON'T GET BACK SOON.
HUFF
THEN GOTOH AND I SHOULD HURRY BACK...
...AND YOU GUYS CAN TAKE YOUR TIME.
HUFF
YEAH, THAT'S A GOOD IDEA.
I'M SLOWING EVERYBODY DOWN.
MEAN-WHILE, THE LITTLE ONES...
BURBLE
OH?

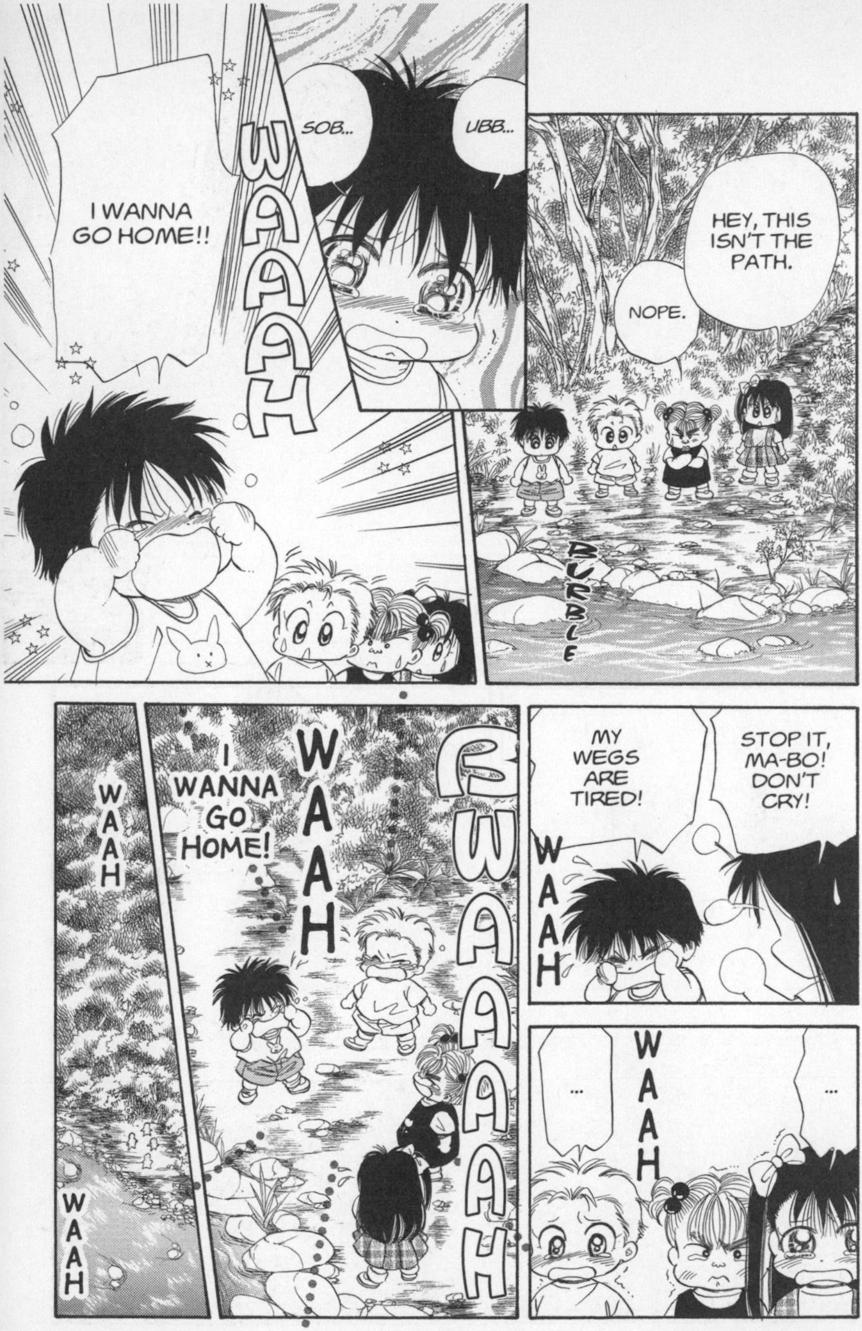
HEY, THIS ISN'T THE PATH.
NOPE.
BURBLE
UBB...
SOB...
WAAAH
I WANNA GO HOME!!
STOP IT, MA-BO! DON'T CRY!
MY WEGS ARE TIRED!
WAAH
...
WAAH
...
BWAAAAH
WAAH
I WANNA GO HOME!
WAAH
WAAH
WAAH

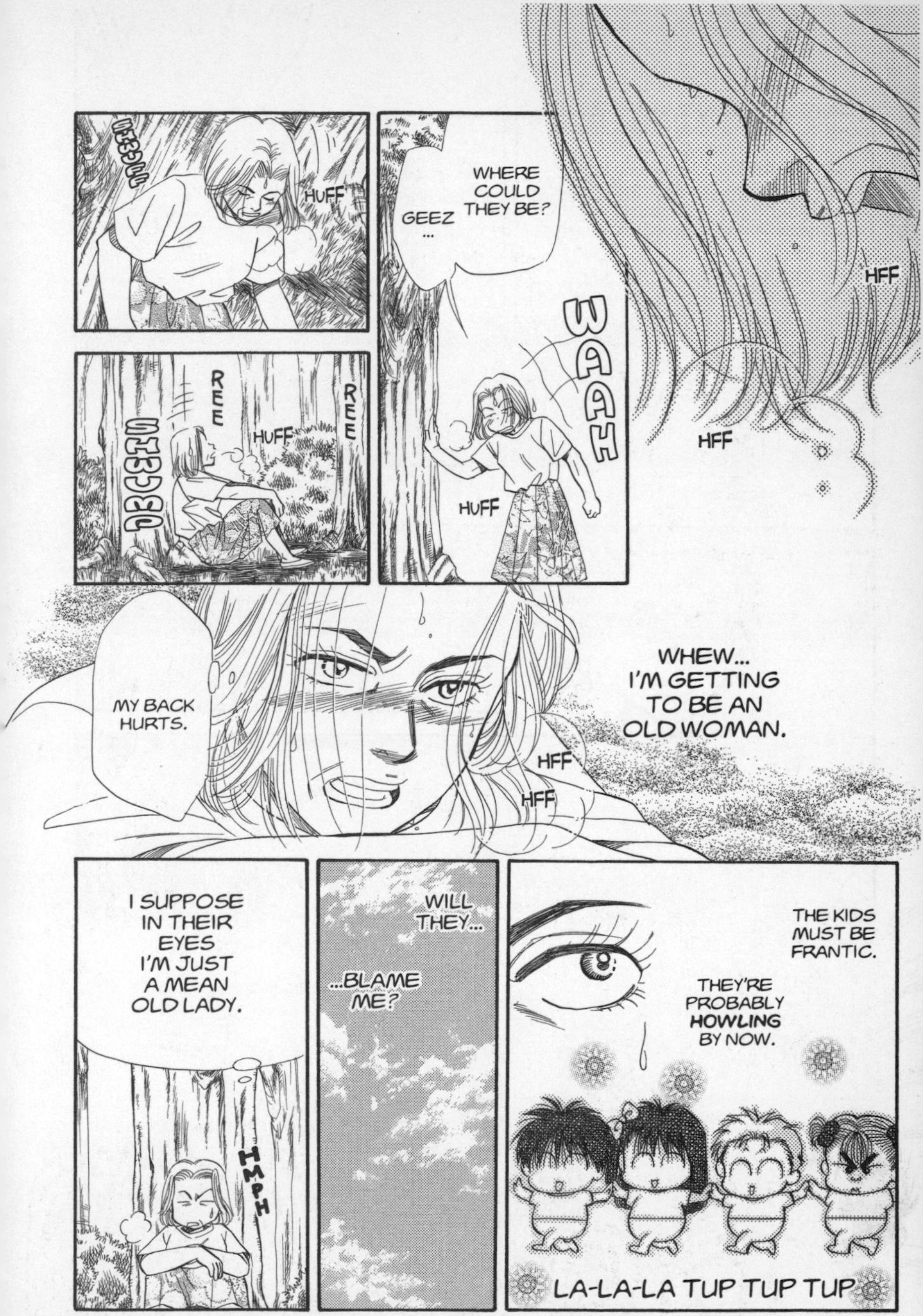
HFF
HFF
WHERE COULD THEY BE?
GEEZ ...
WAAAH
HUFF
SHUFF
HUFF
REE
REE
SHWUMP
HUFF
WHEW... I'M GETTING TO BE AN OLD WOMAN.
MY BACK HURTS.
HFF
HFF
THE KIDS MUST BE FRANTIC.
THEY'RE PROBABLY **HOWLING** BY NOW.
LA-LA-LA TUP TUP TUP
WILL THEY...
...BLAME ME?
I SUPPOSE IN THEIR EYES I'M JUST A MEAN OLD LADY.
HMPH

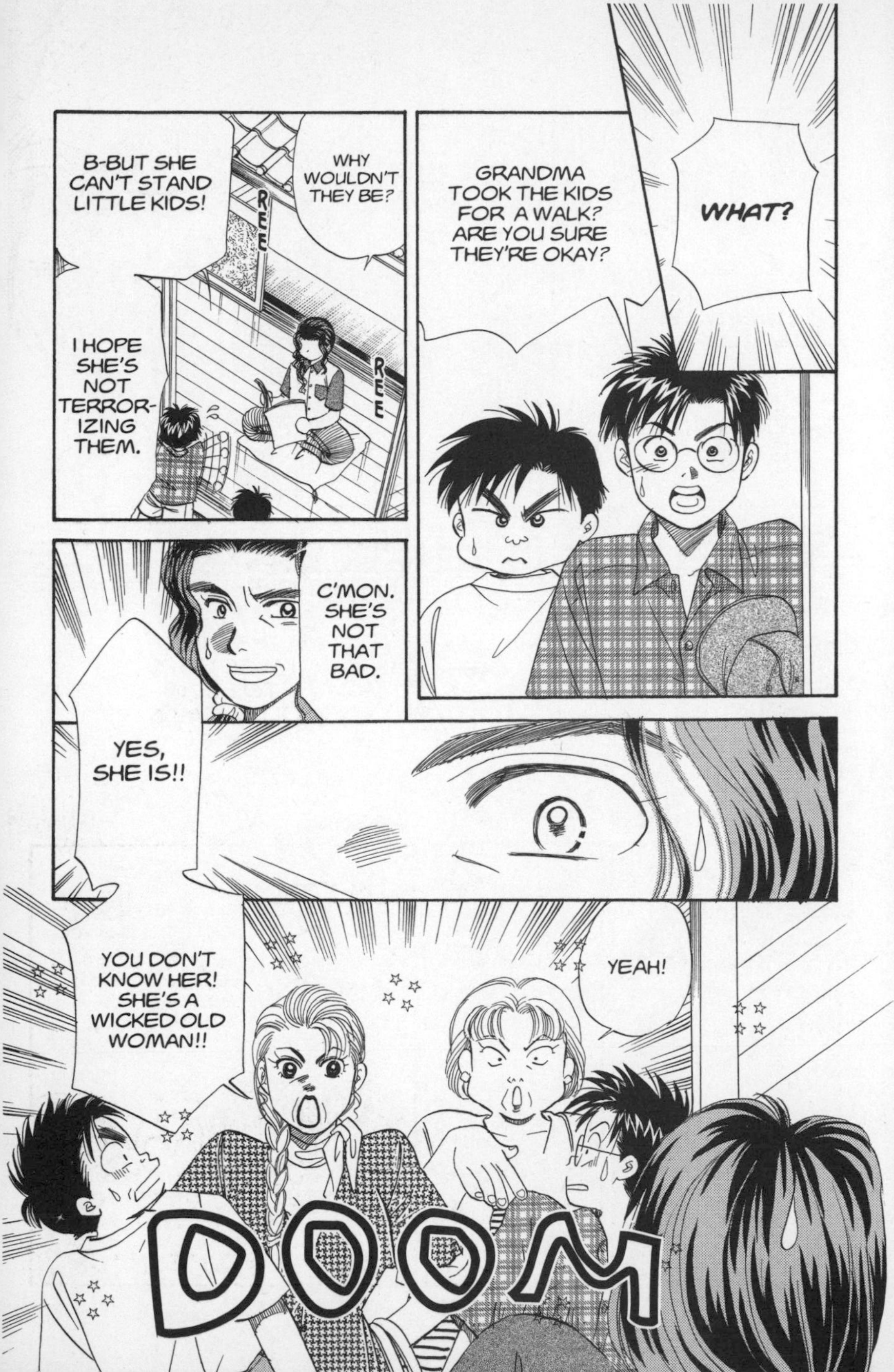
WHAT?
GRANDMA TOOK THE KIDS FOR A WALK? ARE YOU SURE THEY'RE OKAY?
WHY WOULDN'T THEY BE?
B-BUT SHE CAN'T STAND LITTLE KIDS!
REE
REE
I HOPE SHE'S NOT TERROR-IZING THEM.
C'MON. SHE'S NOT THAT BAD.
YES, SHE IS!!
YEAH!
YOU DON'T KNOW HER! SHE'S A WICKED OLD WOMAN!!
DOOM

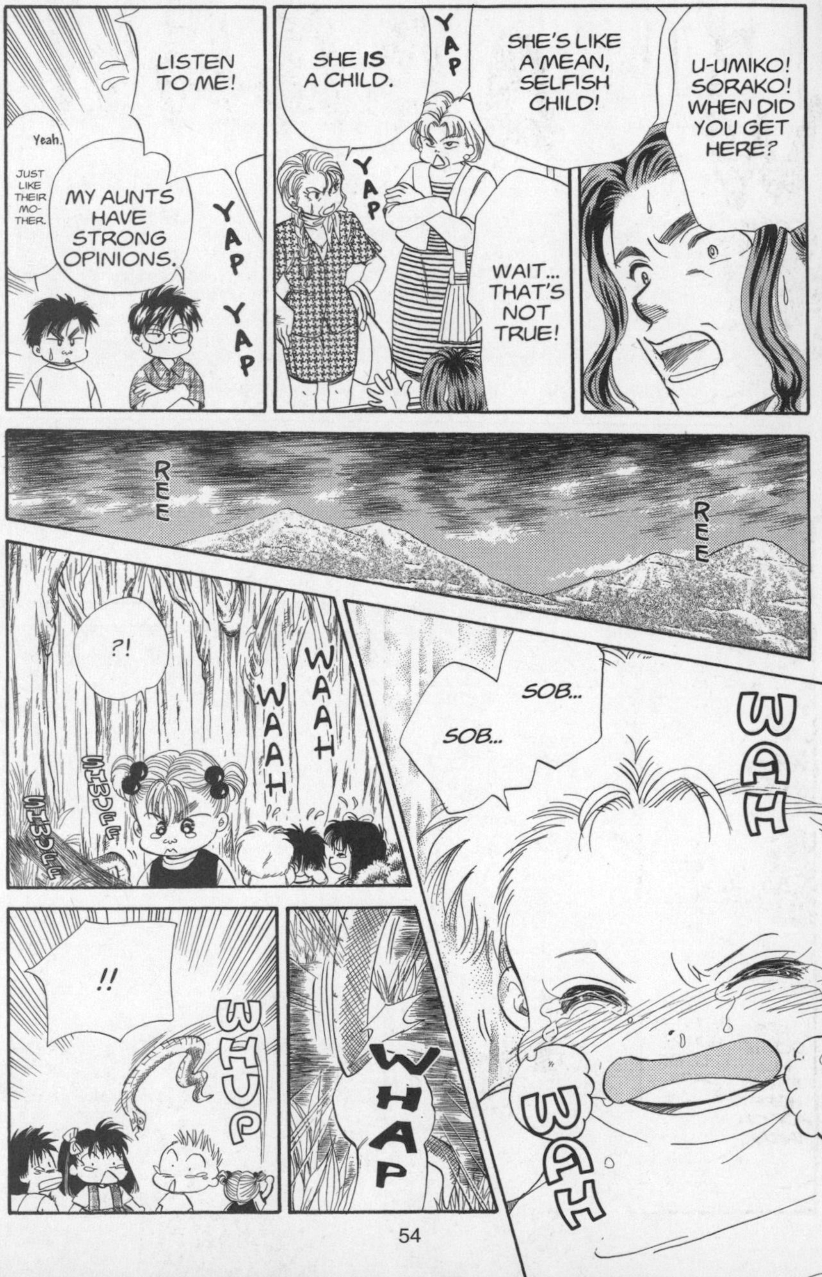
U-UMIKO! SORAKO! WHEN DID YOU GET HERE?
SHE'S LIKE A MEAN, SELFISH CHILD!
YAP
SHE IS A CHILD.
YAP
YAP
WAIT... THAT'S NOT TRUE!
LISTEN TO ME!
YAP YAP
MY AUNTS HAVE STRONG OPINIONS.
Yeah.
JUST LIKE THEIR MO-THER.
REE
REE
SOB...
SOB...
WAH
WAH
?!
WAAH
WAAH
SHWUFF
SHWUFF
WHAP
!!
WHUP

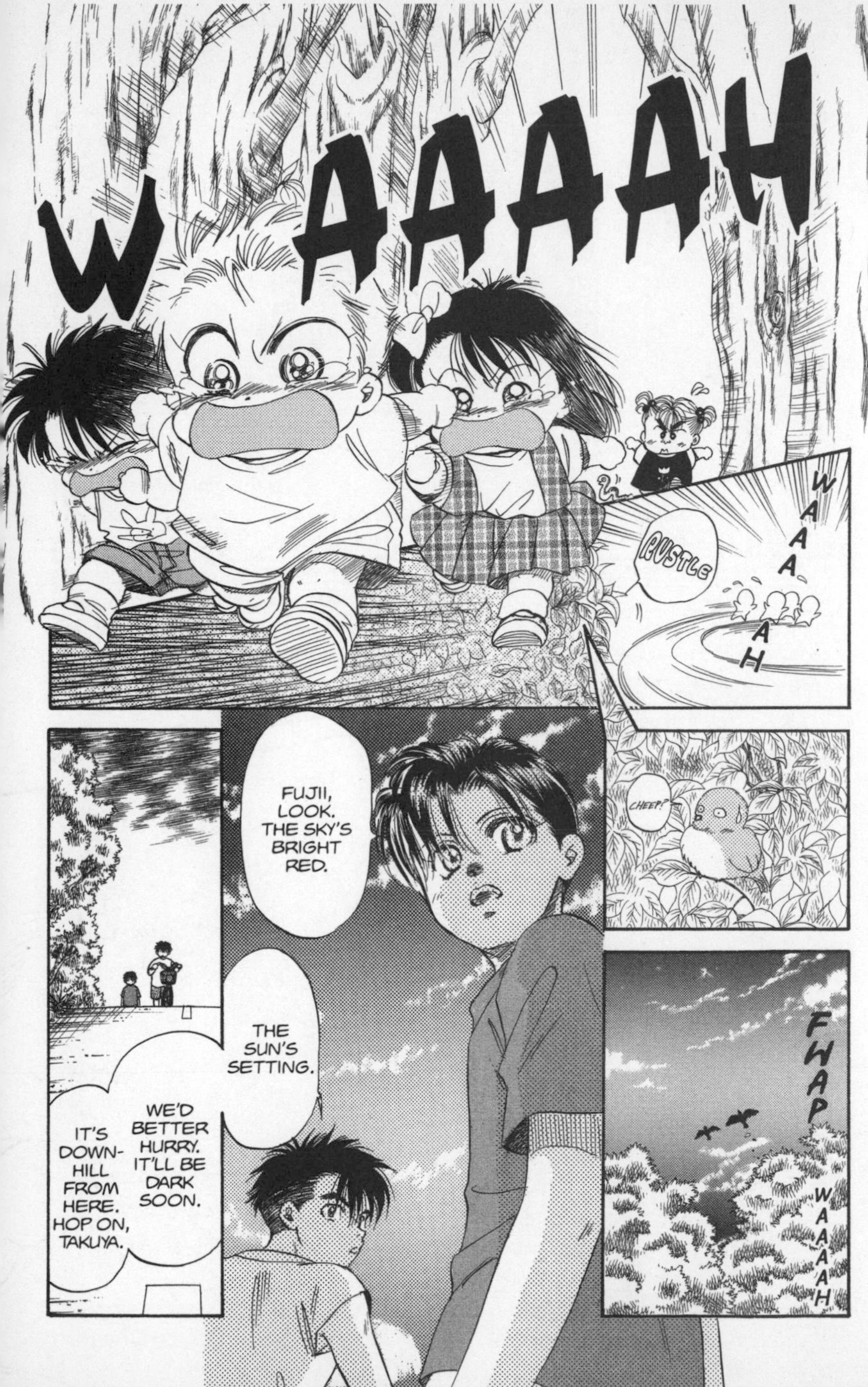
WAAAAH
RUSTLE
WAAAAH
CHEEP?
FWAP
WAAAAH
FUJII, LOOK. THE SKY'S BRIGHT RED.
THE SUN'S SETTING.
WE'D BETTER HURRY. IT'LL BE DARK SOON.
IT'S DOWNHILL FROM HERE. HOP ON, TAKUYA.

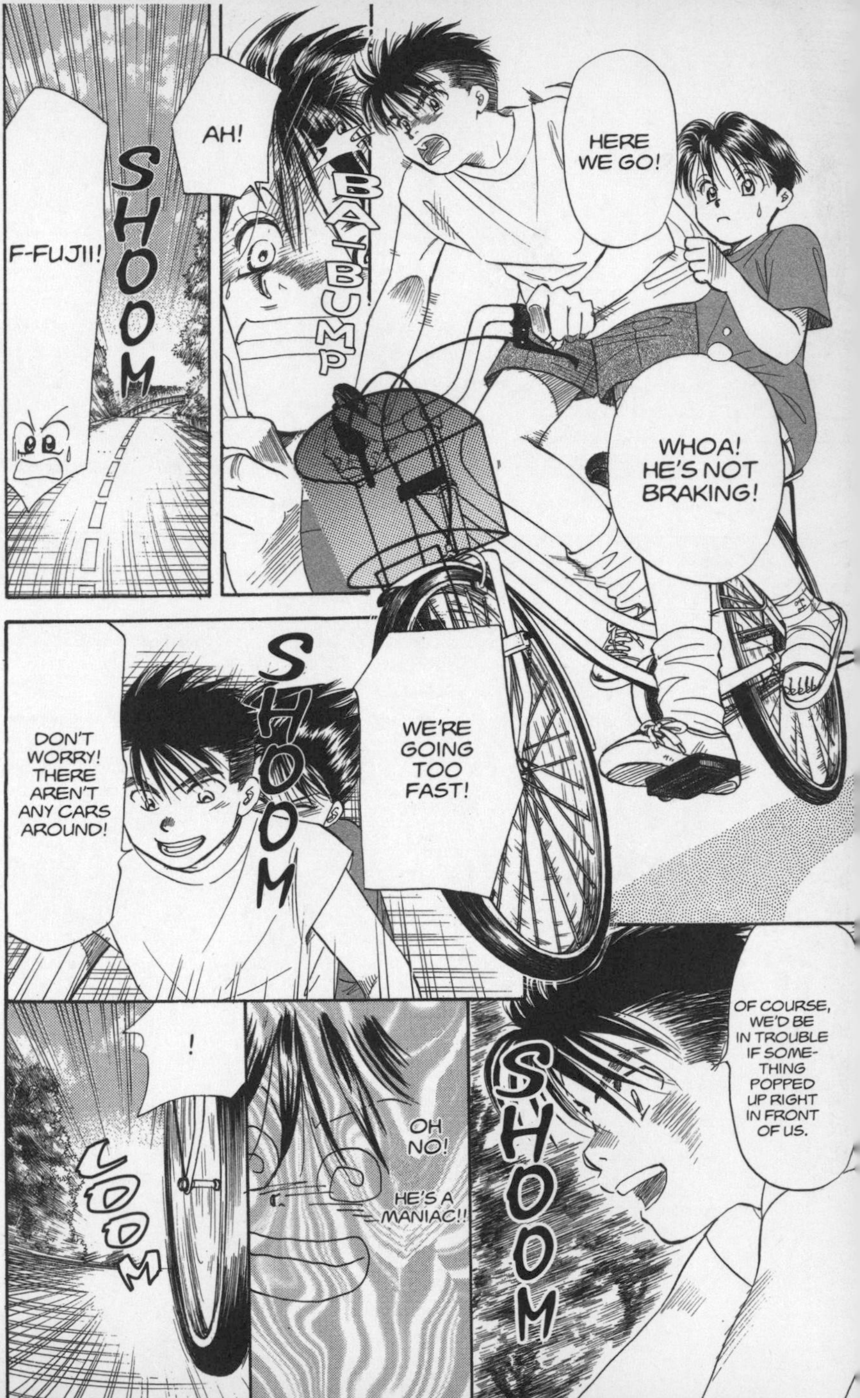
HERE WE GO!
WHOA! HE'S NOT BRAKING!
AH!
BA-BUMP
F-FUJII!
SHOOM
WE'RE GOING TOO FAST!
SHOOM
DON'T WORRY! THERE AREN'T ANY CARS AROUND!
OF COURSE, WE'D BE IN TROUBLE IF SOME-THING POPPED UP RIGHT IN FRONT OF US.
SHOOM
OH NO!
HE'S A MANIAC!!
!
VOOM

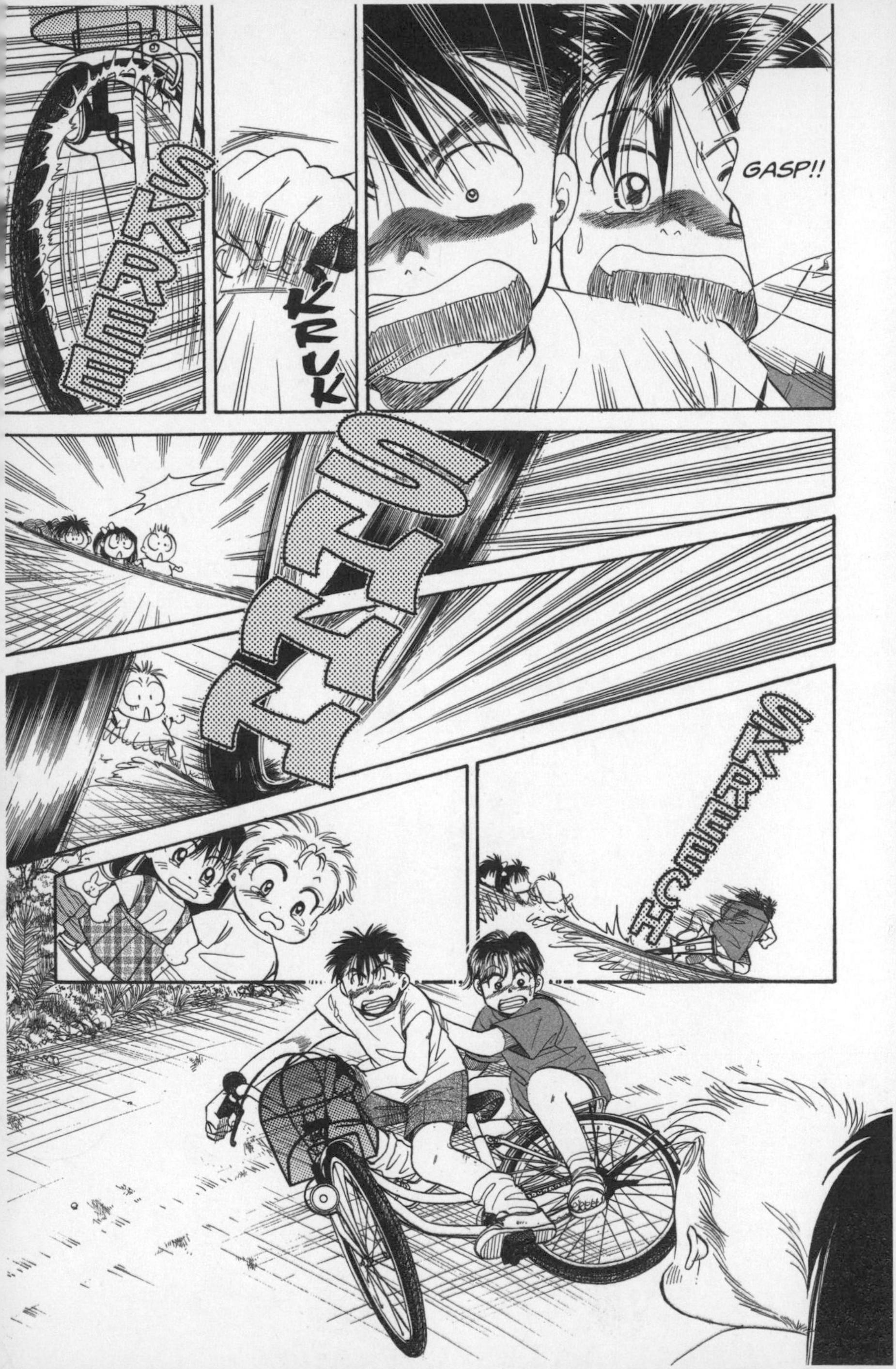
GASP!!
SKRUK
SKREEE
SHHH
SKREEECH

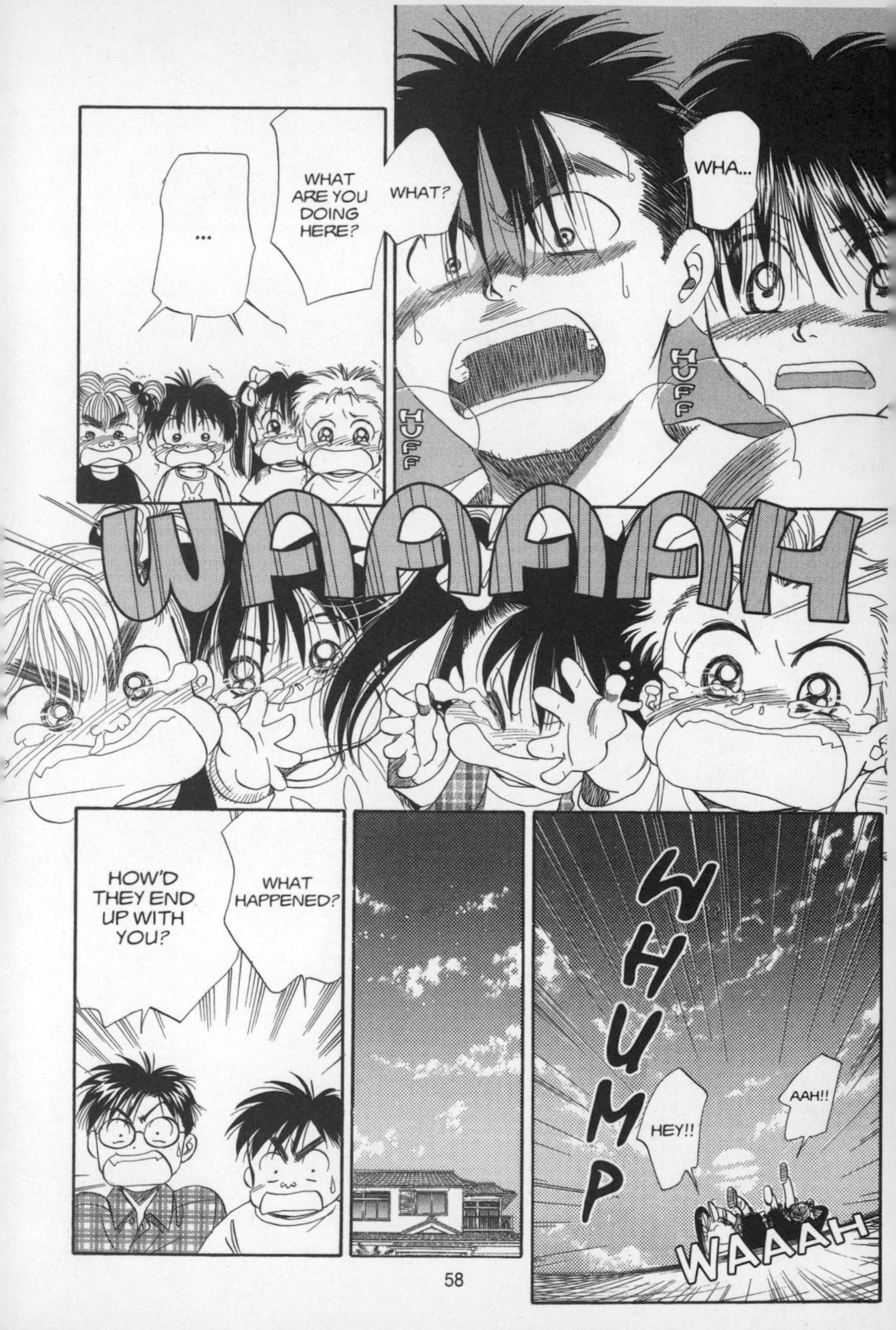
WHA...
HUFF
WHAT?
HUFF
WHAT ARE YOU DOING HERE?
...
WAAAAAH
AAH!!
HEY!!
WHUMP
WAAAH
WHAT HAPPENED?
HOW'D THEY END UP WITH YOU?

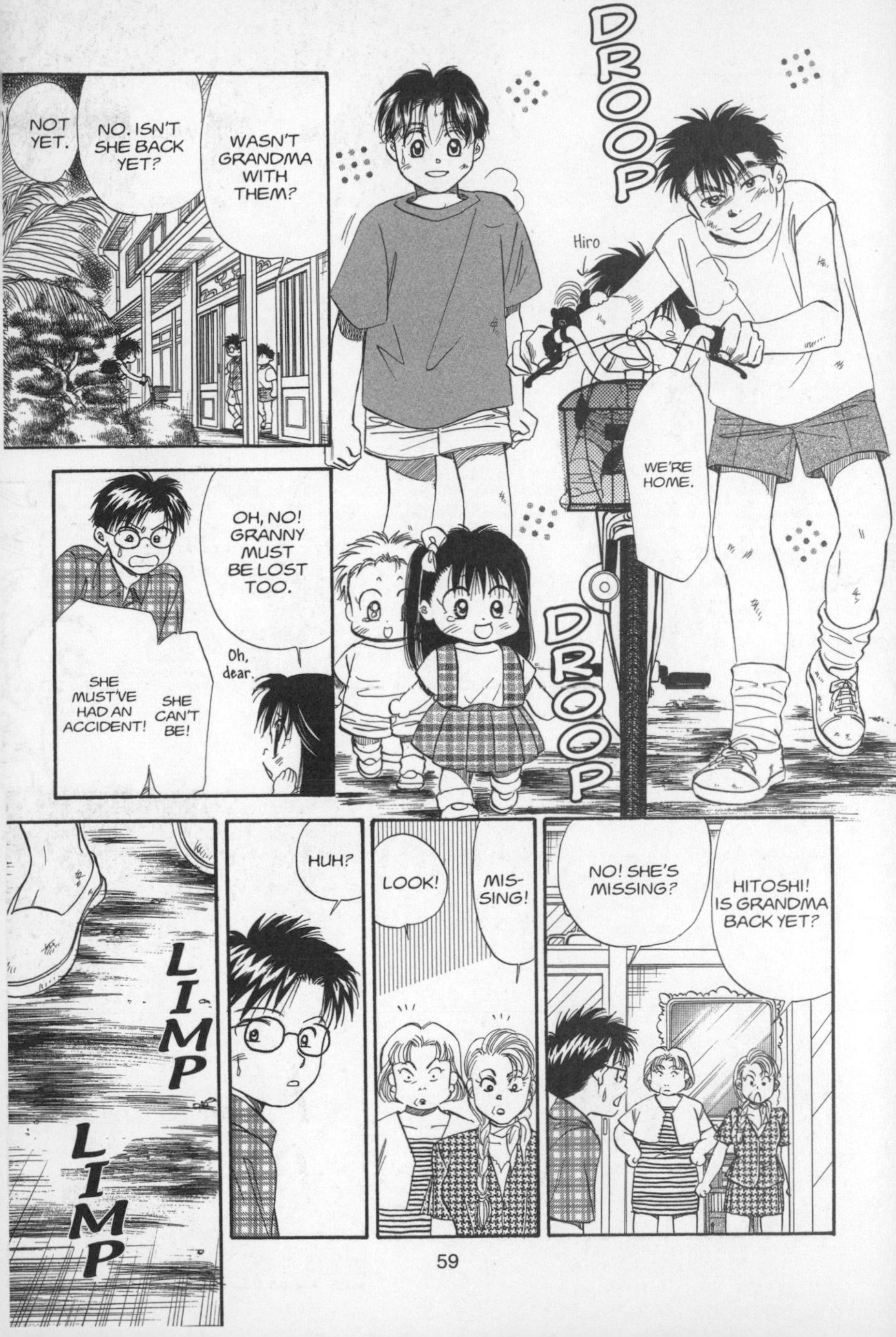
DROOP
Hiro
WE'RE HOME.
DROOP
WASN'T GRANDMA WITH THEM?
NO. ISN'T SHE BACK YET?
NOT YET.
OH, NO! GRANNY MUST BE LOST TOO.
Oh, dear.
SHE CAN'T BE!
SHE MUST'VE HAD AN ACCIDENT!
HITOSHI! IS GRANDMA BACK YET?
NO! SHE'S MISSING?
MIS-SING!
LOOK!
HUH?
LIMP
LIMP

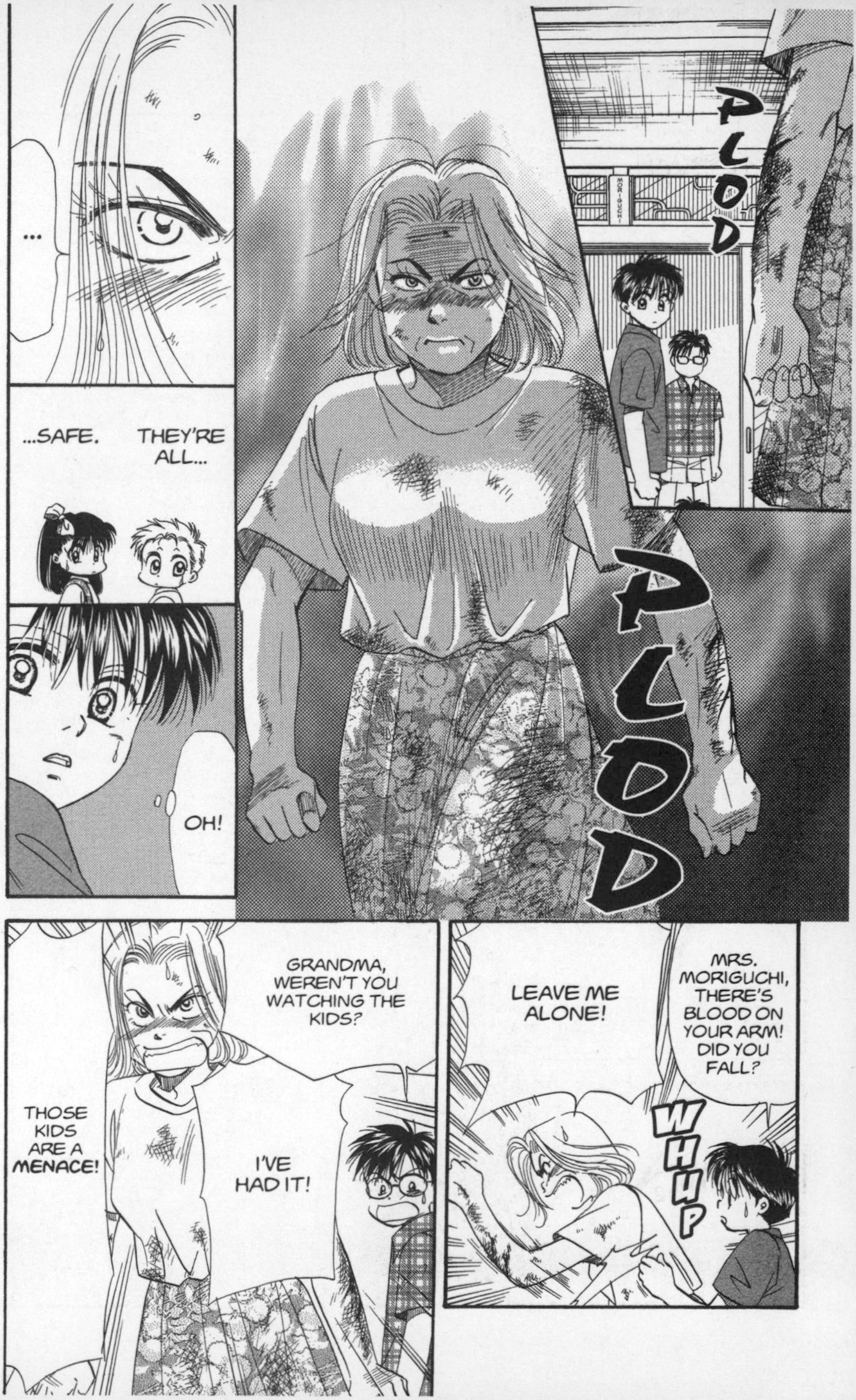
PLOD
MORIGUCHI
PLOD
...
THEY'RE ALL...
...SAFE.
OH!
MRS. MORIGUCHI, THERE'S BLOOD ON YOUR ARM! DID YOU FALL?
WHUP
LEAVE ME ALONE!
GRANDMA, WEREN'T YOU WATCHING THE KIDS?
I'VE HAD IT!
THOSE KIDS ARE A MENACE!

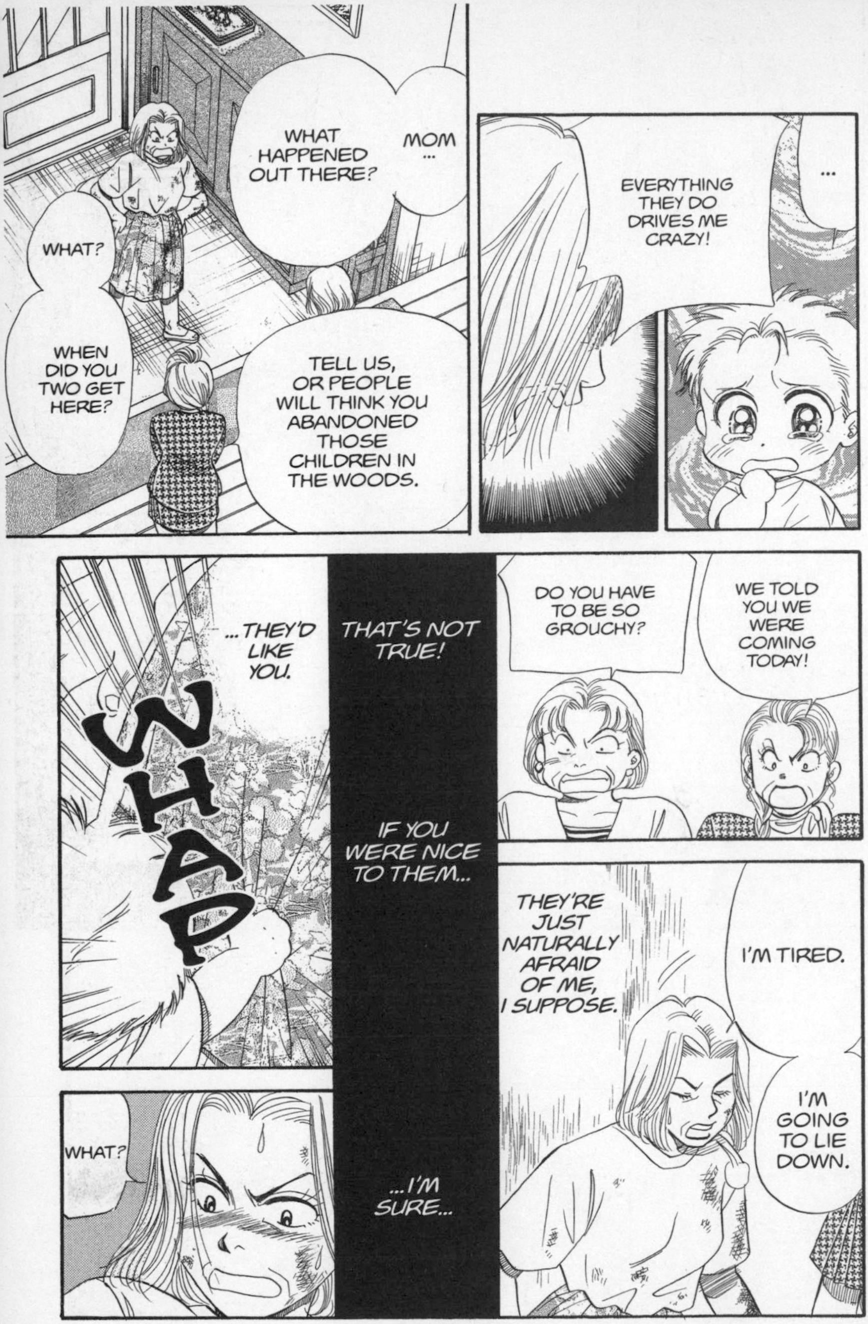
...
EVERYTHING THEY DO DRIVES ME CRAZY!
MOM ...
WHAT HAPPENED OUT THERE?
TELL US, OR PEOPLE WILL THINK YOU ABANDONED THOSE CHILDREN IN THE WOODS.
WHAT?
WHEN DID YOU TWO GET HERE?
WE TOLD YOU WE WERE COMING TODAY!
DO YOU HAVE TO BE SO GROUCHY?
I'M TIRED.
I'M GOING TO LIE DOWN.
THEY'RE JUST NATURALLY AFRAID OF ME, I SUPPOSE.
THAT'S NOT TRUE!
IF YOU WERE NICE TO THEM...
...I'M SURE...
...THEY'D LIKE YOU.
WHAP
WHAT?

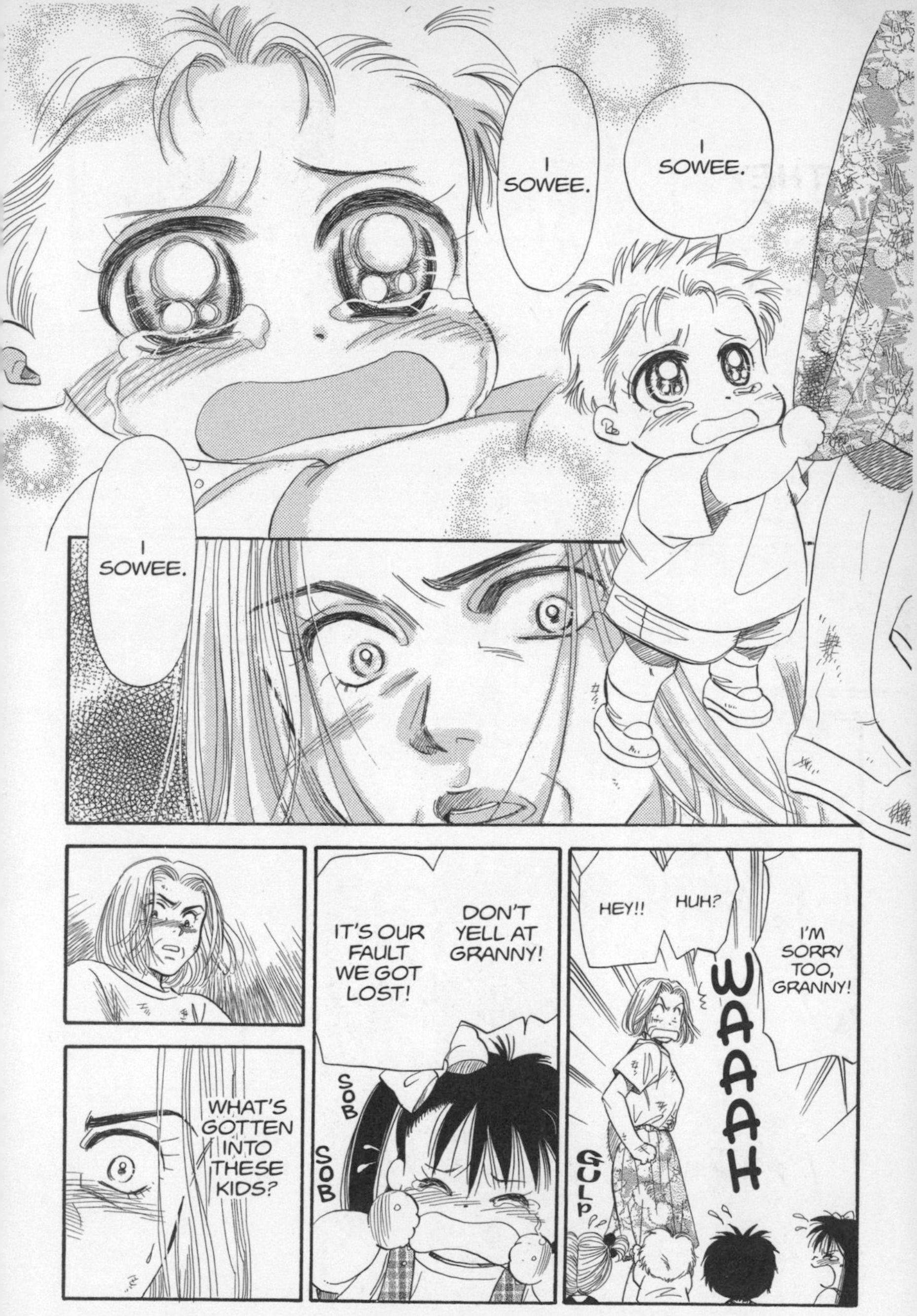
I SOWEE.
I SOWEE.
I SOWEE.
I'M SORRY TOO, GRANNY!
HUH?
HEY!!
WAAAH
GULP
DON'T YELL AT GRANNY!
IT'S OUR FAULT WE GOT LOST!
SOB
SOB
WHAT'S GOTTEN INTO THESE KIDS?

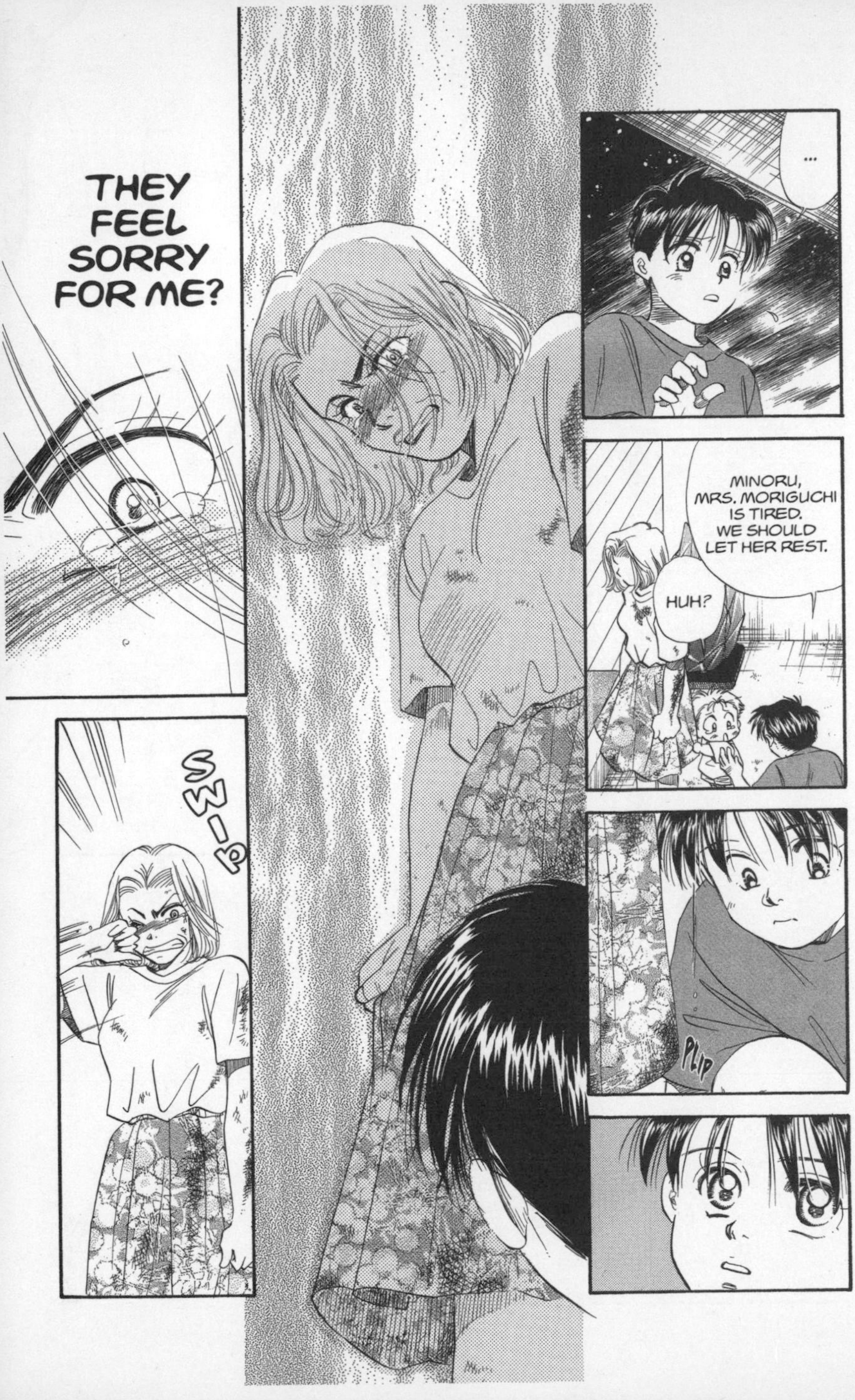
...
MINORU, MRS. MORIGUCHI IS TIRED. WE SHOULD LET HER REST.
HUH?
PLIP
THEY FEEL SORRY FOR ME?
SWIP

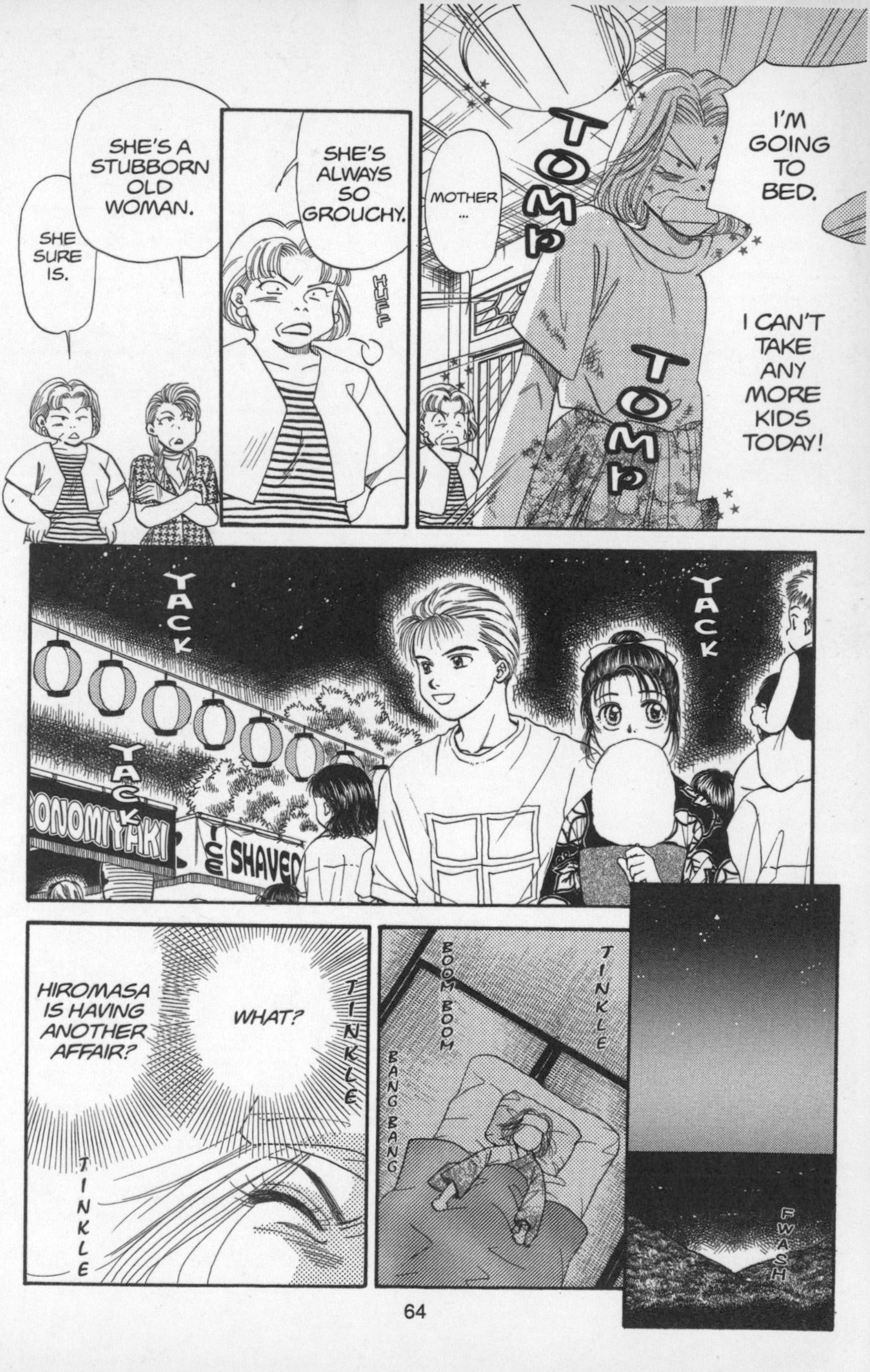
I'M GOING TO BED.
I CAN'T TAKE ANY MORE KIDS TODAY!
TOMP
TOMP
MOTHER ...
SHE'S ALWAYS SO GROUCHY.
HUFF
SHE'S A STUBBORN OLD WOMAN.
SHE SURE IS.
YACK
YACK
YACK
ONOMIYAKI
SHAVED ICE
FWASH
TINKLE
BOOM BOOM
BANG BANG
WHAT?
HIROMASA IS HAVING ANOTHER AFFAIR?
TINKLE
TINKLE

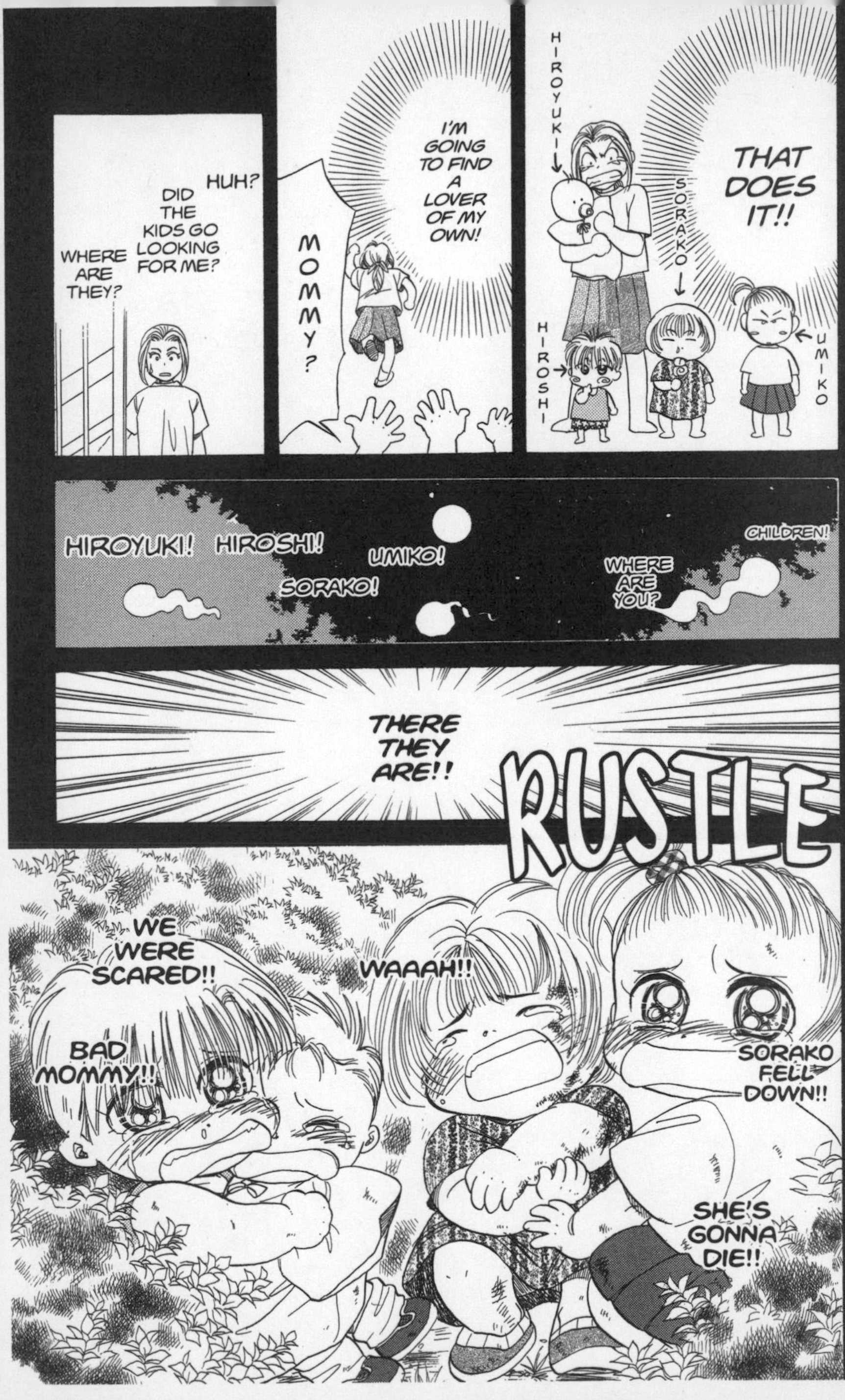
THAT DOES IT!!
HIROYUKI
SORAKO
UMIKO
HIROSHI
I'M GOING TO FIND A LOVER OF MY OWN!
MOMMY?
HUH?
DID THE KIDS GO LOOKING FOR ME?
WHERE ARE THEY?
CHILDREN!
WHERE ARE YOU?
UMIKO!
HIROSHI!
HIROYUKI!
SORAKO!
THERE THEY ARE!!
RUSTLE
SORAKO FELL DOWN!!
SHE'S GONNA DIE!!
WAAAH!!
WE WERE SCARED!!
BAD MOMMY!!

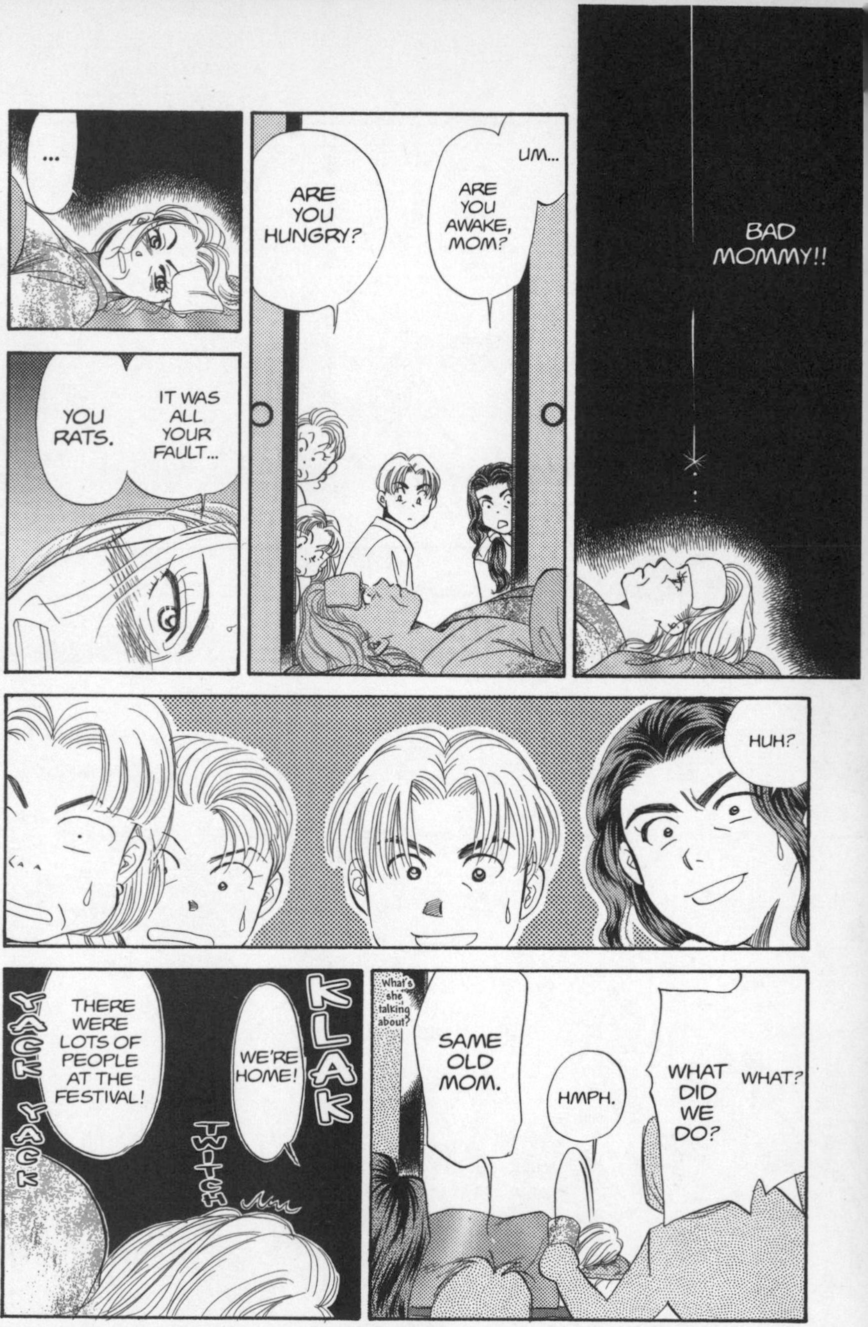

BAD MOMMY!!
UM... ARE YOU AWAKE, MOM?
ARE YOU HUNGRY?
...
IT WAS ALL YOUR FAULT...
YOU RATS.
HUH?
WHAT?
WHAT DID WE DO?
HMPH.
SAME OLD MOM.
What's she talking about?
KLAK
WE'RE HOME!
TWITCH
THERE WERE LOTS OF PEOPLE AT THE FESTIVAL!
YACK YACK

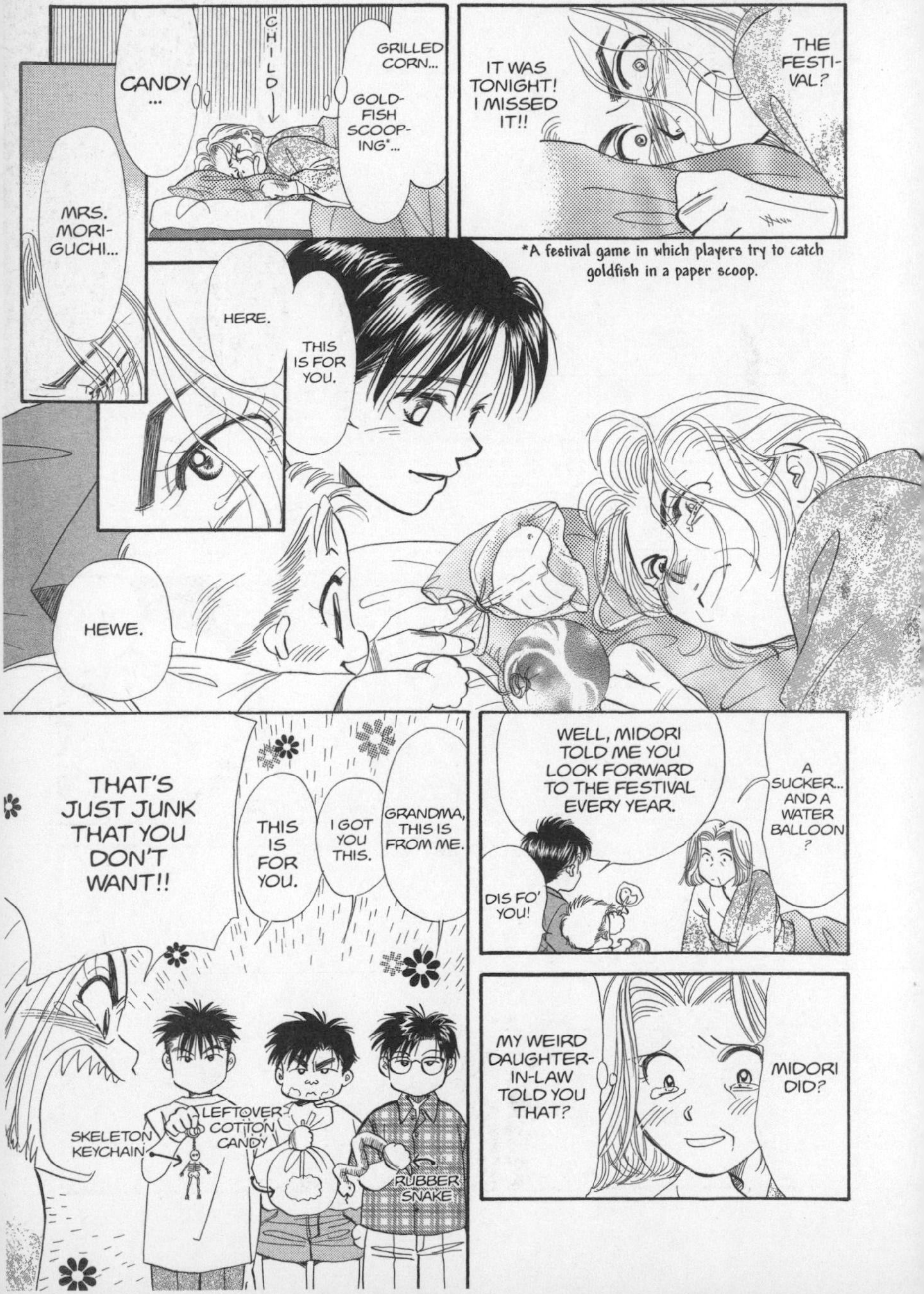
THE FESTI-VAL?
IT WAS TONIGHT! I MISSED IT!!
GRILLED CORN...
GOLD-FISH SCOOP-ING*...
CHILD
CANDY...
MRS. MORI-GUCHI...
HERE.
THIS IS FOR YOU.
HEWE.
A SUCKER... AND A WATER BALLOON?
WELL, MIDORI TOLD ME YOU LOOK FORWARD TO THE FESTIVAL EVERY YEAR.
DIS FO' YOU!
MIDORI DID?
MY WEIRD DAUGHTER-IN-LAW TOLD YOU THAT?
GRANDMA, THIS IS FROM ME.
I GOT YOU THIS.
THIS IS FOR YOU.
THAT'S JUST JUNK THAT YOU DON'T WANT!!
RUBBER SNAKE
LEFTOVER COTTON CANDY
SKELETON KEYCHAIN

*A festival game in which players try to catch goldfish in a paper scoop.

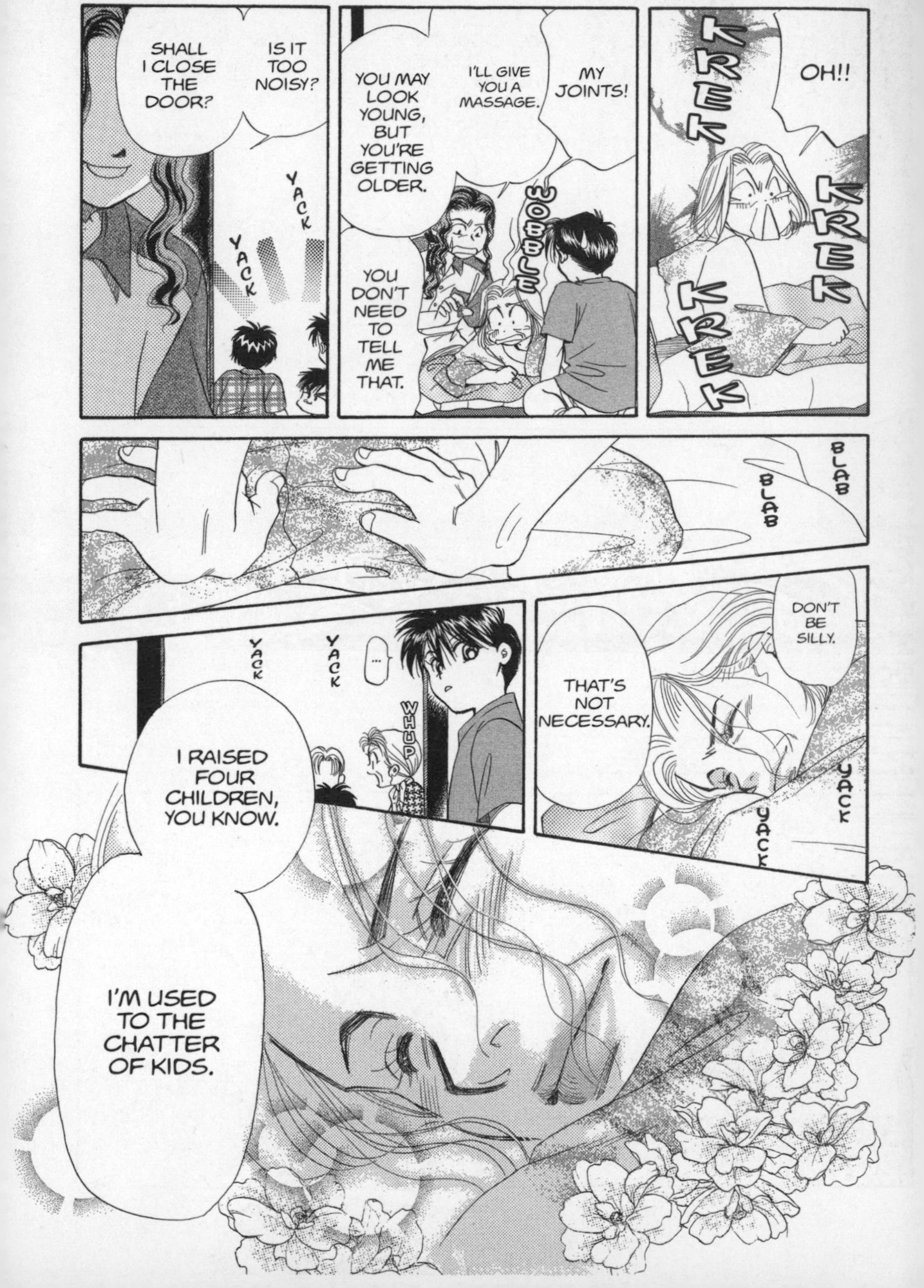
OH!!
KREK
KREK
KREK
MY JOINTS!
I'LL GIVE YOU A MASSAGE.
YOU MAY LOOK YOUNG, BUT YOU'RE GETTING OLDER.
WOBBLE
YOU DON'T NEED TO TELL ME THAT.
IS IT TOO NOISY?
SHALL I CLOSE THE DOOR?
YACK
YACK
BLAB
BLAB
DON'T BE SILLY.
THAT'S NOT NECESSARY.
YACK
YACK
YACK
YACK
...
WHUP
I RAISED FOUR CHILDREN, YOU KNOW.
I'M USED TO THE CHATTER OF KIDS.

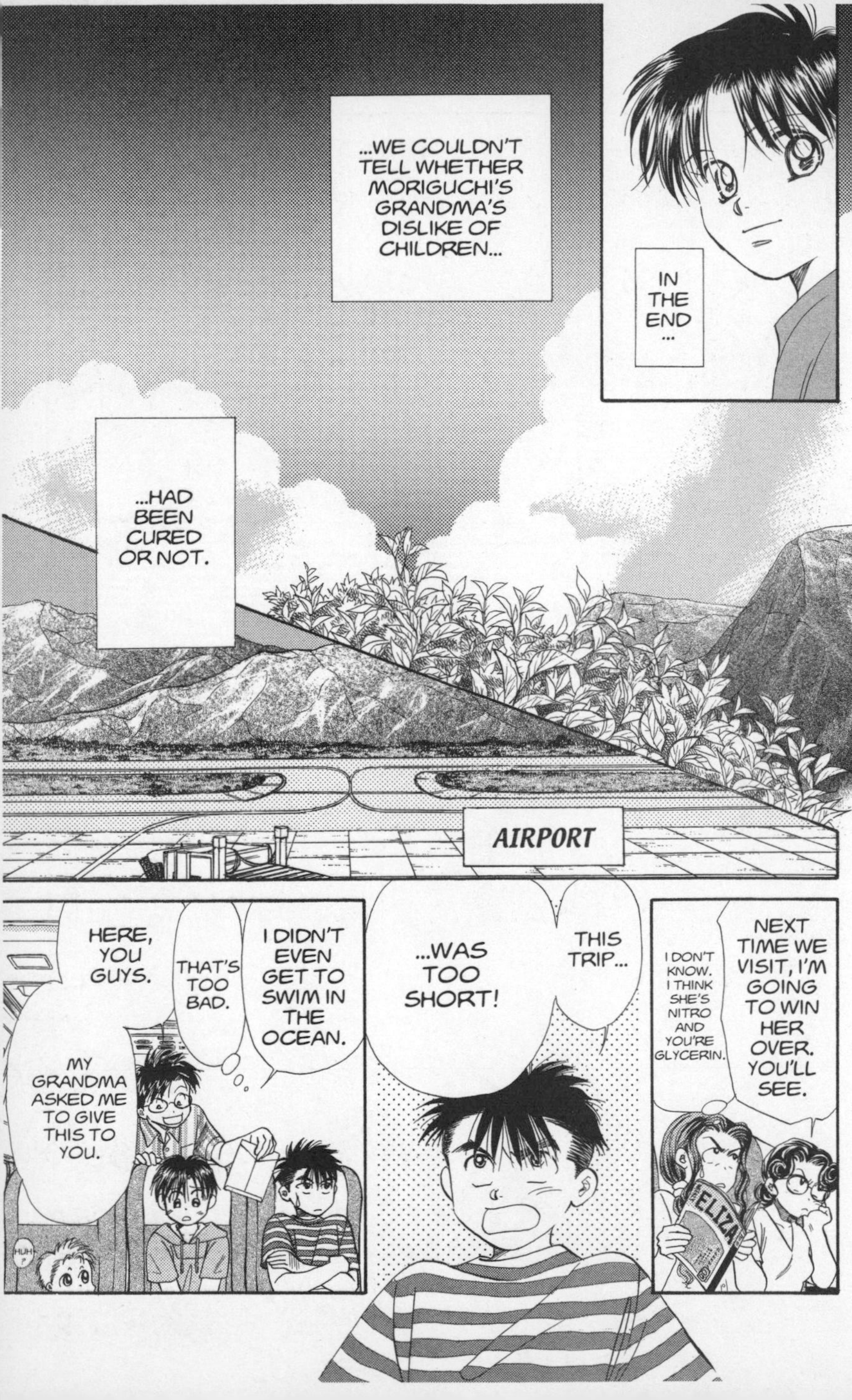
IN THE END...
...WE COULDN'T TELL WHETHER MORIGUCHI'S GRANDMA'S DISLIKE OF CHILDREN...
...HAD BEEN CURED OR NOT.
AIRPORT
NEXT TIME WE VISIT, I'M GOING TO WIN HER OVER. YOU'LL SEE.
I DON'T KNOW. I THINK SHE'S NITRO AND YOU'RE GLYCERIN.
ELIZA
THIS TRIP...
...WAS TOO SHORT!
I DIDN'T EVEN GET TO SWIM IN THE OCEAN.
THAT'S TOO BAD.
HERE, YOU GUYS.
MY GRANDMA ASKED ME TO GIVE THIS TO YOU.
HUH?

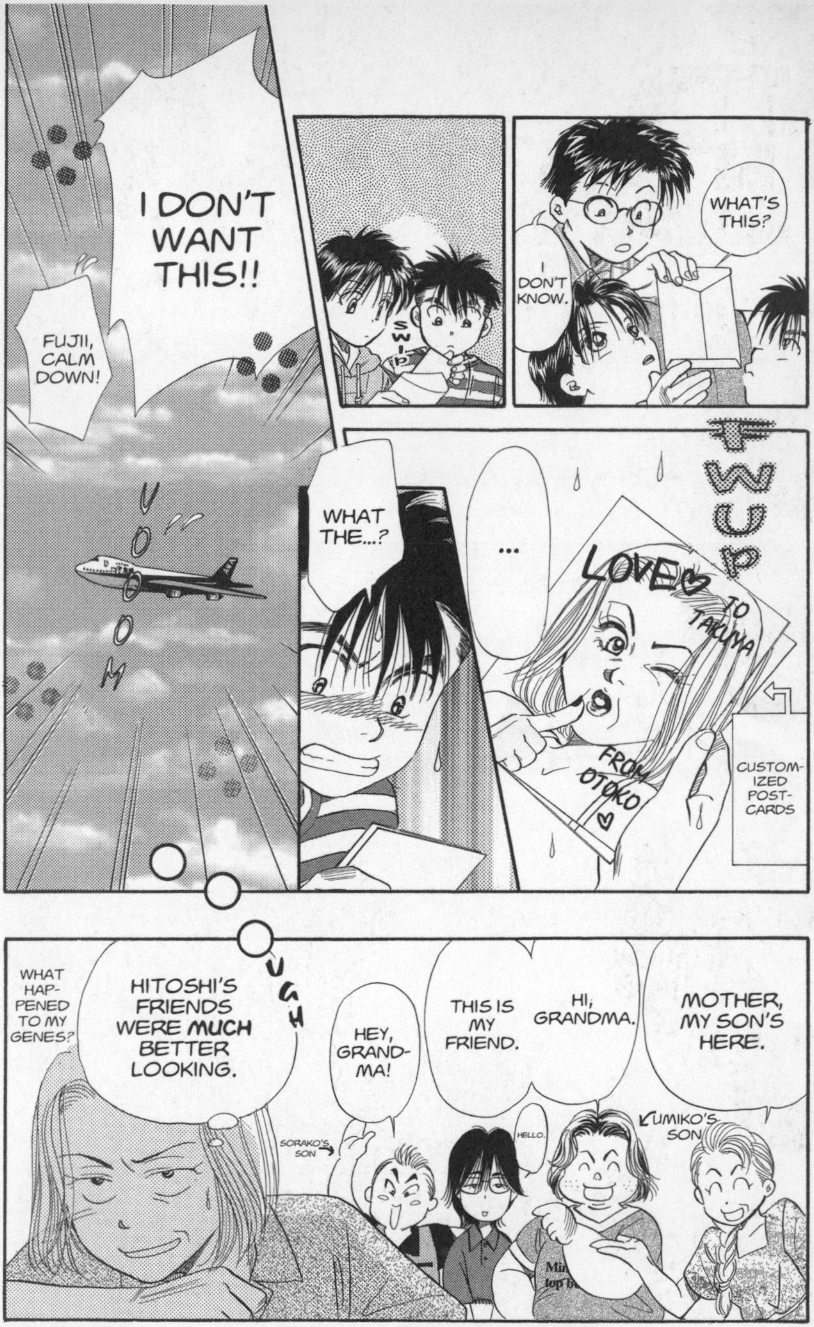
WHAT'S THIS?
I DON'T KNOW.
SWIP
FWUP
...
LOVE♡ TO TAKUYA
FROM OTOKO ♡
CUSTOMIZED POST-CARDS
WHAT THE...?
I DON'T WANT THIS!!
FUJII, CALM DOWN!
VOOOOM
MOTHER, MY SON'S HERE.
UMIKO'S SON
HI, GRANDMA.
THIS IS MY FRIEND.
HELLO.
HEY, GRAND-MA!
SORAKO'S SON
UGH
HITOSHI'S FRIENDS WERE MUCH BETTER LOOKING.
WHAT HAP-PENED TO MY GENES?

Chapter 87 / The End

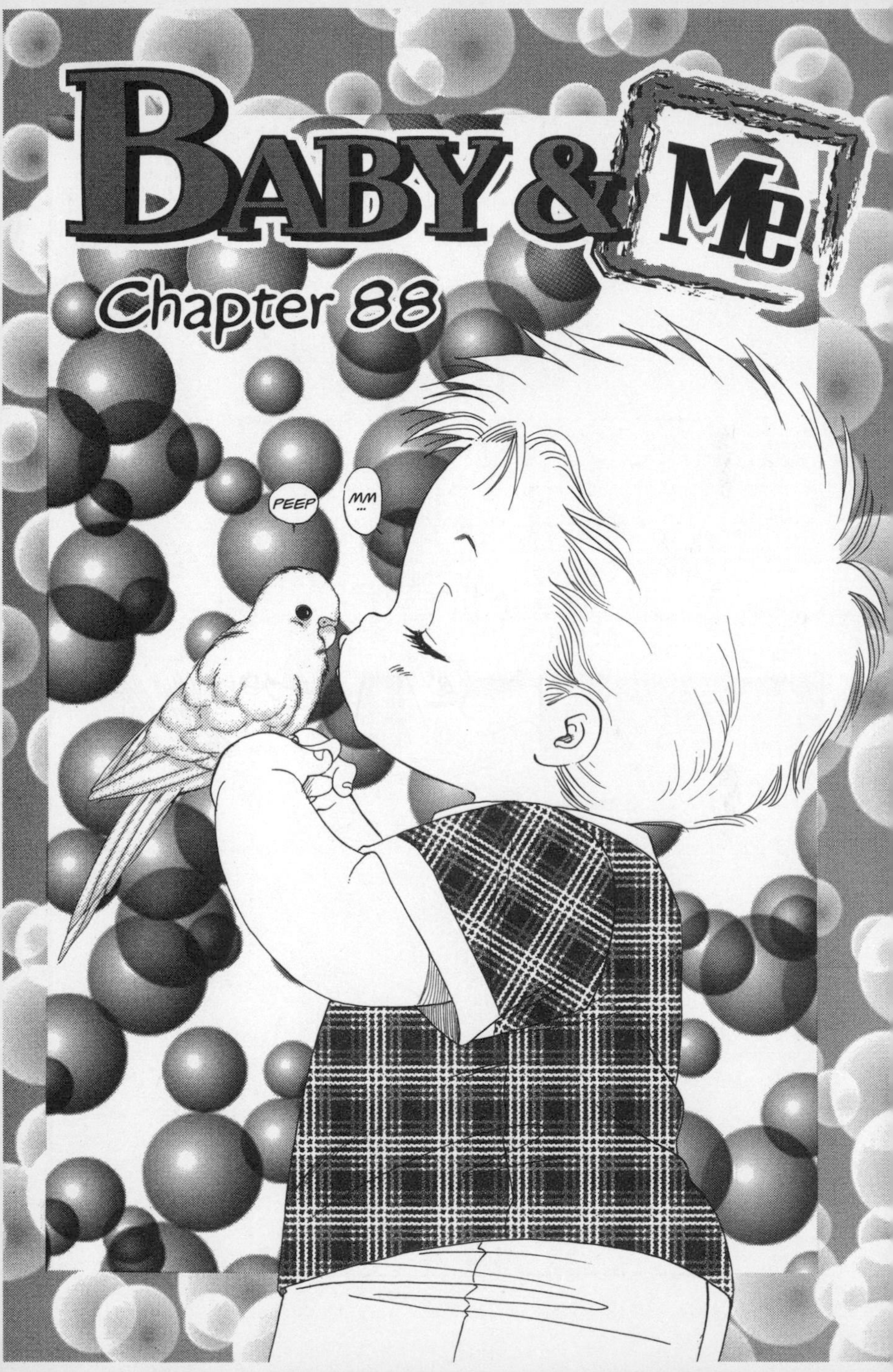
BABY & ME
Chapter 88
MM...
PEEP

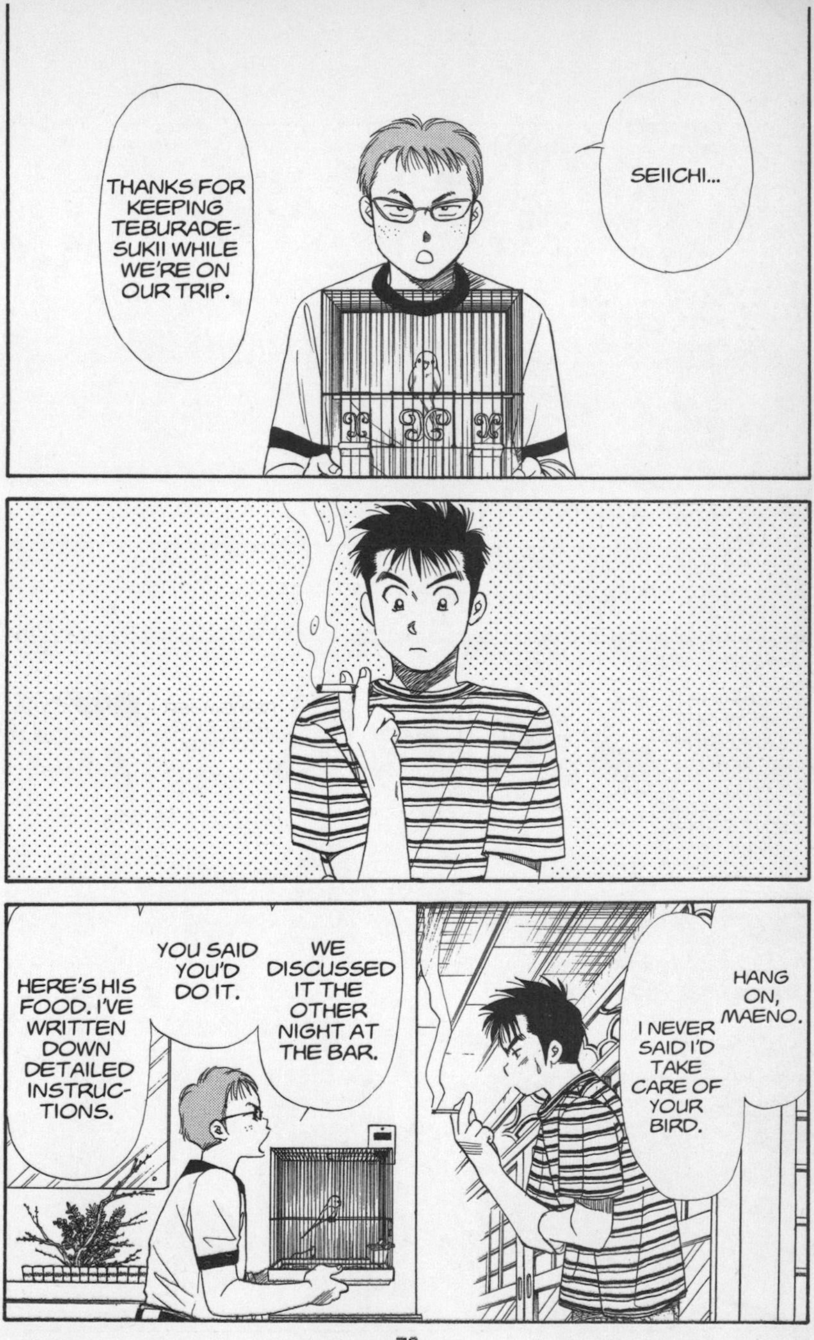
SEIICHI...
THANKS FOR KEEPING TEBURADE-SUKII WHILE WE'RE ON OUR TRIP.
HANG ON, MAENO.
I NEVER SAID I'D TAKE CARE OF YOUR BIRD.
WE DISCUSSED IT THE OTHER NIGHT AT THE BAR.
YOU SAID YOU'D DO IT.
HERE'S HIS FOOD. I'VE WRITTEN DOWN DETAILED INSTRUC-TIONS.

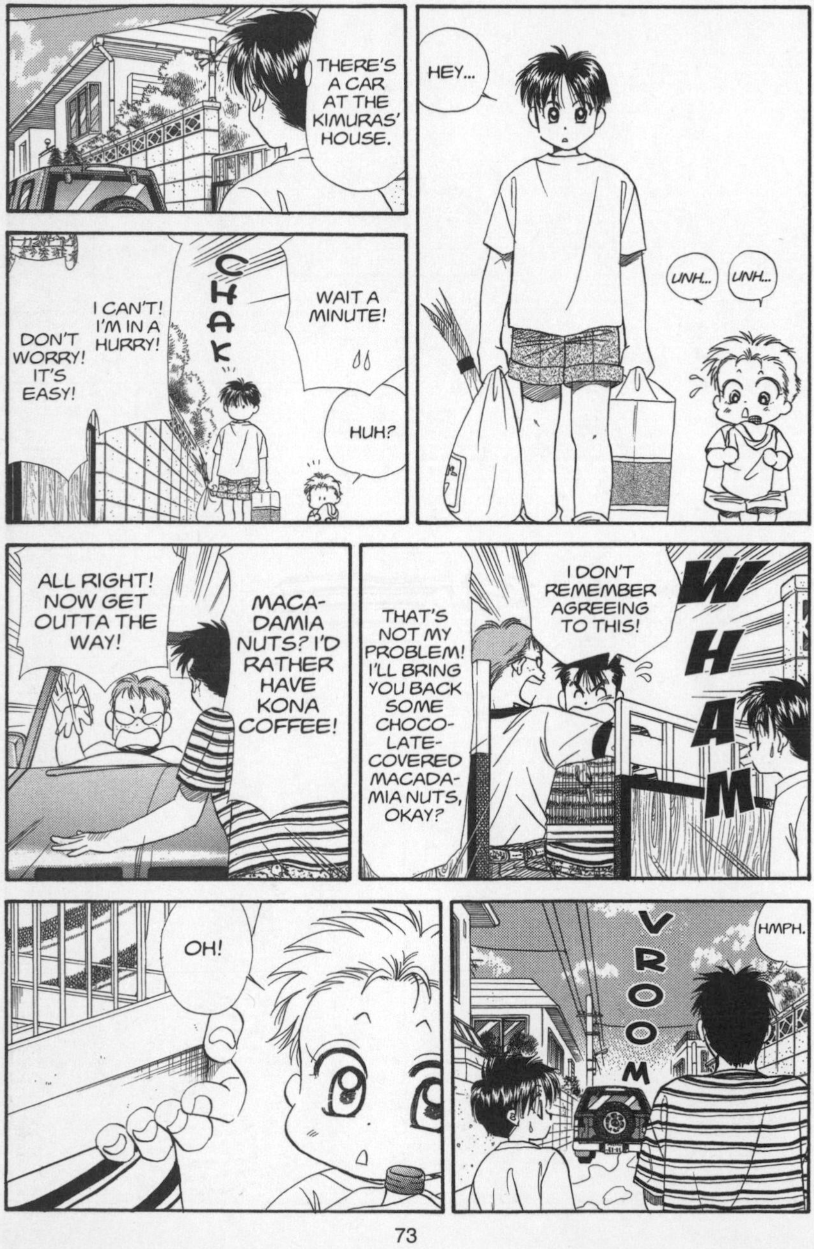
HEY...
UNH...
UNH...
THERE'S A CAR AT THE KIMURAS' HOUSE.
WAIT A MINUTE!
CHAK
I CAN'T! I'M IN A HURRY!
DON'T WORRY! IT'S EASY!
HUH?
WHAM
I DON'T REMEMBER AGREEING TO THIS!
THAT'S NOT MY PROBLEM! I'LL BRING YOU BACK SOME CHOCO-LATE-COVERED MACADA-MIA NUTS, OKAY?
MACA-DAMIA NUTS? I'D RATHER HAVE KONA COFFEE!
ALL RIGHT! NOW GET OUTTA THE WAY!
HMPH.
VROOM
OH!

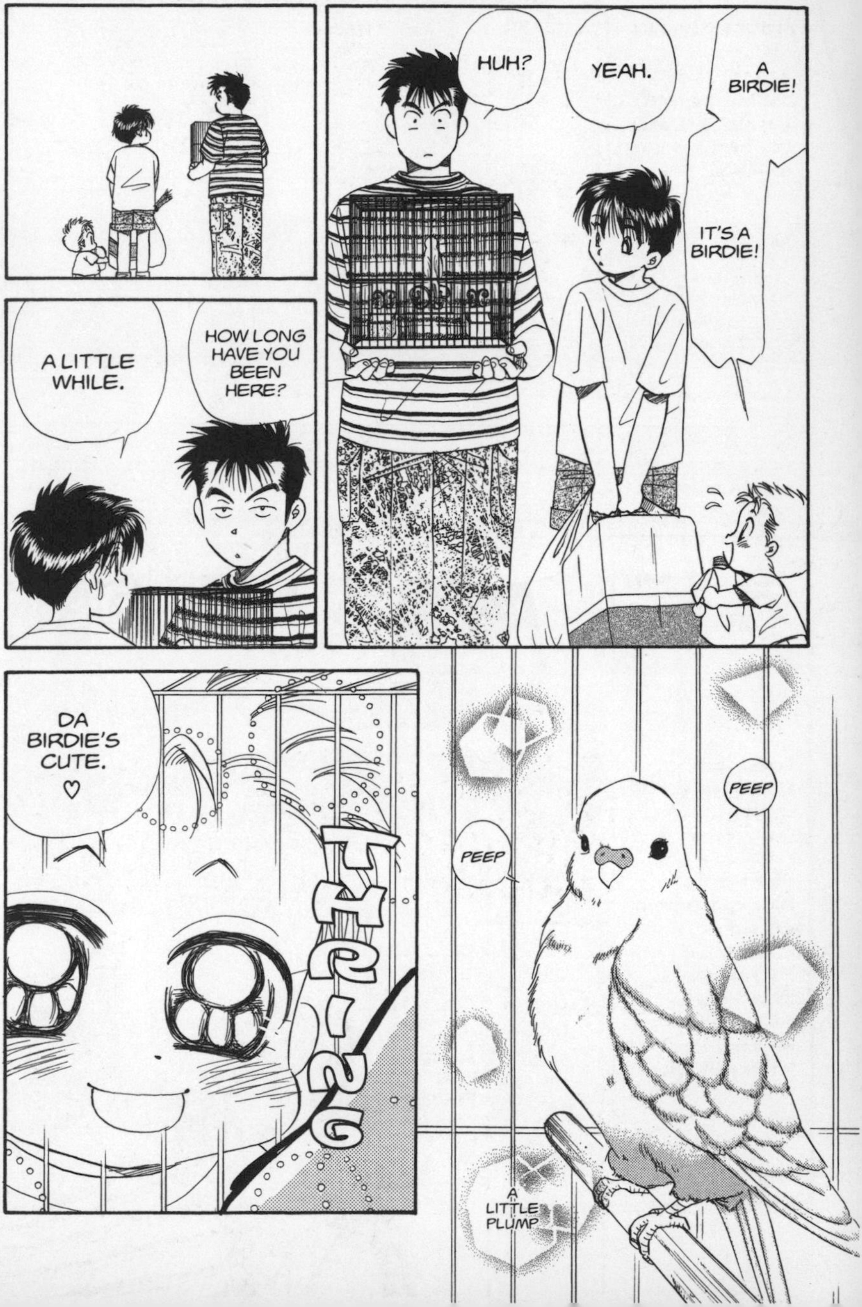
A BIRDIE!
IT'S A BIRDIE!
YEAH.
HUH?
HOW LONG HAVE YOU BEEN HERE?
A LITTLE WHILE.
PEEP
PEEP
A LITTLE PLUMP
DA BIRDIE'S CUTE. ♡
THRING

Author's Note Part 3

As soon as we reached the hotel, I bought a souvenir cup for $8.50 in the dining room.

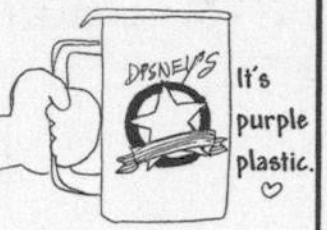
DISNEY'S
It's purple plastic. ♡

I got it because there was a 24-hour bar in the dining room that offered unlimited refills with the cup.

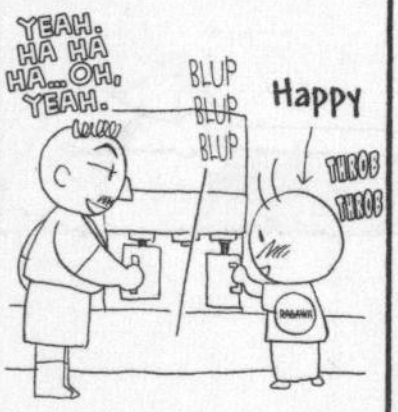
YEAH. HA HA HA...OH. YEAH.
BLUP BLUP BLUP
Happy
THROB THROB

I only had the waiter fill my cup half-way each time (because that's all I could drink), but other people were filling up their cups with coffee or soda. I had breakfast every morning in the dining room, but even though it was a buffet, we had to tell the staff what we wanted to eat — and my English isn't very good.

Continued in Part 4

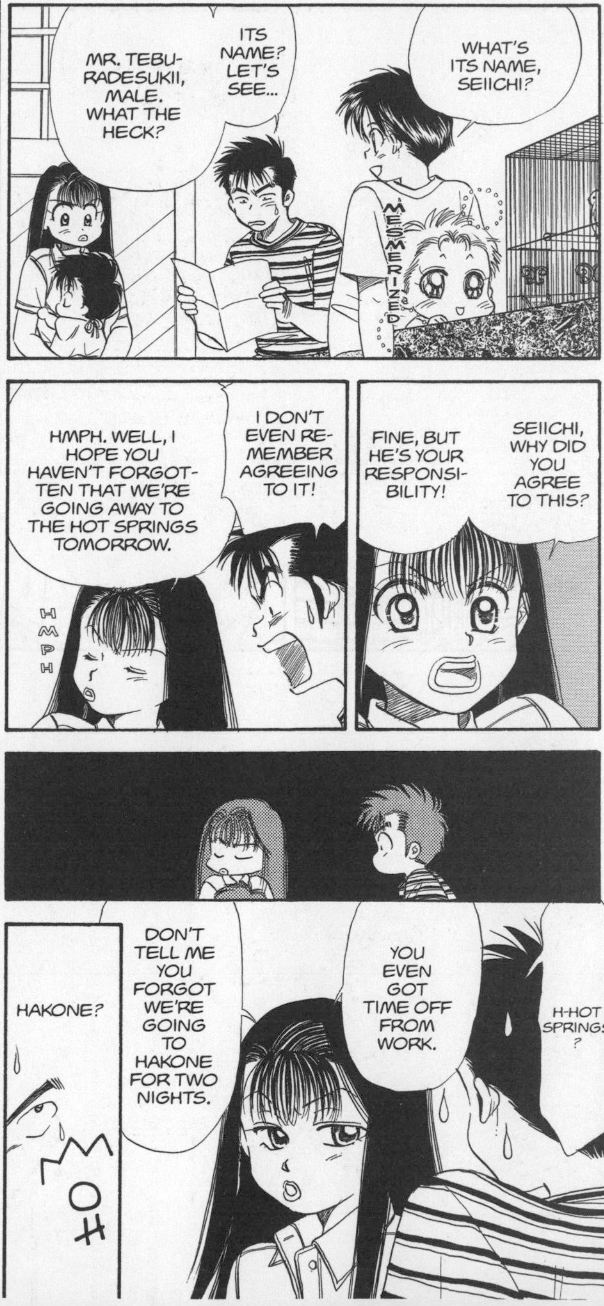
WHAT'S ITS NAME, SEIICHI?
ITS NAME? LET'S SEE...
MR. TEBU-RADESUKII, MALE. WHAT THE HECK?
MESMERIZED
SEIICHI, WHY DID YOU AGREE TO THIS?
FINE, BUT HE'S YOUR RESPONSI-BILITY!
I DON'T EVEN RE-MEMBER AGREEING TO IT!
HMPH. WELL, I HOPE YOU HAVEN'T FORGOT-TEN THAT WE'RE GOING AWAY TO THE HOT SPRINGS TOMORROW.
HMPH
H-HOT SPRINGS?
YOU EVEN GOT TIME OFF FROM WORK.
DON'T TELL ME YOU FORGOT WE'RE GOING TO HAKONE FOR TWO NIGHTS.
HAKONE?
OH

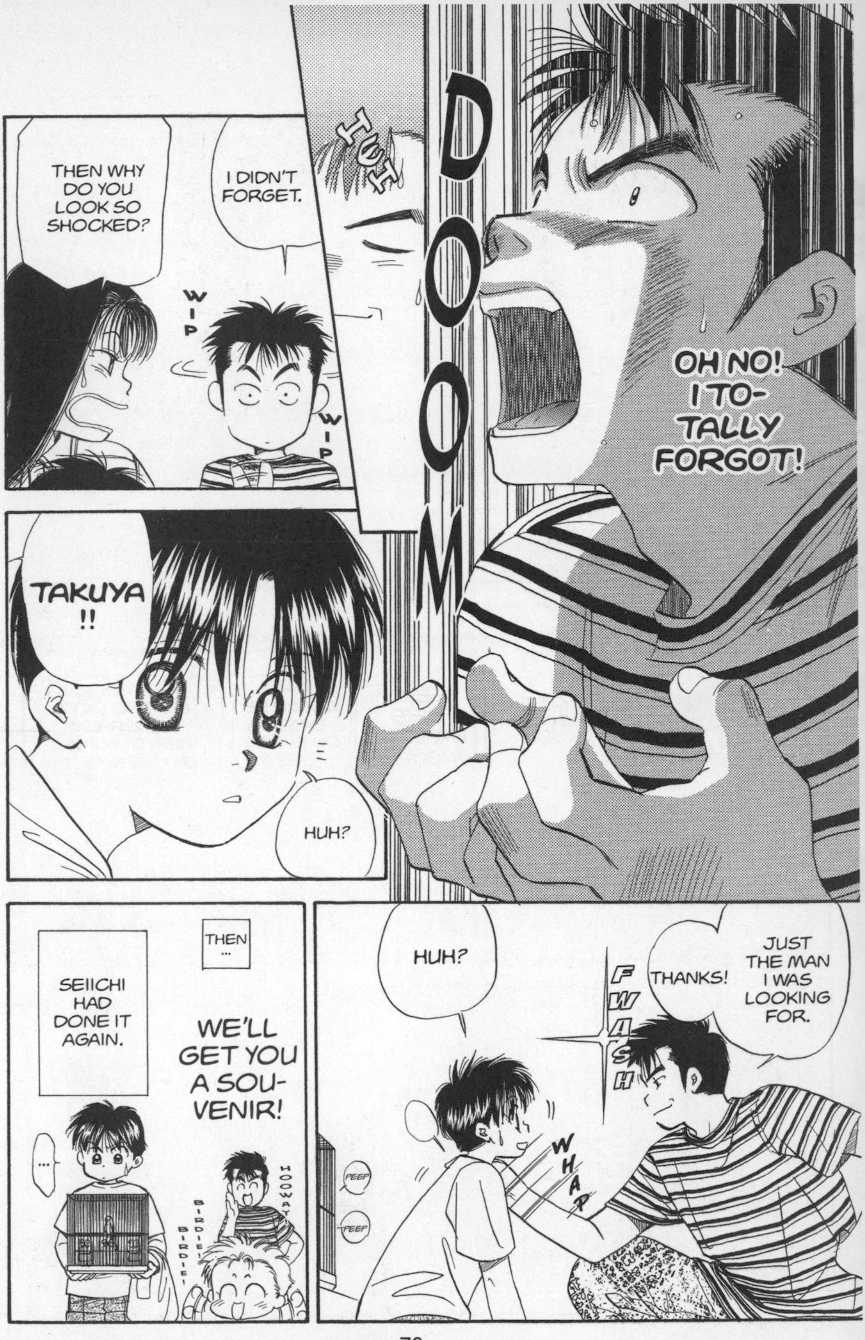
DOOOM
OH NO! I TO-TALLY FORGOT!
I DIDN'T FORGET.
THEN WHY DO YOU LOOK SO SHOCKED?
WIP
WIP
TAKUYA !!
HUH?
JUST THE MAN I WAS LOOKING FOR.
THANKS!
FWASH
HUH?
WHAP
PEEP
PEEP
THEN ...
WE'LL GET YOU A SOU-VENIR!
SEIICHI HAD DONE IT AGAIN.
HOOWAY!
BIRDIE!
BIRDIE!
...

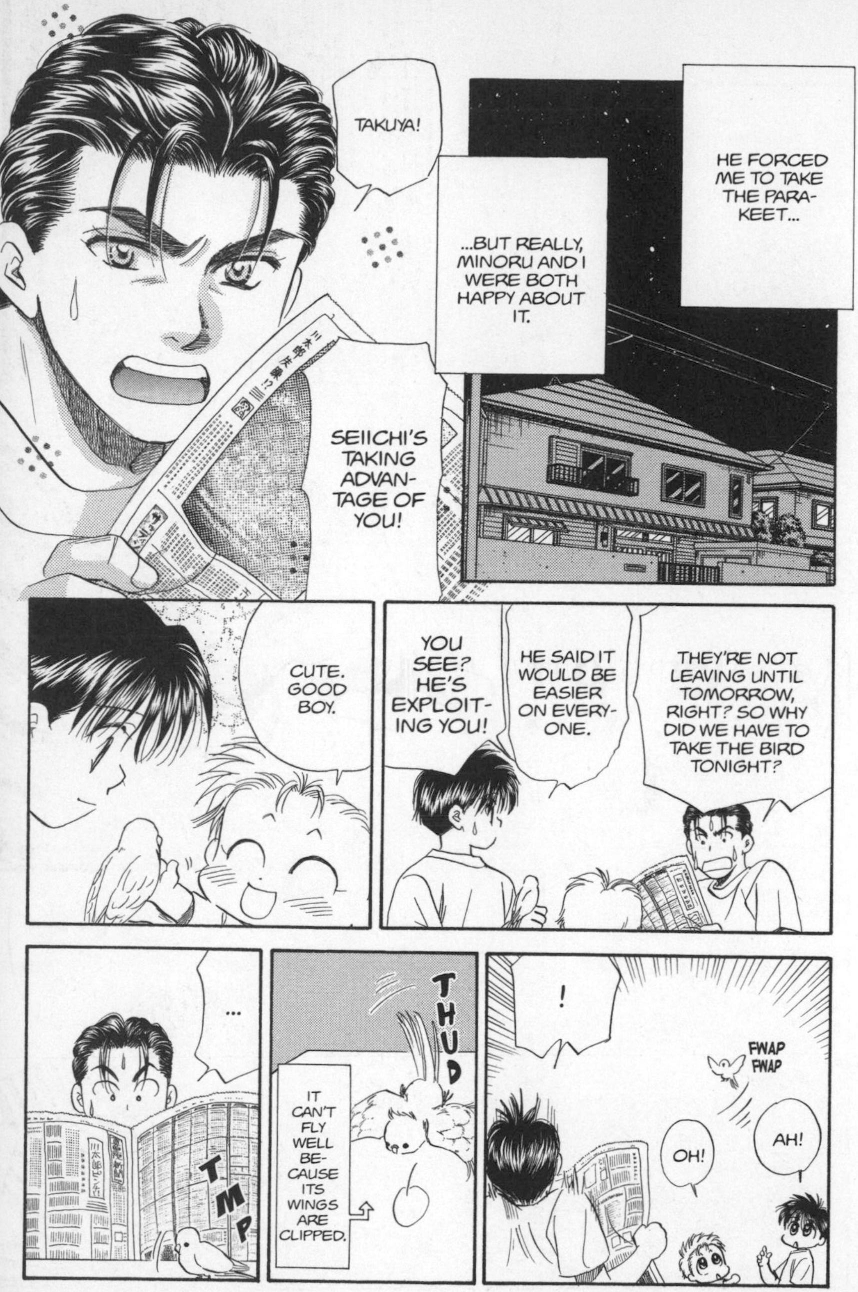
HE FORCED ME TO TAKE THE PARAKEET...
...BUT REALLY, MINORU AND I WERE BOTH HAPPY ABOUT IT.
TAKUYA!
SEIICHI'S TAKING ADVANTAGE OF YOU!
THEY'RE NOT LEAVING UNTIL TOMORROW, RIGHT? SO WHY DID WE HAVE TO TAKE THE BIRD TONIGHT?
HE SAID IT WOULD BE EASIER ON EVERYONE.
YOU SEE? HE'S EXPLOITING YOU!
CUTE. GOOD BOY.
!
FWAP FWAP
AH!
OH!
THUD
IT CAN'T FLY WELL BECAUSE ITS WINGS ARE CLIPPED.
...
TMP

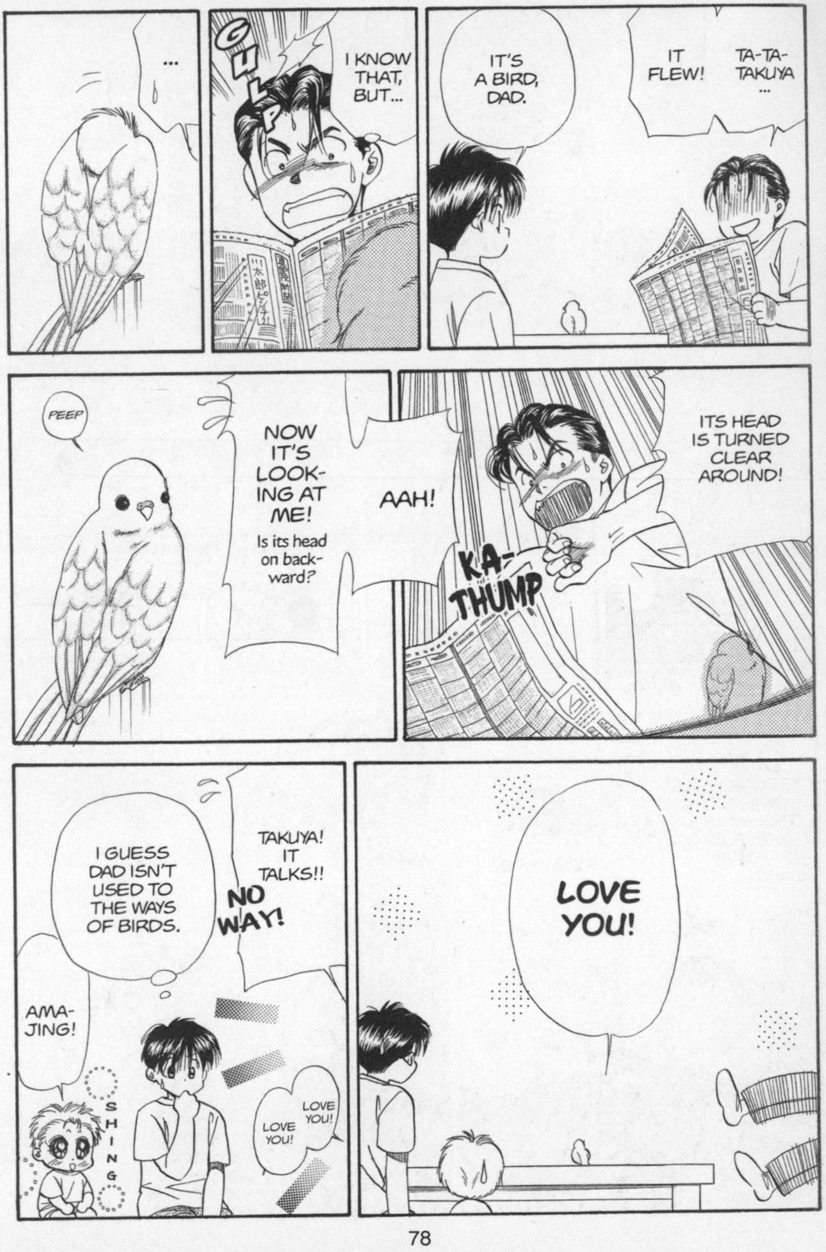
TA-TA-TAKUYA ...
IT FLEW!
IT'S A BIRD, DAD.
GULP
I KNOW THAT, BUT...
...
ITS HEAD IS TURNED CLEAR AROUND!
KA-THUMP
AAH!
NOW IT'S LOOKING AT ME!
Is its head on backward?
PEEP
LOVE YOU!
TAKUYA! IT TALKS!!
NO WAY!
I GUESS DAD ISN'T USED TO THE WAYS OF BIRDS.
LOVE YOU!
LOVE YOU!
AMA-JING!
SHING

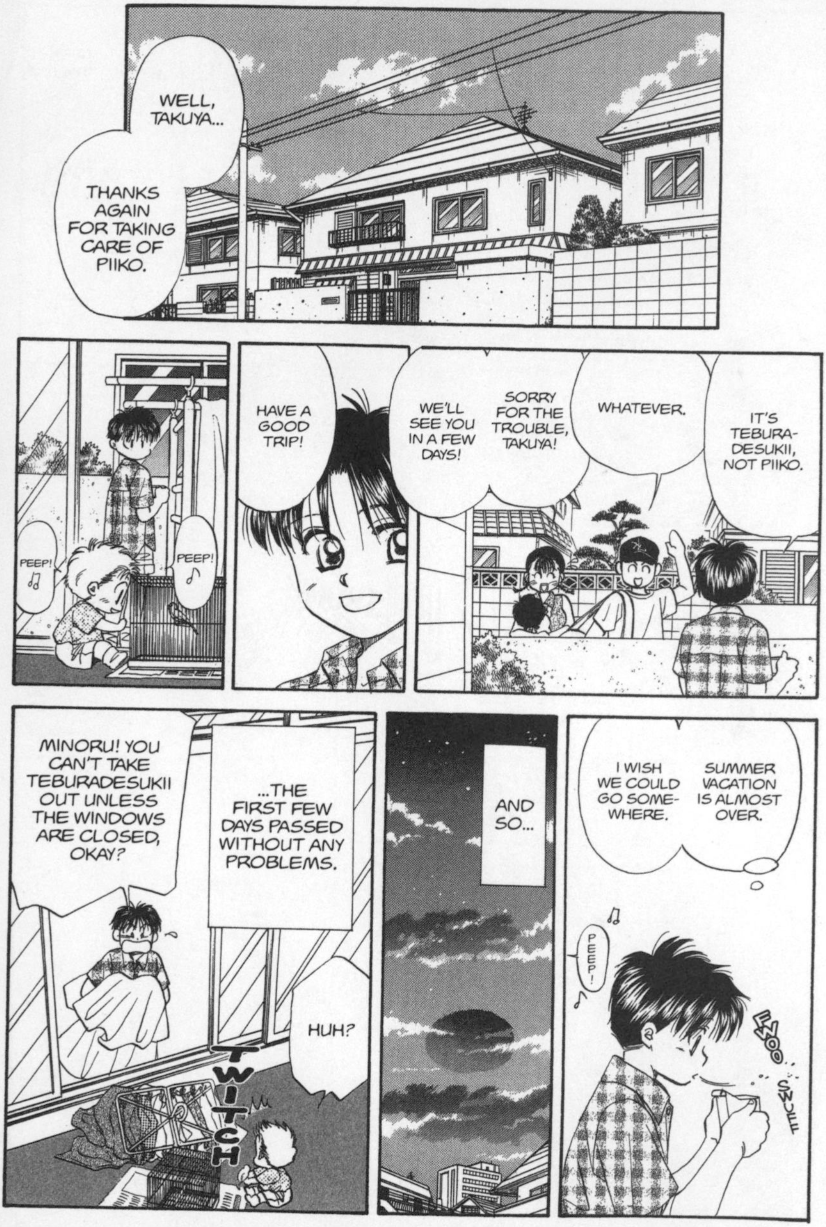
WELL, TAKUYA...
THANKS AGAIN FOR TAKING CARE OF PIIKO.
IT'S TEBURA-DESUKII, NOT PIIKO.
WHATEVER.
SORRY FOR THE TROUBLE, TAKUYA!
WE'LL SEE YOU IN A FEW DAYS!
HAVE A GOOD TRIP!
PEEP!
PEEP!
SUMMER VACATION IS ALMOST OVER.
I WISH WE COULD GO SOMEWHERE.
PEEP!
FWOO
SWUEE
AND SO...
...THE FIRST FEW DAYS PASSED WITHOUT ANY PROBLEMS.
MINORU! YOU CAN'T TAKE TEBURADESUKII OUT UNLESS THE WINDOWS ARE CLOSED, OKAY?
HUH?
TWITCH

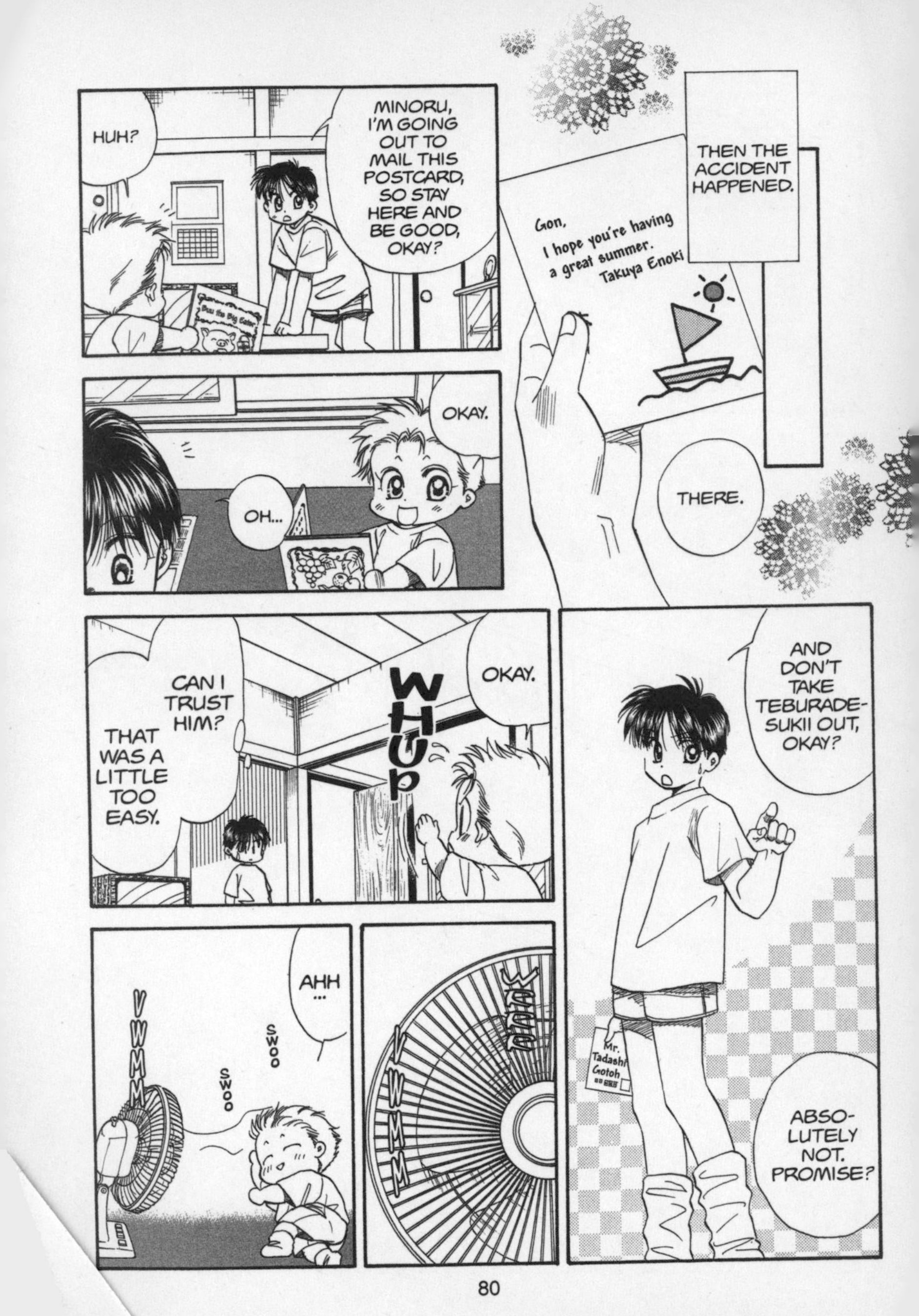
THEN THE ACCIDENT HAPPENED.
Gon,
I hope you're having a great summer.
Takuya Enoki
THERE.
MINORU, I'M GOING OUT TO MAIL THIS POSTCARD, SO STAY HERE AND BE GOOD, OKAY?
HUH?
OKAY.
OH...
AND DON'T TAKE TEBURADE-SUKII OUT, OKAY?
ABSO-LUTELY NOT. PROMISE?
Mr. Tadashi Gotoh
OKAY.
WHUP
CAN I TRUST HIM?
THAT WAS A LITTLE TOO EASY.
VWMMM
AHH...
SWOO
SWOO
VWMMM

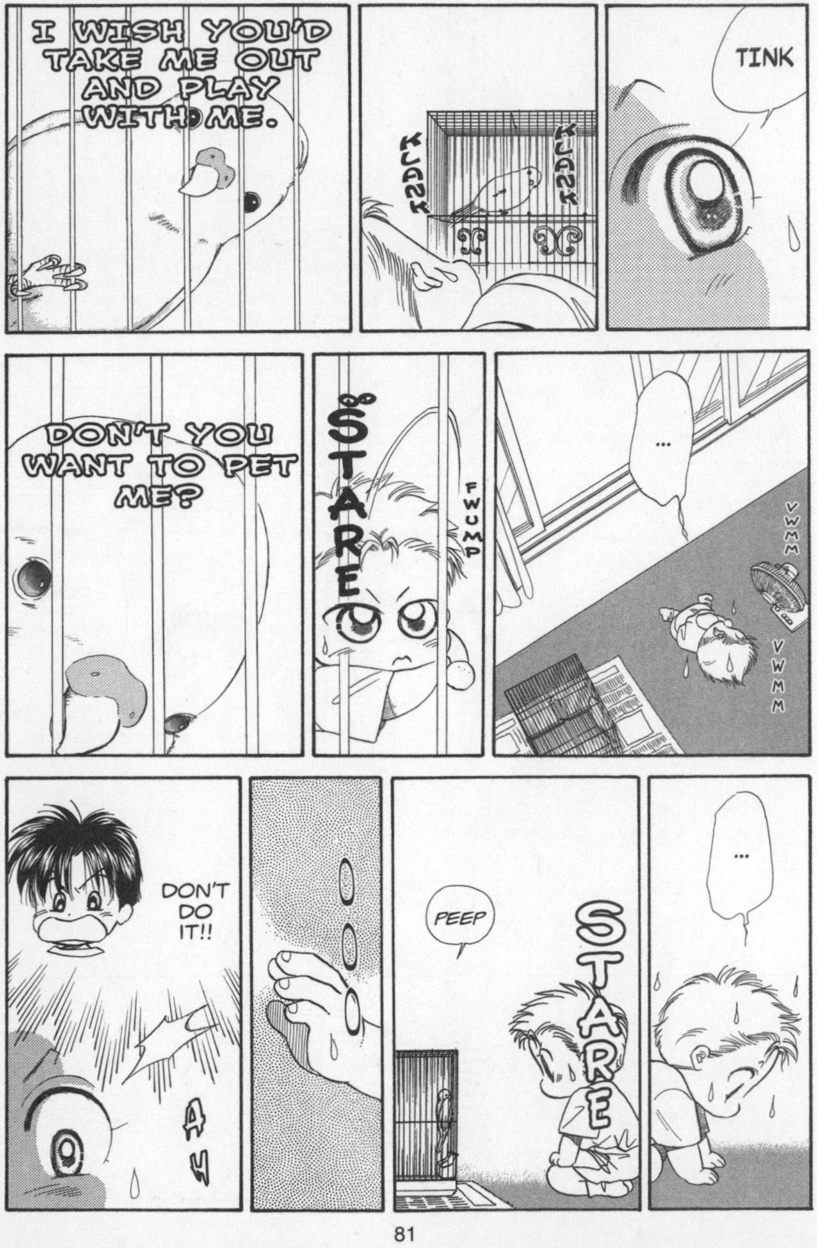
TINK
KLANK
KLANK
I WISH YOU'D TAKE ME OUT AND PLAY WITH ME.
...
VWMM
VWMM
STARE
FWUMP
DON'T YOU WANT TO PET ME?
...
STARE
PEEP
DON'T DO IT!!
AH

PEEP

STARE

A FEW SECONDS LATER...

...

V W M M

V W M M

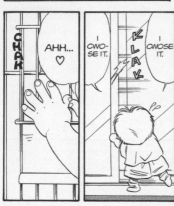

CHAK

AHH... ♡

I CWO-SE IT.

KLAK

I CWOSE IT.

YOU CAN'T TAKE TEBU-RADESUKII OUT UNLESS THE WINDOWS ARE CLOSED, OKAY?

DING

AH!

HEY!!

FWADIEWAP

BLISS

PEEP

82

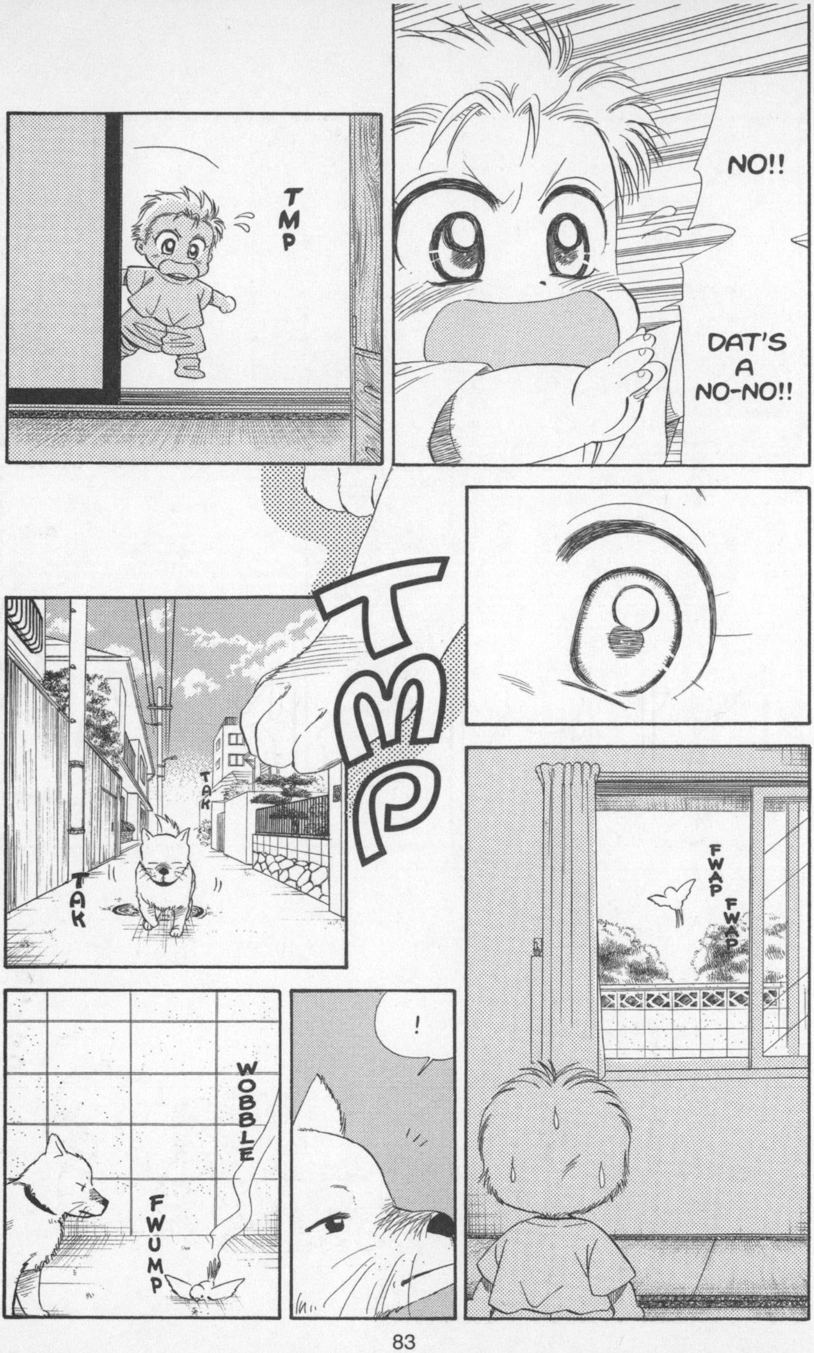

NO!!
DAT'S A NO-NO!!
TMP
TMP
TAK
TAK
FWAP
FWAP
!
WOBBLE
FWUMP

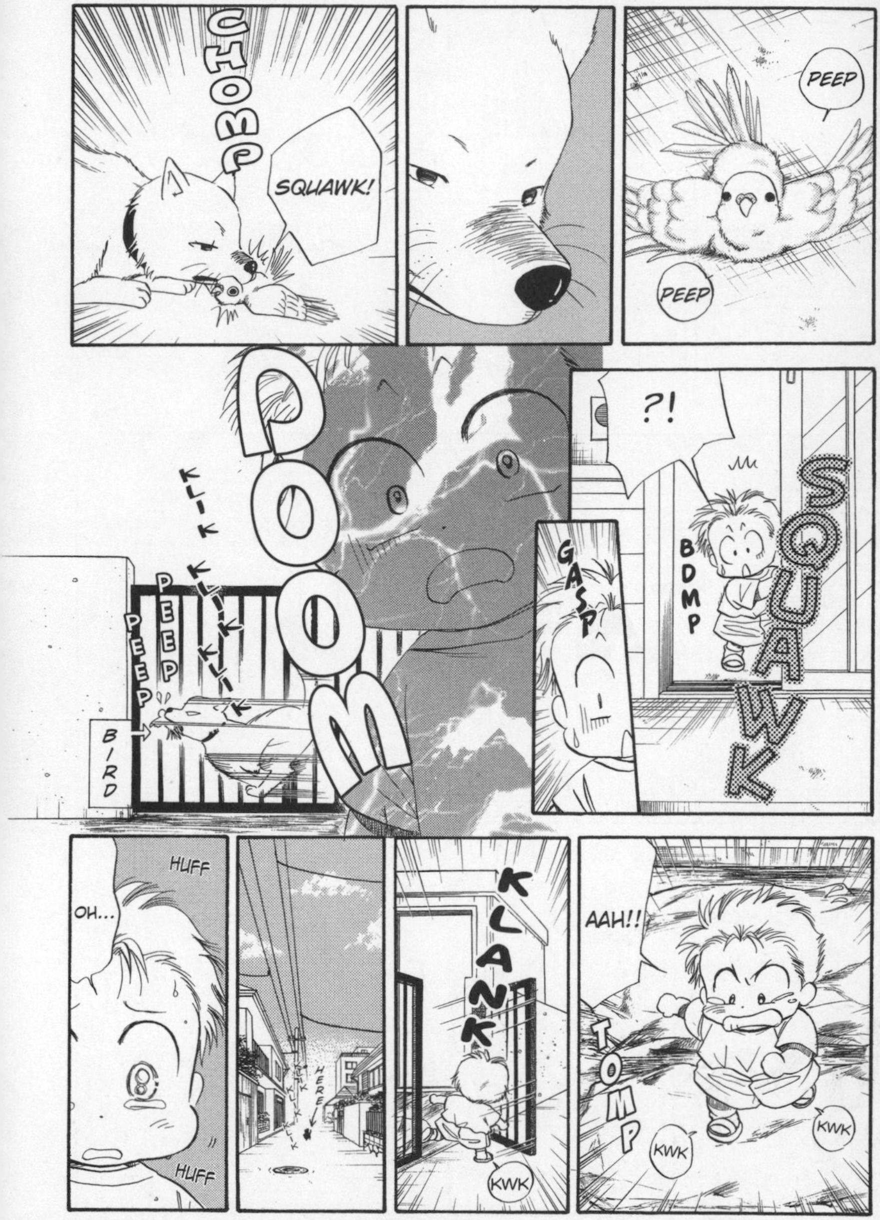
PEEP
PEEP
CHOMP
SQUAWK!
?!
BDMP
SQUAWK
GASP
BOOM
KLIK KLIK KLIK
PEEP PEEP PEEP
BIRD
AAH!!
TOMP
KWK
KWK
KLANK
KWK
HERE
HUFF
OH...
HUFF

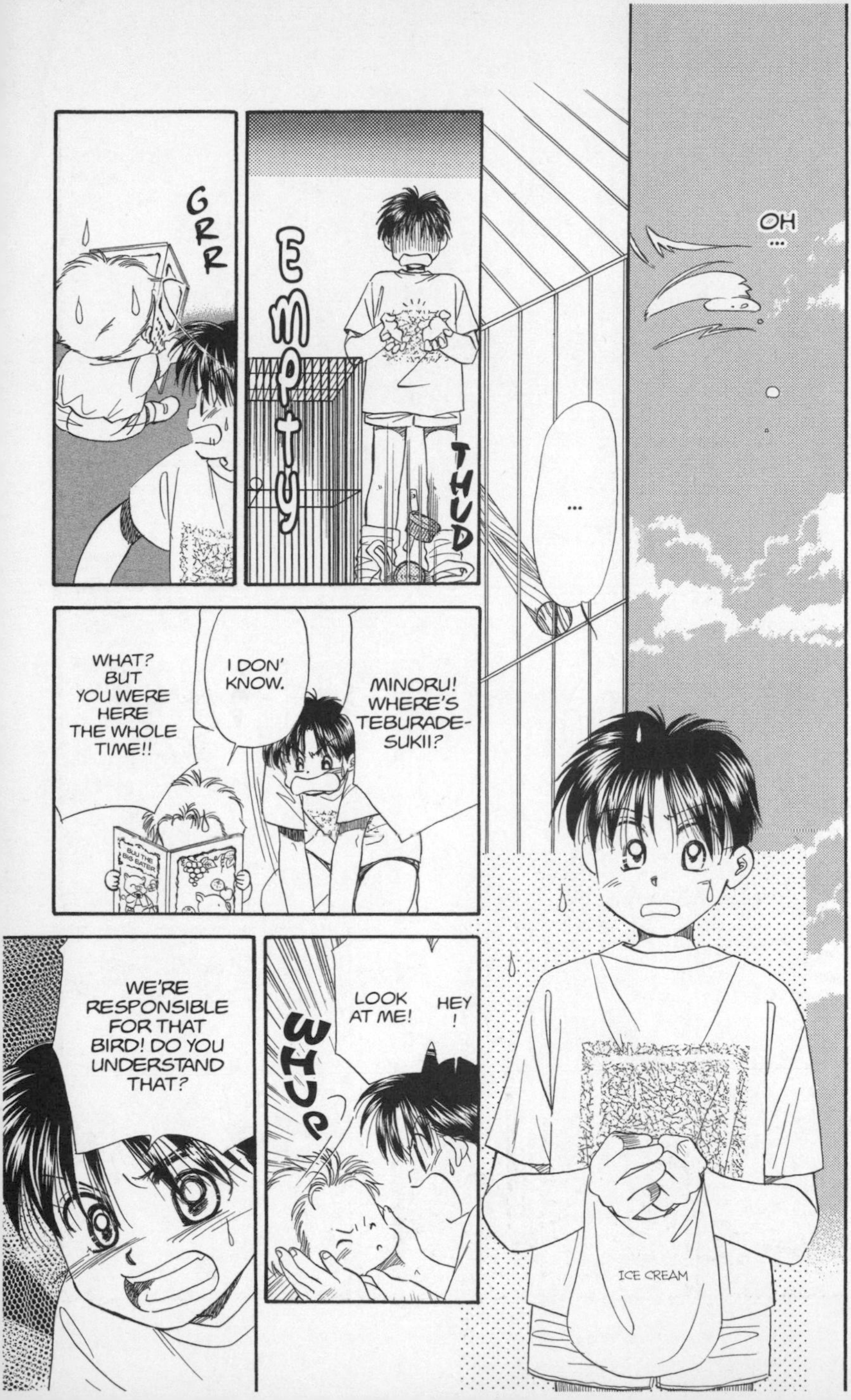

OH ...
...
ICE CREAM
EMPTY
THUD
GRR
MINORU! WHERE'S TEBURADE-SUKII?
I DON' KNOW.
WHAT? BUT YOU WERE HERE THE WHOLE TIME!!
HEY!
LOOK AT ME!
WHUP
WE'RE RESPONSIBLE FOR THAT BIRD! DO YOU UNDERSTAND THAT?

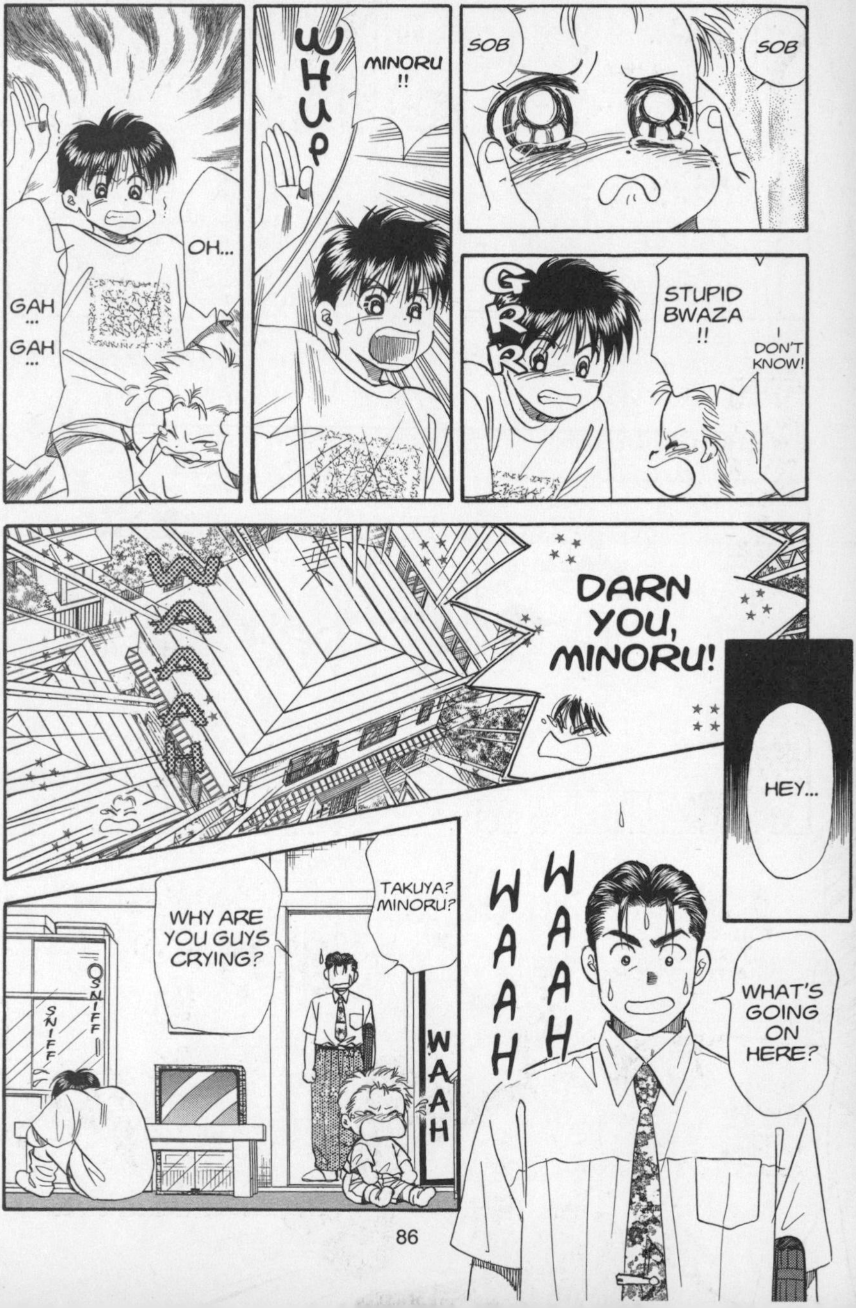
SOB
SOB
STUPID BWAZA!!
I DON'T KNOW!
GRR
MINORU!!
WHUP
OH...
GAH... GAH...
DARN YOU, MINORU!
WAAAH
HEY...
WHAT'S GOING ON HERE?
WAAH
WAAH
TAKUYA? MINORU?
WHY ARE YOU GUYS CRYING?
WAAH
SNIFF
SNIFF

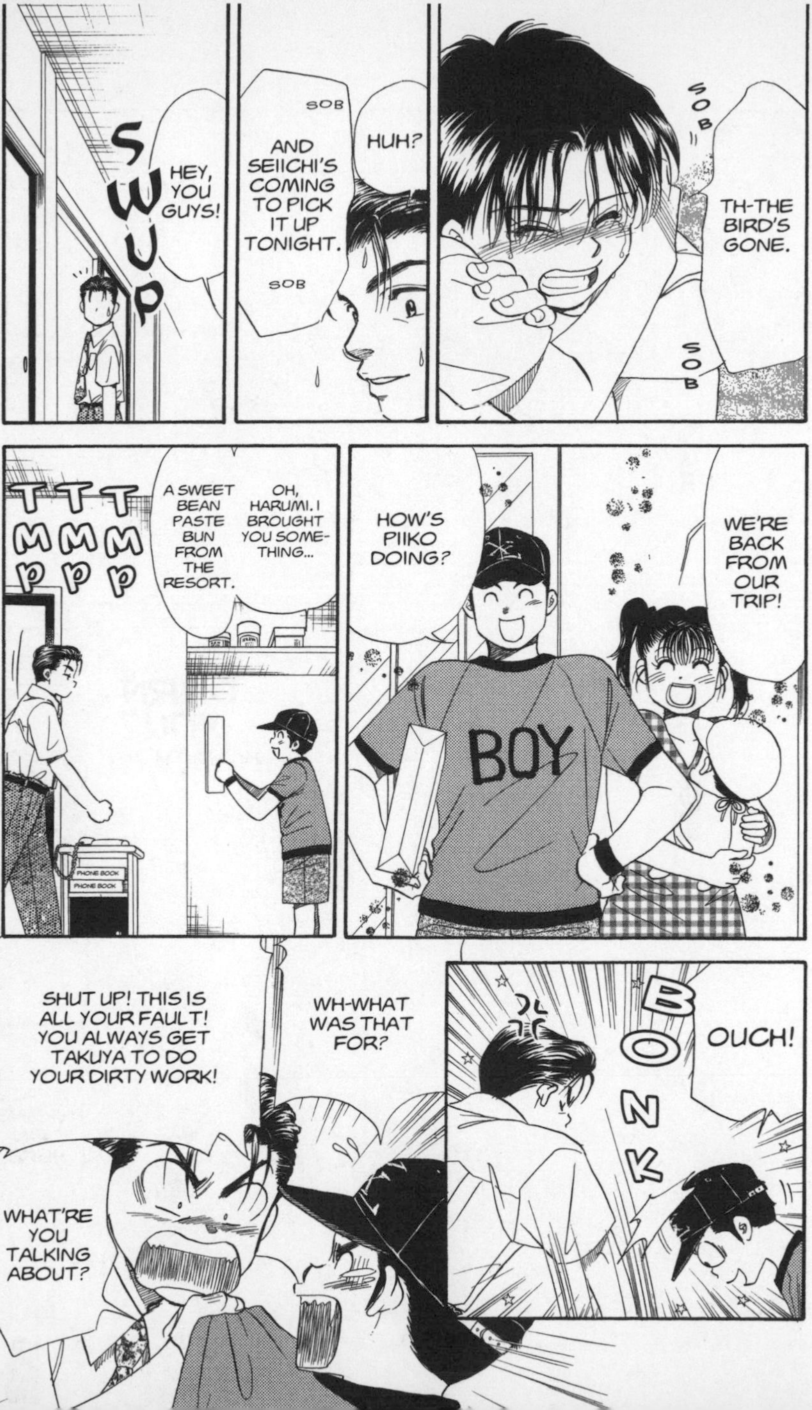
SOB
SOB
TH-THE BIRD'S GONE.
SOB
HUH?
SOB
AND SEIICHI'S COMING TO PICK IT UP TONIGHT.
SOB
HEY, YOU GUYS!
SWUP
WE'RE BACK FROM OUR TRIP!
HOW'S PIIKO DOING?
OH, HARUMI. I BROUGHT YOU SOME-THING...
A SWEET BEAN PASTE BUN FROM THE RESORT.
TMp TMp TMp
BONK
OUCH!
WH-WHAT WAS THAT FOR?
SHUT UP! THIS IS ALL YOUR FAULT! YOU ALWAYS GET TAKUYA TO DO YOUR DIRTY WORK!
WHAT'RE YOU TALKING ABOUT?

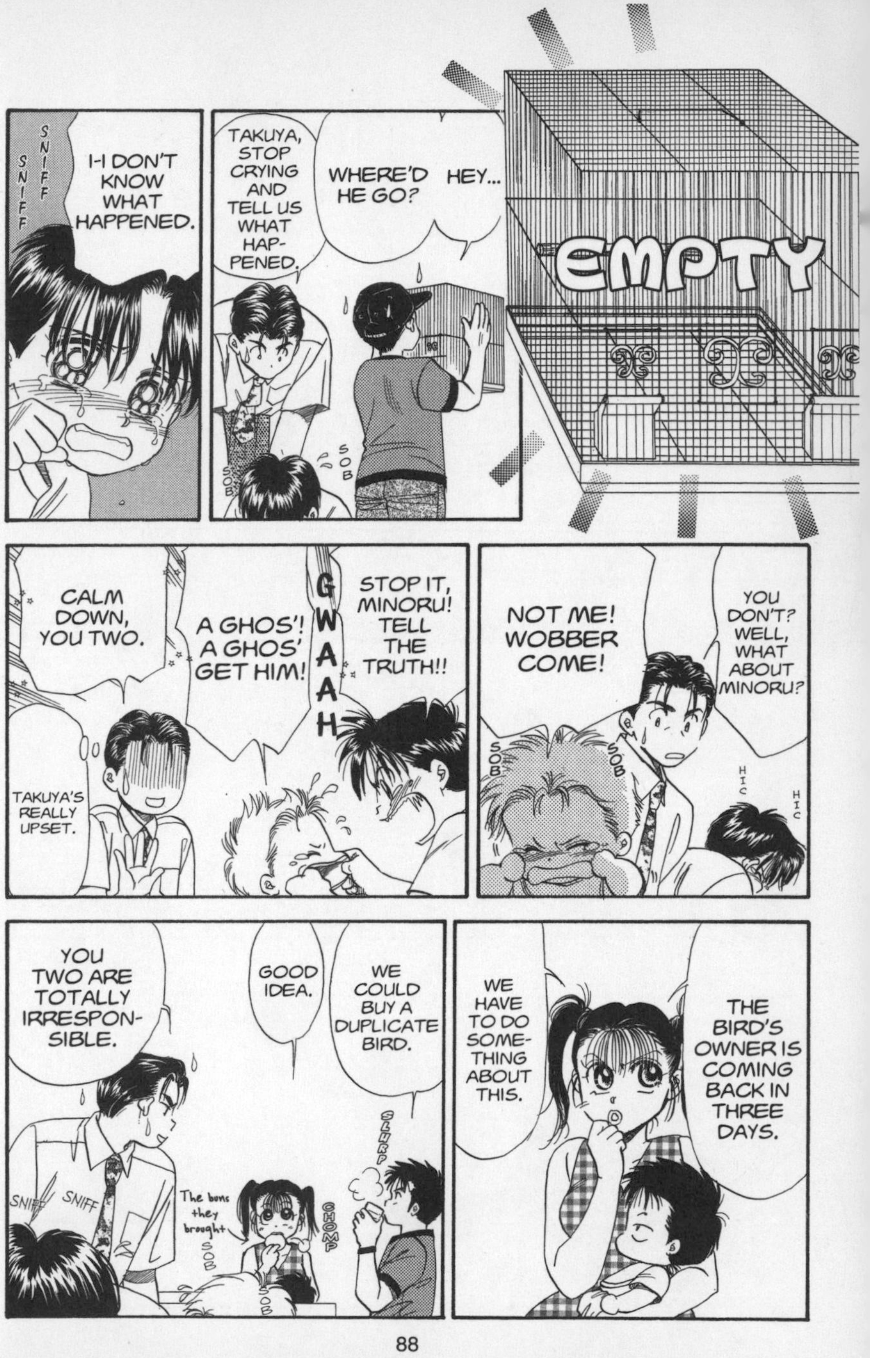
EMPTY
HEY...
WHERE'D HE GO?
TAKUYA, STOP CRYING AND TELL US WHAT HAP-PENED.
SOB SOB
I-I DON'T KNOW WHAT HAPPENED.
SNIFF SNIFF
YOU DON'T? WELL, WHAT ABOUT MINORU?
NOT ME! WOBBER COME!
SOB SOB
HIC HIC
STOP IT, MINORU! TELL THE TRUTH!!
GWAAAH
A GHOS'! A GHOS' GET HIM!
CALM DOWN, YOU TWO.
TAKUYA'S REALLY UPSET.
THE BIRD'S OWNER IS COMING BACK IN THREE DAYS.
WE HAVE TO DO SOME-THING ABOUT THIS.
WE COULD BUY A DUPLICATE BIRD.
SLURP
CHOMP
GOOD IDEA.
The buns they brought
SOB
YOU TWO ARE TOTALLY IRRESPON-SIBLE.
SNIFF SNIFF
SOB

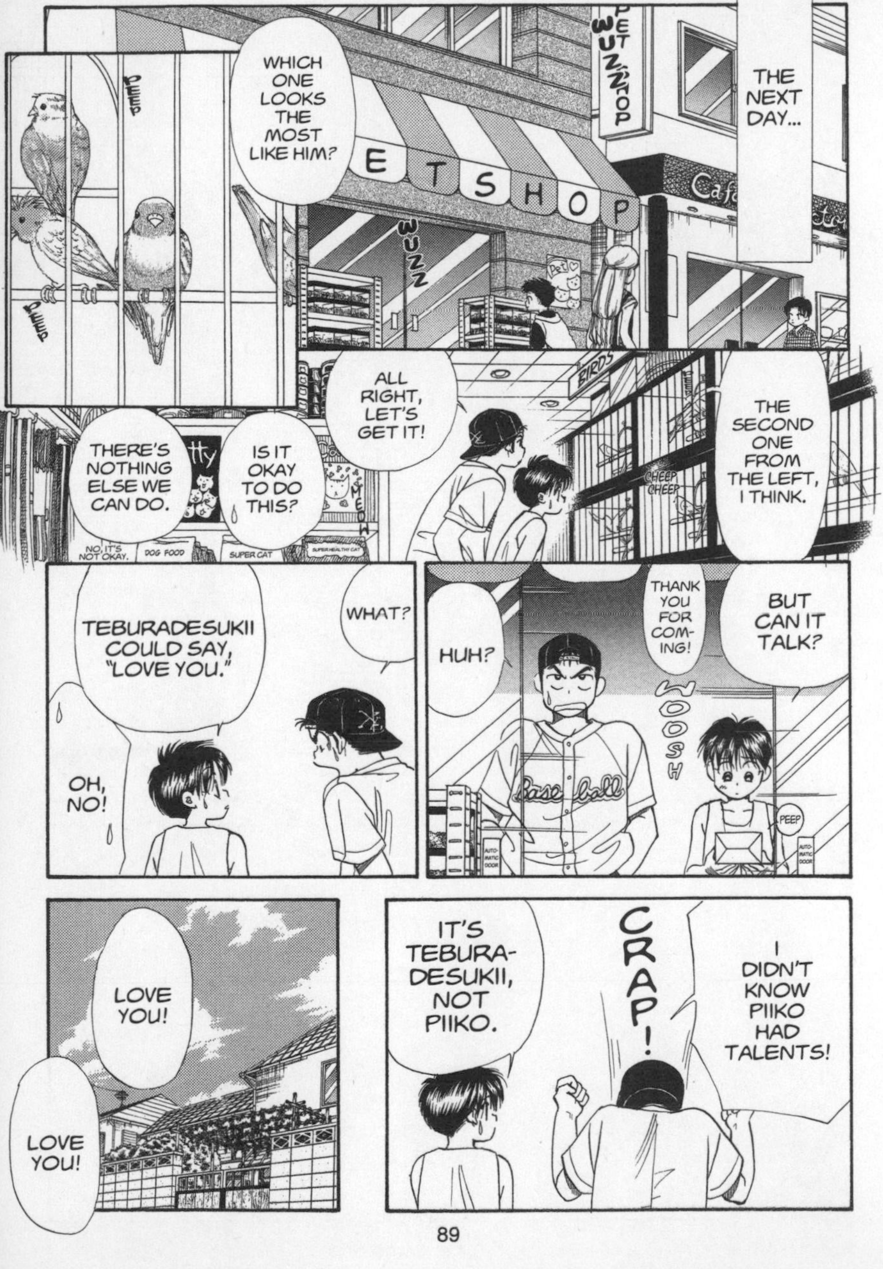
THE NEXT DAY...
PET SHOP
WUZZ
WHICH ONE LOOKS THE MOST LIKE HIM?
PETSHOP
WUZZ
PEEP
PEEP
BIRDS
THE SECOND ONE FROM THE LEFT, I THINK.
CHEEP CHEEP
ALL RIGHT, LET'S GET IT!
IS IT OKAY TO DO THIS?
THERE'S NOTHING ELSE WE CAN DO.
MEOW
NO, IT'S NOT OKAY.
DOG FOOD
SUPER CAT
SUPER HEALTHY CAT
BUT CAN IT TALK?
THANK YOU FOR COMING!
WOOSH
HUH?
PEEP
AUTOMATIC DOOR
AUTOMATIC DOOR
WHAT?
TEBURADESUKII COULD SAY, "LOVE YOU."
OH, NO!
I DIDN'T KNOW PIIKO HAD TALENTS!
CRAP!
IT'S TEBURA-DESUKII, NOT PIIKO.
LOVE YOU!
LOVE YOU!

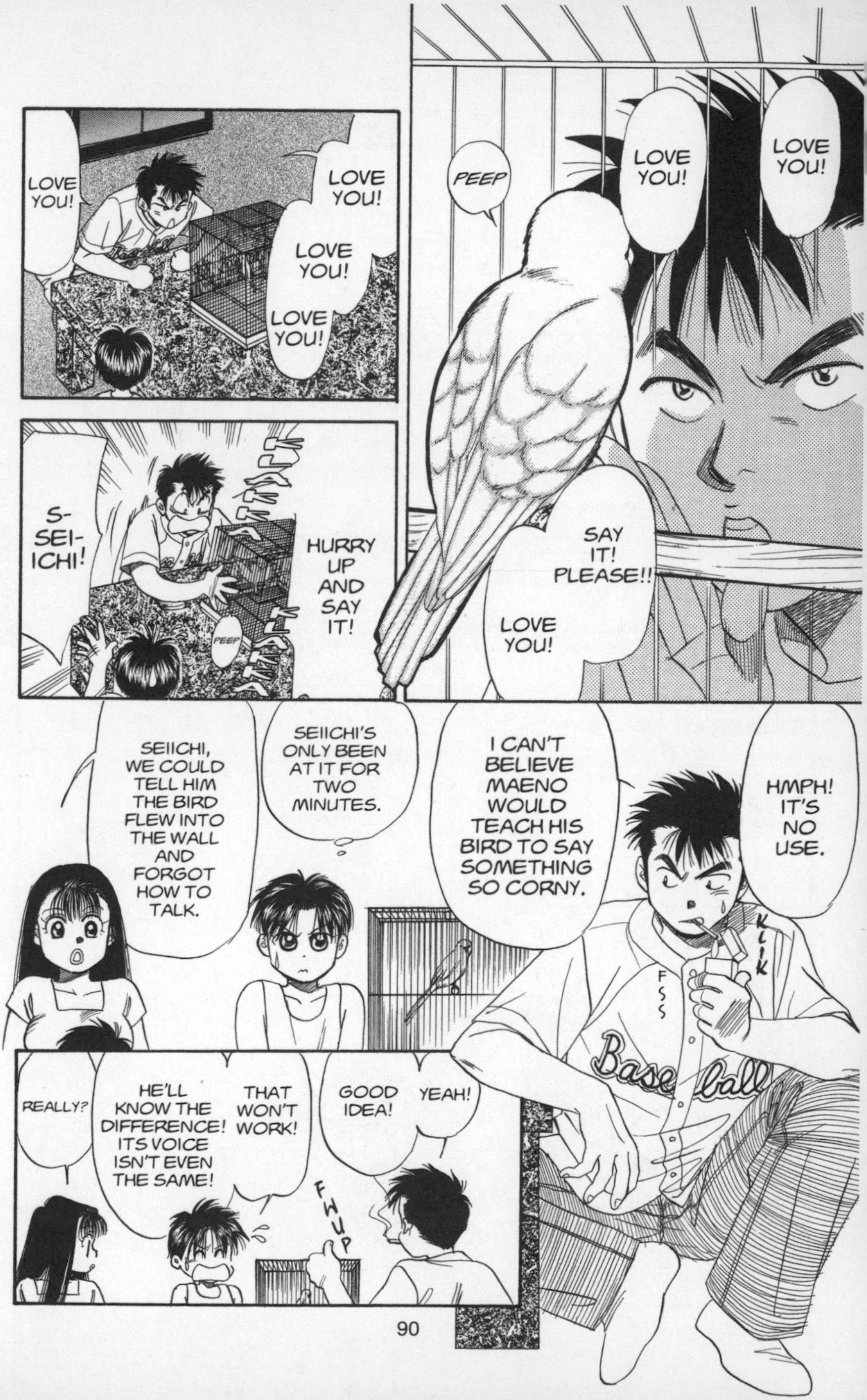
LOVE YOU!
LOVE YOU!
PEEP
SAY IT! PLEASE!!
LOVE YOU!
LOVE YOU!
LOVE YOU!
LOVE YOU!
LOVE YOU!
HURRY UP AND SAY IT!
PEEP
S-SEI-ICHI!
HMPH! IT'S NO USE.
KLIK
FSS
I CAN'T BELIEVE MAENO WOULD TEACH HIS BIRD TO SAY SOMETHING SO CORNY.
SEIICHI'S ONLY BEEN AT IT FOR TWO MINUTES.
SEIICHI, WE COULD TELL HIM THE BIRD FLEW INTO THE WALL AND FORGOT HOW TO TALK.
YEAH!
GOOD IDEA!
FWUP
THAT WON'T WORK!
HE'LL KNOW THE DIFFERENCE! ITS VOICE ISN'T EVEN THE SAME!
REALLY?

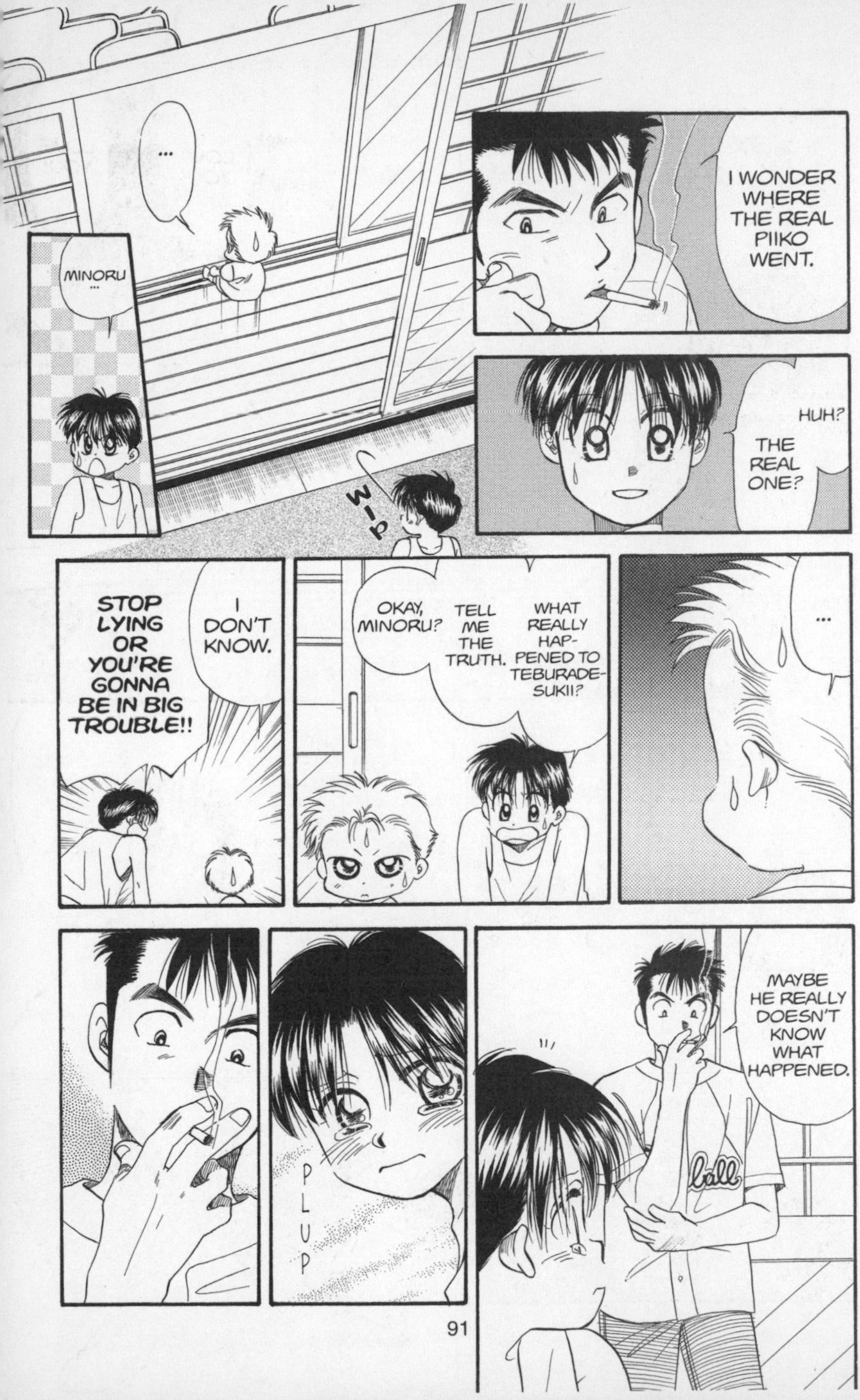
I WONDER WHERE THE REAL PIIKO WENT.
HUH?
THE REAL ONE?
...
MINORU ...
WIP
...
OKAY, MINORU? TELL ME THE TRUTH. WHAT REALLY HAP-PENED TO TEBURADE-SUKI!?
I DON'T KNOW.
STOP LYING OR YOU'RE GONNA BE IN BIG TROUBLE!!
MAYBE HE REALLY DOESN'T KNOW WHAT HAPPENED.
!!
PLUP

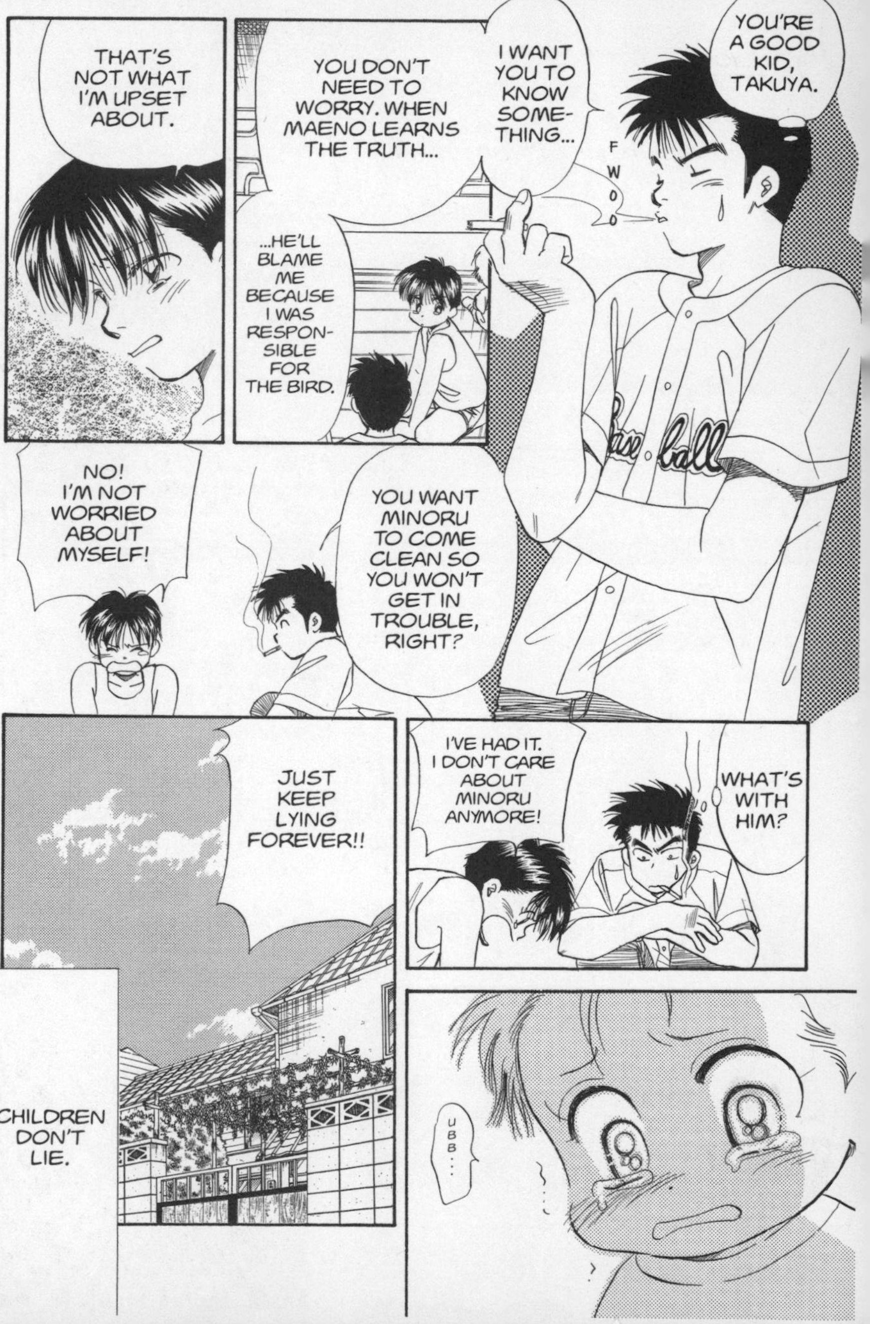

YOU'RE A GOOD KID, TAKUYA.
FWOO
I WANT YOU TO KNOW SOMETHING...
YOU DON'T NEED TO WORRY. WHEN MAENO LEARNS THE TRUTH...
...HE'LL BLAME ME BECAUSE I WAS RESPONSIBLE FOR THE BIRD.
THAT'S NOT WHAT I'M UPSET ABOUT.
YOU WANT MINORU TO COME CLEAN SO YOU WON'T GET IN TROUBLE, RIGHT?
NO! I'M NOT WORRIED ABOUT MYSELF!
WHAT'S WITH HIM?
I'VE HAD IT. I DON'T CARE ABOUT MINORU ANYMORE!
JUST KEEP LYING FOREVER!!
UBB...
CHILDREN DON'T LIE.

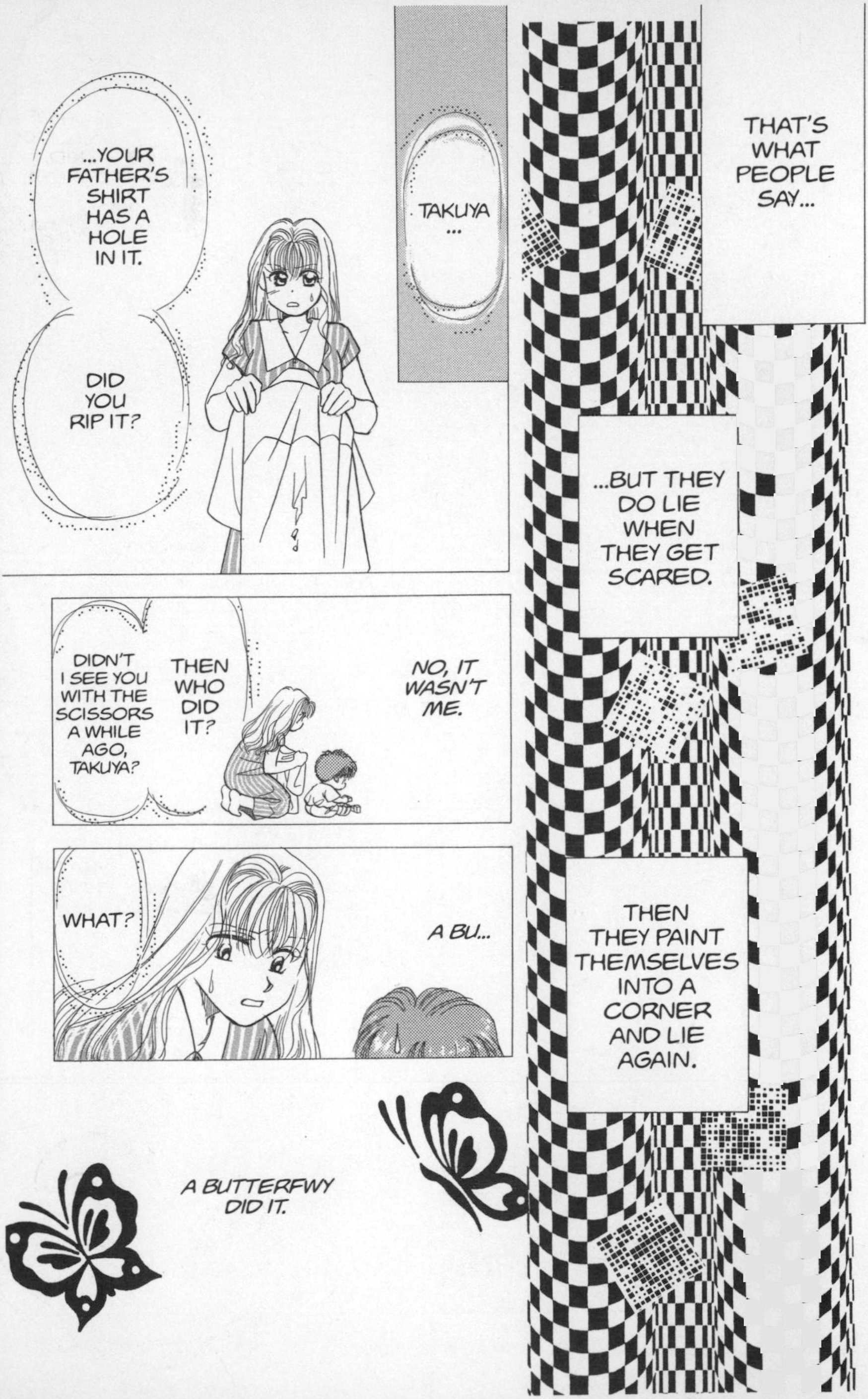
THAT'S WHAT PEOPLE SAY...
...BUT THEY DO LIE WHEN THEY GET SCARED.
THEN THEY PAINT THEMSELVES INTO A CORNER AND LIE AGAIN.
TAKUYA...
...YOUR FATHER'S SHIRT HAS A HOLE IN IT.
DID YOU RIP IT?
NO, IT WASN'T ME.
THEN WHO DID IT?
DIDN'T I SEE YOU WITH THE SCISSORS A WHILE AGO, TAKUYA?
A BU...
WHAT?
A BUTTERFWY DID IT.

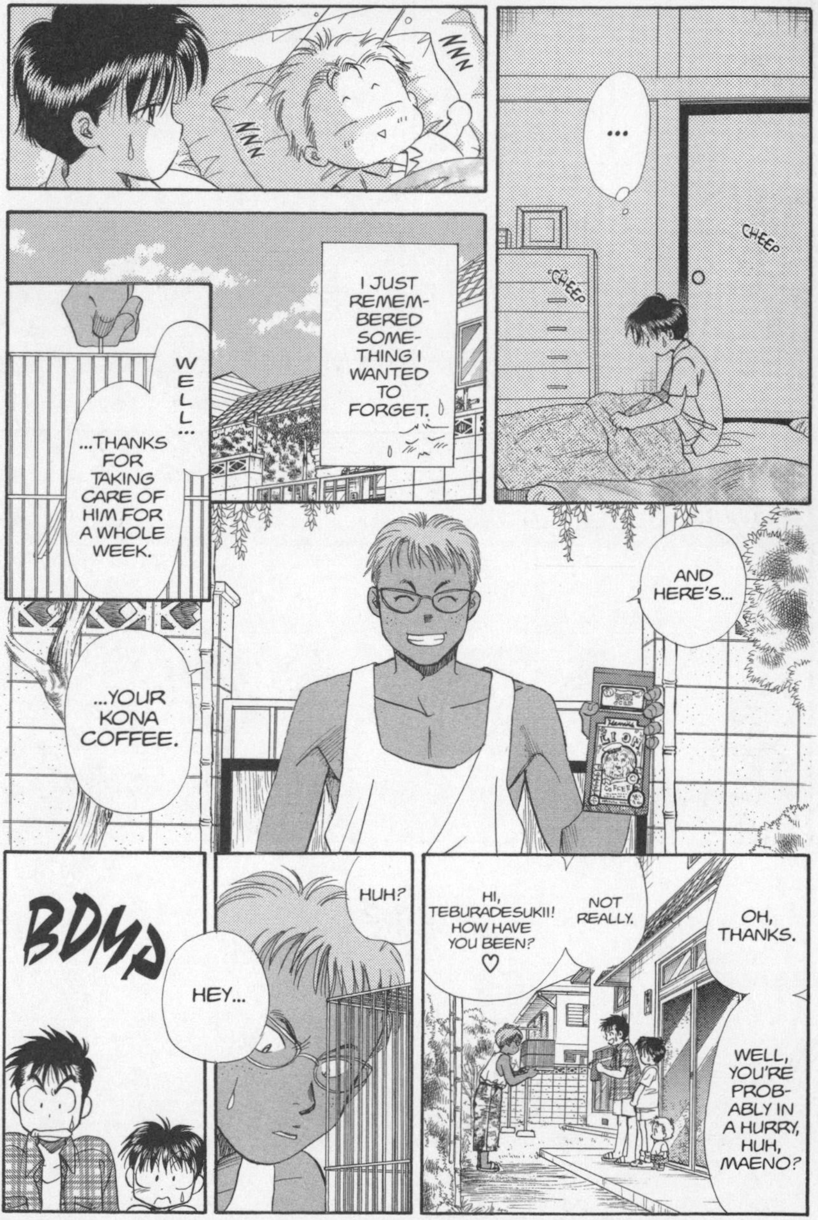
...
CHEEP
CHEEP
NNN
NNN
I JUST REMEMBERED SOMETHING I WANTED TO FORGET.
WELL...
...THANKS FOR TAKING CARE OF HIM FOR A WHOLE WEEK.
AND HERE'S...
...YOUR KONA COFFEE.
OH, THANKS.
WELL, YOU'RE PROBABLY IN A HURRY, HUH, MAENO?
NOT REALLY.
HI, TEBURADESUKII! HOW HAVE YOU BEEN? ♡
HUH?
HEY...
BDMP

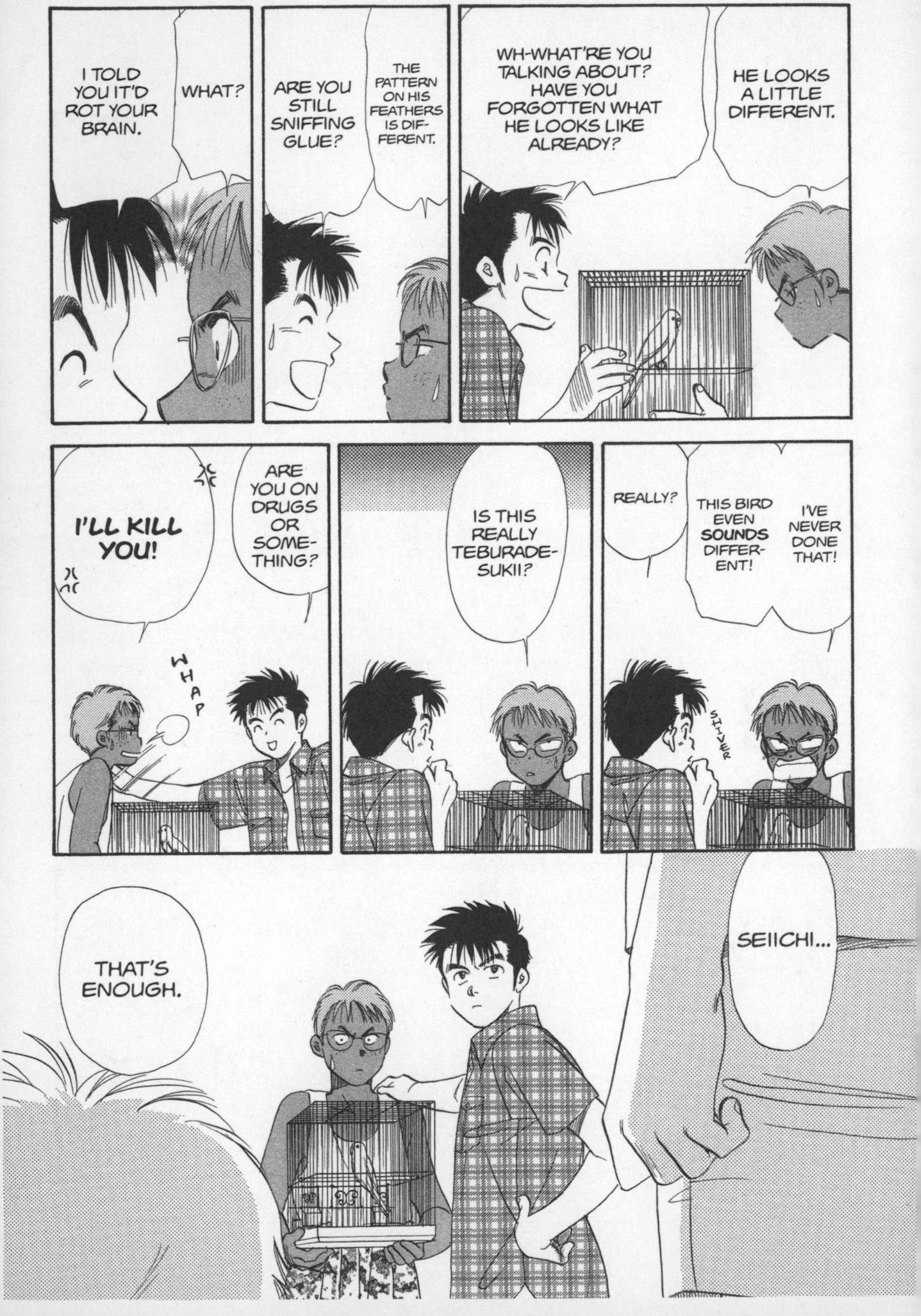
HE LOOKS A LITTLE DIFFERENT.
WH-WHAT'RE YOU TALKING ABOUT? HAVE YOU FORGOTTEN WHAT HE LOOKS LIKE ALREADY?
THE PATTERN ON HIS FEATHERS IS DIF-FERENT.
ARE YOU STILL SNIFFING GLUE?
WHAT?
I TOLD YOU IT'D ROT YOUR BRAIN.
I'VE NEVER DONE THAT!
THIS BIRD EVEN **SOUNDS** DIFFER-ENT!
REALLY?
SHIVER
IS THIS REALLY TEBURADE-SUKII?
ARE YOU ON DRUGS OR SOME-THING?
I'LL KILL YOU!
WHAP
SEIICHI...
THAT'S ENOUGH.

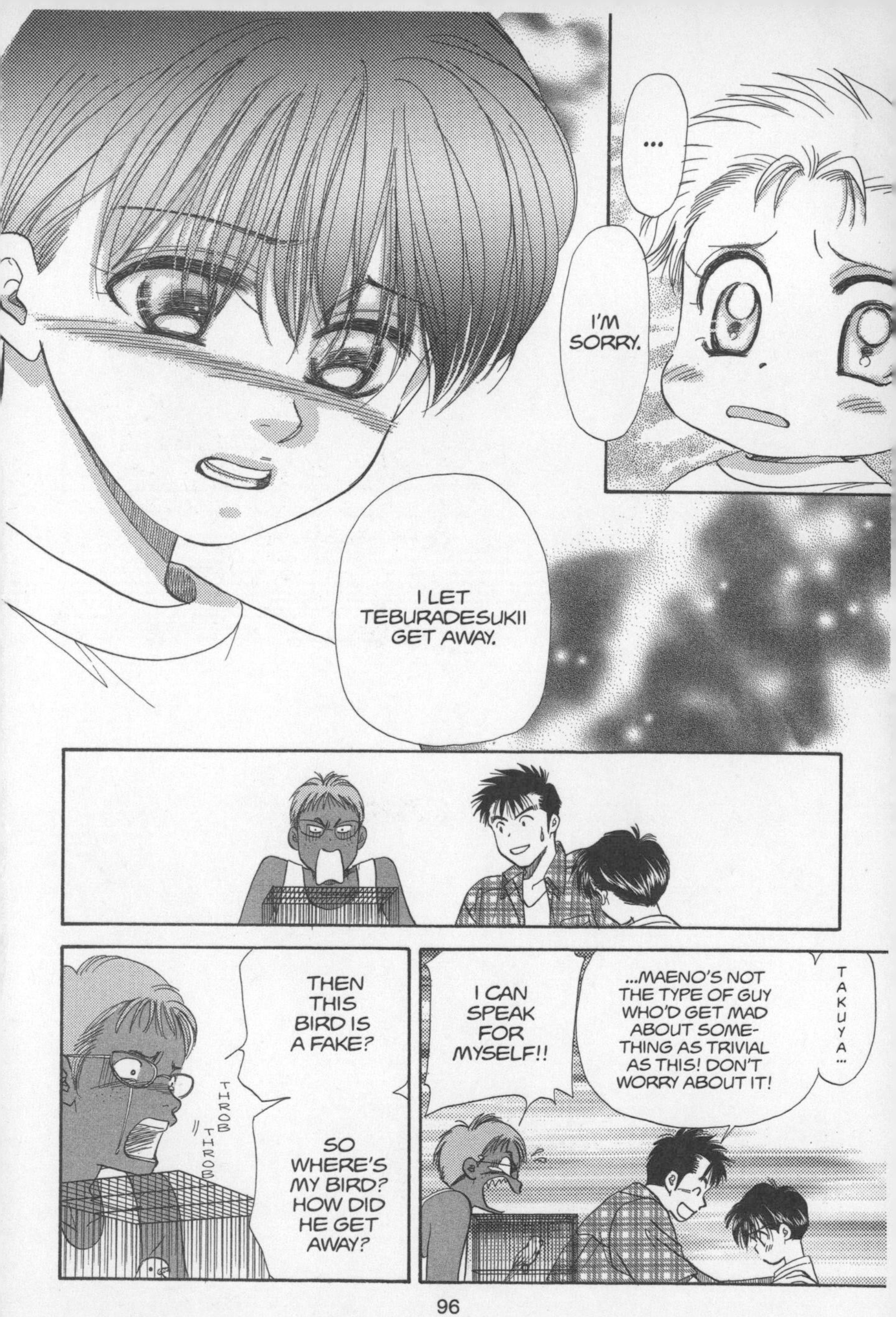
...
I'M SORRY.
I LET TEBURADESUKII GET AWAY.
TAKUYA...
...MAENO'S NOT THE TYPE OF GUY WHO'D GET MAD ABOUT SOMETHING AS TRIVIAL AS THIS! DON'T WORRY ABOUT IT!
I CAN SPEAK FOR MYSELF!!
THEN THIS BIRD IS A FAKE?
THROB THROB
SO WHERE'S MY BIRD? HOW DID HE GET AWAY?

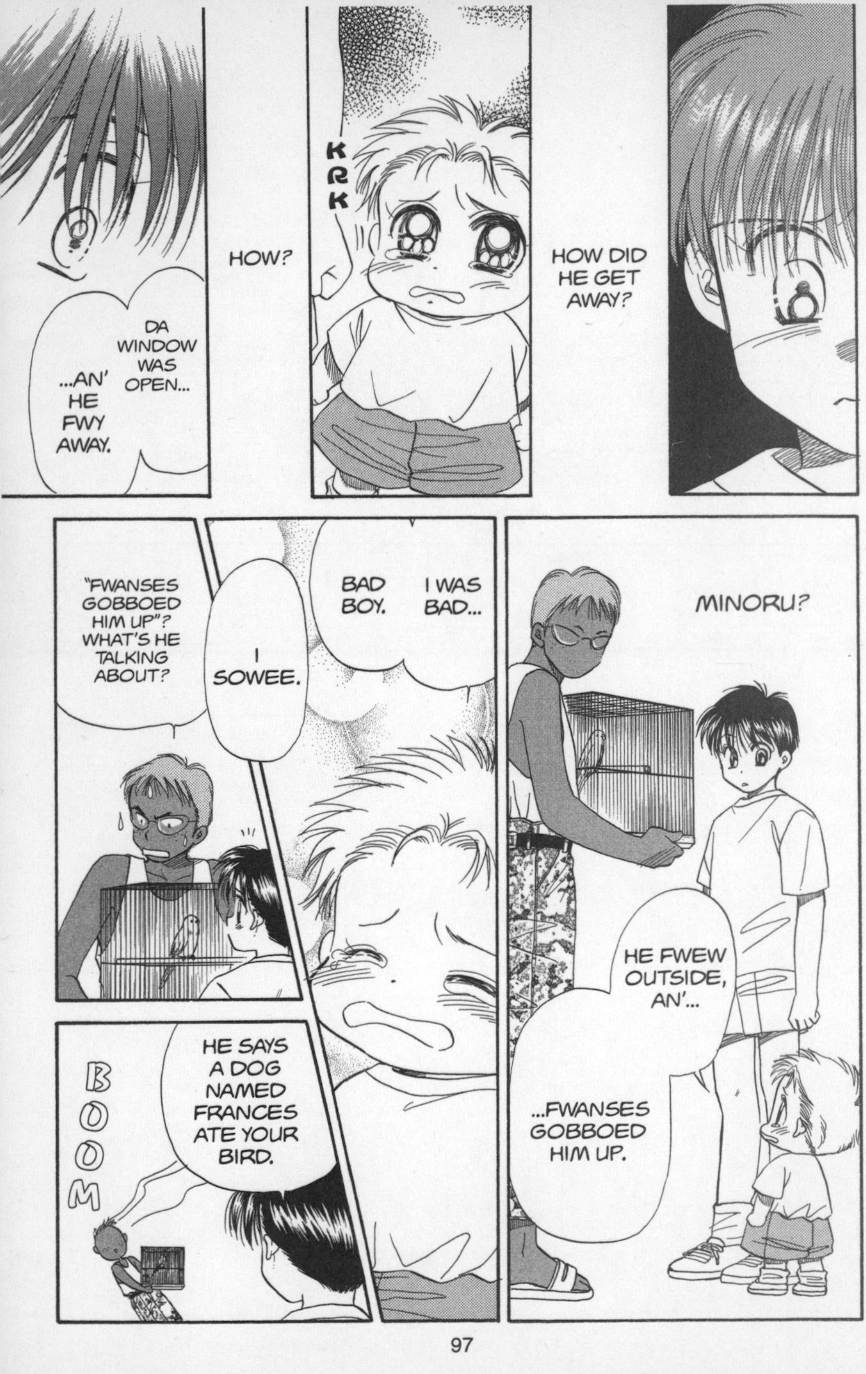
HOW DID HE GET AWAY?
KRK
HOW?
DA WINDOW WAS OPEN...
...AN' HE FWY AWAY.
MINORU?
HE FWEW OUTSIDE, AN'...
...FWANSES GOBBOED HIM UP.
I WAS BAD...
BAD BOY.
I SOWEE.
"FWANSES GOBBOED HIM UP"? WHAT'S HE TALKING ABOUT?
HE SAYS A DOG NAMED FRANCES ATE YOUR BIRD.
BOOM

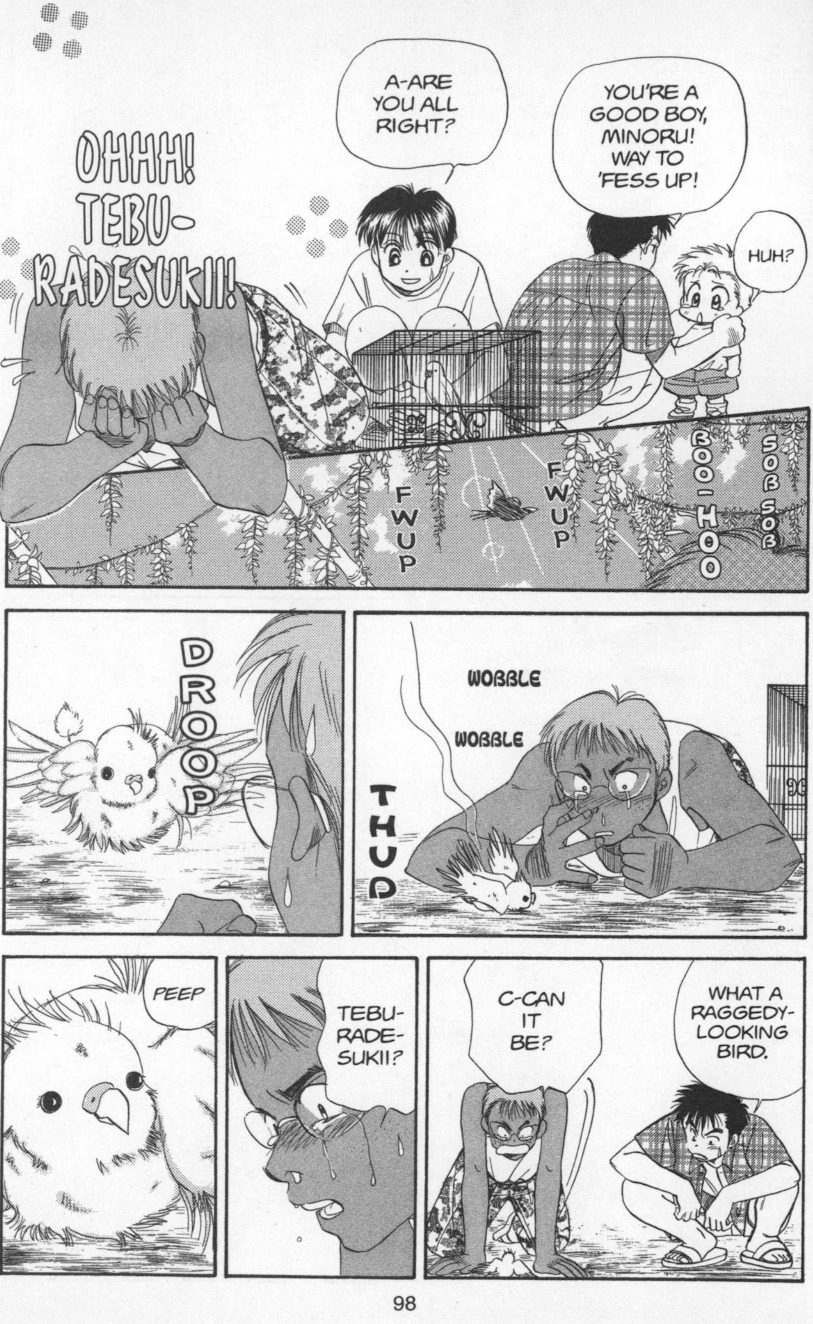

YOU'RE A GOOD BOY, MINORU! WAY TO 'FESS UP!
HUH?
A-ARE YOU ALL RIGHT?
SOB SOB
BOO-HOO
FWUP
FWUP
OHHH! TEBU-RADESUKII!
WOBBLE
WOBBLE
THUD
DROOP
WHAT A RAGGEDY-LOOKING BIRD.
C-CAN IT BE?
TEBU-RADE-SUKII?
PEEP

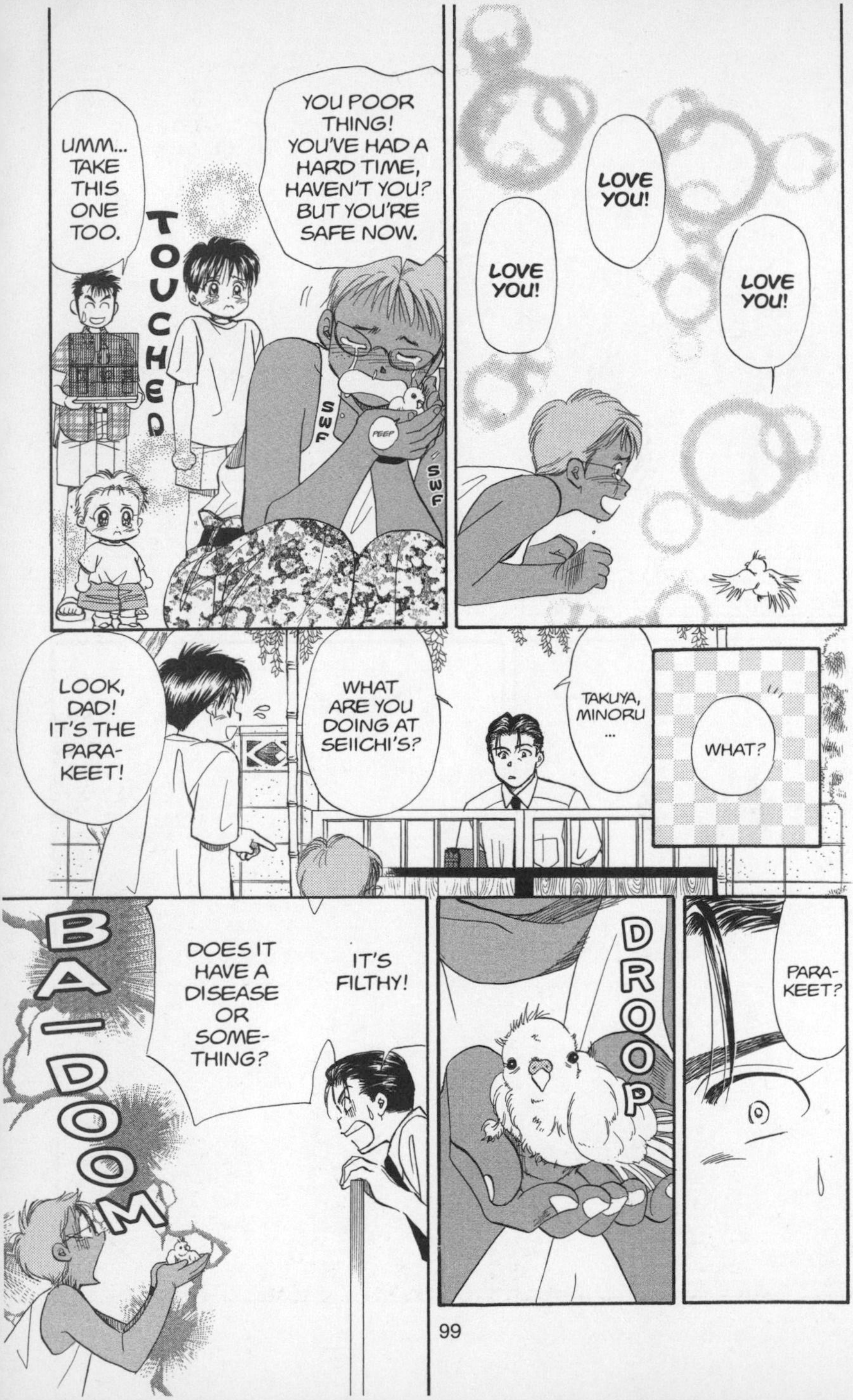
LOVE YOU!
LOVE YOU!
LOVE YOU!
YOU POOR THING! YOU'VE HAD A HARD TIME, HAVEN'T YOU? BUT YOU'RE SAFE NOW.
TOUCHED
UMM... TAKE THIS ONE TOO.
SWF
PEEP
SWF
WHAT?
TAKUYA, MINORU ...
WHAT ARE YOU DOING AT SEIICHI'S?
LOOK, DAD! IT'S THE PARA-KEET!
PARA-KEET?
DROOP
IT'S FILTHY!
DOES IT HAVE A DISEASE OR SOME-THING?
BA-DOOM

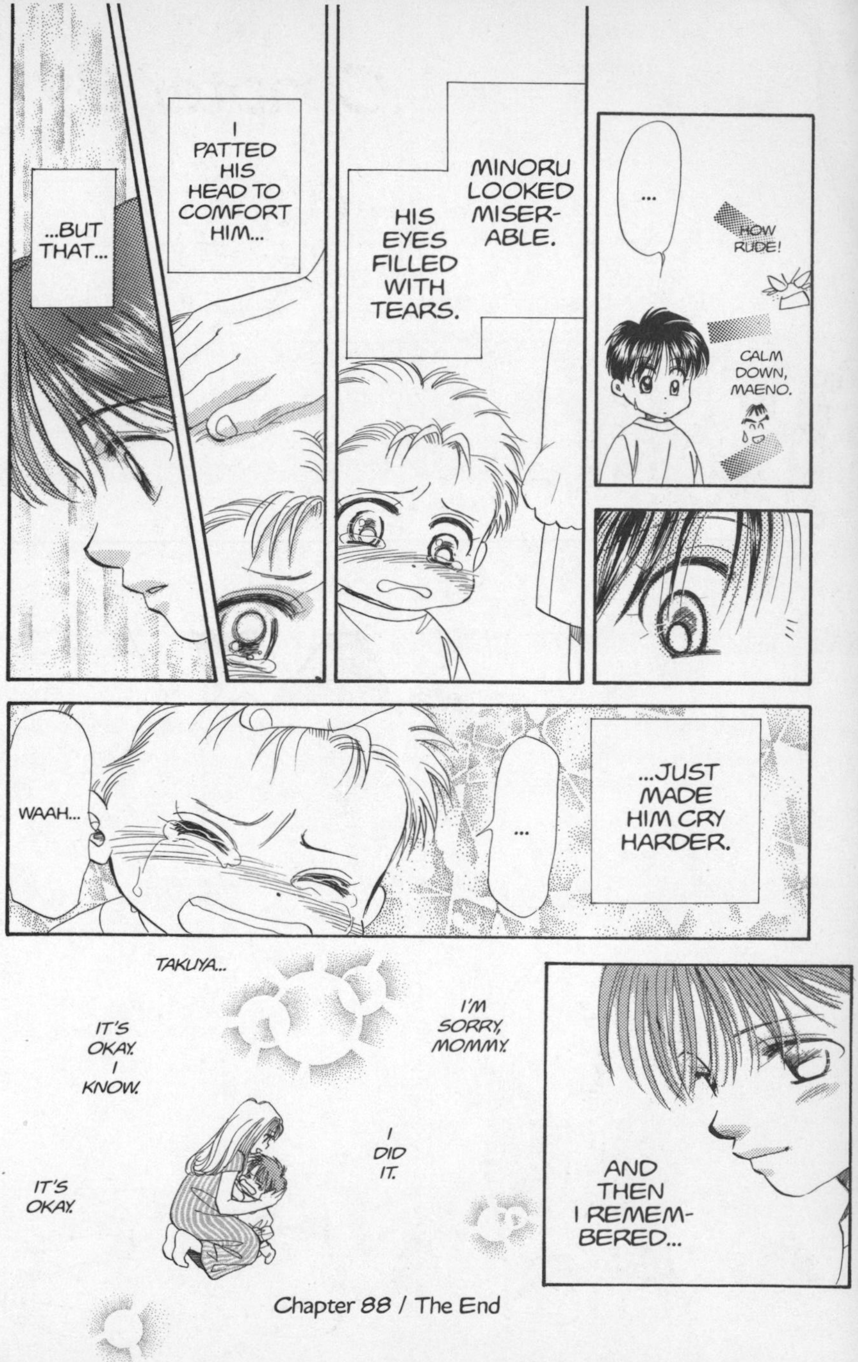
...
HOW RUDE!
CALM DOWN, MAENO.
MINORU LOOKED MISERABLE.
HIS EYES FILLED WITH TEARS.
I PATTED HIS HEAD TO COMFORT HIM...
...BUT THAT...
...JUST MADE HIM CRY HARDER.
...
WAAH...
AND THEN I REMEMBERED...
TAKUYA...
I'M SORRY, MOMMY.
IT'S OKAY. I KNOW.
I DID IT.
IT'S OKAY.

Chapter 88 / The End

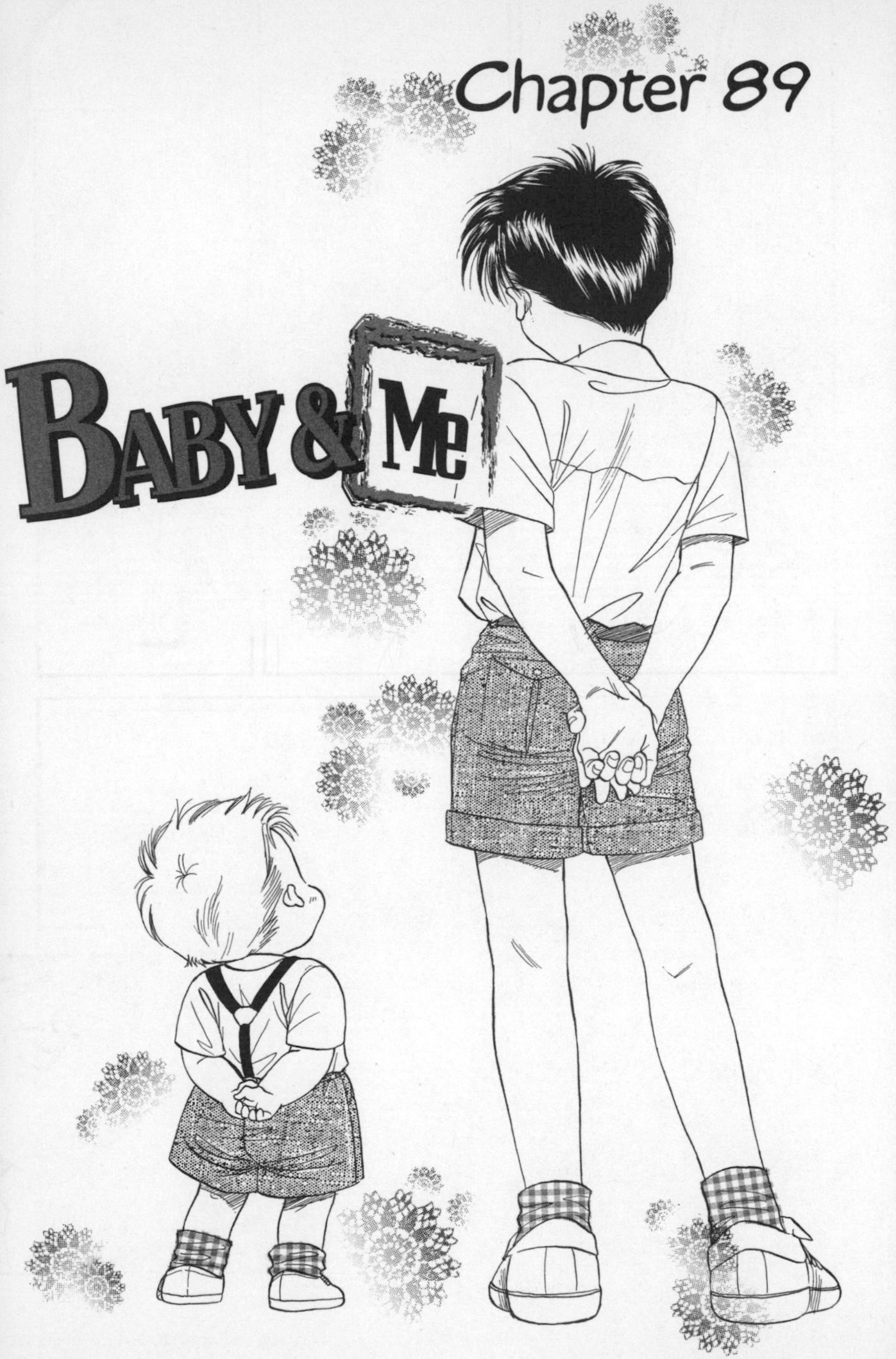
Chapter 89
BABY & ME

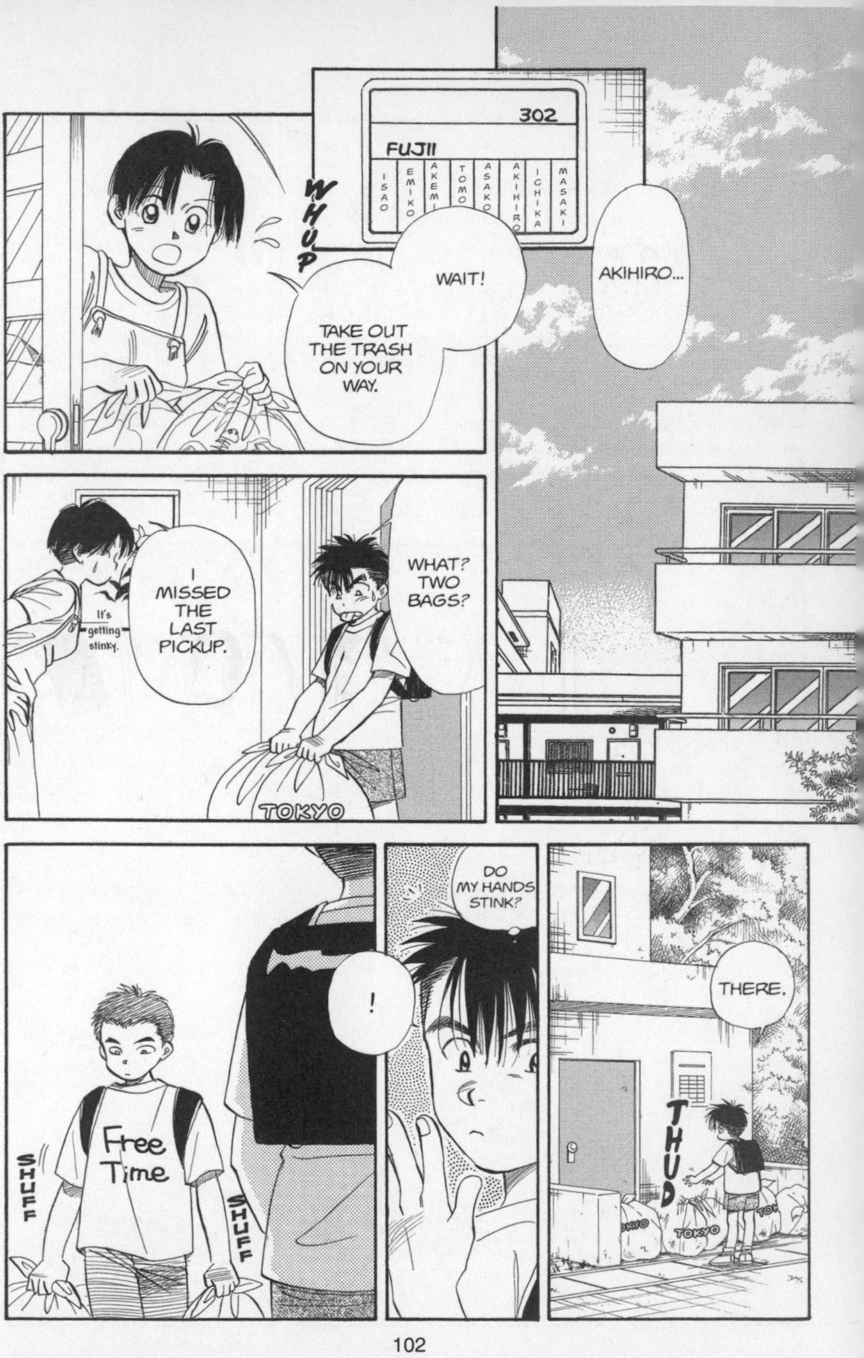
302
FUJII
ISAO
EMIKO
AKEMI
TOMO
ASAKO
AKIHIRO
ICHIKA
MASAKI
AKIHIRO...
WHUP
WAIT!
TAKE OUT THE TRASH ON YOUR WAY.
WHAT? TWO BAGS?
I MISSED THE LAST PICKUP.
It's getting stinky.
TOKYO
THERE.
THUD
TOKYO
TOKYO
DO MY HANDS STINK?
!
Free Time
SHUFF
SHUFF

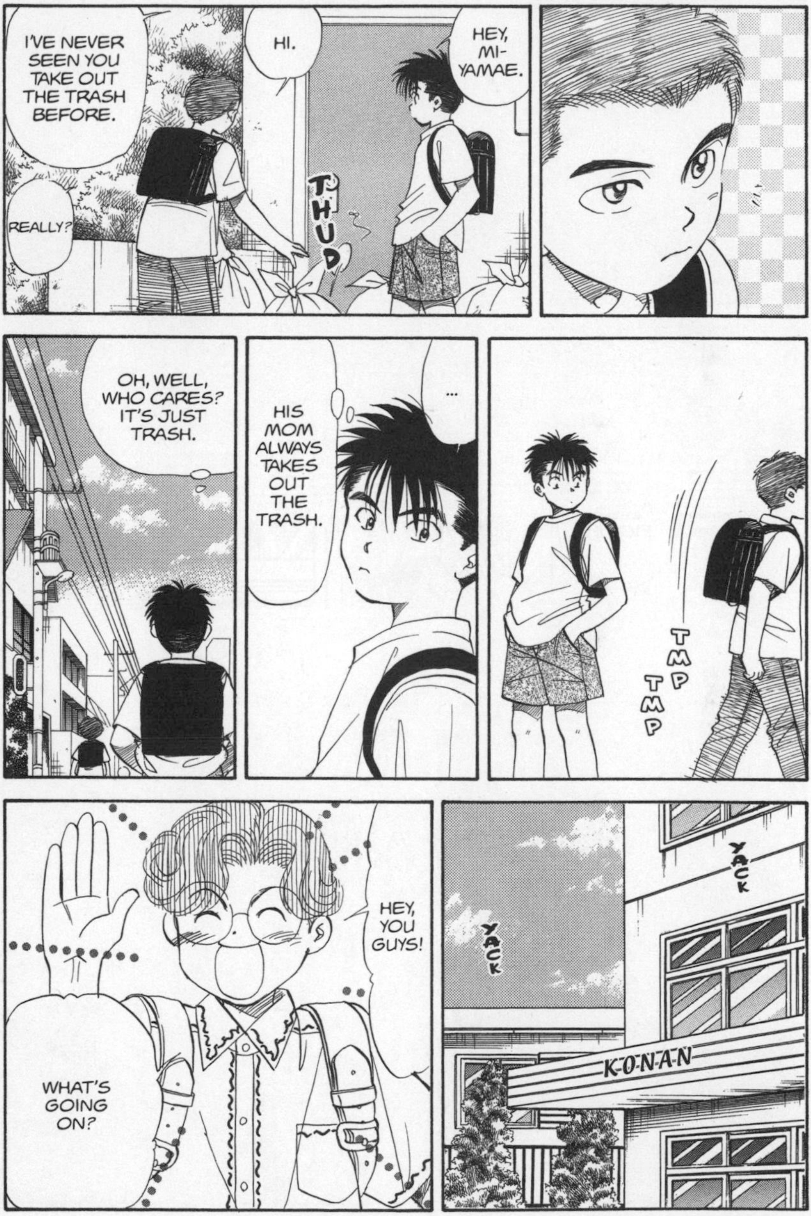
HEY, MI-YAMAE.
HI.
I'VE NEVER SEEN YOU TAKE OUT THE TRASH BEFORE.
THUD
REALLY?
TMP TMP
...
HIS MOM ALWAYS TAKES OUT THE TRASH.
OH, WELL, WHO CARES? IT'S JUST TRASH.
YACK
YACK
KONAN
HEY, YOU GUYS!
WHAT'S GOING ON?

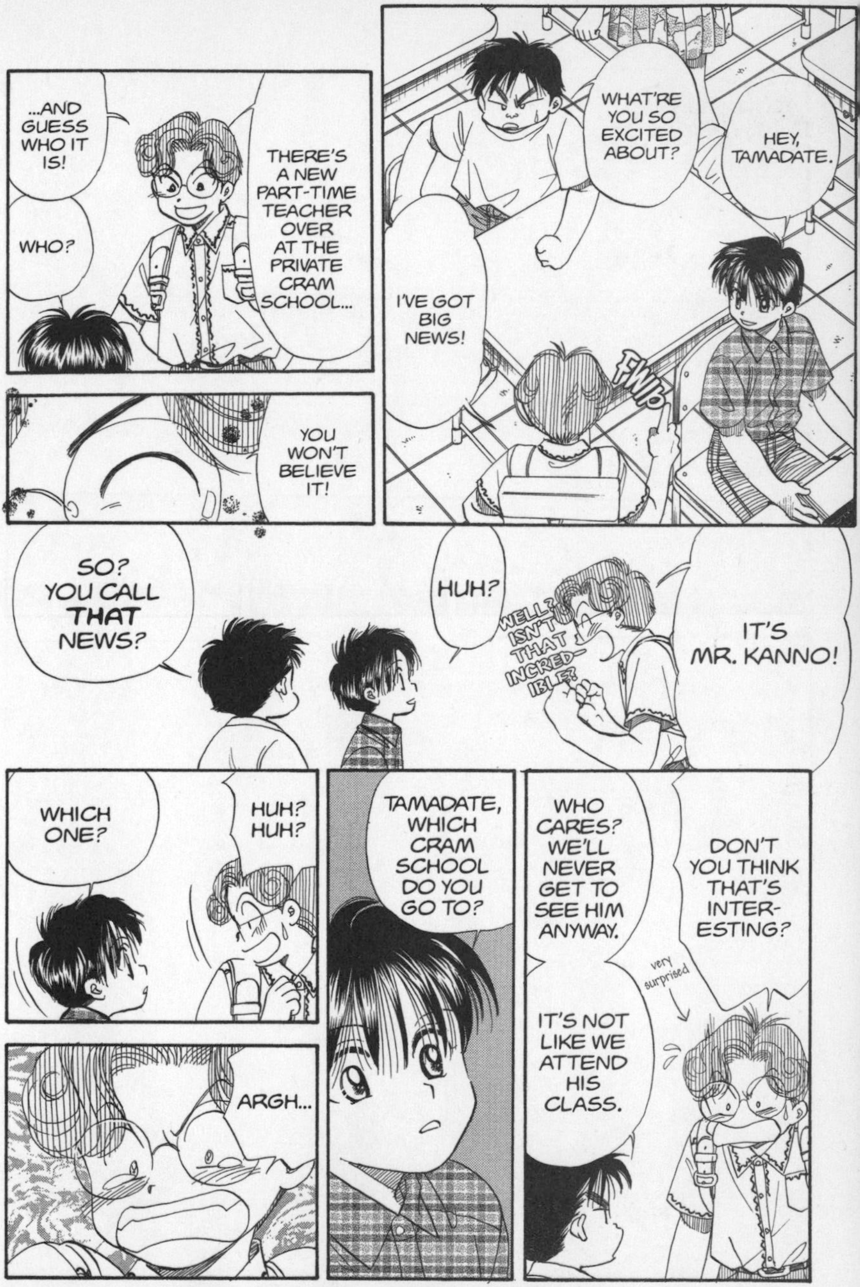
HEY, TAMADATE.
WHAT'RE YOU SO EXCITED ABOUT?
I'VE GOT BIG NEWS!
FWIP
THERE'S A NEW PART-TIME TEACHER OVER AT THE PRIVATE CRAM SCHOOL...
...AND GUESS WHO IT IS!
WHO?
YOU WON'T BELIEVE IT!
IT'S MR. KANNO!
WELL? ISN'T THAT INCREDIBLE?
HUH?
SO? YOU CALL THAT NEWS?
DON'T YOU THINK THAT'S INTERESTING?
very surprised
WHO CARES? WE'LL NEVER GET TO SEE HIM ANYWAY.
IT'S NOT LIKE WE ATTEND HIS CLASS.
TAMADATE, WHICH CRAM SCHOOL DO YOU GO TO?
HUH? HUH?
WHICH ONE?
ARGH...

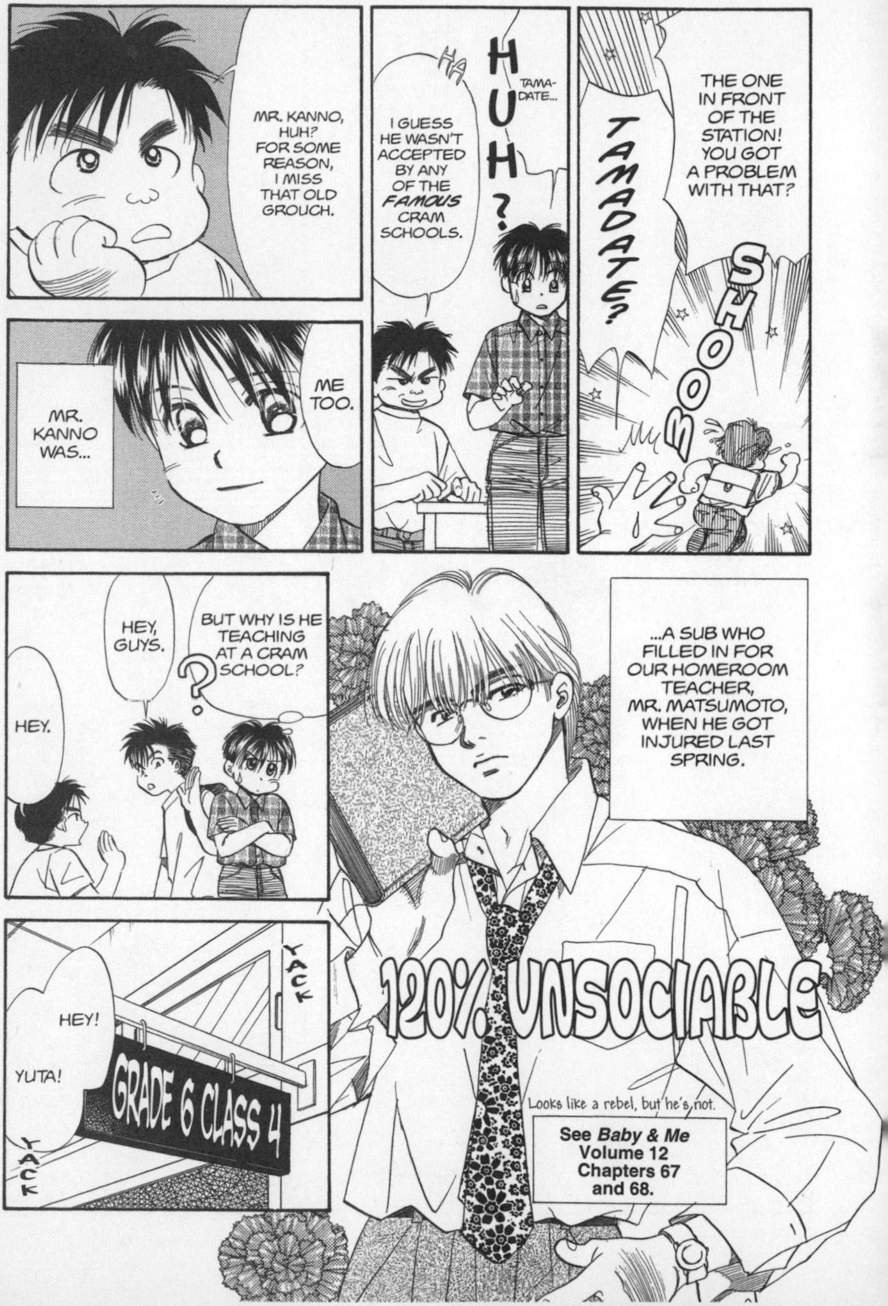
THE ONE IN FRONT OF THE STATION! YOU GOT A PROBLEM WITH THAT?
TAMADATE?
SHOOOOM
HA
HUH?
TAMA-DATE...
I GUESS HE WASN'T ACCEPTED BY ANY OF THE *FAMOUS* CRAM SCHOOLS.
MR. KANNO, HUH? FOR SOME REASON, I MISS THAT OLD GROUCH.
ME TOO.
MR. KANNO WAS...
...A SUB WHO FILLED IN FOR OUR HOMEROOM TEACHER, MR. MATSUMOTO, WHEN HE GOT INJURED LAST SPRING.
120% UNSOCIABLE
Looks like a rebel, but he's not.
See *Baby & Me* Volume 12 Chapters 67 and 68.
BUT WHY IS HE TEACHING AT A CRAM SCHOOL?
HEY, GUYS.
HEY.
YACK
HEY!
YUTA!
GRADE 6 CLASS 4
YACK

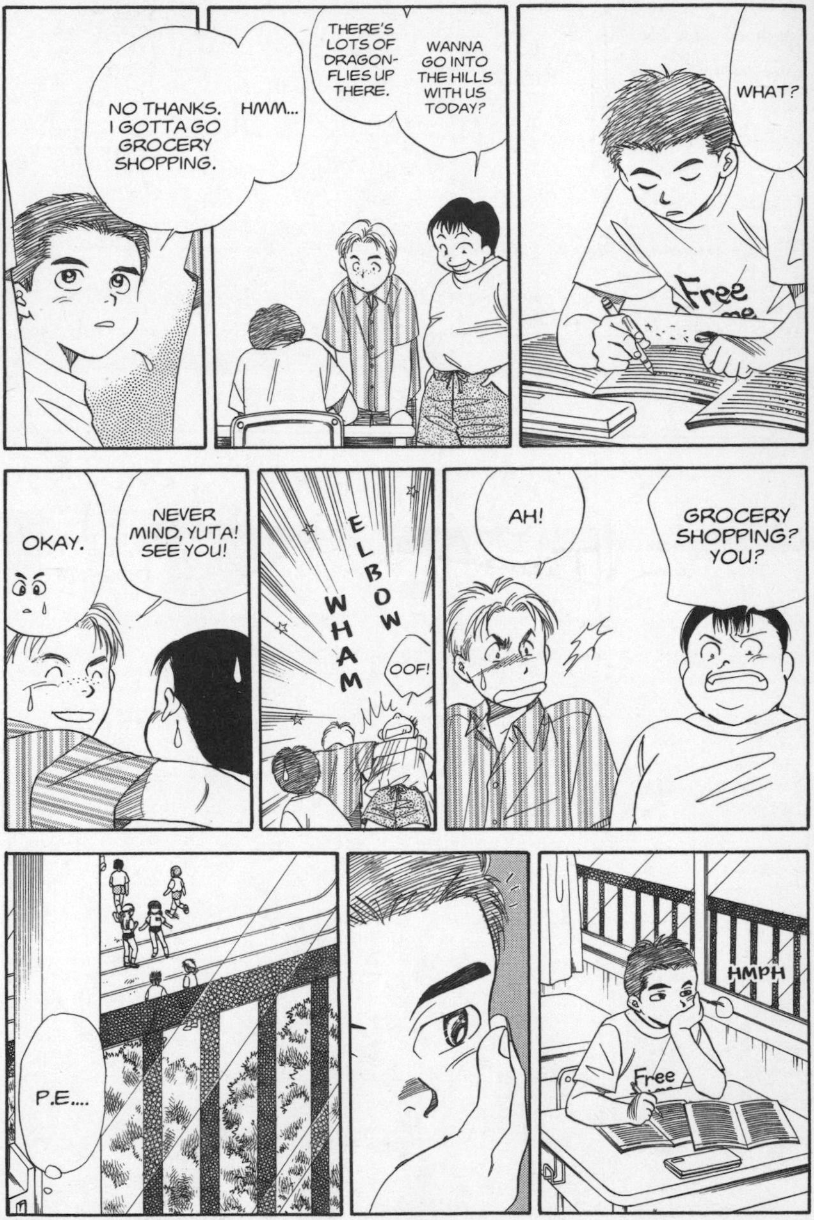
WHAT?
WANNA GO INTO THE HILLS WITH US TODAY?
THERE'S LOTS OF DRAGON-FLIES UP THERE.
HMM...
NO THANKS. I GOTTA GO GROCERY SHOPPING.
GROCERY SHOPPING? YOU?
AH!
ELBOW
WHAM
OOF!
NEVER MIND, YUTA! SEE YOU!
OKAY.
HMPH
P.E....

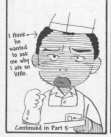

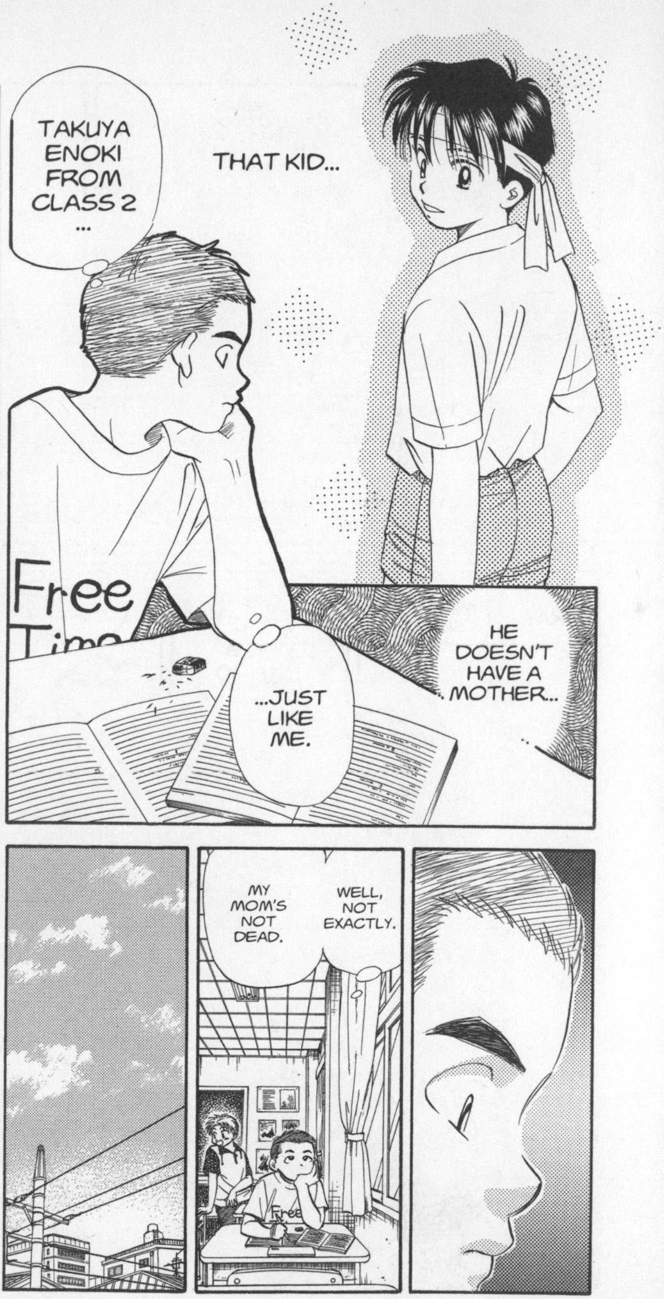
THAT KID...
TAKUYA ENOKI FROM CLASS 2 ...
Free Time
HE DOESN'T HAVE A MOTHER...
...JUST LIKE ME.
WELL, NOT EXACTLY.
MY MOM'S NOT DEAD.

Author's Note Part 4

They pronounce things very differently in Japan and the U.S.

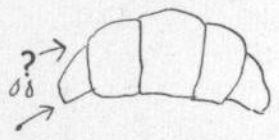

I tried to order a croissant and failed. They call it something like "Kurossan," not "Kurowassan." (My pronunciation was close, so why couldn't they understand me?) On the first day, I made a mistake. I kept nodding yes to all of the waiter's suggestions, so my first American meal was gigantic!

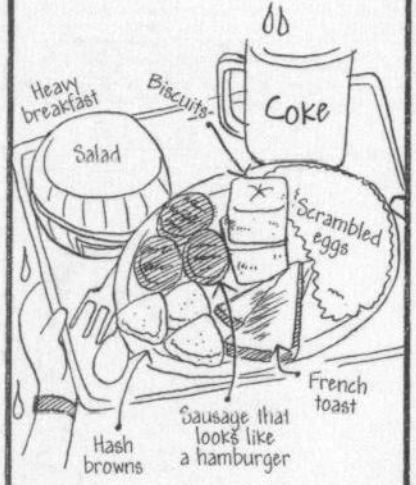
Heavy breakfast
Biscuits
Coke
Salad
Scrambled eggs
French toast
Sausage that looks like a hamburger
Hash browns

There was no way I could eat it all. Another day, based on the lesson I'd learned, I said, "No, thank you," to refuse the food items I didn't want. The waiter looked puzzled.

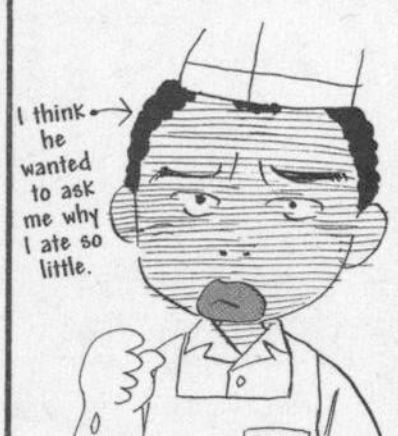
I think he wanted to ask me why I ate so little.

Continued in Part 5

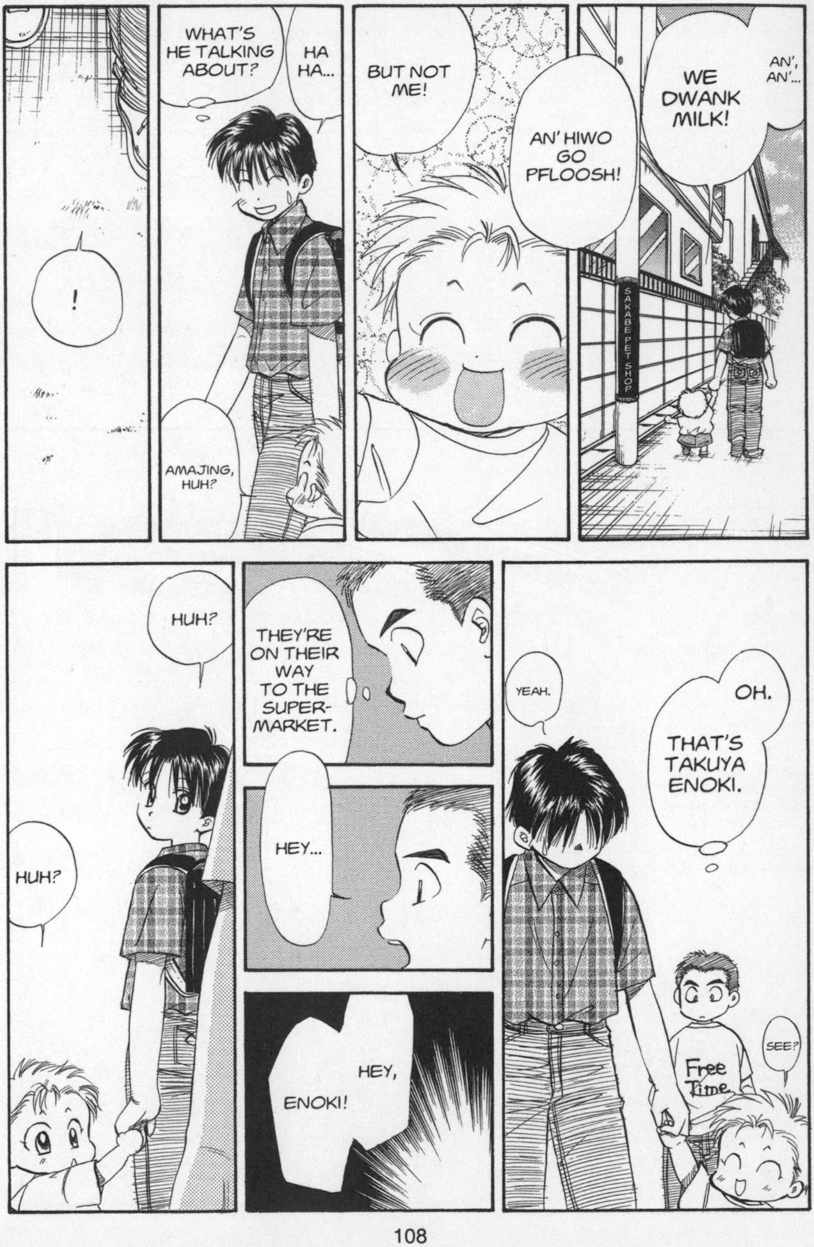
AN', AN'...
WE DWANK MILK!
AN' HIWO GO PFLOOSH!
SAKABE PET SHOP
BUT NOT ME!
HA HA...
WHAT'S HE TALKING ABOUT?
AMAJING, HUH?
!
OH.
THAT'S TAKUYA ENOKI.
YEAH.
SEE?
Free Time
THEY'RE ON THEIR WAY TO THE SUPER-MARKET.
HEY...
HEY, ENOKI!
HUH?
HUH?

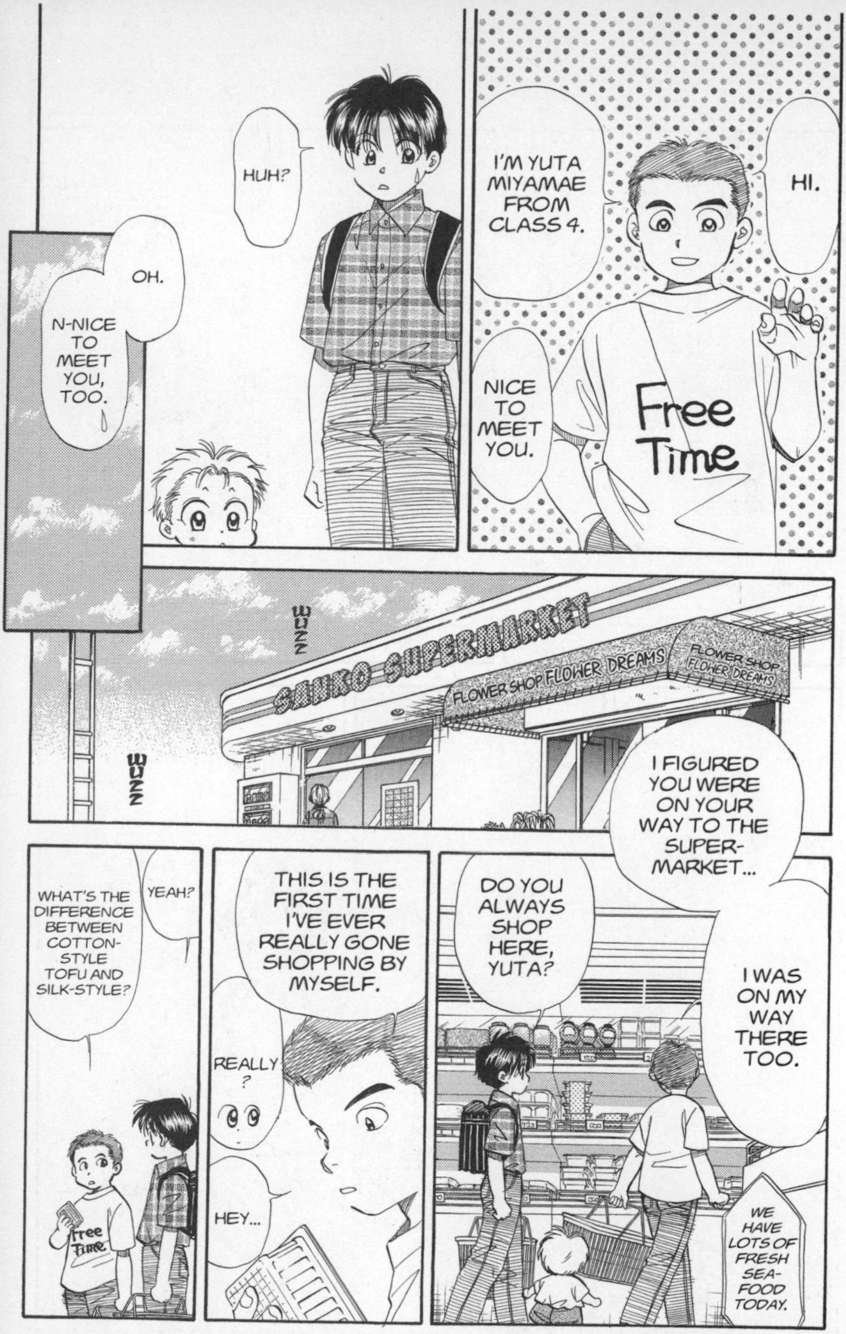
HI.
I'M YUTA MIYAMAE FROM CLASS 4.
NICE TO MEET YOU.
Free Time
HUH?
OH.
N-NICE TO MEET YOU, TOO.
WUZZ
WUZZ
SANKO SUPERMARKET
FLOWER SHOP FLOWER DREAMS
FLOWER SHOP FLOWER DREAMS
I FIGURED YOU WERE ON YOUR WAY TO THE SUPER-MARKET...
I WAS ON MY WAY THERE TOO.
DO YOU ALWAYS SHOP HERE, YUTA?
WE HAVE LOTS OF FRESH SEA-FOOD TODAY.
THIS IS THE FIRST TIME I'VE EVER REALLY GONE SHOPPING BY MYSELF.
REALLY?
HEY...
YEAH?
WHAT'S THE DIFFERENCE BETWEEN COTTON-STYLE TOFU AND SILK-STYLE?
Free Time

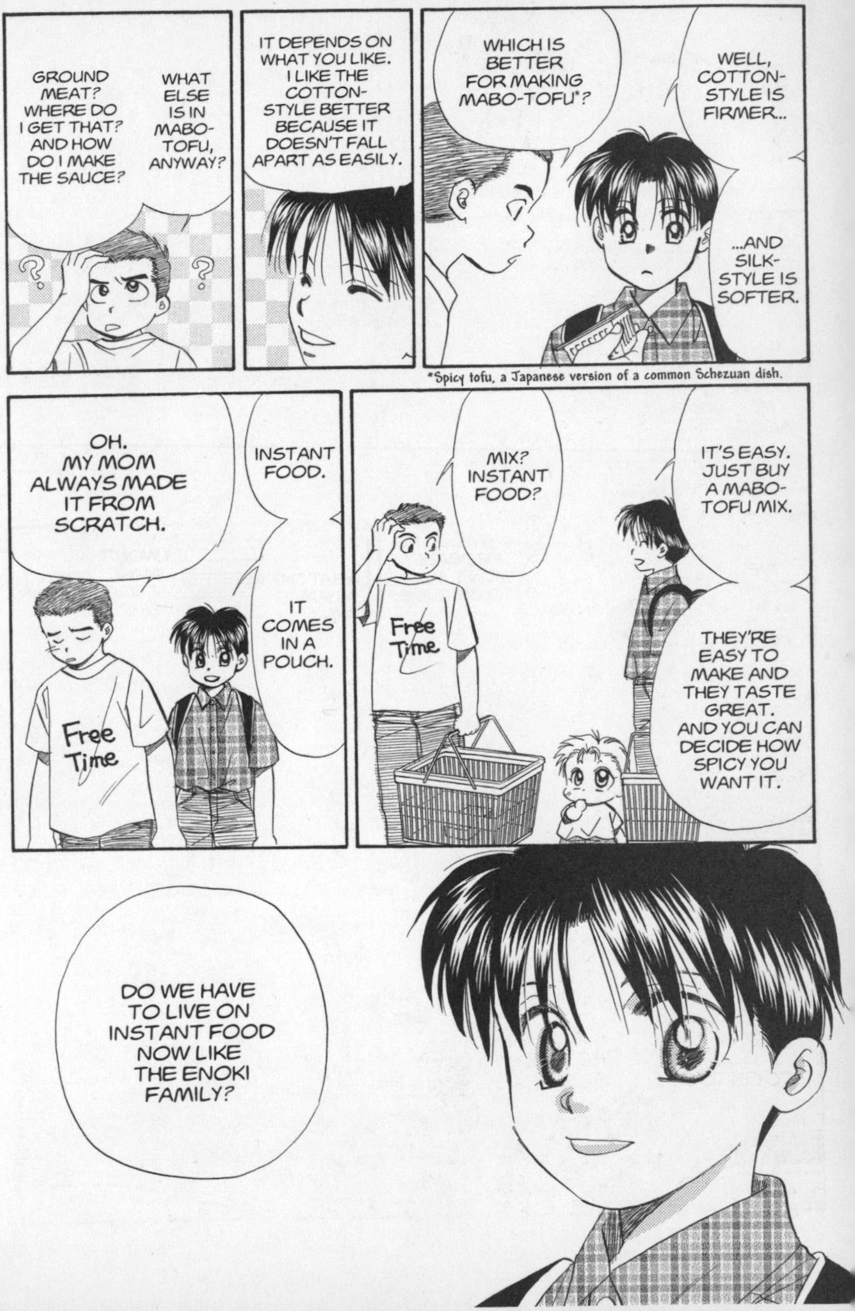
WHICH IS BETTER FOR MAKING MABO-TOFU*?
WELL, COTTON-STYLE IS FIRMER...
...AND SILK-STYLE IS SOFTER.
IT DEPENDS ON WHAT YOU LIKE. I LIKE THE COTTON-STYLE BETTER BECAUSE IT DOESN'T FALL APART AS EASILY.
WHAT ELSE IS IN MABO-TOFU, ANYWAY?
GROUND MEAT? WHERE DO I GET THAT? AND HOW DO I MAKE THE SAUCE?
IT'S EASY. JUST BUY A MABO-TOFU MIX.
MIX? INSTANT FOOD?
THEY'RE EASY TO MAKE AND THEY TASTE GREAT. AND YOU CAN DECIDE HOW SPICY YOU WANT IT.
Free Time
INSTANT FOOD.
IT COMES IN A POUCH.
OH. MY MOM ALWAYS MADE IT FROM SCRATCH.
Free Time
DO WE HAVE TO LIVE ON INSTANT FOOD NOW LIKE THE ENOKI FAMILY?
*Spicy tofu, a Japanese version of a common Schezuan dish.

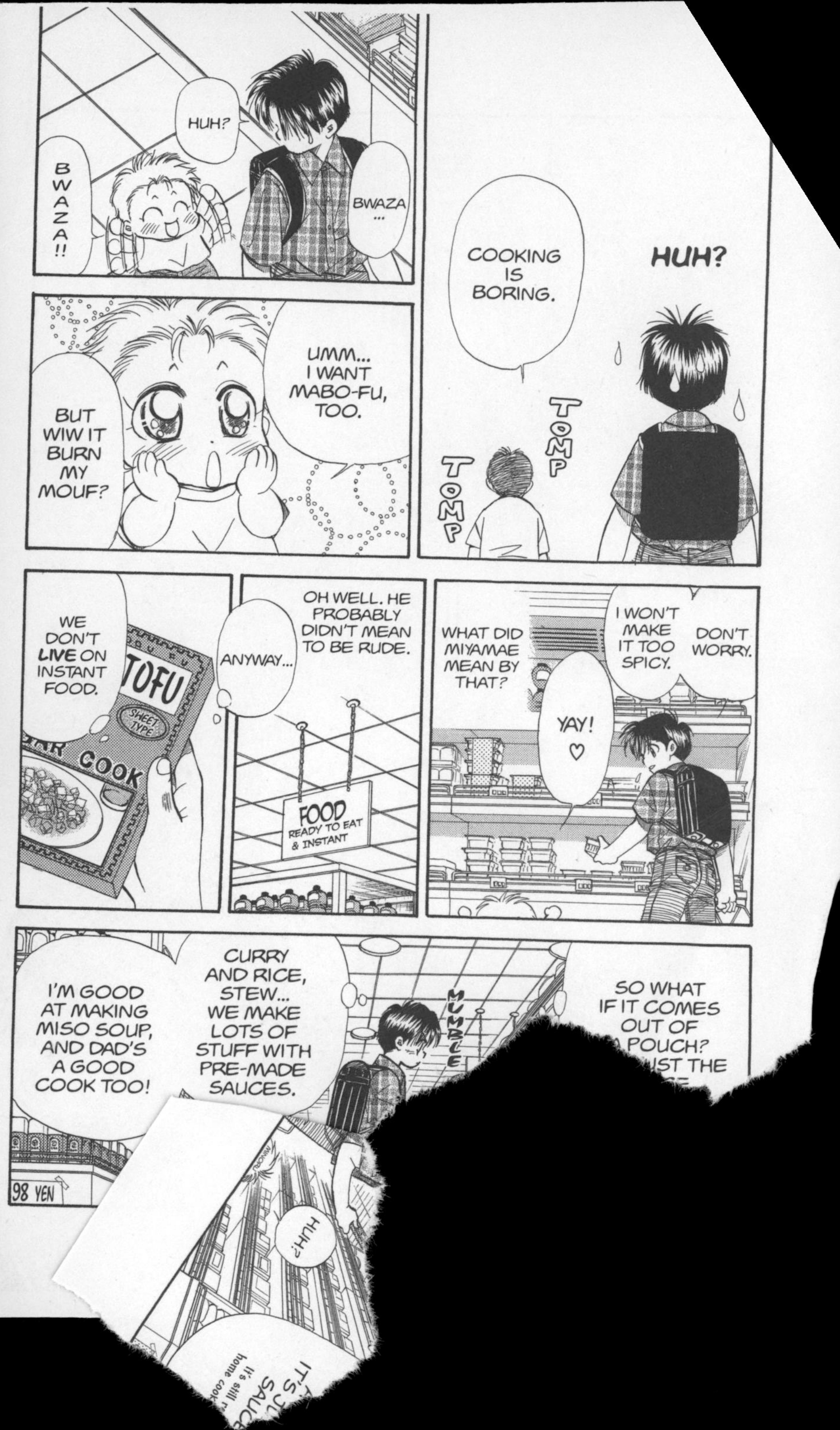
HUH?
COOKING IS BORING.
TOMP
TOMP
HUH?
BWAZA...
BWAZA!!
UMM... I WANT MABO-FU, TOO.
BUT WIW IT BURN MY MOUF?
DON'T WORRY.
I WON'T MAKE IT TOO SPICY.
WHAT DID MIYAMAE MEAN BY THAT?
YAY! ♡
OH WELL. HE PROBABLY DIDN'T MEAN TO BE RUDE.
ANYWAY...
FOOD READY TO EAT & INSTANT
WE DON'T **LIVE** ON INSTANT FOOD.
TOFU
SWEET TYPE
COOK
SO WHAT IF IT COMES OUT OF A POUCH?
MUMBLE
CURRY AND RICE, STEW... WE MAKE LOTS OF STUFF WITH PRE-MADE SAUCES.
I'M GOOD AT MAKING MISO SOUP, AND DAD'S A GOOD COOK TOO!
98 YEN
HUH?

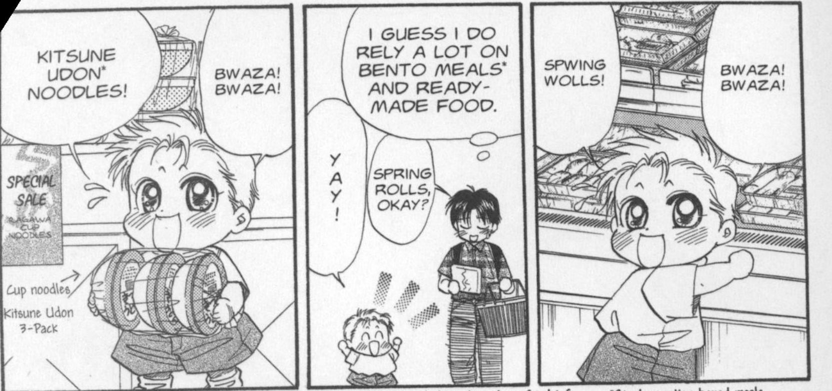
BWAZA! BWAZA!
SPWING WOLLS!
I GUESS I DO RELY A LOT ON BENTO MEALS* AND READY-MADE FOOD.
SPRING ROLLS, OKAY?
YAY!
BWAZA! BWAZA!
KITSUNE UDON* NOODLES!
SPECIAL SALE
Cup noodles
Kitsune Udon 3-Pack

*"Fox udon." This is udon with sweetened deep-fried tofu. According to legend, foxes love deep-fried tofu.

*Single-portion boxed meals.

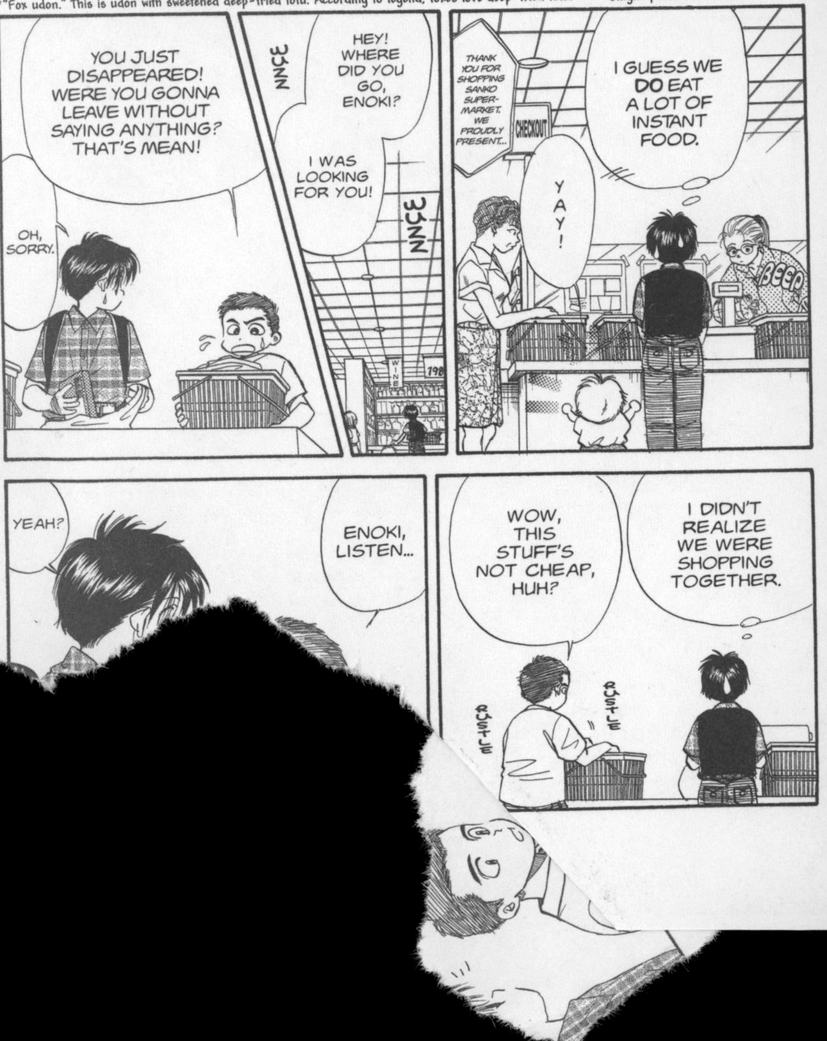
I GUESS WE DO EAT A LOT OF INSTANT FOOD.
THANK YOU FOR SHOPPING SANKO SUPER-MARKET. WE PROUDLY PRESENT...
CHECKOUT
YAY!
BEEP
HEY! WHERE DID YOU GO, ENOKI?
I WAS LOOKING FOR YOU!
WINE
198
YOU JUST DISAPPEARED! WERE YOU GONNA LEAVE WITHOUT SAYING ANYTHING? THAT'S MEAN!
OH, SORRY.
I DIDN'T REALIZE WE WERE SHOPPING TOGETHER.
WOW, THIS STUFF'S NOT CHEAP, HUH?
RUSTLE
RUSTLE
ENOKI, LISTEN...
YEAH?

HUH?

BWAZA!!

BWAZA...

COOKING IS BORING.

HUH?

TOMP

TOMP

UMM... I WANT MABO-FU, TOO.

BUT WIW IT BURN MY MOUF?

WE DON'T **LIVE** ON INSTANT FOOD.

TOFU
SHEET TYPE

COOK

ANYWAY...

OH WELL. HE PROBABLY DIDN'T MEAN TO BE RUDE.

FOOD
READY TO EAT
& INSTANT

WHAT DID MIYAMAE MEAN BY THAT?

I WON'T MAKE IT TOO SPICY.

DON'T WORRY.

YAY! ♡

I'M GOOD AT MAKING MISO SOUP, AND DAD'S A GOOD COOK TOO!

CURRY AND RICE, STEW... WE MAKE LOTS OF STUFF WITH PRE-MADE SAUCES.

MUMBLE

SO WHAT IF IT COMES OUT OF A PAROUCH? IT'S JUST LIKE THE SAUSAGE. It's still real home cooking!

HUH?

98 YEN

MINORU

SUGAR

KITSUNE UDON* NOODLES!

BWAZA! BWAZA!

SPECIAL SALE
SAKAWA CUP NOODLES

Cup noodles

Kitsune Udon 3-Pack

I GUESS I DO RELY A LOT ON BENTO MEALS* AND READY-MADE FOOD.

YAY!

SPRING ROLLS, OKAY?

SPWING WOLLS!

BWAZA! BWAZA!

*"Fox udon." This is udon with sweetened deep-fried tofu. According to legend, foxes love deep-fried tofu.   *Single-portion boxed meals.

YOU JUST DISAPPEARED! WERE YOU GONNA LEAVE WITHOUT SAYING ANYTHING? THAT'S MEAN!

NNGE

HEY! WHERE DID YOU GO, ENOKI?

I WAS LOOKING FOR YOU!

NNGE

OH, SORRY.

THANK YOU FOR SHOPPING SANKO SUPER-MARKET. WE PROUDLY PRESENT...

CHECKOUT

I GUESS WE DO EAT A LOT OF INSTANT FOOD.

YAY!

BEEP

YEAH?

ENOKI, LISTEN...

WOW, THIS STUFF'S NOT CHEAP, HUH?

I DIDN'T REALIZE WE WERE SHOPPING TOGETHER.

RUSTLE

RUSTLE

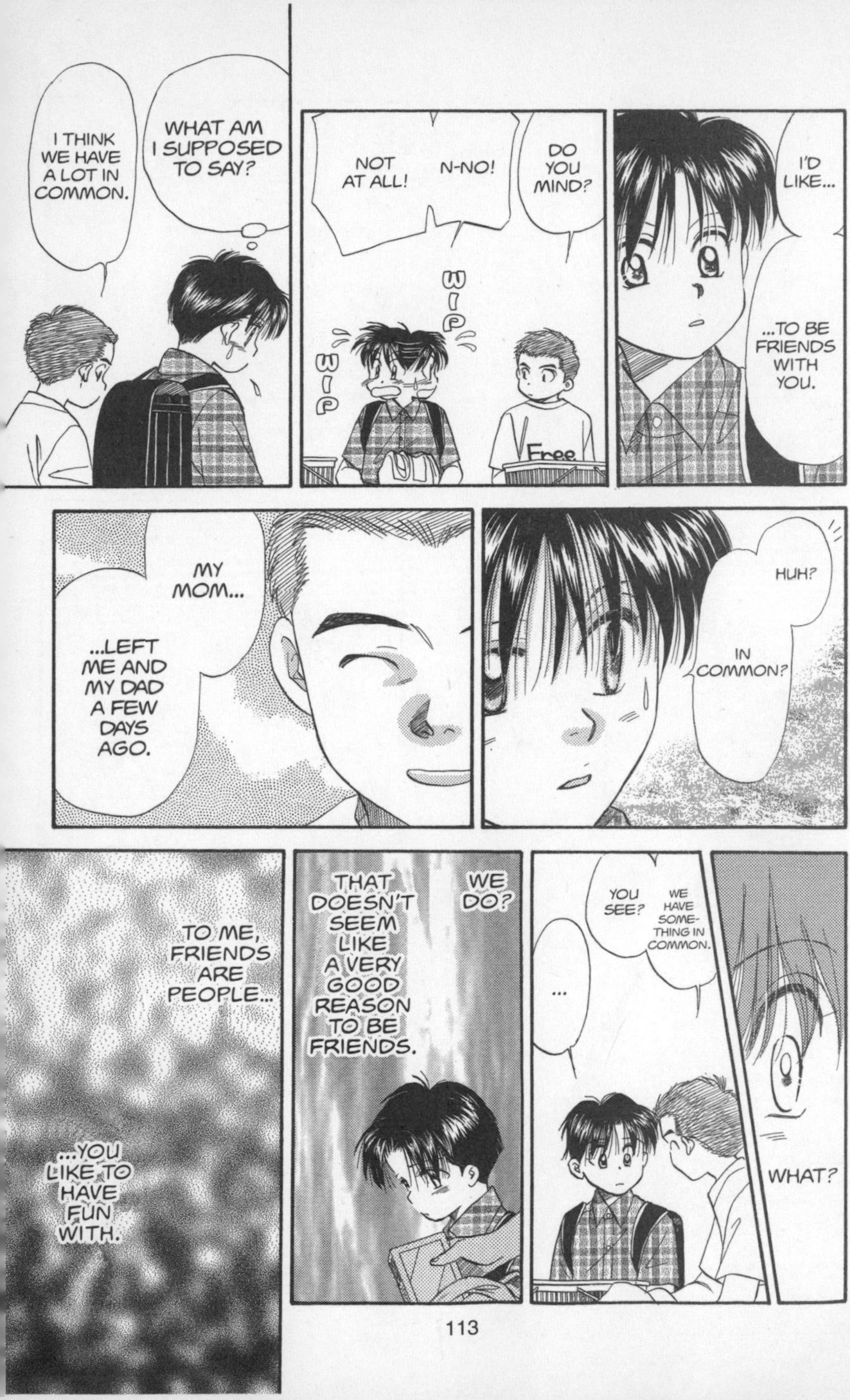
I'D LIKE...
...TO BE FRIENDS WITH YOU.
DO YOU MIND?
N-NO!
NOT AT ALL!
WIP
WIP
WHAT AM I SUPPOSED TO SAY?
I THINK WE HAVE A LOT IN COMMON.
HUH?
IN COMMON?
MY MOM...
...LEFT ME AND MY DAD A FEW DAYS AGO.
WHAT?
YOU SEE? WE HAVE SOME-THING IN COMMON.
...
WE DO?
THAT DOESN'T SEEM LIKE A VERY GOOD REASON TO BE FRIENDS.
TO ME, FRIENDS ARE PEOPLE...
...YOU LIKE TO HAVE FUN WITH.

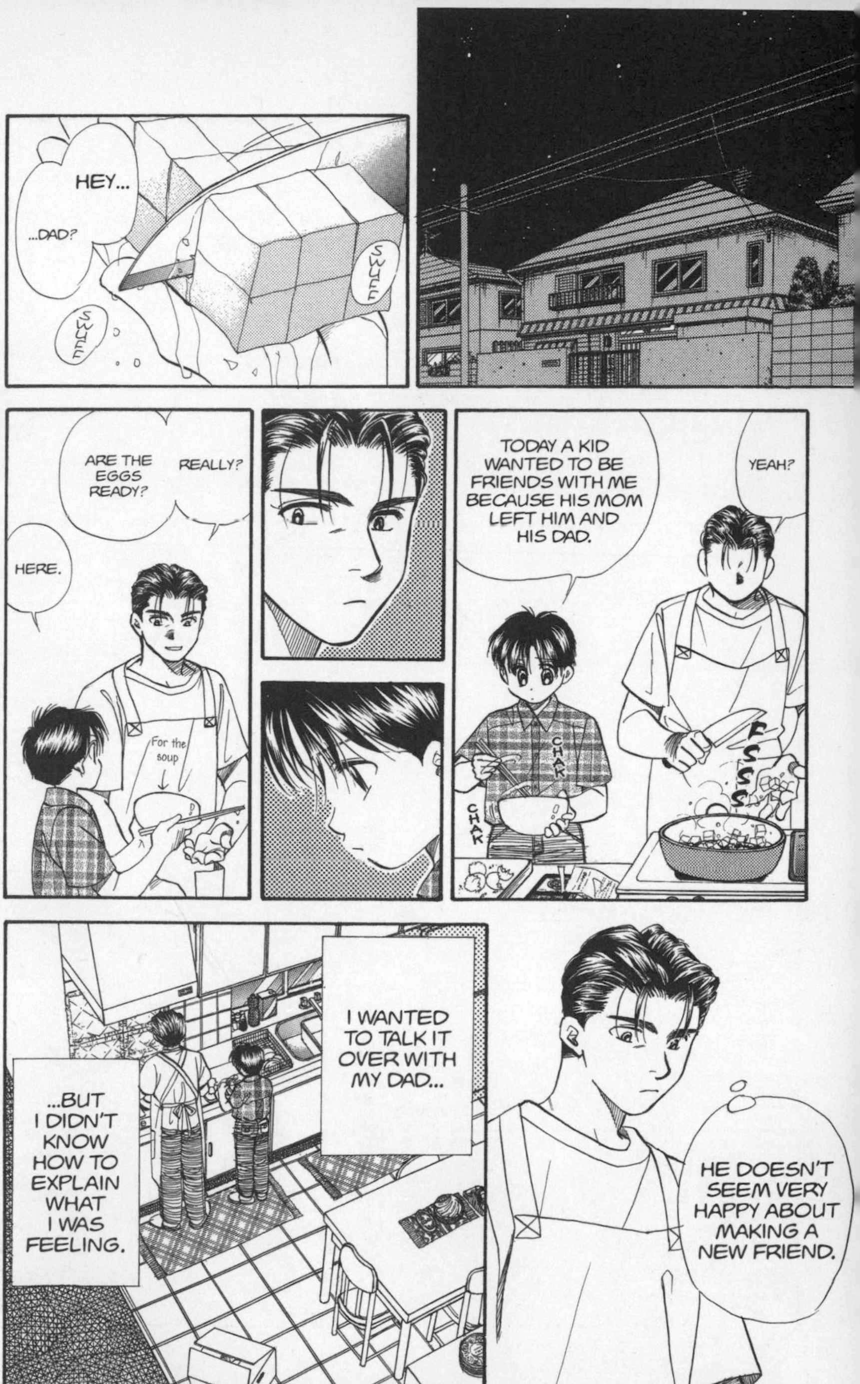
HEY...
...DAD?
SWUFF
SWUFF
TODAY A KID WANTED TO BE FRIENDS WITH ME BECAUSE HIS MOM LEFT HIM AND HIS DAD.
YEAH?
CHAK
CHAK
FSSSS
REALLY?
ARE THE EGGS READY?
HERE.
For the soup
HE DOESN'T SEEM VERY HAPPY ABOUT MAKING A NEW FRIEND.
I WANTED TO TALK IT OVER WITH MY DAD...
...BUT I DIDN'T KNOW HOW TO EXPLAIN WHAT I WAS FEELING.

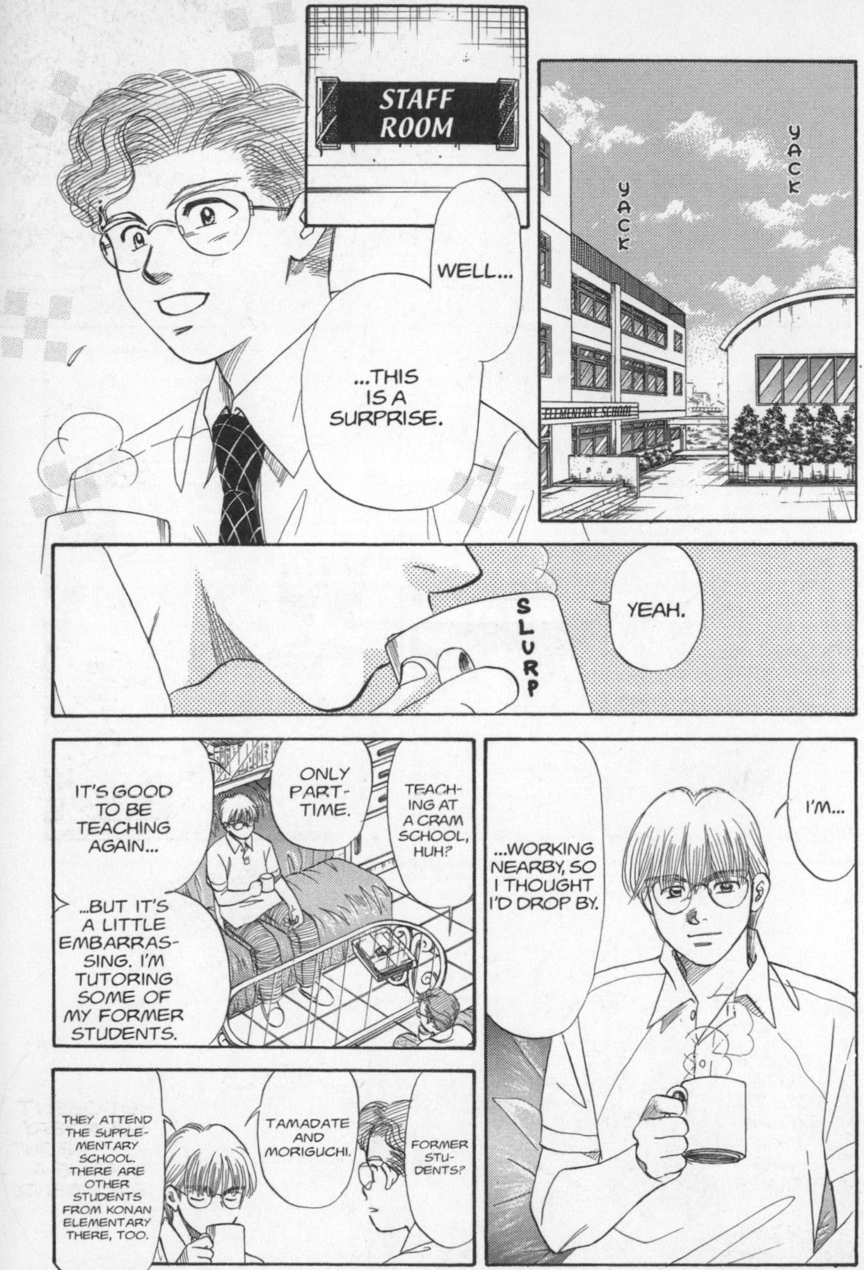
YACK
YACK
STAFF ROOM
WELL...
...THIS IS A SURPRISE.
SLURP
YEAH.
I'M...
...WORKING NEARBY, SO I THOUGHT I'D DROP BY.
TEACHING AT A CRAM SCHOOL, HUH?
ONLY PART-TIME.
IT'S GOOD TO BE TEACHING AGAIN...
...BUT IT'S A LITTLE EMBARRASSING. I'M TUTORING SOME OF MY FORMER STUDENTS.
FORMER STUDENTS?
TAMADATE AND MORIGUCHI.
THEY ATTEND THE SUPPLEMENTARY SCHOOL. THERE ARE OTHER STUDENTS FROM KONAN ELEMENTARY THERE, TOO.

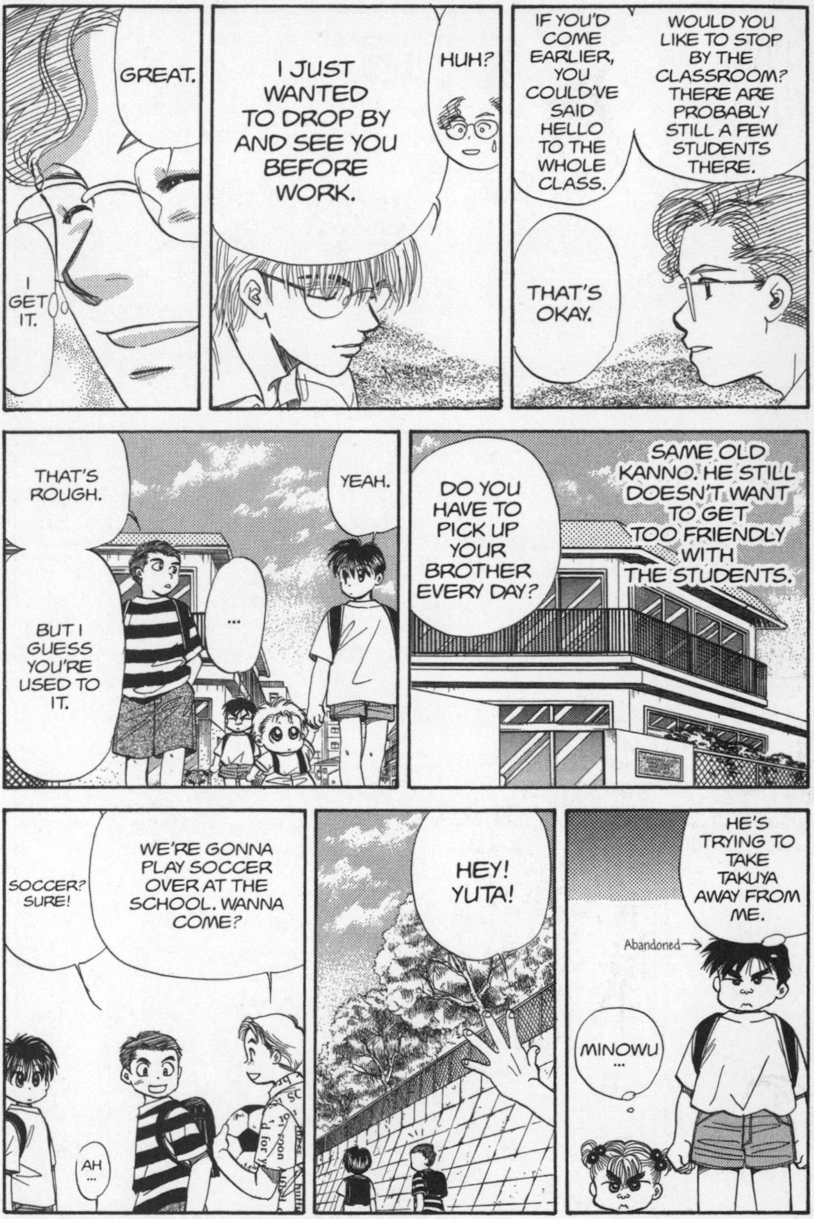
WOULD YOU LIKE TO STOP BY THE CLASSROOM? THERE ARE PROBABLY STILL A FEW STUDENTS THERE.
IF YOU'D COME EARLIER, YOU COULD'VE SAID HELLO TO THE WHOLE CLASS.
THAT'S OKAY.
HUH?
I JUST WANTED TO DROP BY AND SEE YOU BEFORE WORK.
GREAT.
I GET IT.
SAME OLD KANNO. HE STILL DOESN'T WANT TO GET TOO FRIENDLY WITH THE STUDENTS.
DO YOU HAVE TO PICK UP YOUR BROTHER EVERY DAY?
YEAH.
...
THAT'S ROUGH.
BUT I GUESS YOU'RE USED TO IT.
HE'S TRYING TO TAKE TAKUYA AWAY FROM ME.
Abandoned
MINOWU ...
HEY! YUTA!
WE'RE GONNA PLAY SOCCER OVER AT THE SCHOOL. WANNA COME?
SOCCER? SURE!
AH ...

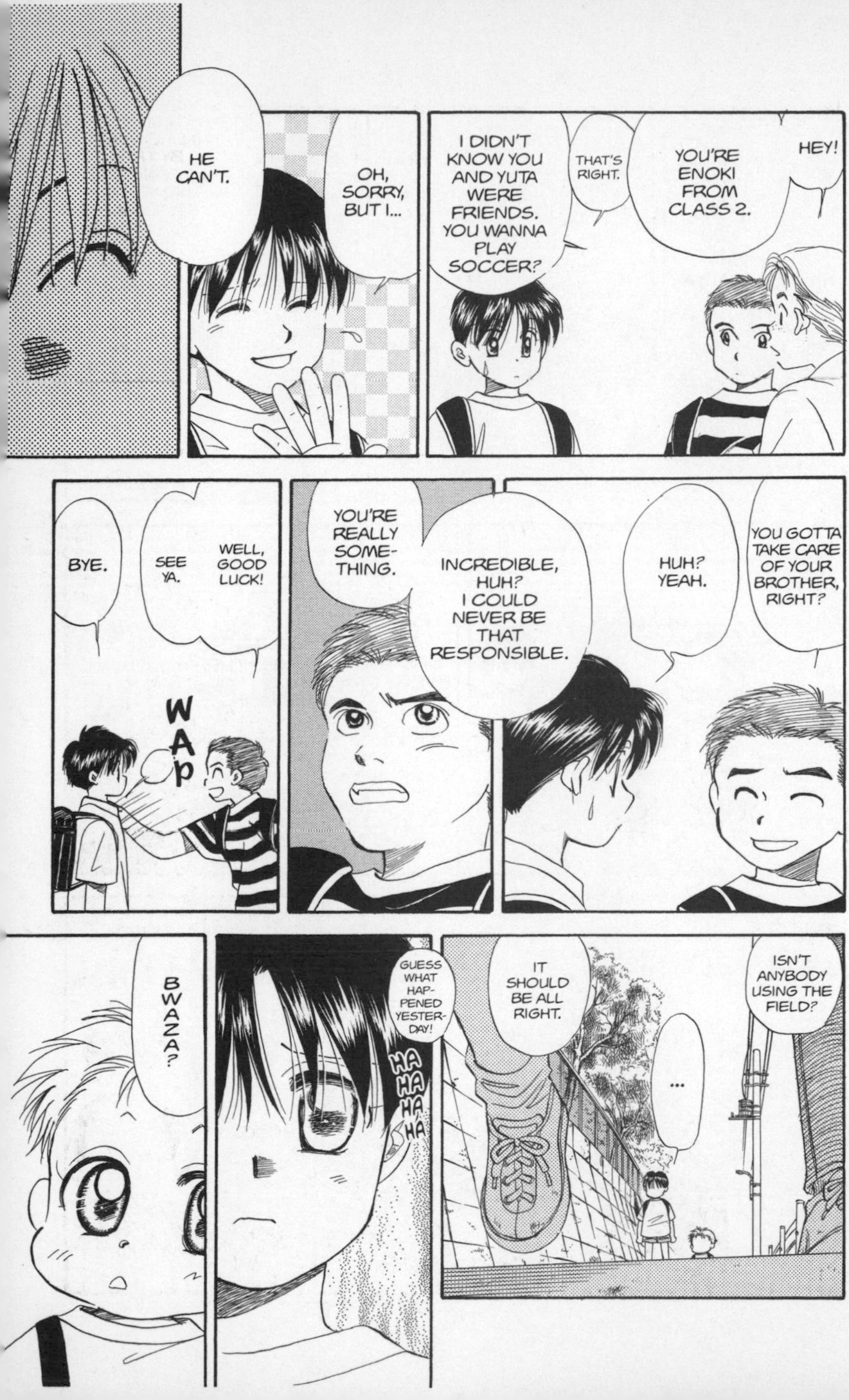
HEY!
YOU'RE ENOKI FROM CLASS 2.
THAT'S RIGHT.
I DIDN'T KNOW YOU AND YUTA WERE FRIENDS. YOU WANNA PLAY SOCCER?
OH, SORRY, BUT I...
HE CAN'T.
YOU GOTTA TAKE CARE OF YOUR BROTHER, RIGHT?
HUH? YEAH.
YOU'RE REALLY SOME-THING.
INCREDIBLE, HUH? I COULD NEVER BE THAT RESPONSIBLE.
WELL, GOOD LUCK!
SEE YA.
BYE.
WAp
ISN'T ANYBODY USING THE FIELD?
IT SHOULD BE ALL RIGHT.
...
GUESS WHAT HAP-PENED YESTER-DAY!
HA HA HA HA
BWAZA?

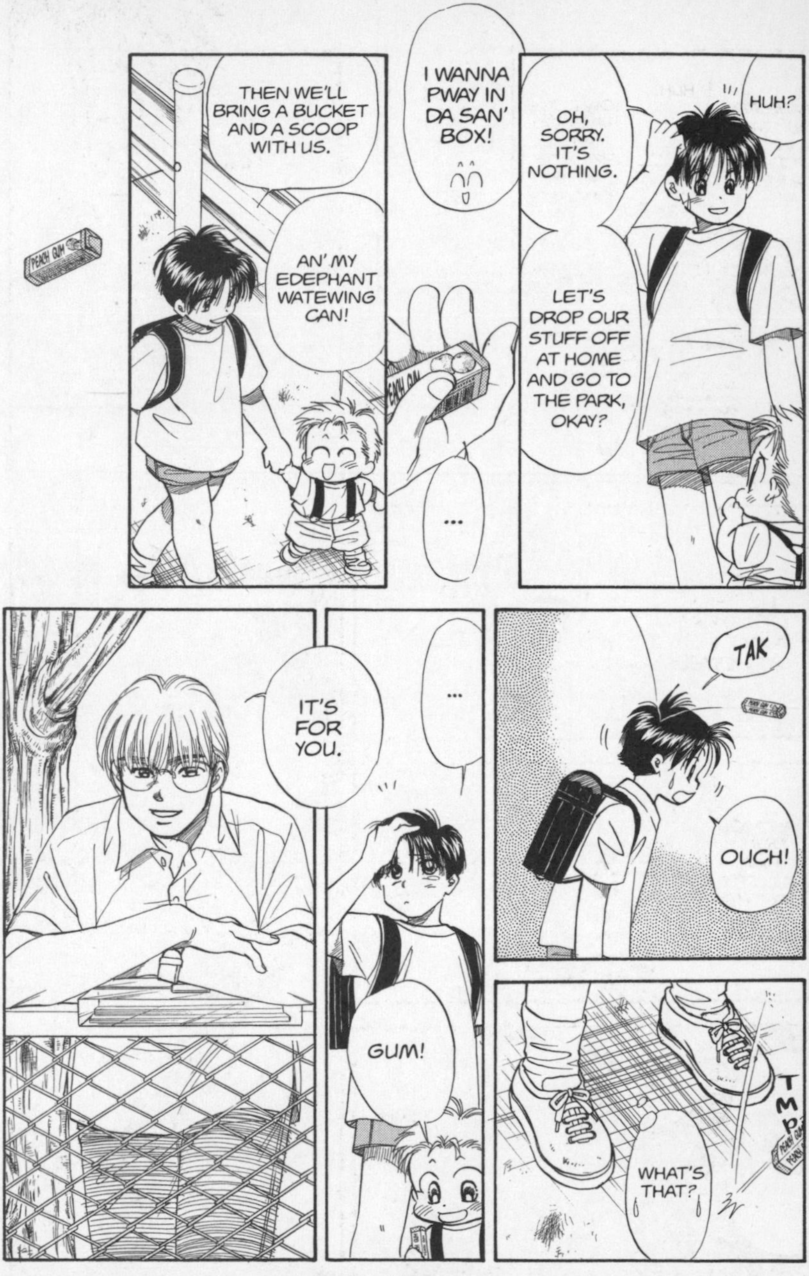
HUH?
OH, SORRY. IT'S NOTHING.
LET'S DROP OUR STUFF OFF AT HOME AND GO TO THE PARK, OKAY?
I WANNA PWAY IN DA SAN' BOX!
THEN WE'LL BRING A BUCKET AND A SCOOP WITH US.
AN' MY EDEPHANT WATEWING CAN!
PEACH GUM
...
TAK
OUCH!
TMP
WHAT'S THAT?
...
GUM!
IT'S FOR YOU.

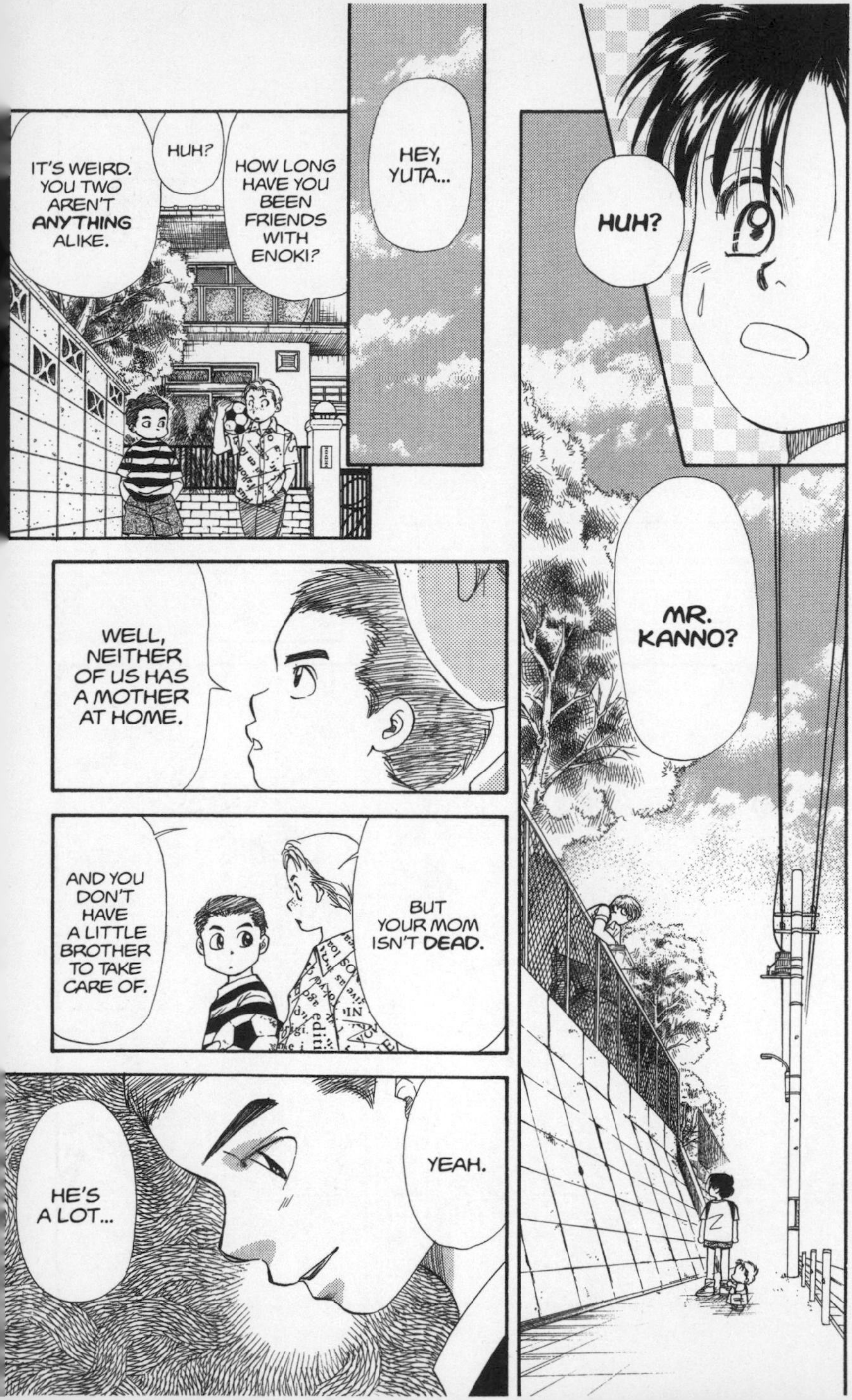
HUH?
MR. KANNO?
HEY, YUTA...
HOW LONG HAVE YOU BEEN FRIENDS WITH ENOKI?
HUH?
IT'S WEIRD. YOU TWO AREN'T **ANYTHING** ALIKE.
WELL, NEITHER OF US HAS A MOTHER AT HOME.
BUT YOUR MOM ISN'T **DEAD**.
AND YOU DON'T HAVE A LITTLE BROTHER TO TAKE CARE OF.
YEAH.
HE'S A LOT...

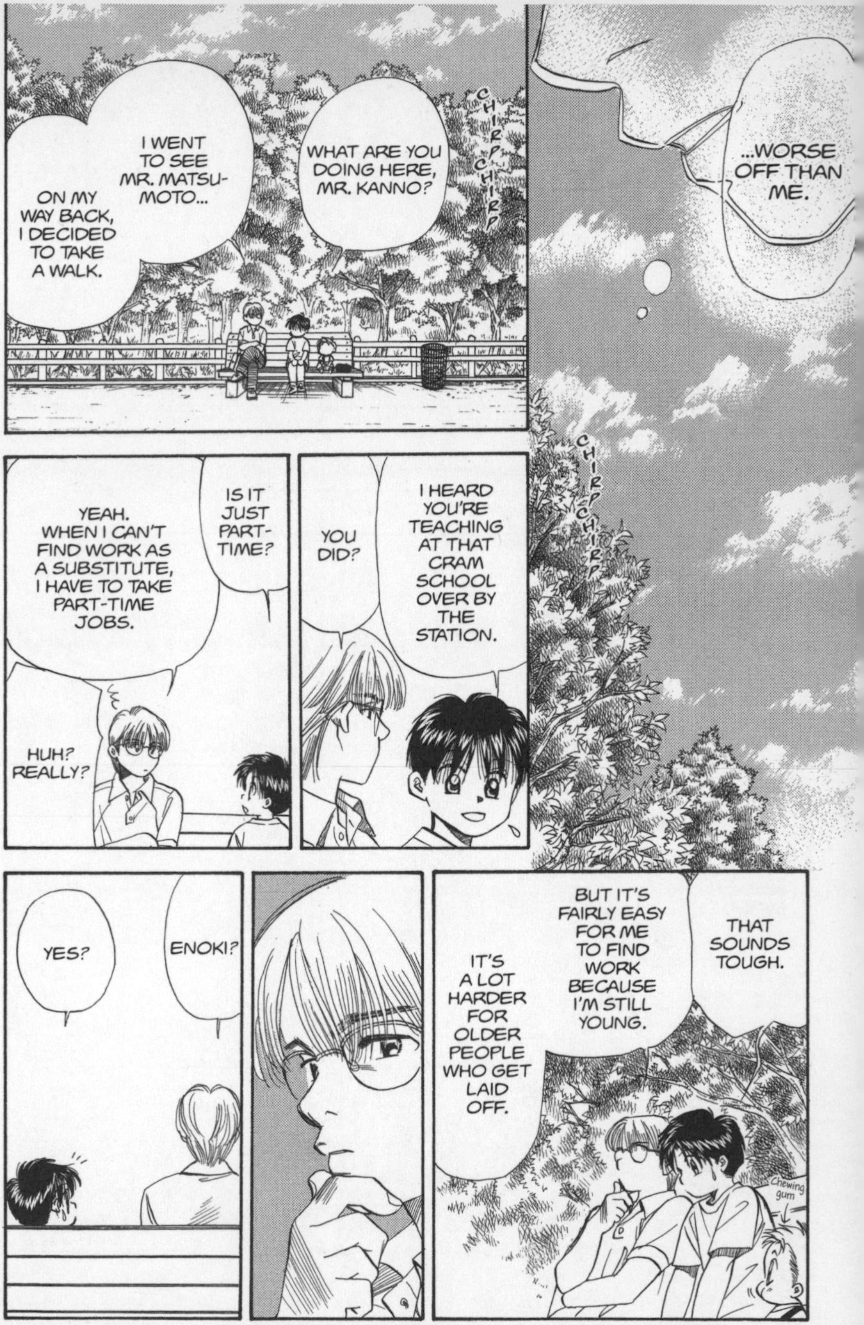
...WORSE OFF THAN ME.
CHIRP CHIRP
WHAT ARE YOU DOING HERE, MR. KANNO?
CHIRP CHIRP
I WENT TO SEE MR. MATSU-MOTO...
ON MY WAY BACK, I DECIDED TO TAKE A WALK.
I HEARD YOU'RE TEACHING AT THAT CRAM SCHOOL OVER BY THE STATION.
YOU DID?
IS IT JUST PART-TIME?
YEAH. WHEN I CAN'T FIND WORK AS A SUBSTITUTE, I HAVE TO TAKE PART-TIME JOBS.
HUH? REALLY?
THAT SOUNDS TOUGH.
BUT IT'S FAIRLY EASY FOR ME TO FIND WORK BECAUSE I'M STILL YOUNG.
IT'S A LOT HARDER FOR OLDER PEOPLE WHO GET LAID OFF.
Chewing gum
ENOKI?
YES?

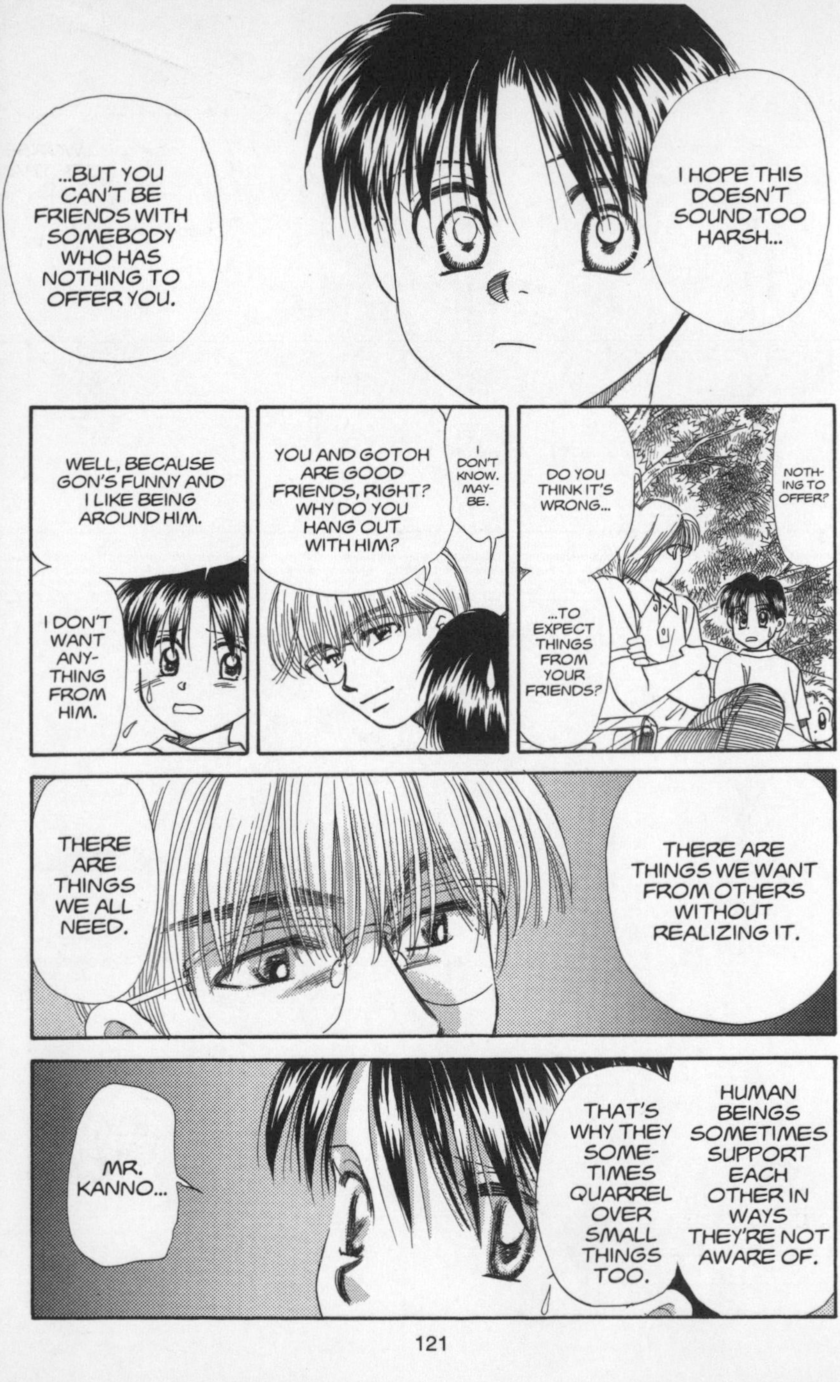

I HOPE THIS DOESN'T SOUND TOO HARSH...
...BUT YOU CAN'T BE FRIENDS WITH SOMEBODY WHO HAS NOTHING TO OFFER YOU.
NOTHING TO OFFER?
DO YOU THINK IT'S WRONG...
...TO EXPECT THINGS FROM YOUR FRIENDS?
I DON'T KNOW. MAYBE.
YOU AND GOTOH ARE GOOD FRIENDS, RIGHT? WHY DO YOU HANG OUT WITH HIM?
WELL, BECAUSE GON'S FUNNY AND I LIKE BEING AROUND HIM.
I DON'T WANT ANYTHING FROM HIM.
THERE ARE THINGS WE WANT FROM OTHERS WITHOUT REALIZING IT.
THERE ARE THINGS WE ALL NEED.
HUMAN BEINGS SOMETIMES SUPPORT EACH OTHER IN WAYS THEY'RE NOT AWARE OF.
THAT'S WHY THEY SOMETIMES QUARREL OVER SMALL THINGS TOO.
MR. KANNO...

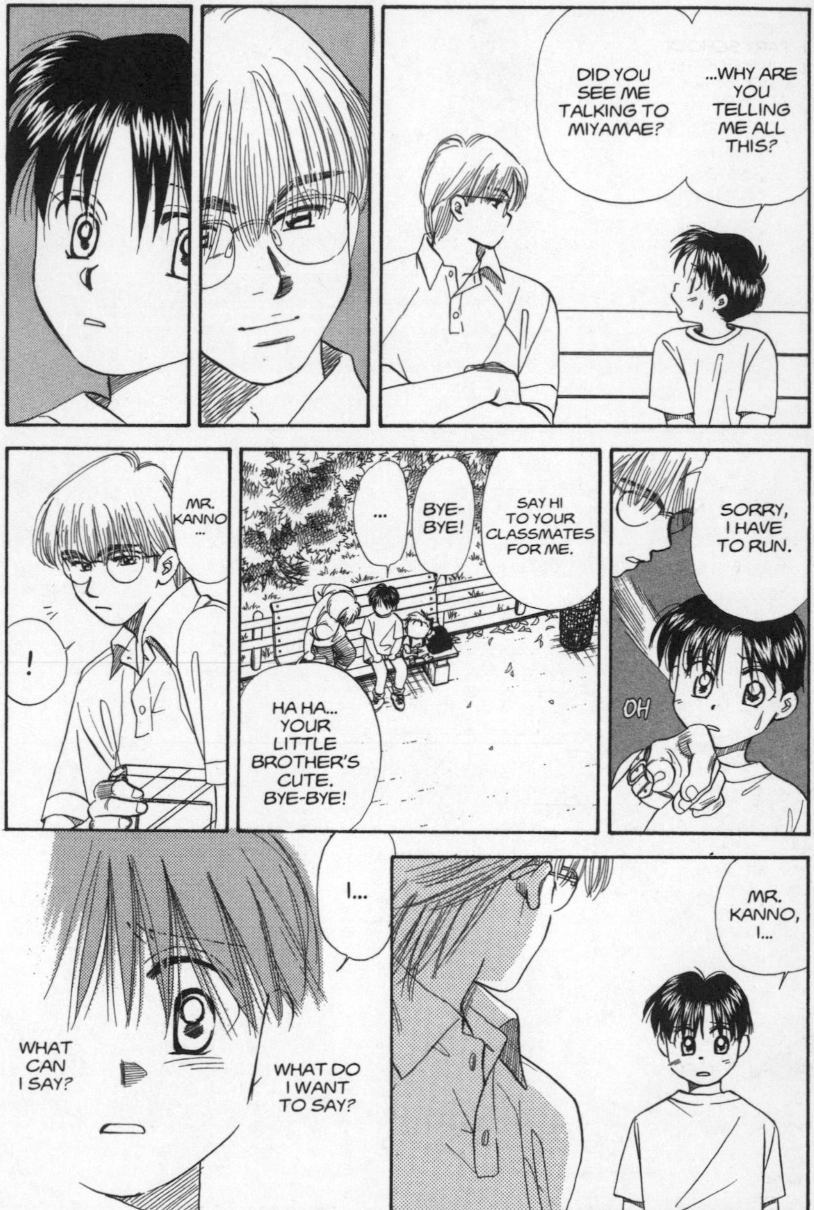
...WHY ARE YOU TELLING ME ALL THIS?
DID YOU SEE ME TALKING TO MIYAMAE?
SORRY, I HAVE TO RUN.
OH
SAY HI TO YOUR CLASSMATES FOR ME.
BYE-BYE!
...
HA HA... YOUR LITTLE BROTHER'S CUTE. BYE-BYE!
MR. KANNO ...
!
MR. KANNO, I...
I...
WHAT DO I WANT TO SAY?
WHAT CAN I SAY?

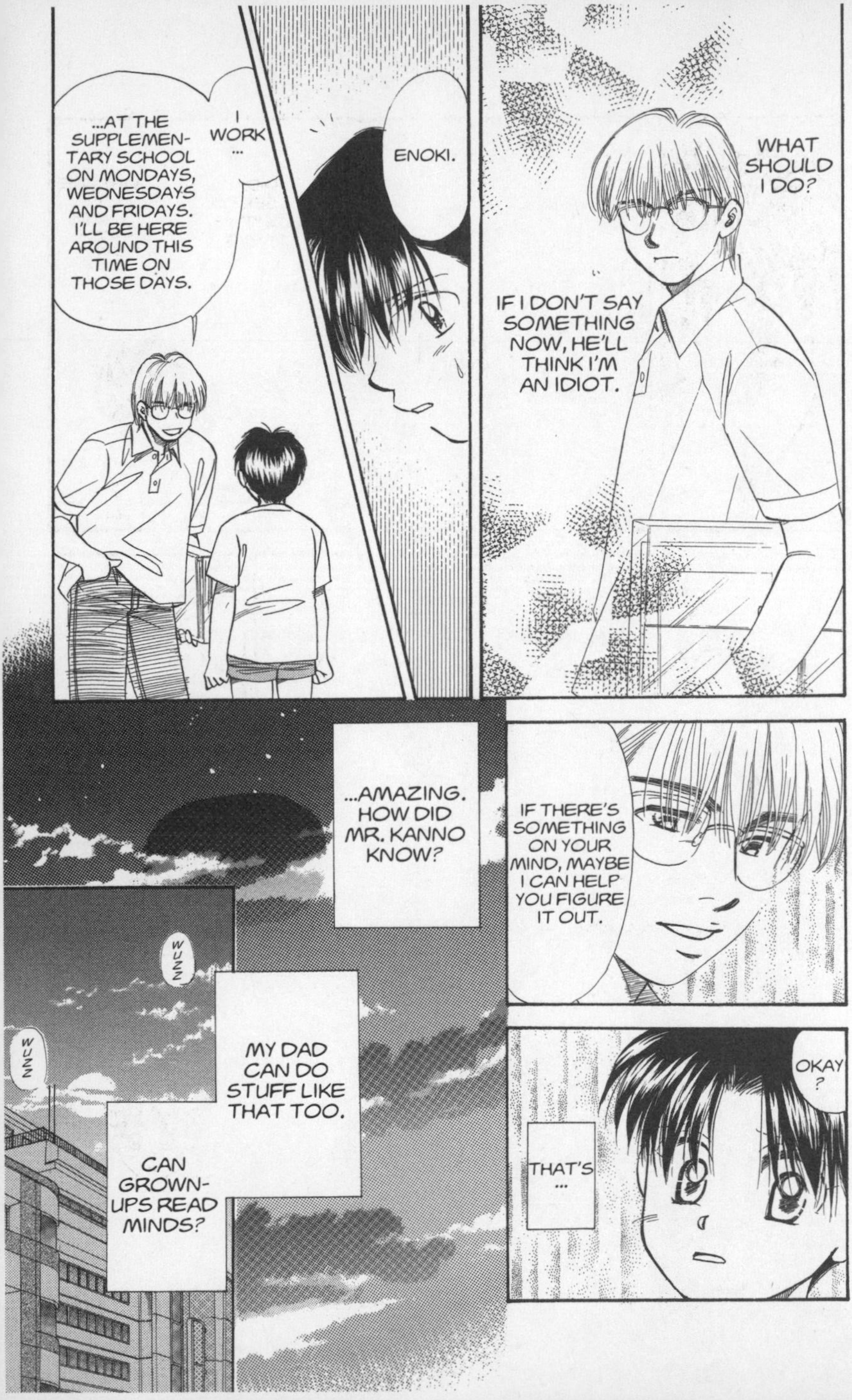
WHAT SHOULD I DO?
IF I DON'T SAY SOMETHING NOW, HE'LL THINK I'M AN IDIOT.
ENOKI.
I WORK ...
...AT THE SUPPLEMENTARY SCHOOL ON MONDAYS, WEDNESDAYS AND FRIDAYS. I'LL BE HERE AROUND THIS TIME ON THOSE DAYS.
IF THERE'S SOMETHING ON YOUR MIND, MAYBE I CAN HELP YOU FIGURE IT OUT.
OKAY?
THAT'S ...
...AMAZING. HOW DID MR. KANNO KNOW?
WUZZ
MY DAD CAN DO STUFF LIKE THAT TOO.
WUZZ
CAN GROWN-UPS READ MINDS?

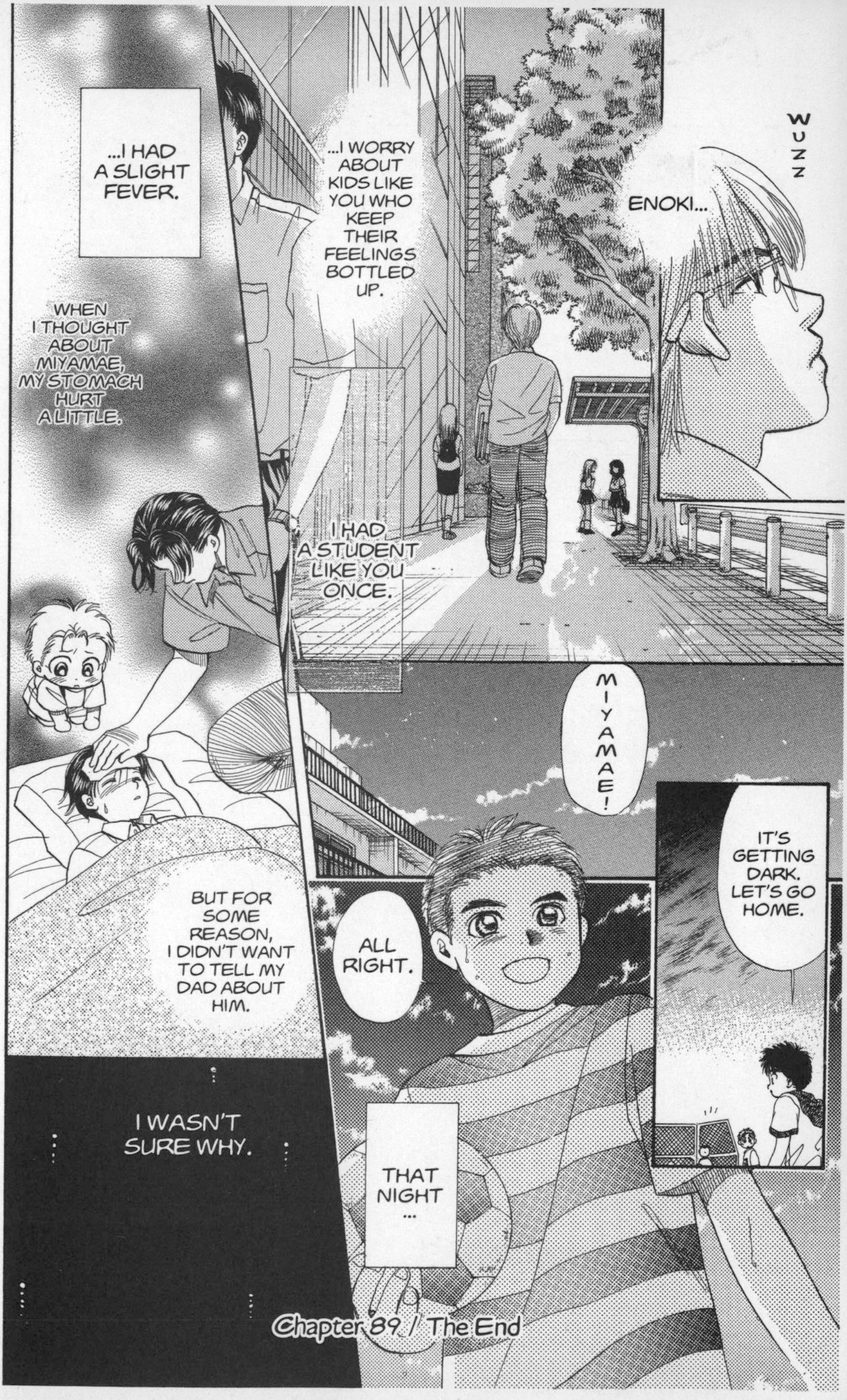
WUZZ
ENOKI...
...I WORRY ABOUT KIDS LIKE YOU WHO KEEP THEIR FEELINGS BOTTLED UP.
I HAD A STUDENT LIKE YOU ONCE.
MIYAMAE!
IT'S GETTING DARK. LET'S GO HOME.
ALL RIGHT.
THAT NIGHT ...
...I HAD A SLIGHT FEVER.
WHEN I THOUGHT ABOUT MIYAMAE, MY STOMACH HURT A LITTLE.
BUT FOR SOME REASON, I DIDN'T WANT TO TELL MY DAD ABOUT HIM.
I WASN'T SURE WHY.
Chapter 89 / The End

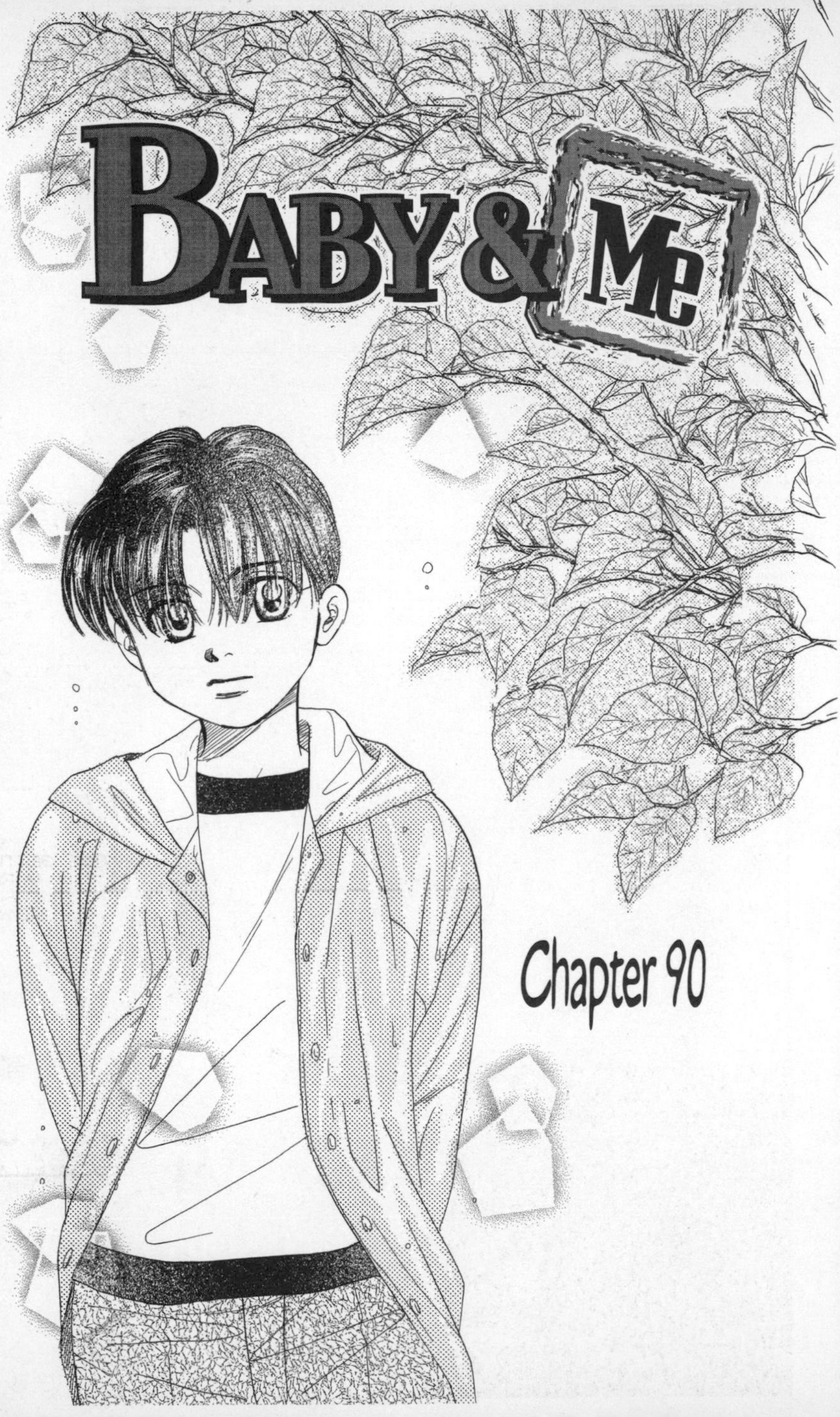
BABY & Me
Chapter 90

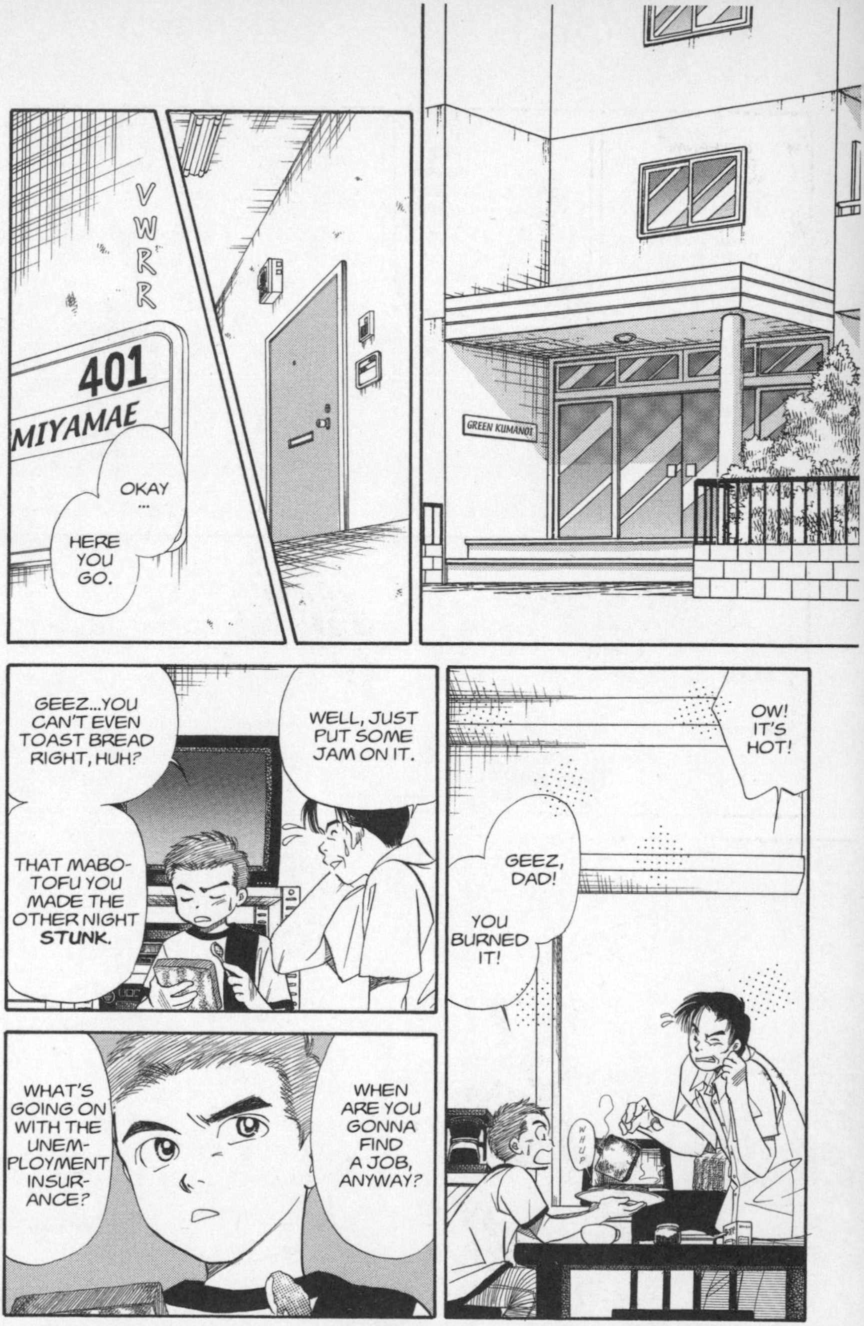
GREEN KUMANOI
401
MIYAMAE
VWRR
OKAY ...
HERE YOU GO.
OW! IT'S HOT!
GEEZ, DAD!
YOU BURNED IT!
WHUP
WELL, JUST PUT SOME JAM ON IT.
GEEZ...YOU CAN'T EVEN TOAST BREAD RIGHT, HUH?
THAT MABO-TOFU YOU MADE THE OTHER NIGHT **STUNK**.
WHEN ARE YOU GONNA FIND A JOB, ANYWAY?
WHAT'S GOING ON WITH THE UNEMPLOYMENT INSURANCE?

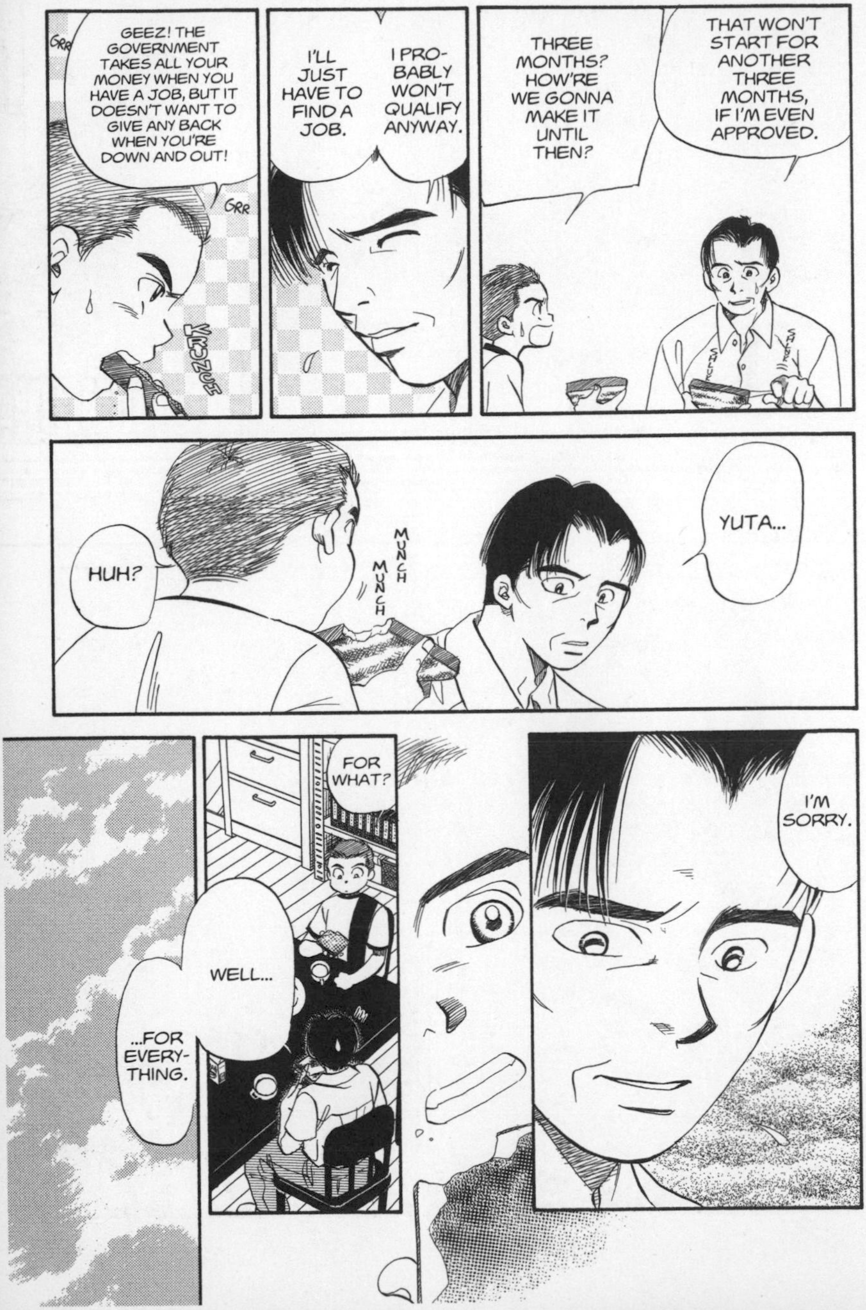
THAT WON'T START FOR ANOTHER THREE MONTHS, IF I'M EVEN APPROVED.
THREE MONTHS? HOW'RE WE GONNA MAKE IT UNTIL THEN?
I PRO-BABLY WON'T QUALIFY ANYWAY.
I'LL JUST HAVE TO FIND A JOB.
GRR
GEEZ! THE GOVERNMENT TAKES ALL YOUR MONEY WHEN YOU HAVE A JOB, BUT IT DOESN'T WANT TO GIVE ANY BACK WHEN YOU'RE DOWN AND OUT!
GRR
KRUNCH
YUTA...
MUNCH
MUNCH
HUH?
I'M SORRY.
FOR WHAT?
WELL...
...FOR EVERY-THING.

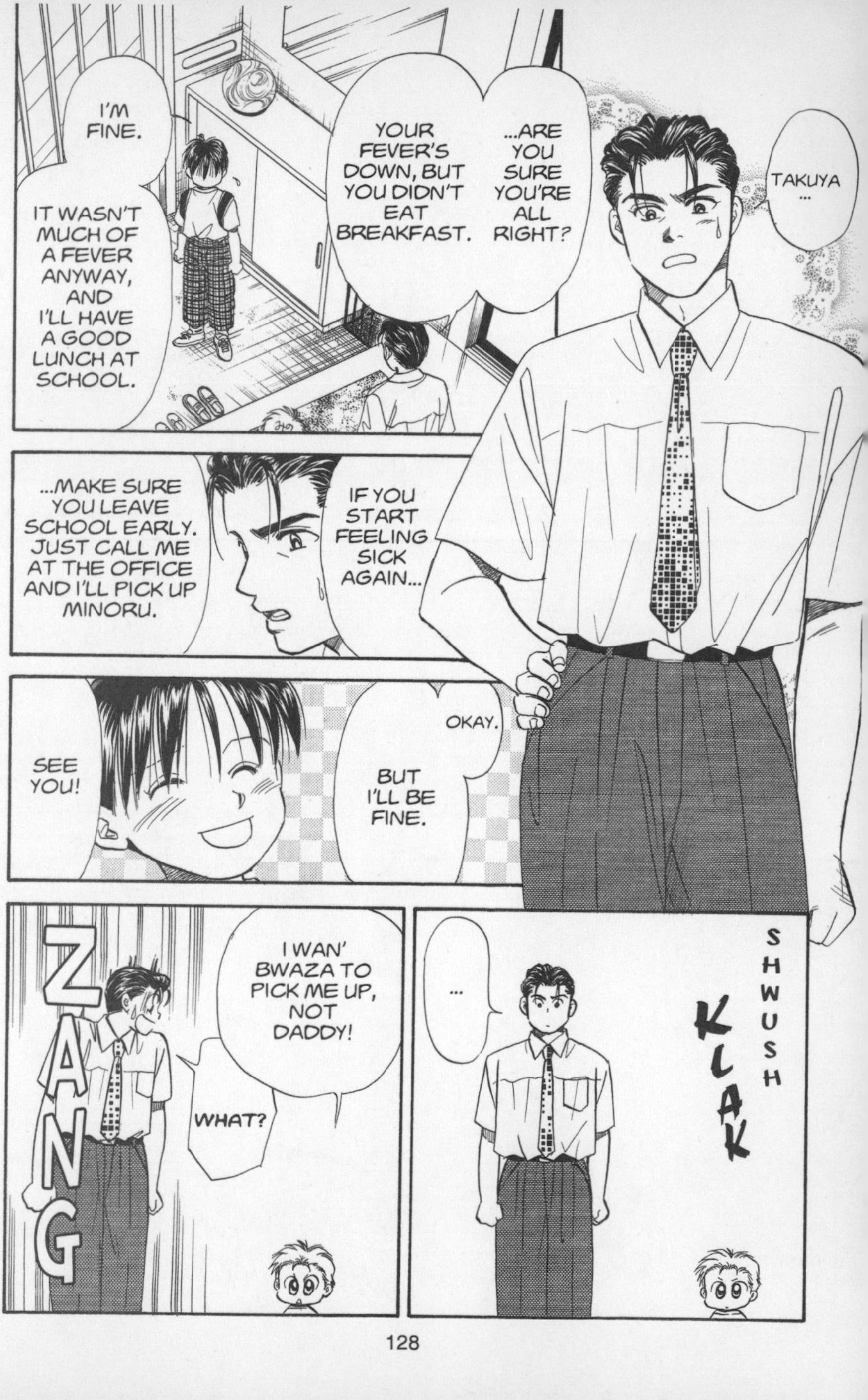

TAKUYA ...
...ARE YOU SURE YOU'RE ALL RIGHT?
YOUR FEVER'S DOWN, BUT YOU DIDN'T EAT BREAKFAST.
I'M FINE.
IT WASN'T MUCH OF A FEVER ANYWAY, AND I'LL HAVE A GOOD LUNCH AT SCHOOL.
IF YOU START FEELING SICK AGAIN...
...MAKE SURE YOU LEAVE SCHOOL EARLY. JUST CALL ME AT THE OFFICE AND I'LL PICK UP MINORU.
OKAY.
BUT I'LL BE FINE.
SEE YOU!
SHWUSH
KLAK
...
I WAN' BWAZA TO PICK ME UP, NOT DADDY!
WHAT?
ZANG

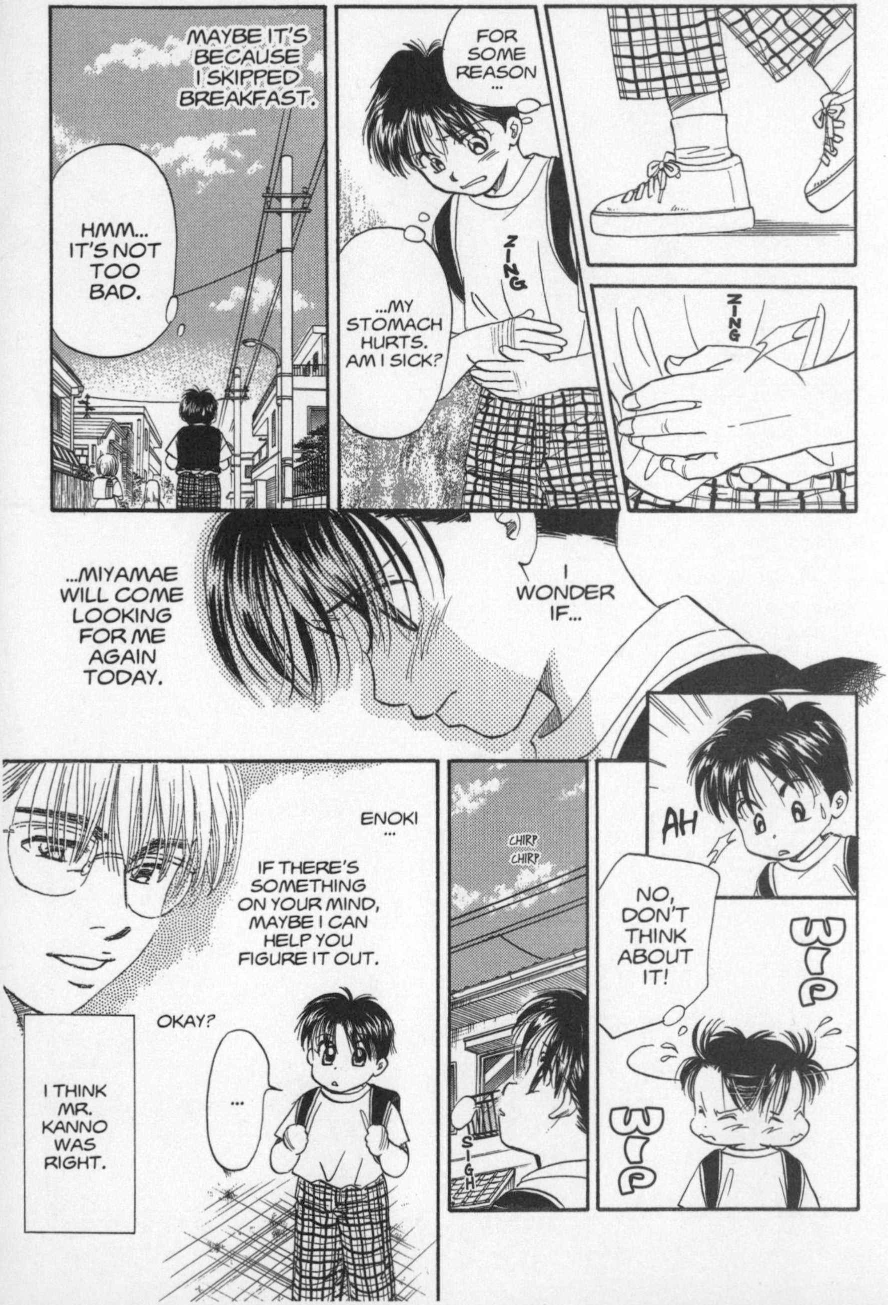
ZING
FOR SOME REASON...
...MY STOMACH HURTS. AM I SICK?
ZING
MAYBE IT'S BECAUSE I SKIPPED BREAKFAST.
HMM... IT'S NOT TOO BAD.
I WONDER IF...
...MIYAMAE WILL COME LOOKING FOR ME AGAIN TODAY.
AH
NO, DON'T THINK ABOUT IT!
WIP
WIP
CHIRP
CHIRP
SIGH
ENOKI...
IF THERE'S SOMETHING ON YOUR MIND, MAYBE I CAN HELP YOU FIGURE IT OUT.
OKAY?
...
I THINK MR. KANNO WAS RIGHT.

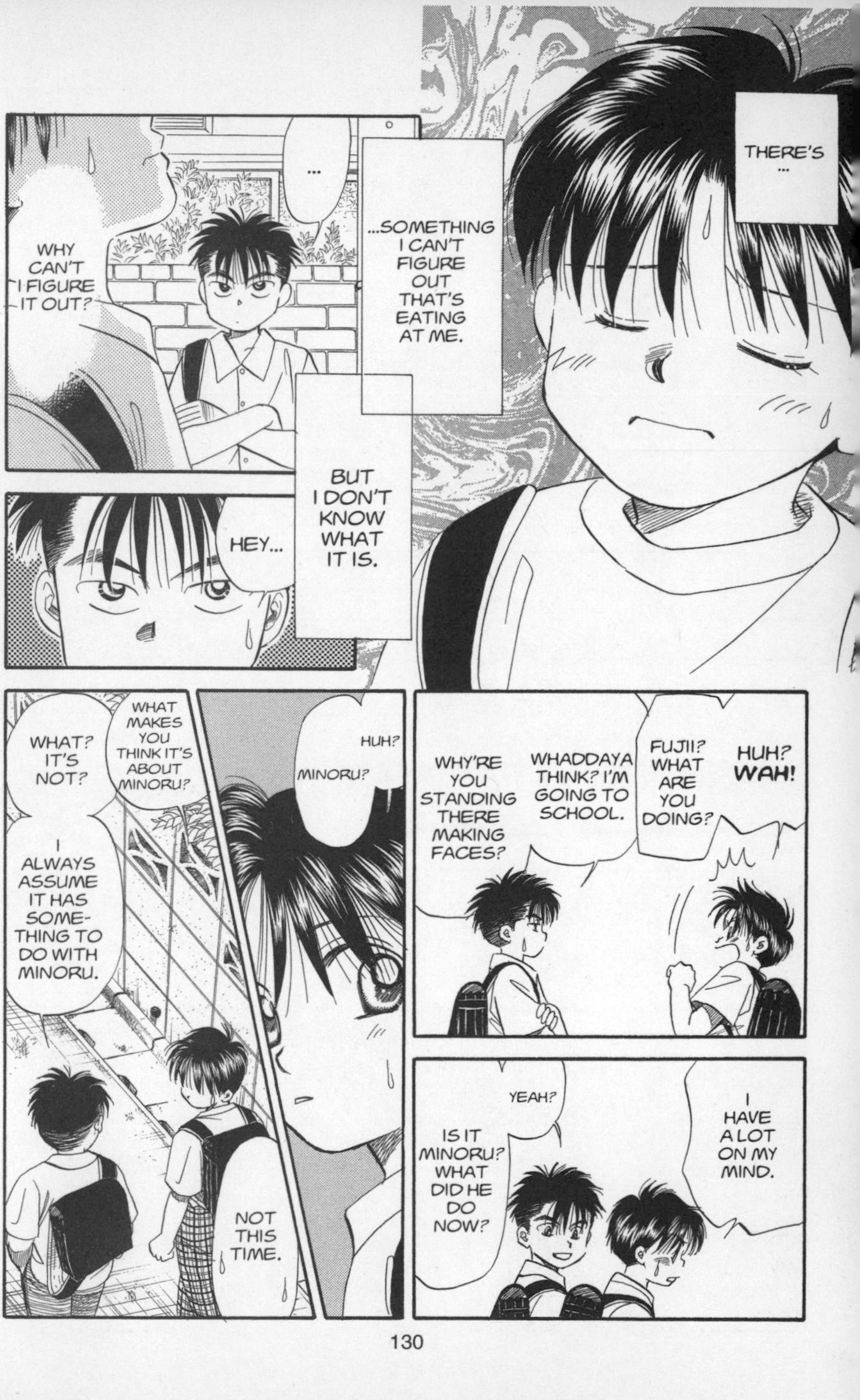
THERE'S ...
...SOMETHING I CAN'T FIGURE OUT THAT'S EATING AT ME.
BUT I DON'T KNOW WHAT IT IS.
...
WHY CAN'T I FIGURE IT OUT?
HEY...
HUH? WAH!
FUJII? WHAT ARE YOU DOING?
WHADDAYA THINK? I'M GOING TO SCHOOL.
WHY'RE YOU STANDING THERE MAKING FACES?
I HAVE A LOT ON MY MIND.
YEAH?
IS IT MINORU? WHAT DID HE DO NOW?
HUH?
MINORU?
NOT THIS TIME.
WHAT MAKES YOU THINK IT'S ABOUT MINORU?
WHAT? IT'S NOT?
I ALWAYS ASSUME IT HAS SOME-THING TO DO WITH MINORU.

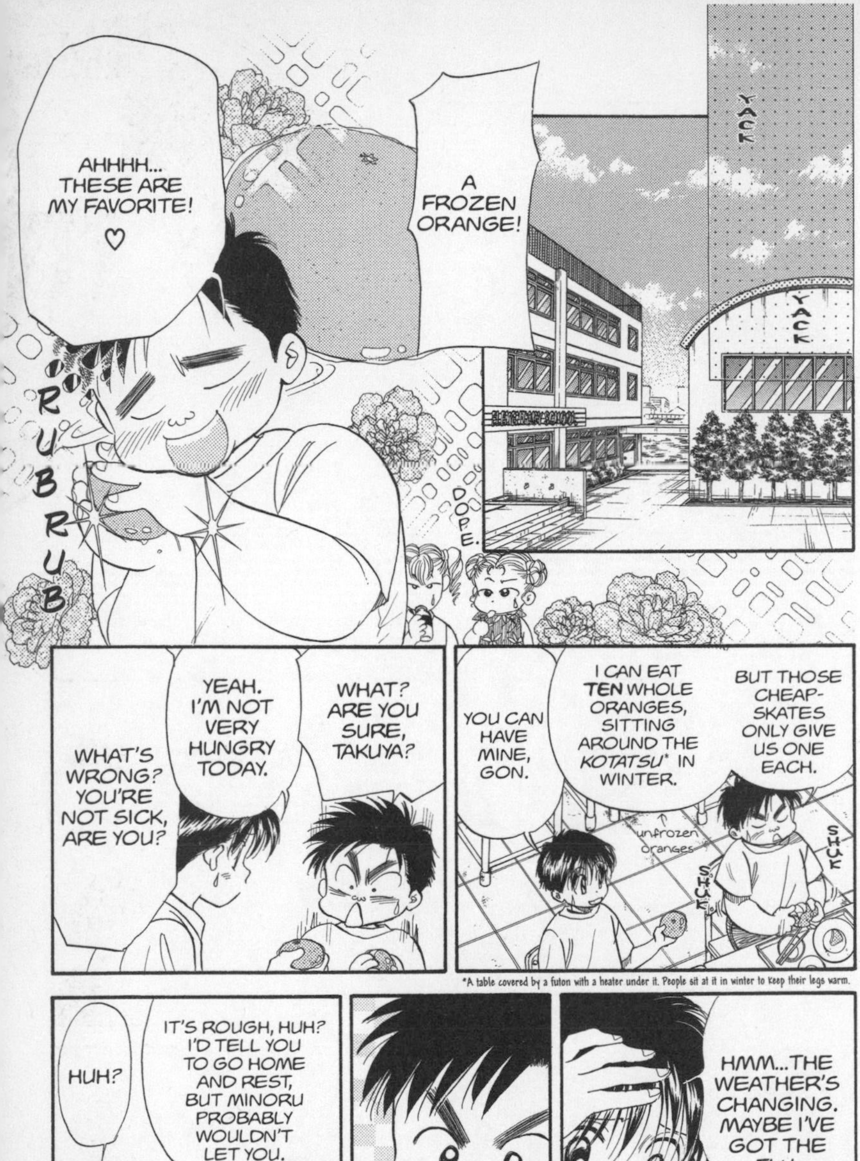
YACK
YACK
A FROZEN ORANGE!
AHHHH... THESE ARE MY FAVORITE! ♡
RUB RUB
RUB RUB
DOPE.
BUT THOSE CHEAP-SKATES ONLY GIVE US ONE EACH.
I CAN EAT TEN WHOLE ORANGES, SITTING AROUND THE KOTATSU* IN WINTER.
YOU CAN HAVE MINE, GON.
unfrozen oranges
SHUK
SHUK
WHAT? ARE YOU SURE, TAKUYA?
YEAH. I'M NOT VERY HUNGRY TODAY.
WHAT'S WRONG? YOU'RE NOT SICK, ARE YOU?

*A table covered by a futon with a heater under it. People sit at it in winter to keep their legs warm.

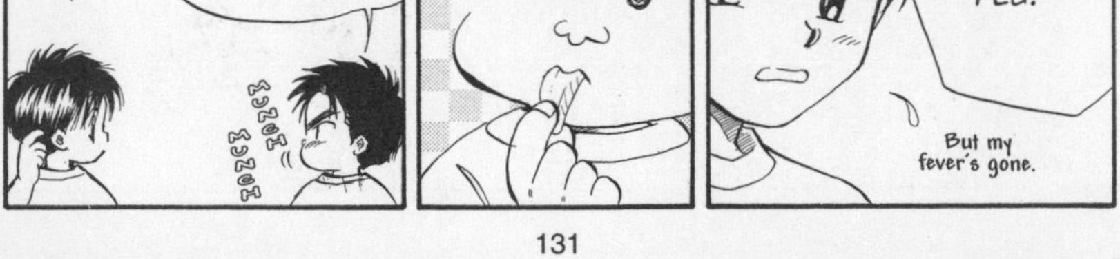
HMM...THE WEATHER'S CHANGING. MAYBE I'VE GOT THE FLU.
But my fever's gone.
IT'S ROUGH, HUH? I'D TELL YOU TO GO HOME AND REST, BUT MINORU PROBABLY WOULDN'T LET YOU.
HUH?
MUNCH MUNCH

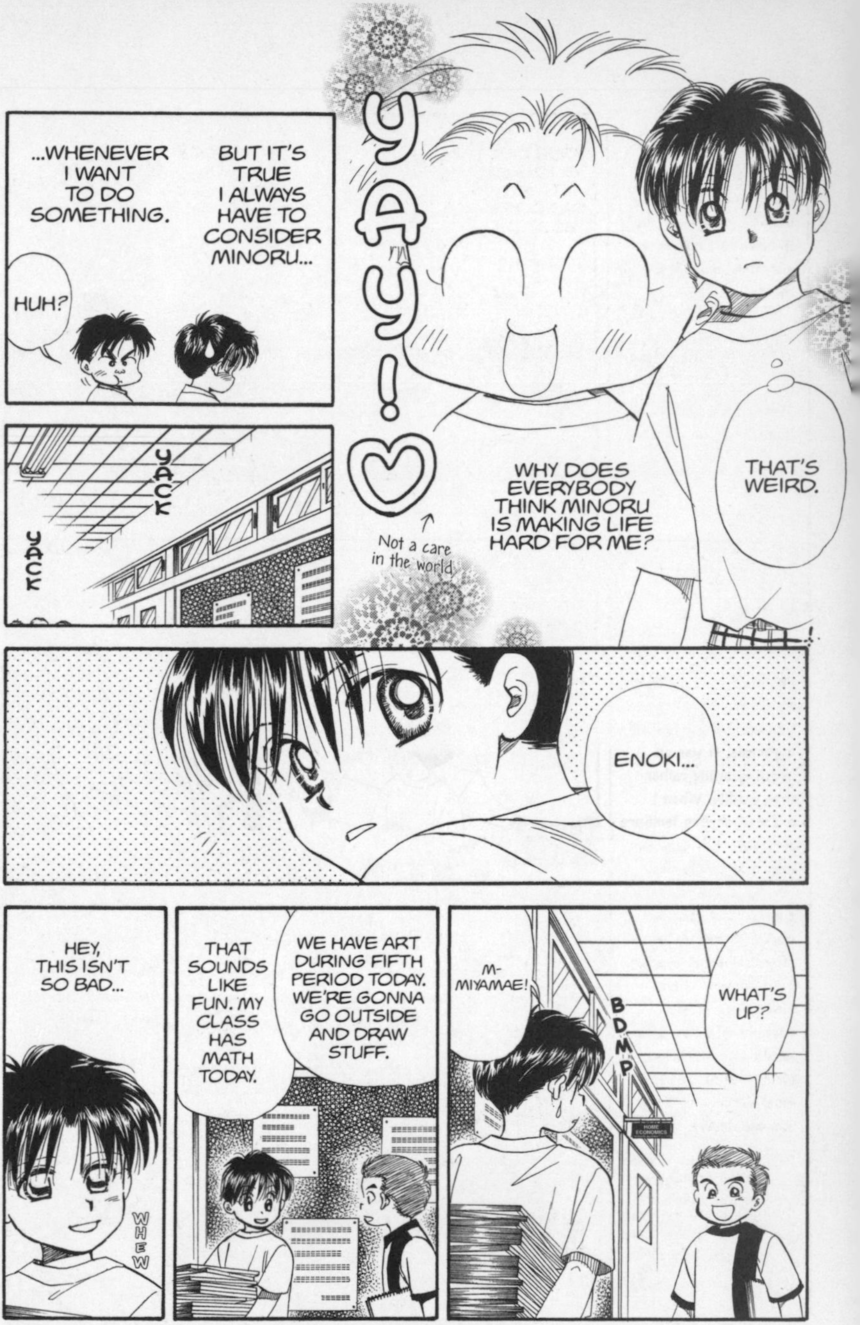
THAT'S WEIRD.
WHY DOES EVERYBODY THINK MINORU IS MAKING LIFE HARD FOR ME?
YAY! ♥
Not a care in the world
BUT IT'S TRUE I ALWAYS HAVE TO CONSIDER MINORU...
...WHENEVER I WANT TO DO SOMETHING.
HUH?
YACK
YACK
ENOKI...
WHAT'S UP?
M-MIYAMAE!
BDMP
HOME ECONOMICS
WE HAVE ART DURING FIFTH PERIOD TODAY. WE'RE GONNA GO OUTSIDE AND DRAW STUFF.
THAT SOUNDS LIKE FUN. MY CLASS HAS MATH TODAY.
HEY, THIS ISN'T SO BAD...
WHEW

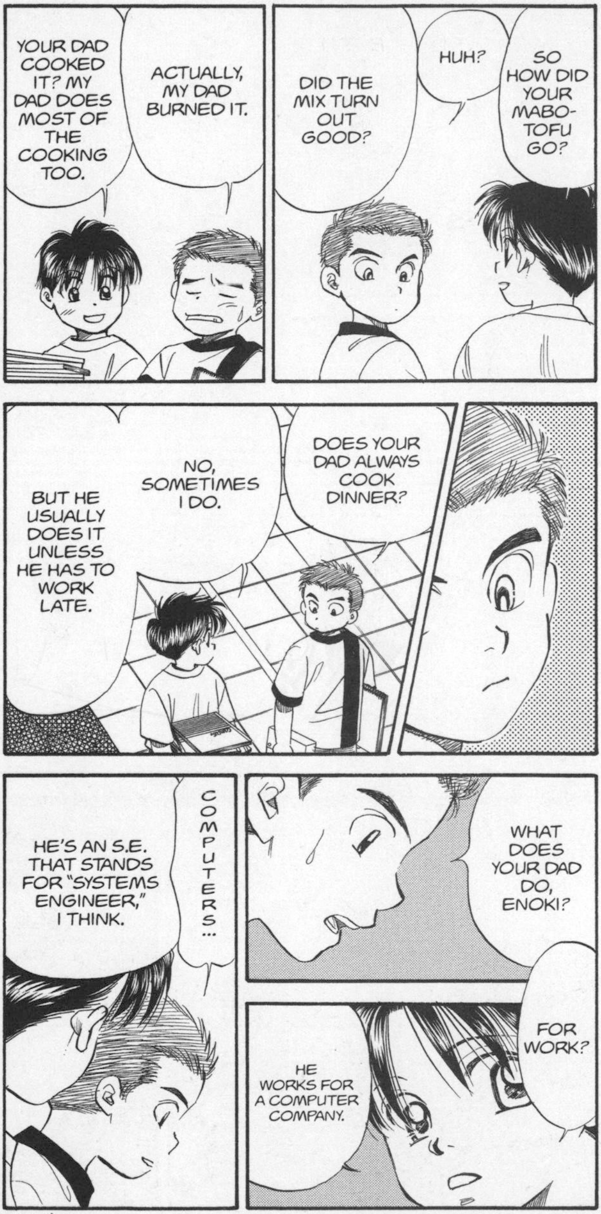
SO HOW DID YOUR MABO-TOFU GO?
HUH?
DID THE MIX TURN OUT GOOD?
ACTUALLY, MY DAD BURNED IT.
YOUR DAD COOKED IT? MY DAD DOES MOST OF THE COOKING TOO.
DOES YOUR DAD ALWAYS COOK DINNER?
NO, SOMETIMES I DO.
BUT HE USUALLY DOES IT UNLESS HE HAS TO WORK LATE.
WHAT DOES YOUR DAD DO, ENOKI?
FOR WORK?
HE WORKS FOR A COMPUTER COMPANY.
COMPUTERS...
HE'S AN S.E. THAT STANDS FOR "SYSTEMS ENGINEER," I THINK.

Author's Note Part 5

I ordered scrambled eggs, sausage and hash browns, just those three things. So I was very surprised when I saw the tray.

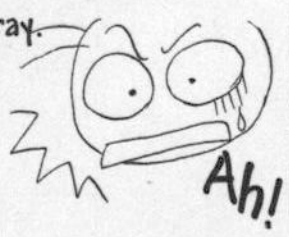
Ah!

There was a heap of all three items on my plate.

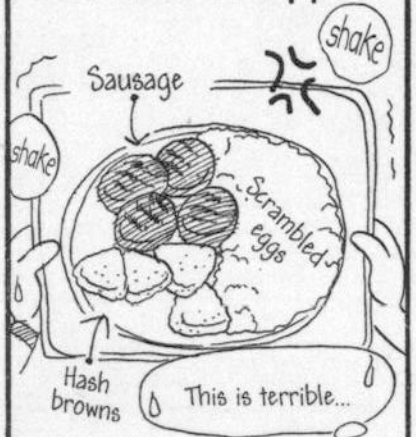
shake
Sausage
shake
Scrambled eggs
Hash browns
This is terrible...

The servings were huge no matter where we ate. I couldn't finish any of my meals. It was all about quantity rather than quality. When I ordered shrimp tempura at Epcot, they gave me five huge pieces of shrimp! I was flabber-gasted. And when we visited Planet Hollywood after Universal Studios, I got another shock. There were huge portions of soup, fish, mashed potatoes and string beans, but the most surprising thing was the dessert.

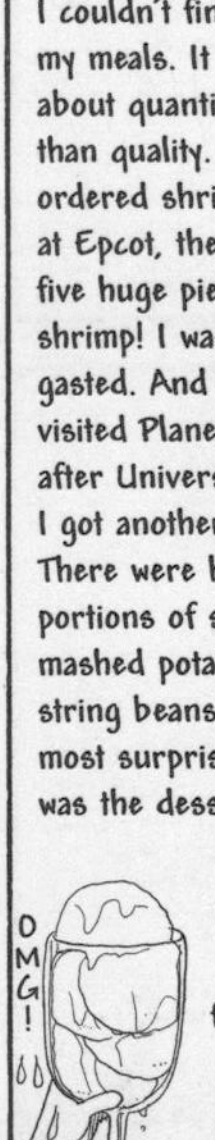
OMG!

Five scoops of ice cream each! The foreigners finished them all. Just amazing. Continued in Part 6

In fact, the ice cream was in a cone, not a glass. I remembered that after I drew this. Sorry.

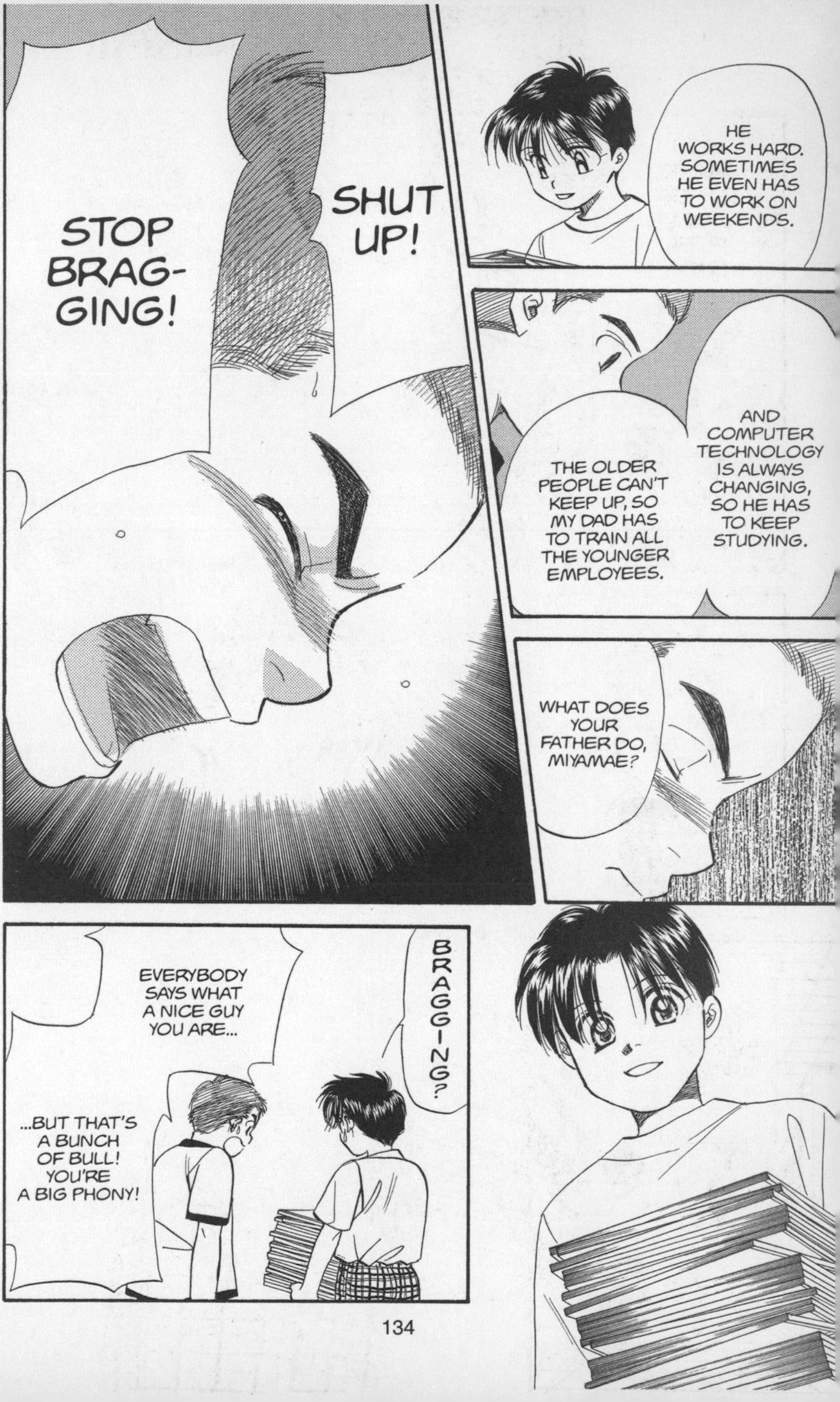
HE WORKS HARD. SOMETIMES HE EVEN HAS TO WORK ON WEEKENDS.
AND COMPUTER TECHNOLOGY IS ALWAYS CHANGING, SO HE HAS TO KEEP STUDYING.
THE OLDER PEOPLE CAN'T KEEP UP, SO MY DAD HAS TO TRAIN ALL THE YOUNGER EMPLOYEES.
WHAT DOES YOUR FATHER DO, MIYAMAE?
SHUT UP!
STOP BRAG-GING!
BRAGGING?
EVERYBODY SAYS WHAT A NICE GUY YOU ARE...
...BUT THAT'S A BUNCH OF BULL! YOU'RE A BIG PHONY!

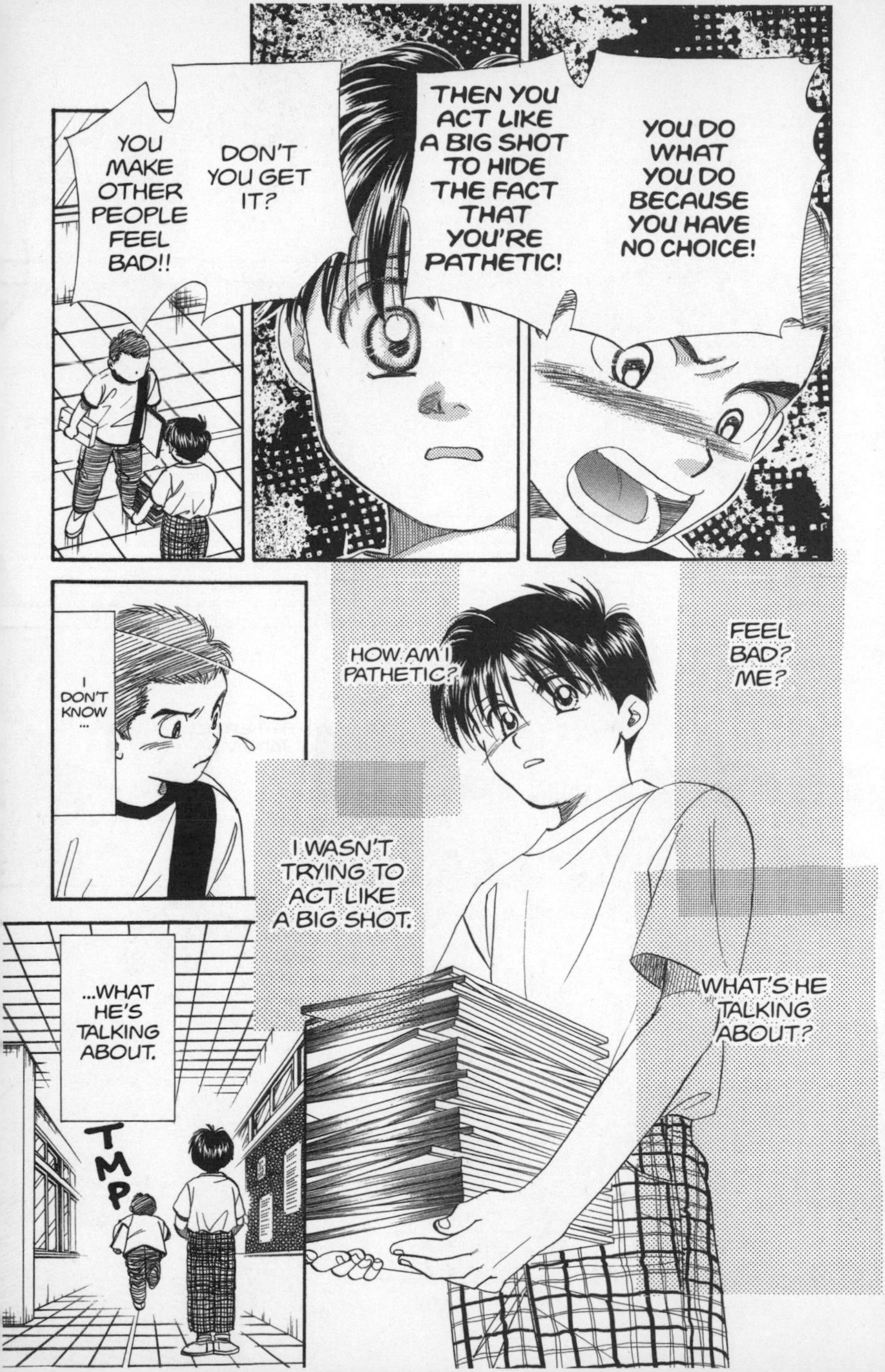
YOU DO WHAT YOU DO BECAUSE YOU HAVE NO CHOICE!
THEN YOU ACT LIKE A BIG SHOT TO HIDE THE FACT THAT YOU'RE PATHETIC!
DON'T YOU GET IT?
YOU MAKE OTHER PEOPLE FEEL BAD!!
FEEL BAD? ME?
HOW AM I PATHETIC?
WHAT'S HE TALKING ABOUT?
I WASN'T TRYING TO ACT LIKE A BIG SHOT.
I DON'T KNOW ...
...WHAT HE'S TALKING ABOUT.
TMP

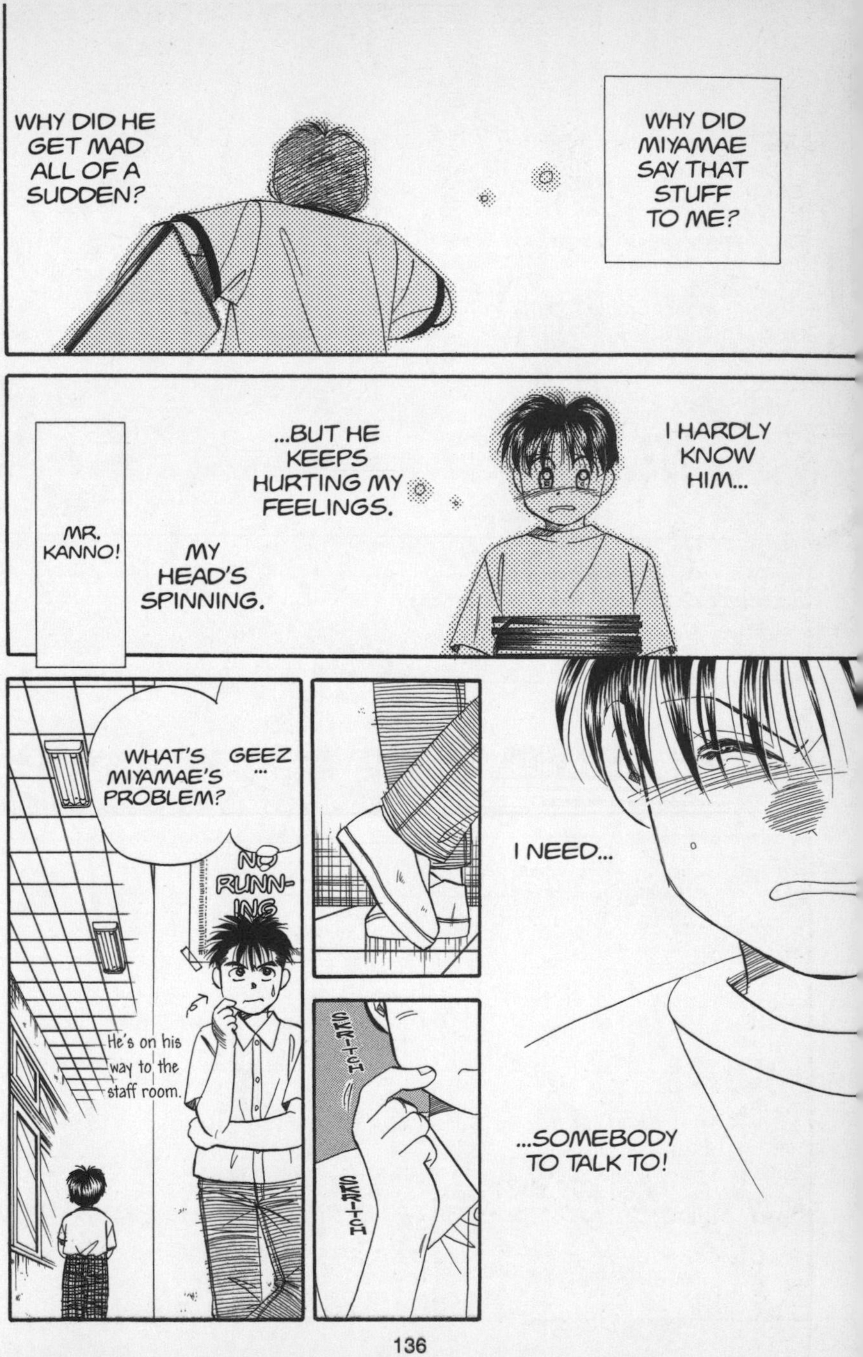
WHY DID MIYAMAE SAY THAT STUFF TO ME?
WHY DID HE GET MAD ALL OF A SUDDEN?
I HARDLY KNOW HIM...
...BUT HE KEEPS HURTING MY FEELINGS.
MY HEAD'S SPINNING.
MR. KANNO!
I NEED...
...SOMEBODY TO TALK TO!
SKRITCH
SKRITCH
GEEZ...
WHAT'S MIYAMAE'S PROBLEM?
NO RUNNING
He's on his way to the staff room.

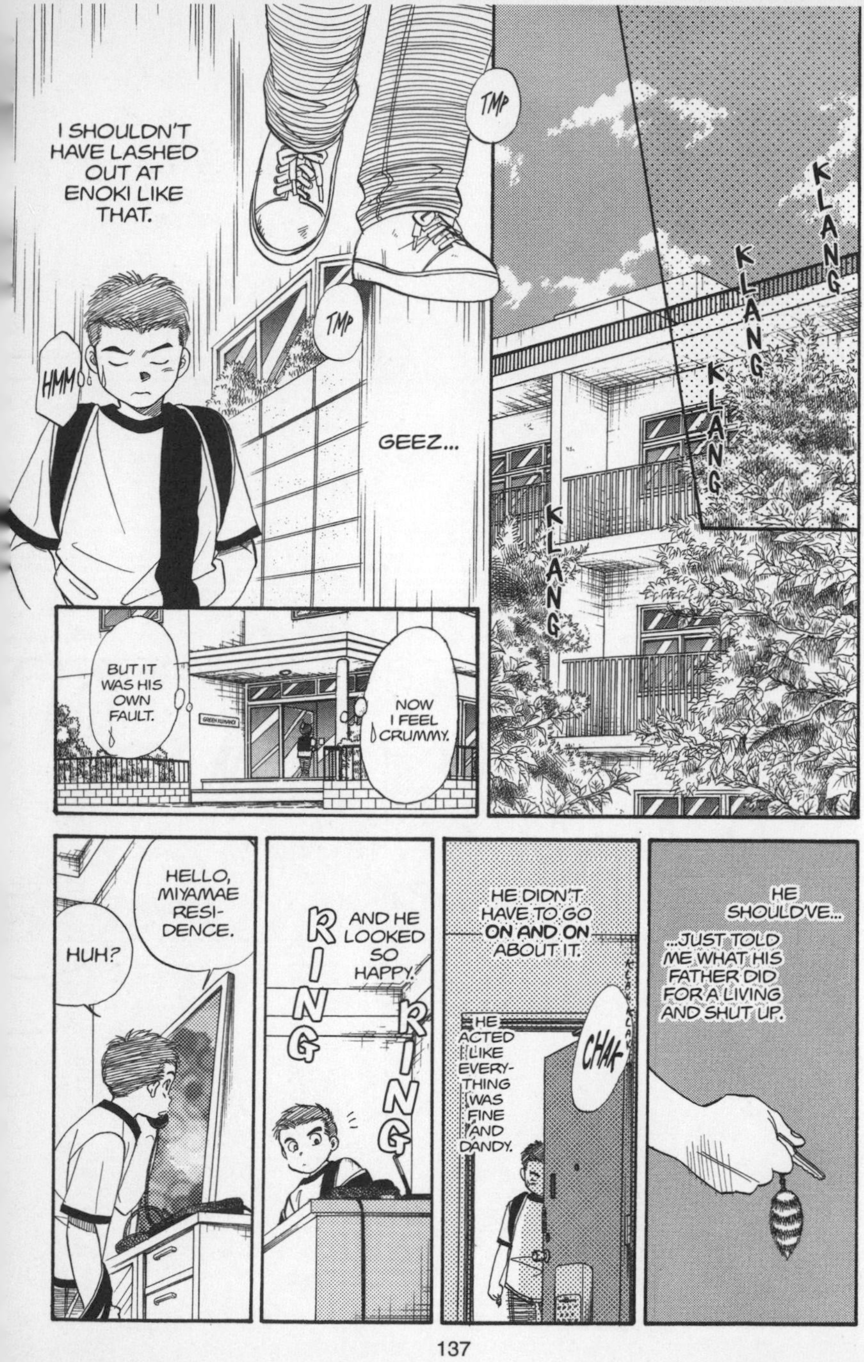
KLANG
KLANG
KLANG
KLANG
TMP
TMP
I SHOULDN'T HAVE LASHED OUT AT ENOKI LIKE THAT.
HMM
GEEZ...
NOW I FEEL CRUMMY.
BUT IT WAS HIS OWN FAULT.
HE SHOULD'VE...
...JUST TOLD ME WHAT HIS FATHER DID FOR A LIVING AND SHUT UP.
HE DIDN'T HAVE TO GO ON AND ON ABOUT IT.
KLAK KLAK
CHAK
HE ACTED LIKE EVERYTHING WAS FINE AND DANDY.
AND HE LOOKED SO HAPPY.
RING
RING
HELLO, MIYAMAE RESIDENCE.
HUH?

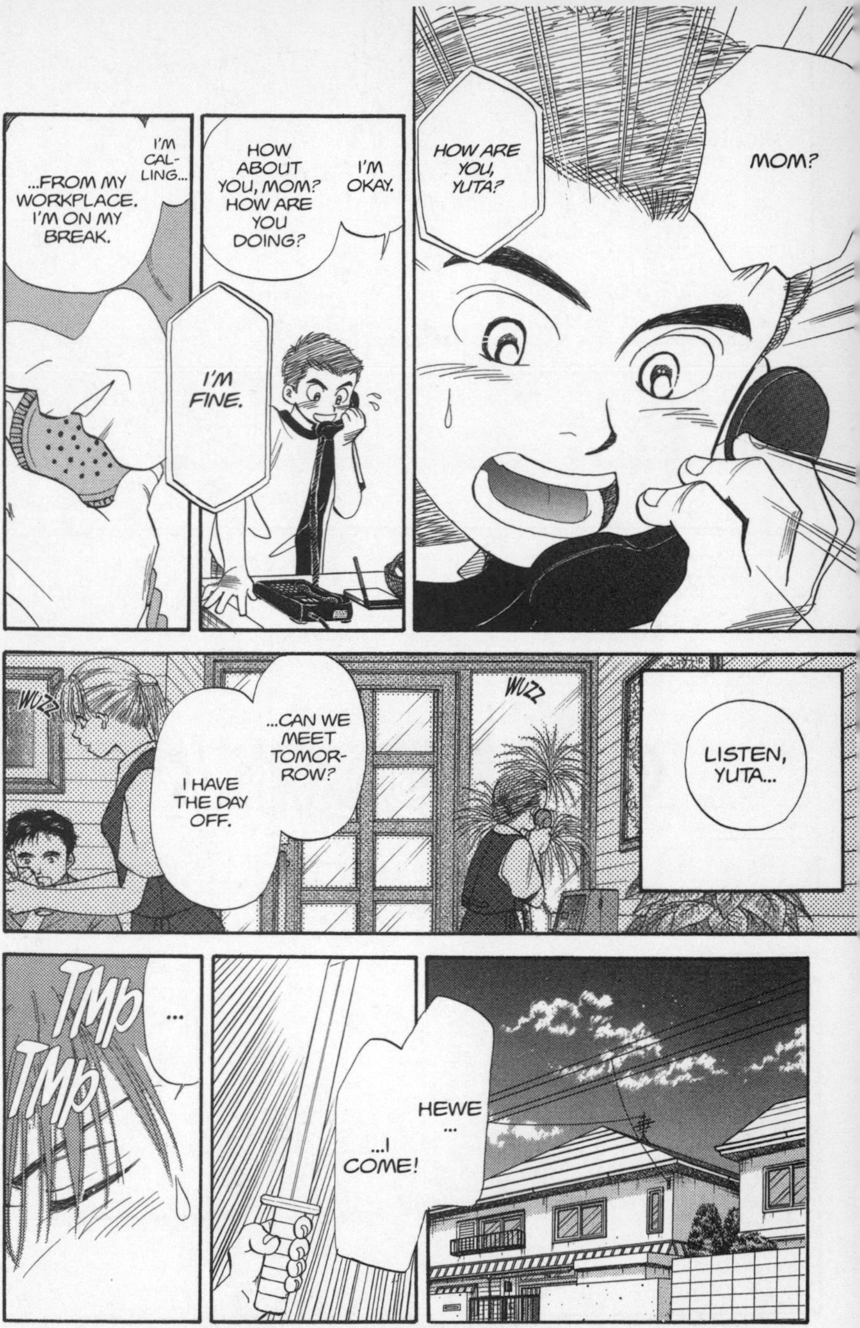
MOM?
HOW ARE YOU, YUTA?
I'M OKAY.
HOW ABOUT YOU, MOM? HOW ARE YOU DOING?
I'M FINE.
I'M CALLING...
...FROM MY WORKPLACE. I'M ON MY BREAK.
LISTEN, YUTA...
WUZZ
...CAN WE MEET TOMORROW?
I HAVE THE DAY OFF.
WUZZ
HEWE...
...I COME!
TMp
TMp
...

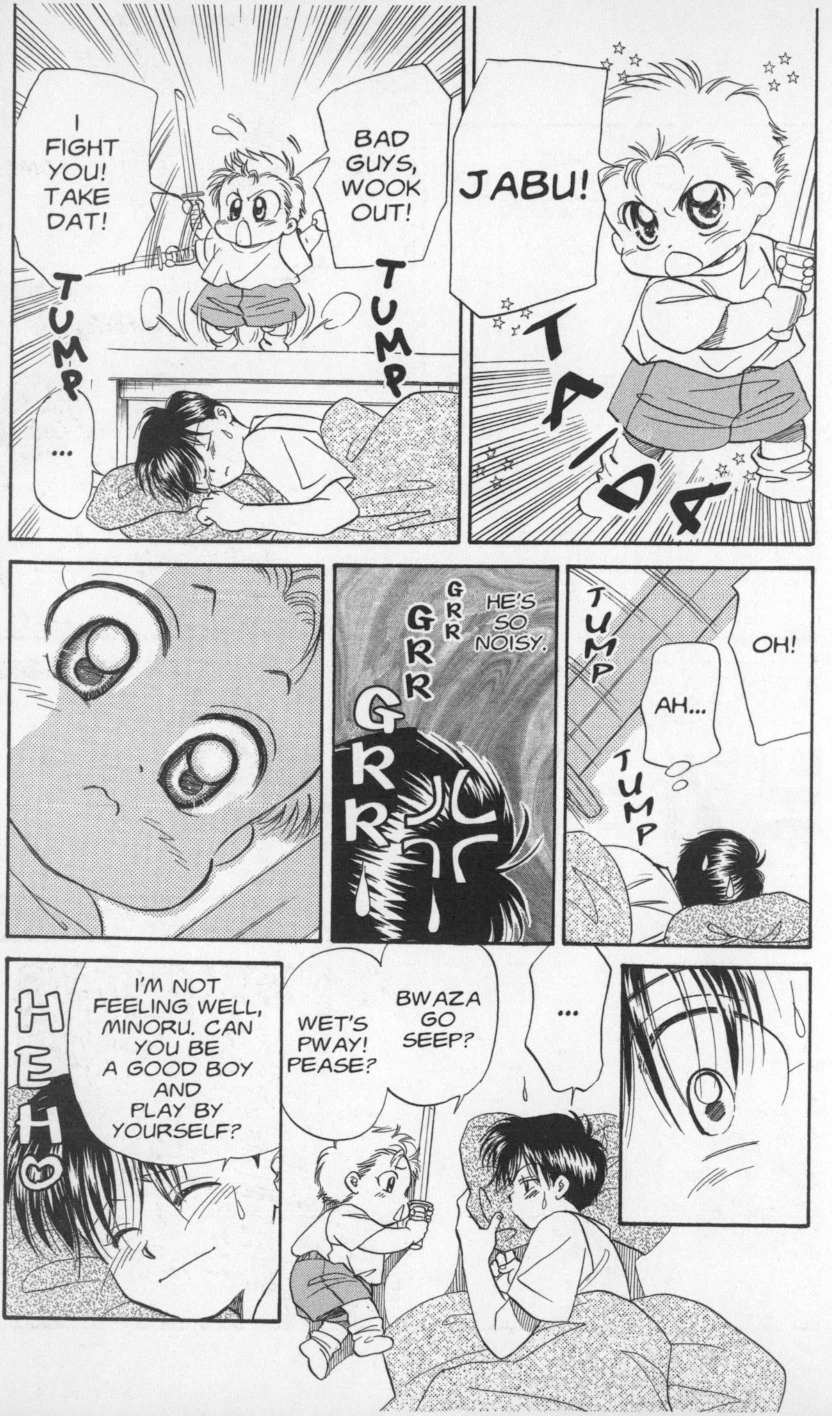
JABU!
TA-DA
BAD GUYS, WOOK OUT!
I FIGHT YOU! TAKE DAT!
TUMP
TUMP
...
OH!
AH...
TUMP
TUMP
HE'S SO NOISY.
GRR
GRR
GRRR
GRRR
...
BWAZA GO SEEP?
WET'S PWAY! PEASE?
I'M NOT FEELING WELL, MINORU. CAN YOU BE A GOOD BOY AND PLAY BY YOURSELF?
HEH♡

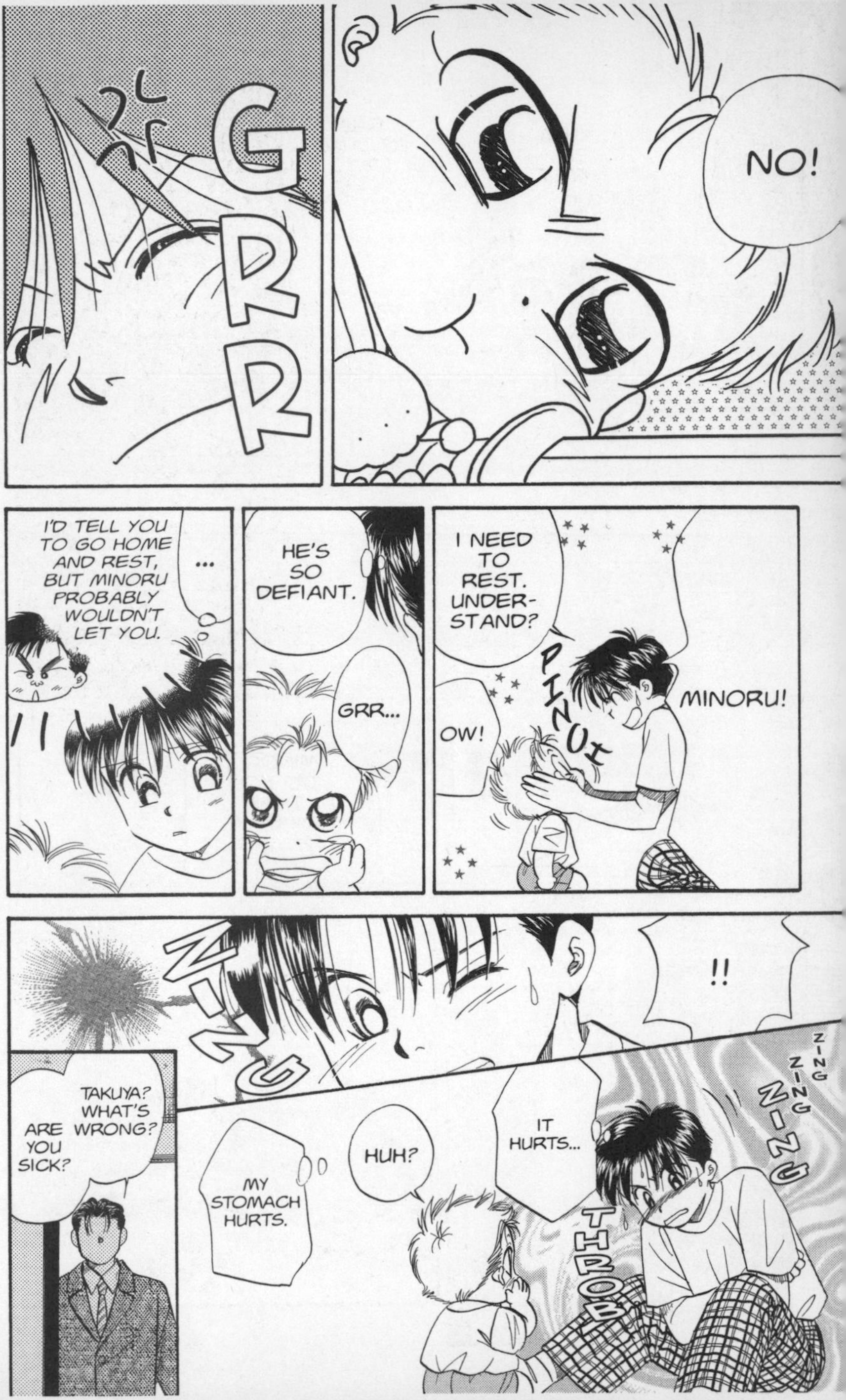
NO!
GRR
MINORU!
PINCH
I NEED TO REST. UNDERSTAND?
OW!
HE'S SO DEFIANT.
GRR...
I'D TELL YOU TO GO HOME AND REST, BUT MINORU PROBABLY WOULDN'T LET YOU.
...
!!
ZING
ZING ZING
ZING
IT HURTS...
THROB
HUH?
MY STOMACH HURTS.
TAKUYA? WHAT'S WRONG? ARE YOU SICK?

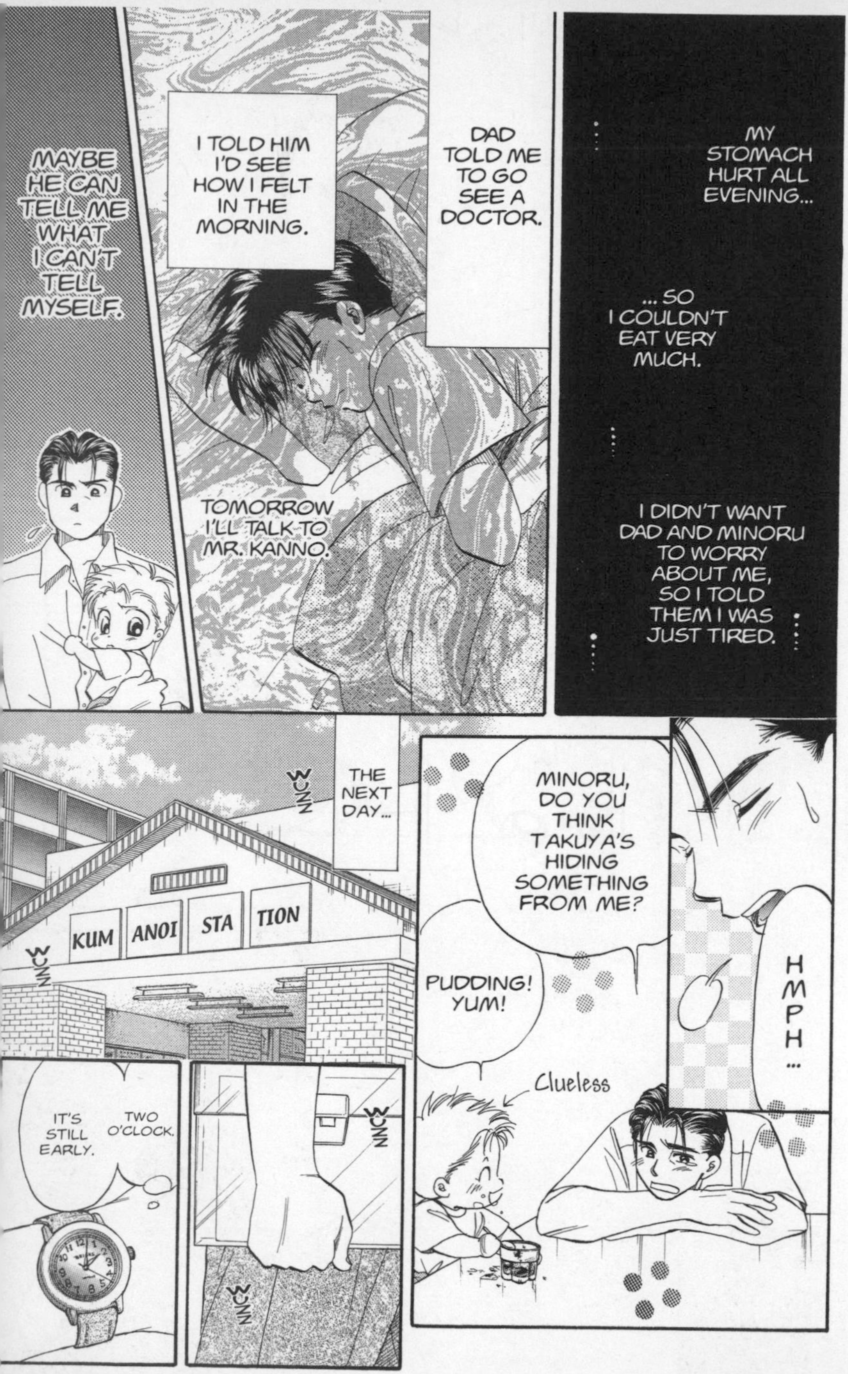
MY STOMACH HURT ALL EVENING...
... SO I COULDN'T EAT VERY MUCH.
I DIDN'T WANT DAD AND MINORU TO WORRY ABOUT ME, SO I TOLD THEM I WAS JUST TIRED.
DAD TOLD ME TO GO SEE A DOCTOR.
I TOLD HIM I'D SEE HOW I FELT IN THE MORNING.
TOMORROW I'LL TALK TO MR. KANNO.
MAYBE HE CAN TELL ME WHAT I CAN'T TELL MYSELF.
HMPH...
MINORU, DO YOU THINK TAKUYA'S HIDING SOMETHING FROM ME?
PUDDING! YUM!
Clueless
THE NEXT DAY...
WUZZ
KUM ANOI STA TION
WUZZ
WUZZ
WUZZ
TWO O'CLOCK.
IT'S STILL EARLY.

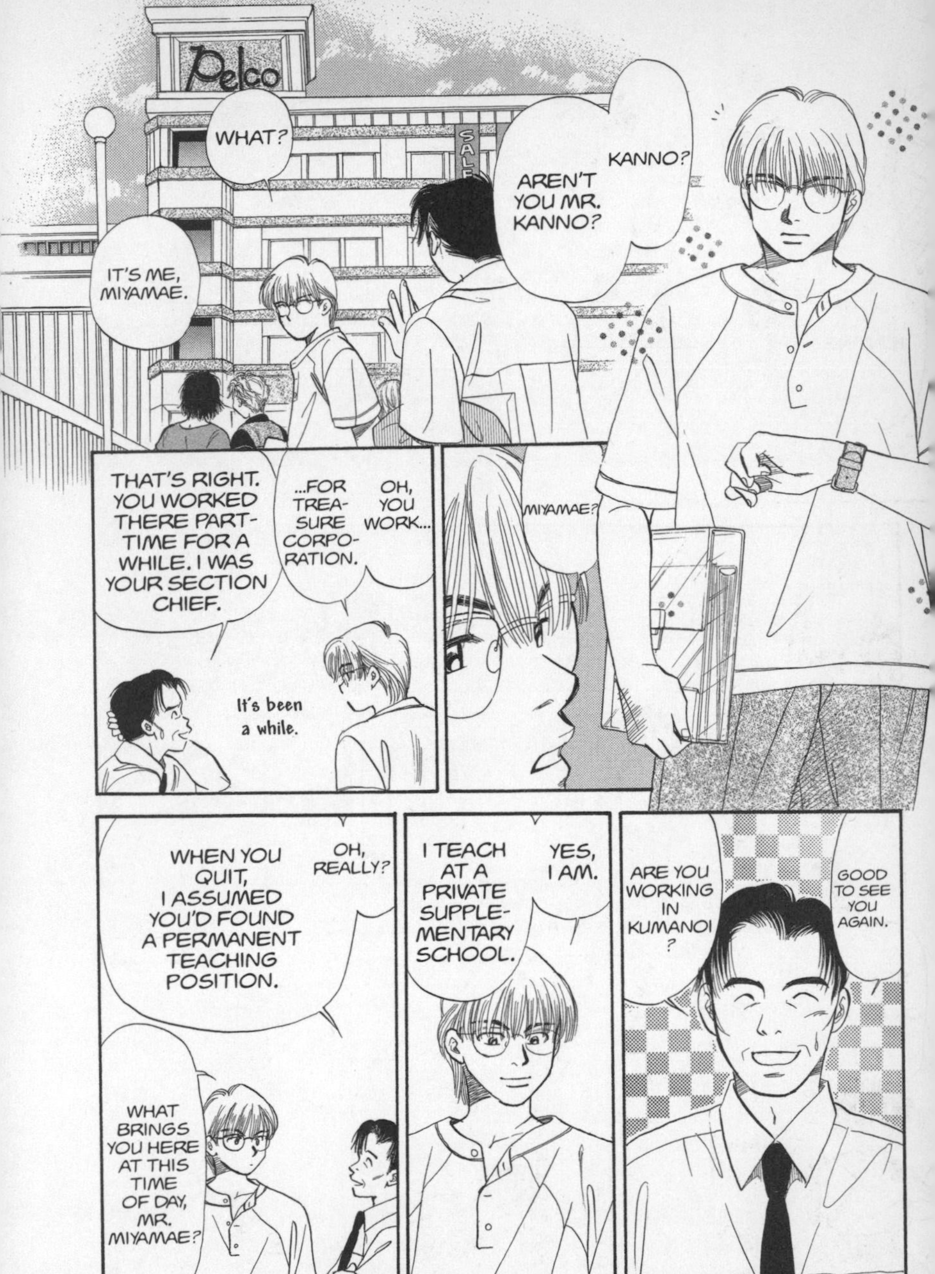
KANNO?
AREN'T YOU MR. KANNO?
WHAT?
IT'S ME, MIYAMAE.
MIYAMAE?
OH, YOU WORK...
...FOR TREASURE CORPORATION.
THAT'S RIGHT. YOU WORKED THERE PART-TIME FOR A WHILE. I WAS YOUR SECTION CHIEF.
It's been a while.
GOOD TO SEE YOU AGAIN.
ARE YOU WORKING IN KUMANOI?
YES, I AM.
I TEACH AT A PRIVATE SUPPLEMENTARY SCHOOL.
OH, REALLY?
WHEN YOU QUIT, I ASSUMED YOU'D FOUND A PERMANENT TEACHING POSITION.
WHAT BRINGS YOU HERE AT THIS TIME OF DAY, MR. MIYAMAE?

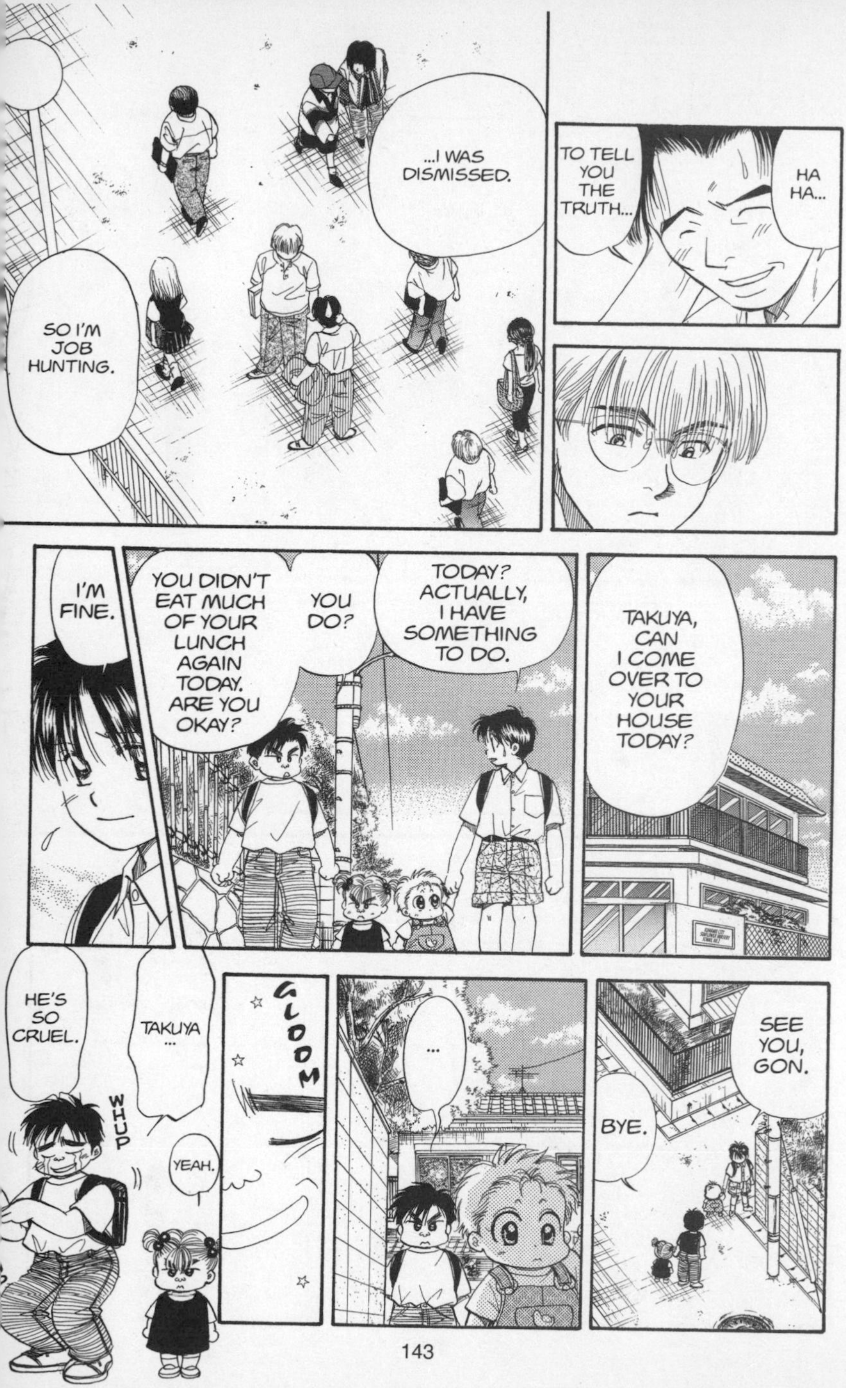
HA HA...
TO TELL YOU THE TRUTH...
...I WAS DISMISSED.
SO I'M JOB HUNTING.
TAKUYA, CAN I COME OVER TO YOUR HOUSE TODAY?
TODAY? ACTUALLY, I HAVE SOMETHING TO DO.
YOU DO?
YOU DIDN'T EAT MUCH OF YOUR LUNCH AGAIN TODAY. ARE YOU OKAY?
I'M FINE.
SEE YOU, GON.
BYE.
...
GLOOM
YEAH.
TAKUYA ...
HE'S SO CRUEL.
WHUP

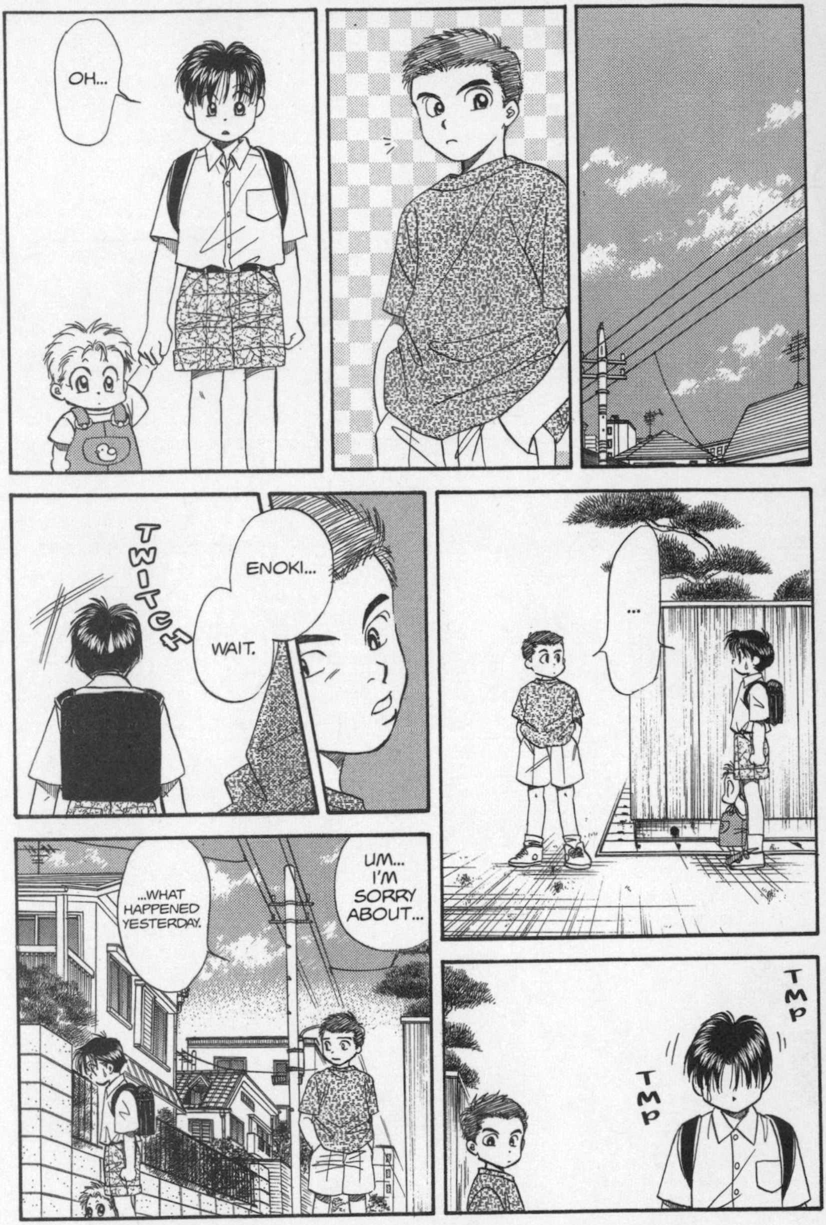
OH...
...
ENOKI...
WAIT.
TWITCH
TMP
TMP
UM... I'M SORRY ABOUT...
...WHAT HAPPENED YESTERDAY.

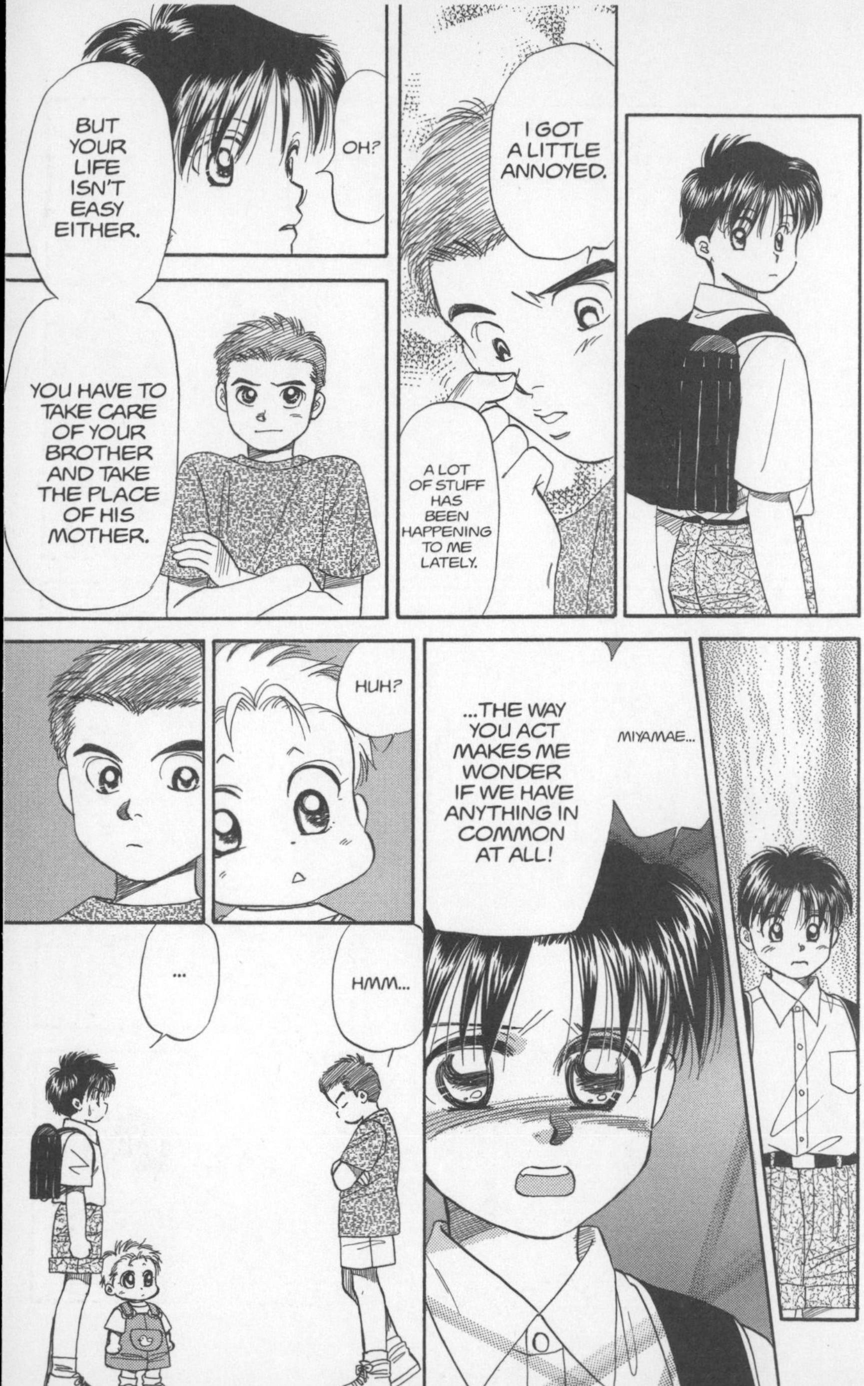
I GOT A LITTLE ANNOYED.
A LOT OF STUFF HAS BEEN HAPPENING TO ME LATELY.
OH?
BUT YOUR LIFE ISN'T EASY EITHER.
YOU HAVE TO TAKE CARE OF YOUR BROTHER AND TAKE THE PLACE OF HIS MOTHER.
MIYAMAE...
...THE WAY YOU ACT MAKES ME WONDER IF WE HAVE ANYTHING IN COMMON AT ALL!
HUH?
HMM...
...

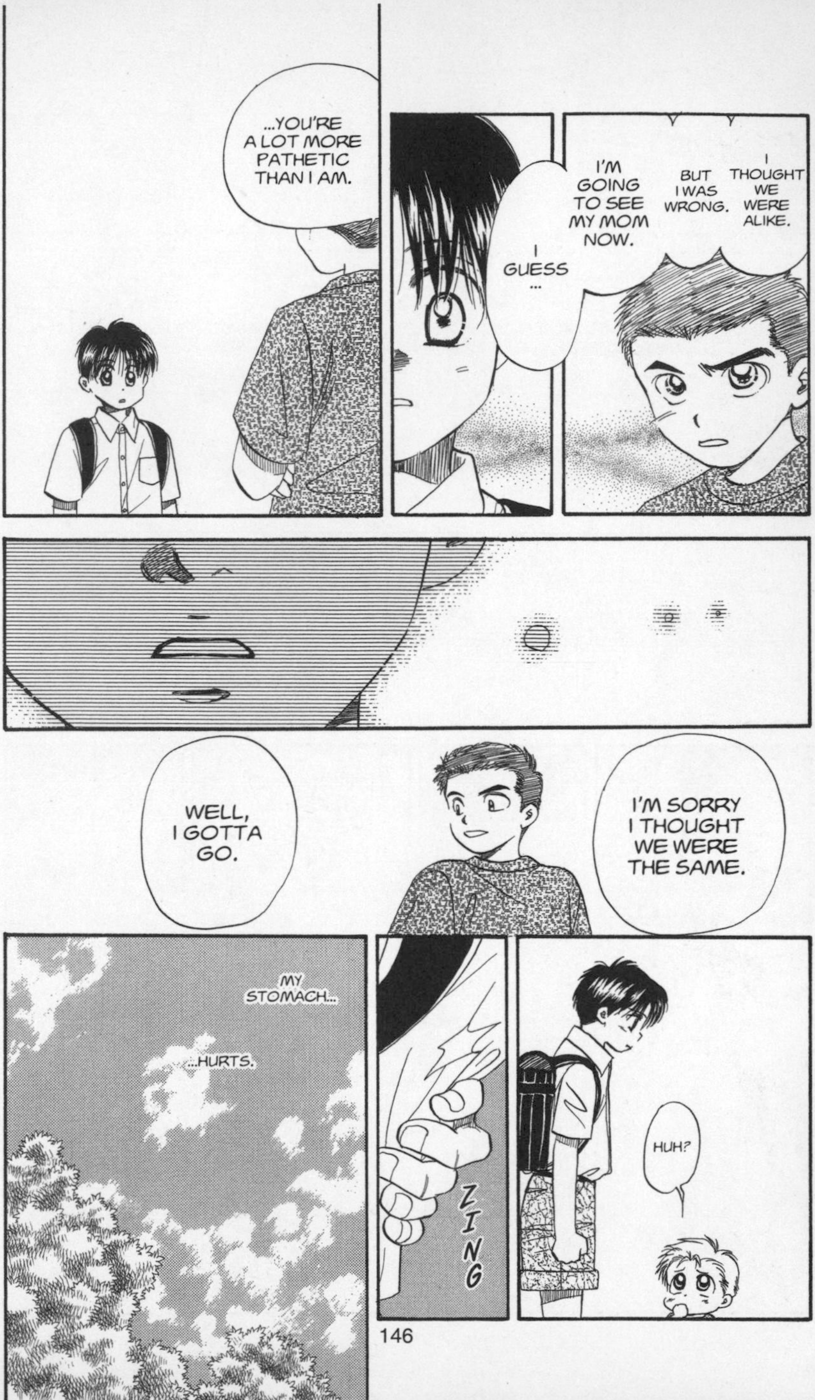
I THOUGHT WE WERE ALIKE.
BUT I WAS WRONG.
I'M GOING TO SEE MY MOM NOW.
I GUESS ...
...YOU'RE A LOT MORE PATHETIC THAN I AM.
I'M SORRY I THOUGHT WE WERE THE SAME.
WELL, I GOTTA GO.
HUH?
ZING
MY STOMACH...
...HURTS.

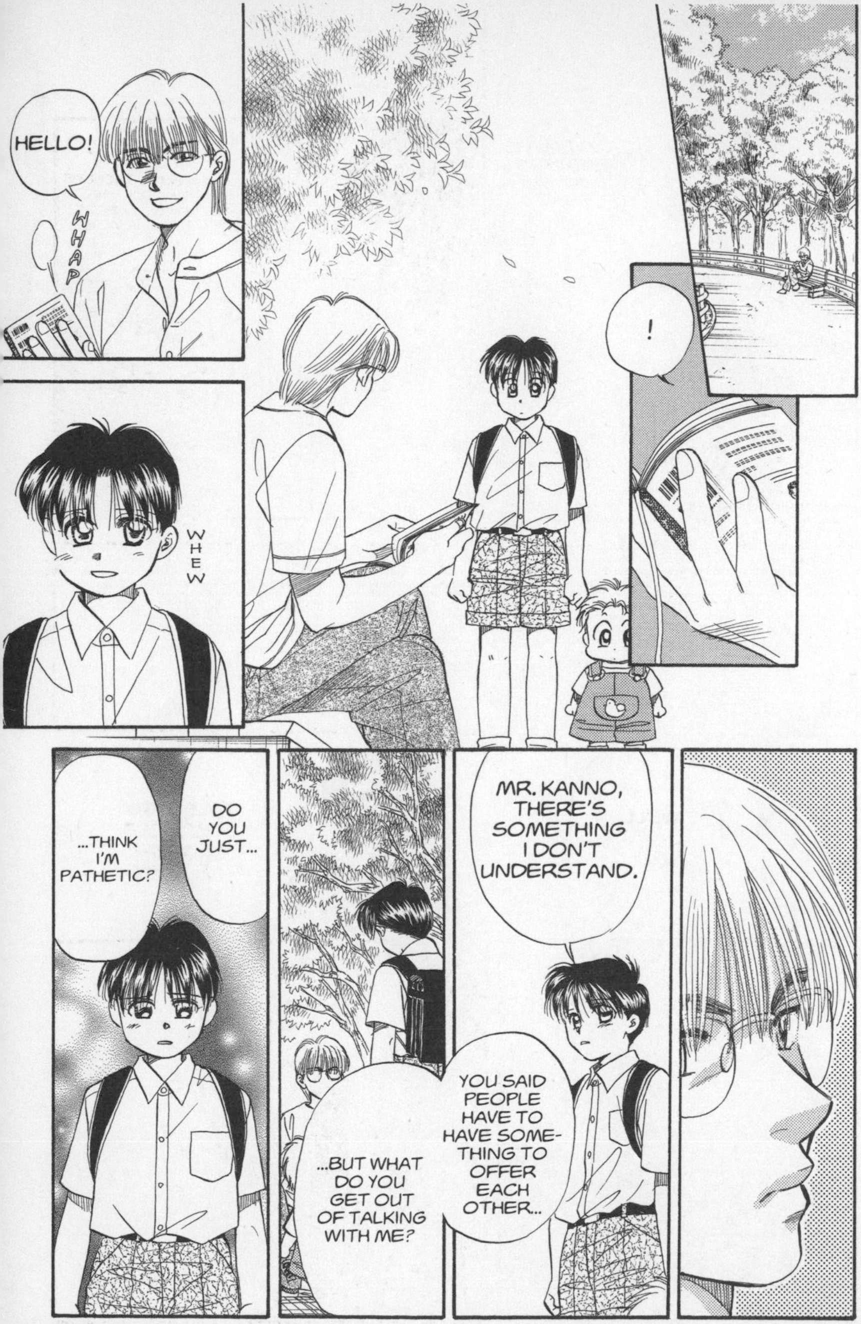
!
HELLO!
WHAP
WHEW
MR. KANNO, THERE'S SOMETHING I DON'T UNDERSTAND.
YOU SAID PEOPLE HAVE TO HAVE SOME-THING TO OFFER EACH OTHER...
...BUT WHAT DO YOU GET OUT OF TALKING WITH ME?
DO YOU JUST...
...THINK I'M PATHETIC?

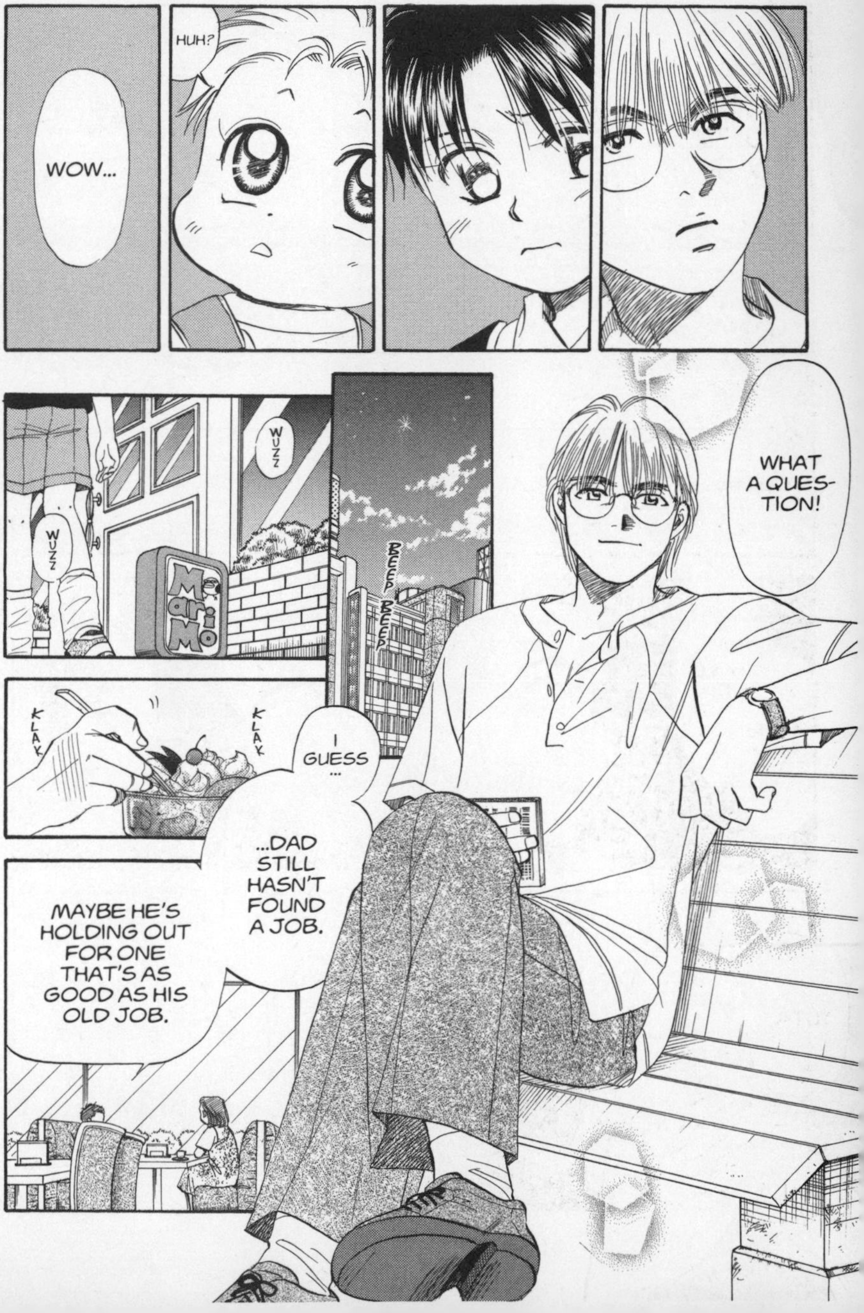
HUH?
WOW...
WHAT A QUES-TION!
BEEP BEEP BEEP
WUZZ
WUZZ
KLAK
KLAK
I GUESS...
...DAD STILL HASN'T FOUND A JOB.
MAYBE HE'S HOLDING OUT FOR ONE THAT'S AS GOOD AS HIS OLD JOB.
Mari Mo

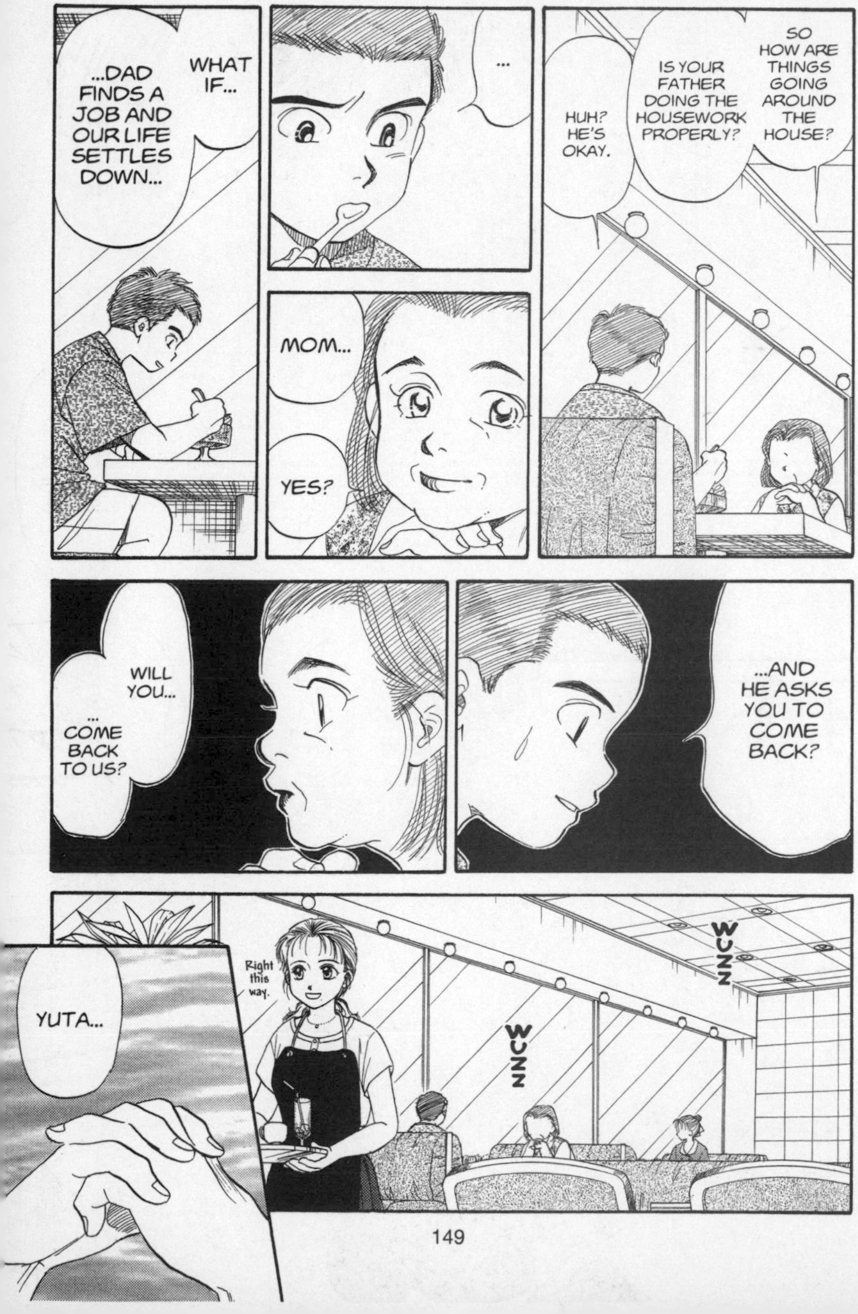
SO HOW ARE THINGS GOING AROUND THE HOUSE?
IS YOUR FATHER DOING THE HOUSEWORK PROPERLY?
HUH? HE'S OKAY.
...
MOM...
YES?
WHAT IF...
...DAD FINDS A JOB AND OUR LIFE SETTLES DOWN...
...AND HE ASKS YOU TO COME BACK?
WILL YOU...
...COME BACK TO US?
WUZZ
WUZZ
Right this way.
YUTA...

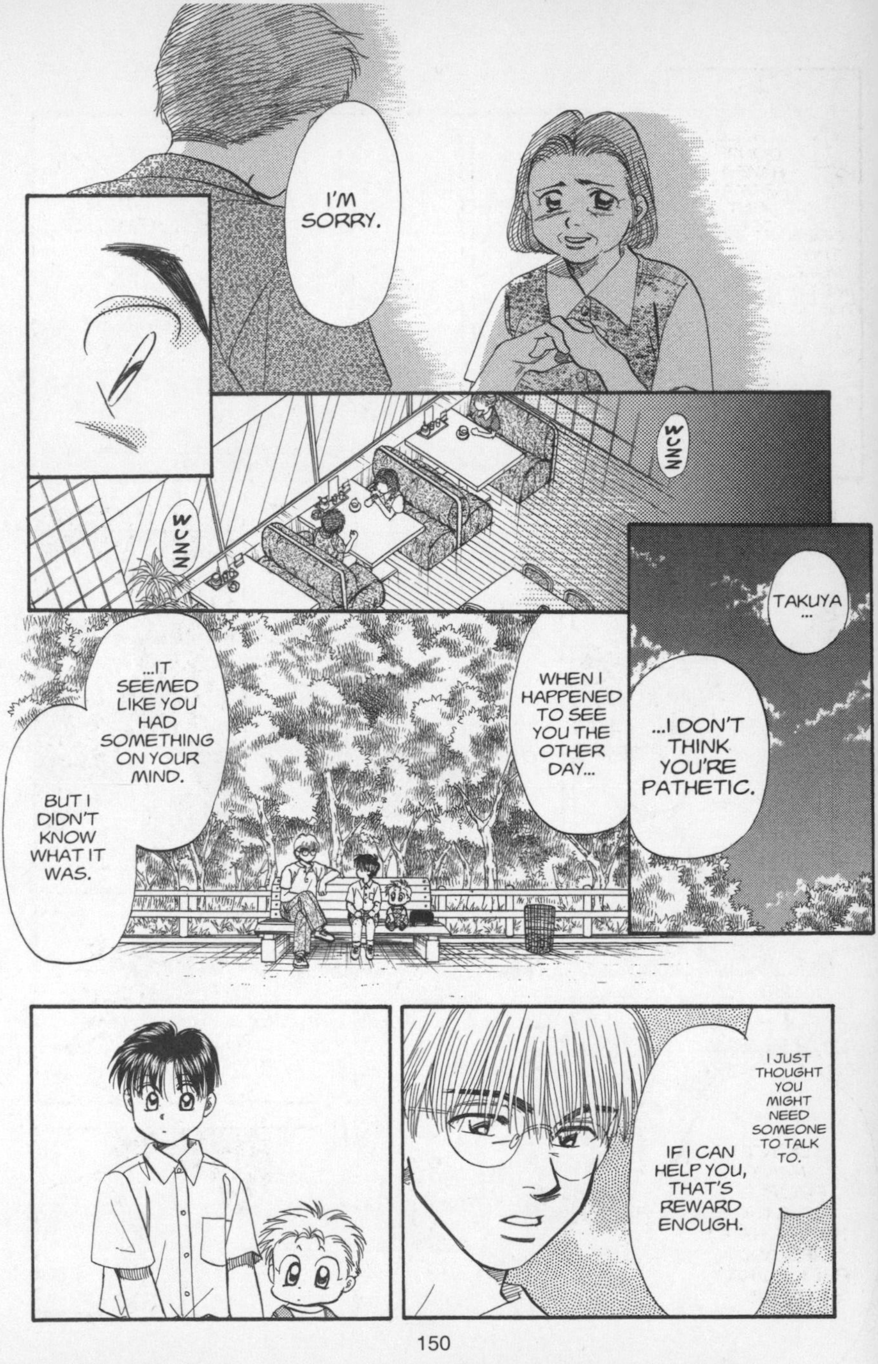
I'M SORRY.
WUNN
WUNN
TAKUYA...
...I DON'T THINK YOU'RE PATHETIC.
WHEN I HAPPENED TO SEE YOU THE OTHER DAY...
...IT SEEMED LIKE YOU HAD SOMETHING ON YOUR MIND.
BUT I DIDN'T KNOW WHAT IT WAS.
I JUST THOUGHT YOU MIGHT NEED SOMEONE TO TALK TO.
IF I CAN HELP YOU, THAT'S REWARD ENOUGH.

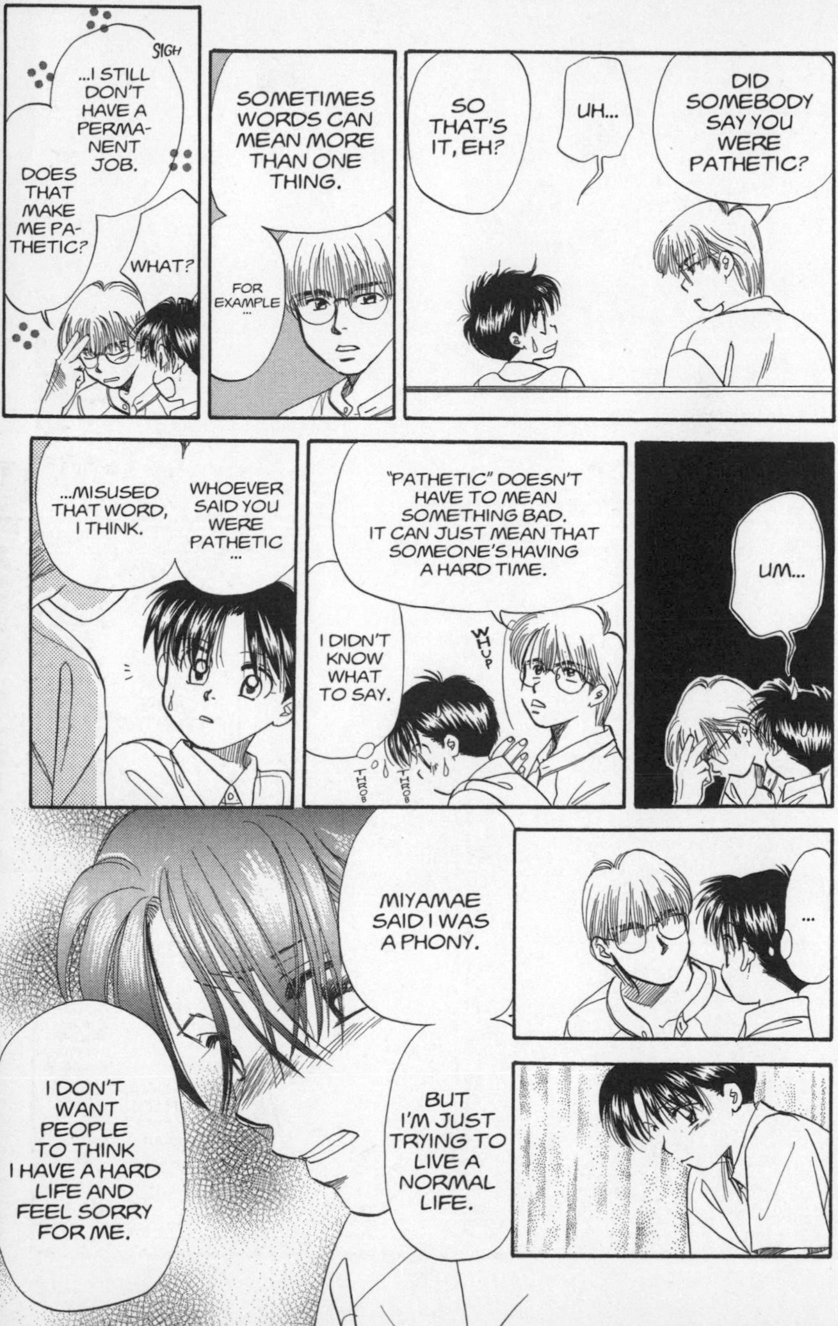
DID SOMEBODY SAY YOU WERE PATHETIC?
UH...
SO THAT'S IT, EH?
SOMETIMES WORDS CAN MEAN MORE THAN ONE THING.
FOR EXAMPLE...
SIGH
...I STILL DON'T HAVE A PERMANENT JOB.
DOES THAT MAKE ME PATHETIC?
WHAT?
UM...
"PATHETIC" DOESN'T HAVE TO MEAN SOMETHING BAD. IT CAN JUST MEAN THAT SOMEONE'S HAVING A HARD TIME.
WHUP
I DIDN'T KNOW WHAT TO SAY.
THROB
THROB
WHOEVER SAID YOU WERE PATHETIC...
...MISUSED THAT WORD, I THINK.
...
MIYAMAE SAID I WAS A PHONY.
BUT I'M JUST TRYING TO LIVE A NORMAL LIFE.
I DON'T WANT PEOPLE TO THINK I HAVE A HARD LIFE AND FEEL SORRY FOR ME.

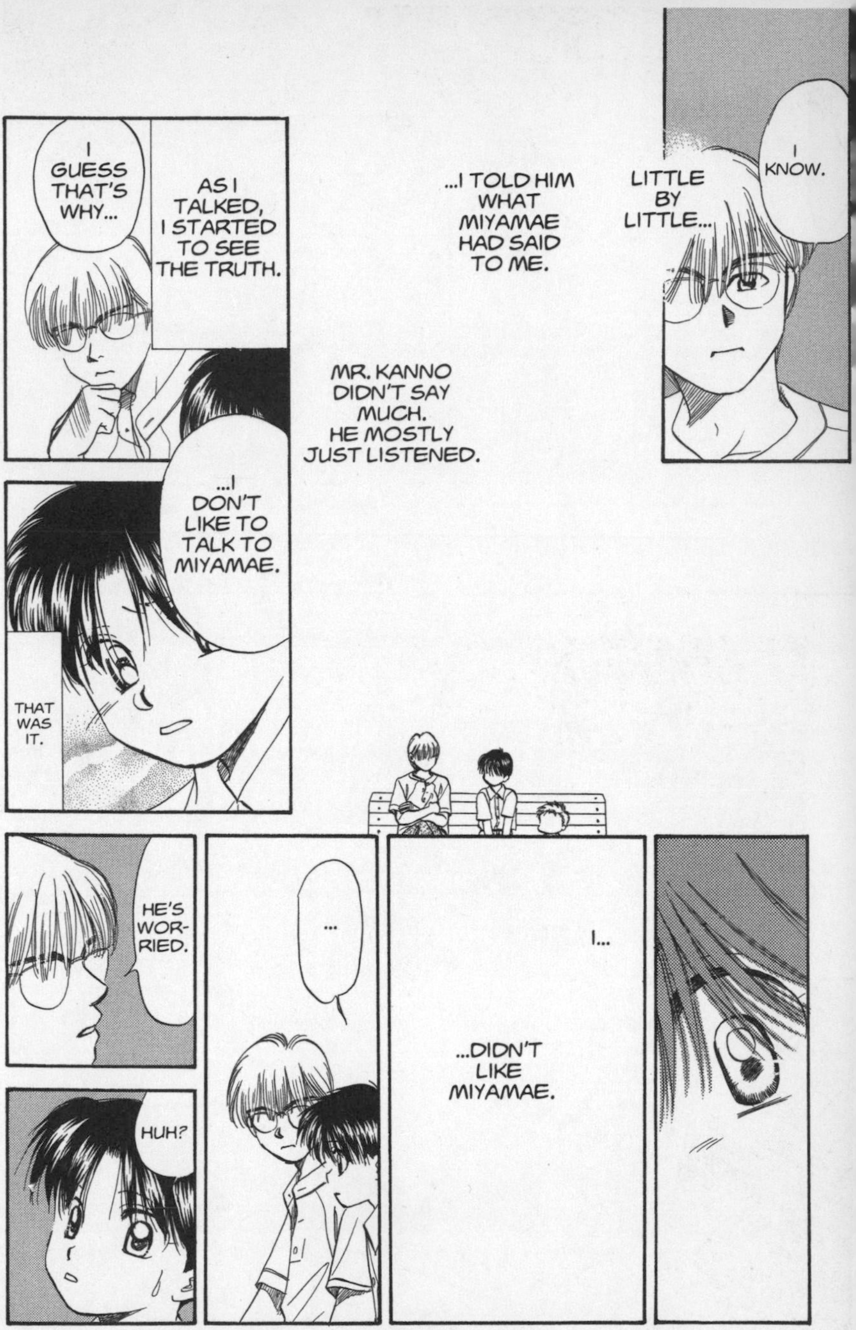
I KNOW.
LITTLE BY LITTLE...
...I TOLD HIM WHAT MIYAMAE HAD SAID TO ME.
MR. KANNO DIDN'T SAY MUCH. HE MOSTLY JUST LISTENED.
I GUESS THAT'S WHY...
AS I TALKED, I STARTED TO SEE THE TRUTH.
...I DON'T LIKE TO TALK TO MIYAMAE.
THAT WAS IT.
I...
...DIDN'T LIKE MIYAMAE.
...
HE'S WOR-RIED.
HUH?

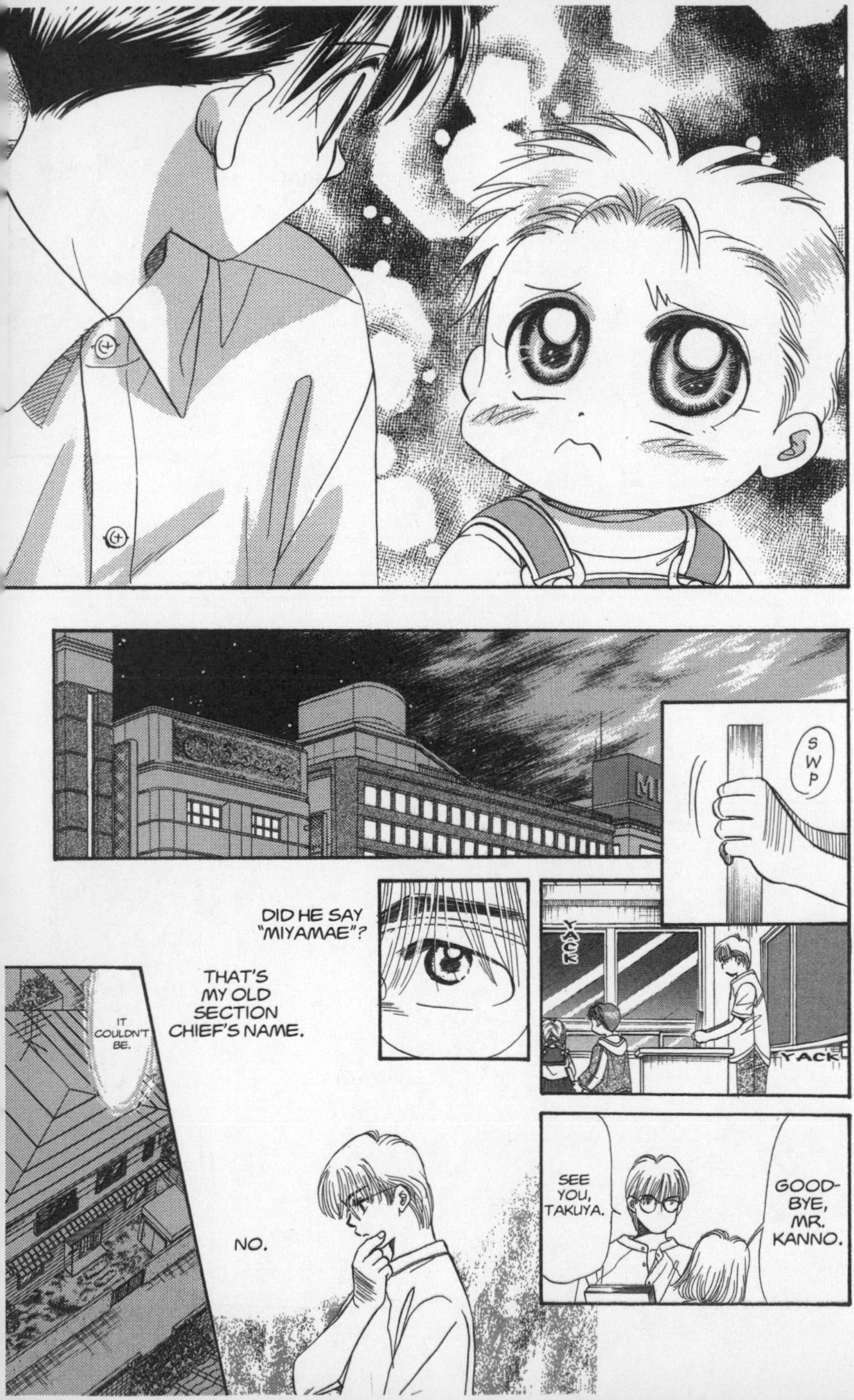
SWP
YACK
YACK
GOOD-BYE, MR. KANNO.
SEE YOU, TAKUYA.
DID HE SAY "MIYAMAE"?
THAT'S MY OLD SECTION CHIEF'S NAME.
IT COULDN'T BE.
NO.

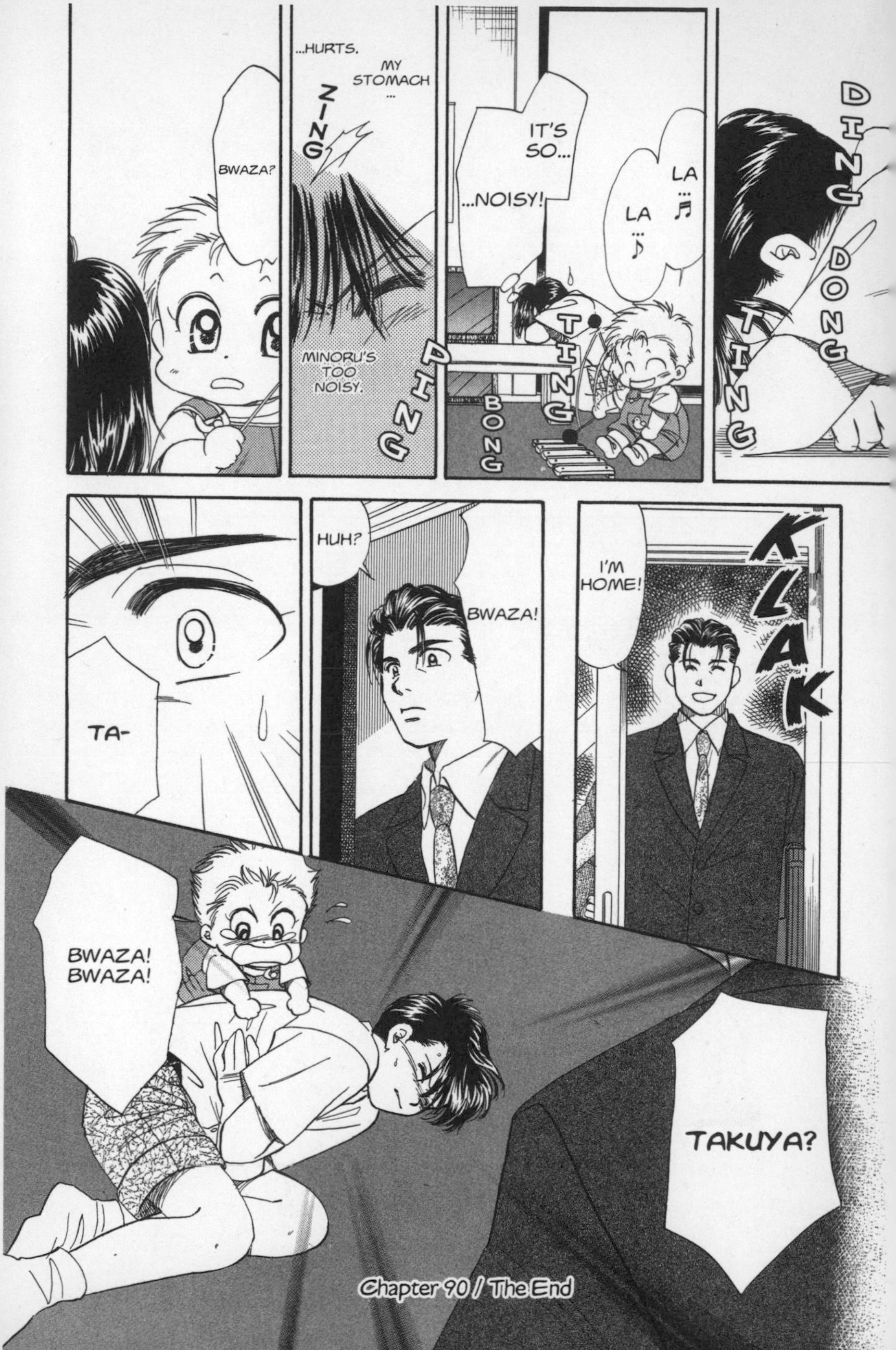
DING DONG
TING TING
LA... ♬
LA... ♪
IT'S SO...
...NOISY!
TING
BONG
MY STOMACH...
...HURTS.
ZING
MINORU'S TOO NOISY.
PING
BWAZA?
KLAK
I'M HOME!
HUH?
BWAZA!
TA-
TAKUYA?
BWAZA! BWAZA!
Chapter 90 / The End

Chapter 91

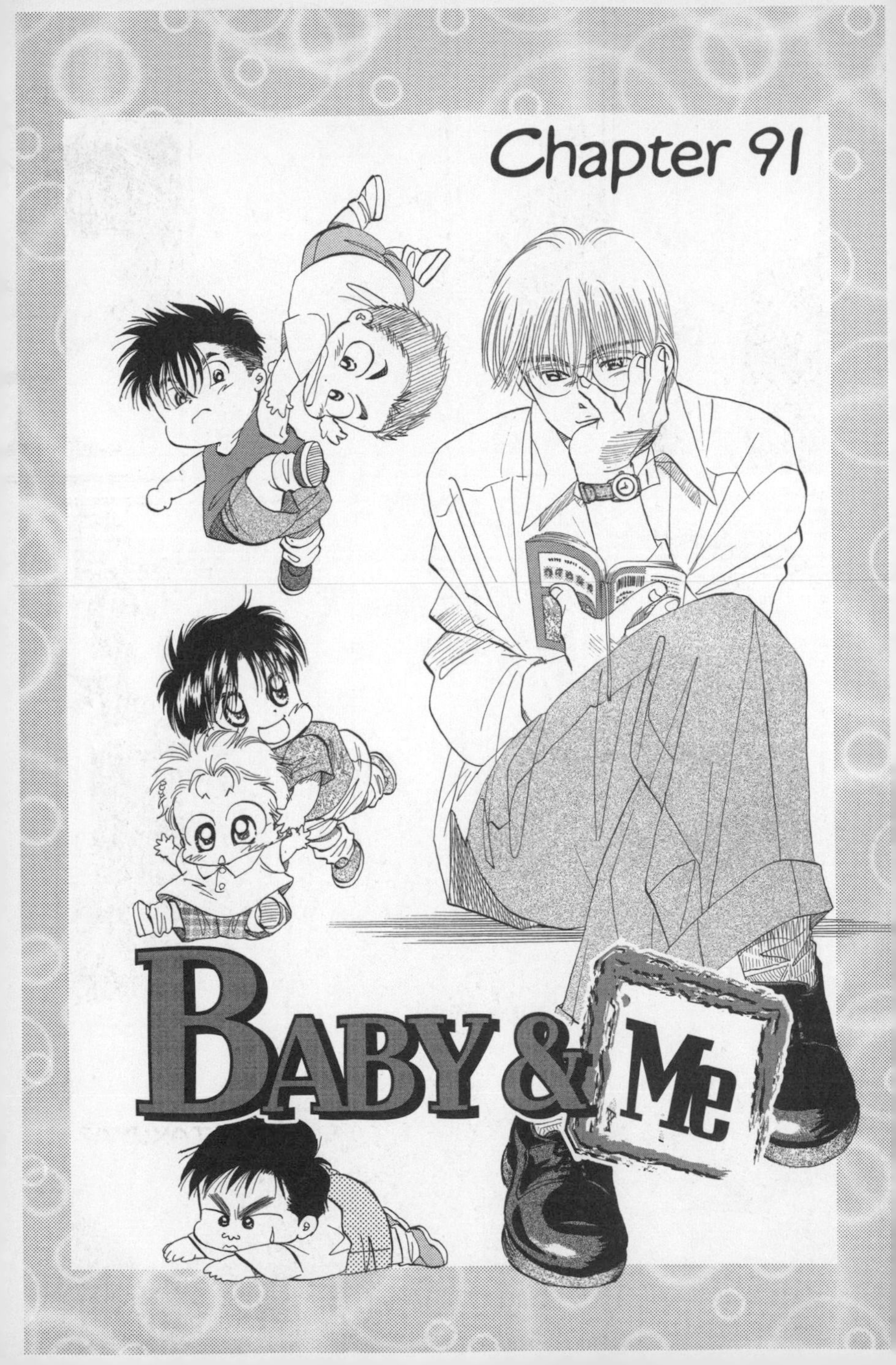
BABY & Me

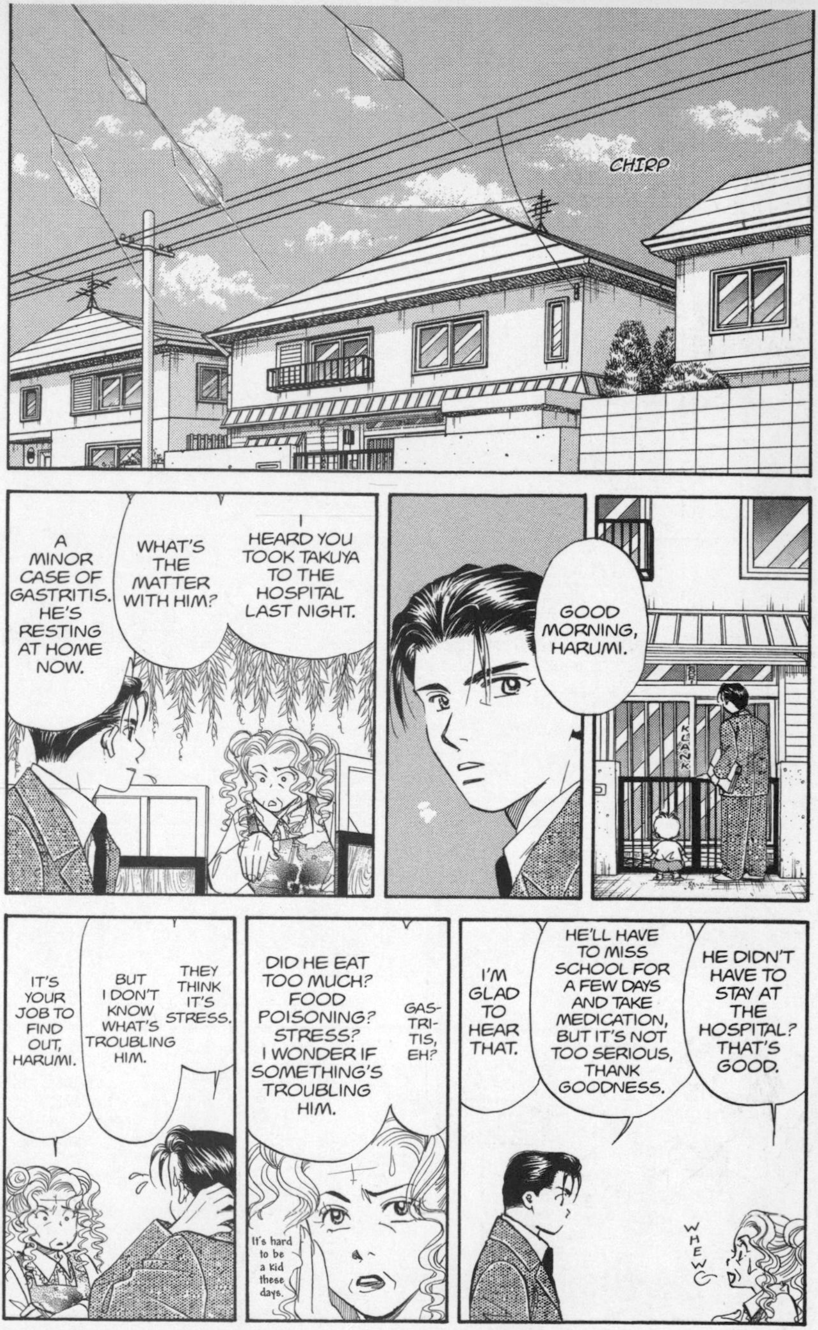
CHIRP
KLANK
GOOD MORNING, HARUMI.
I HEARD YOU TOOK TAKUYA TO THE HOSPITAL LAST NIGHT.
WHAT'S THE MATTER WITH HIM?
A MINOR CASE OF GASTRITIS. HE'S RESTING AT HOME NOW.
HE DIDN'T HAVE TO STAY AT THE HOSPITAL? THAT'S GOOD.
HE'LL HAVE TO MISS SCHOOL FOR A FEW DAYS AND TAKE MEDICATION, BUT IT'S NOT TOO SERIOUS, THANK GOODNESS.
I'M GLAD TO HEAR THAT.
WHEW
GAS-TRI-TIS, EH?
DID HE EAT TOO MUCH? FOOD POISONING? STRESS? I WONDER IF SOMETHING'S TROUBLING HIM.
It's hard to be a kid these days.
THEY THINK IT'S STRESS.
BUT I DON'T KNOW WHAT'S TROUBLING HIM.
IT'S YOUR JOB TO FIND OUT, HARUMI.

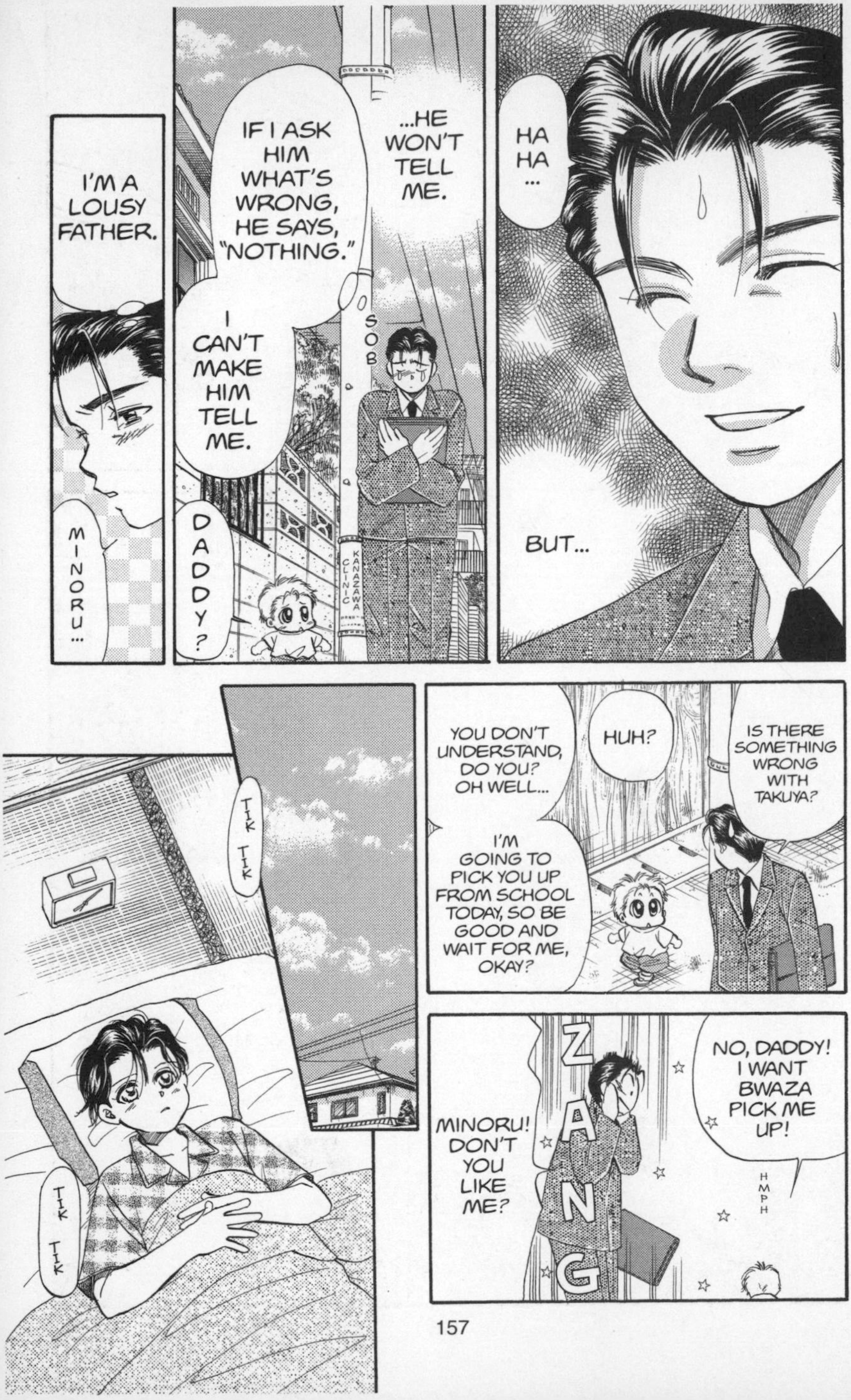
HA HA ...
BUT...
...HE WON'T TELL ME.
IF I ASK HIM WHAT'S WRONG, HE SAYS, "NOTHING."
I CAN'T MAKE HIM TELL ME.
SOB
KANAZAWA CLINIC
DADDY?
I'M A LOUSY FATHER.
MINORU...
IS THERE SOMETHING WRONG WITH TAKUYA?
HUH?
YOU DON'T UNDERSTAND, DO YOU? OH WELL...
I'M GOING TO PICK YOU UP FROM SCHOOL TODAY, SO BE GOOD AND WAIT FOR ME, OKAY?
NO, DADDY! I WANT BWAZA PICK ME UP!
HMPH
ZANG
MINORU! DON'T YOU LIKE ME?
TIK TIK
TIK TIK

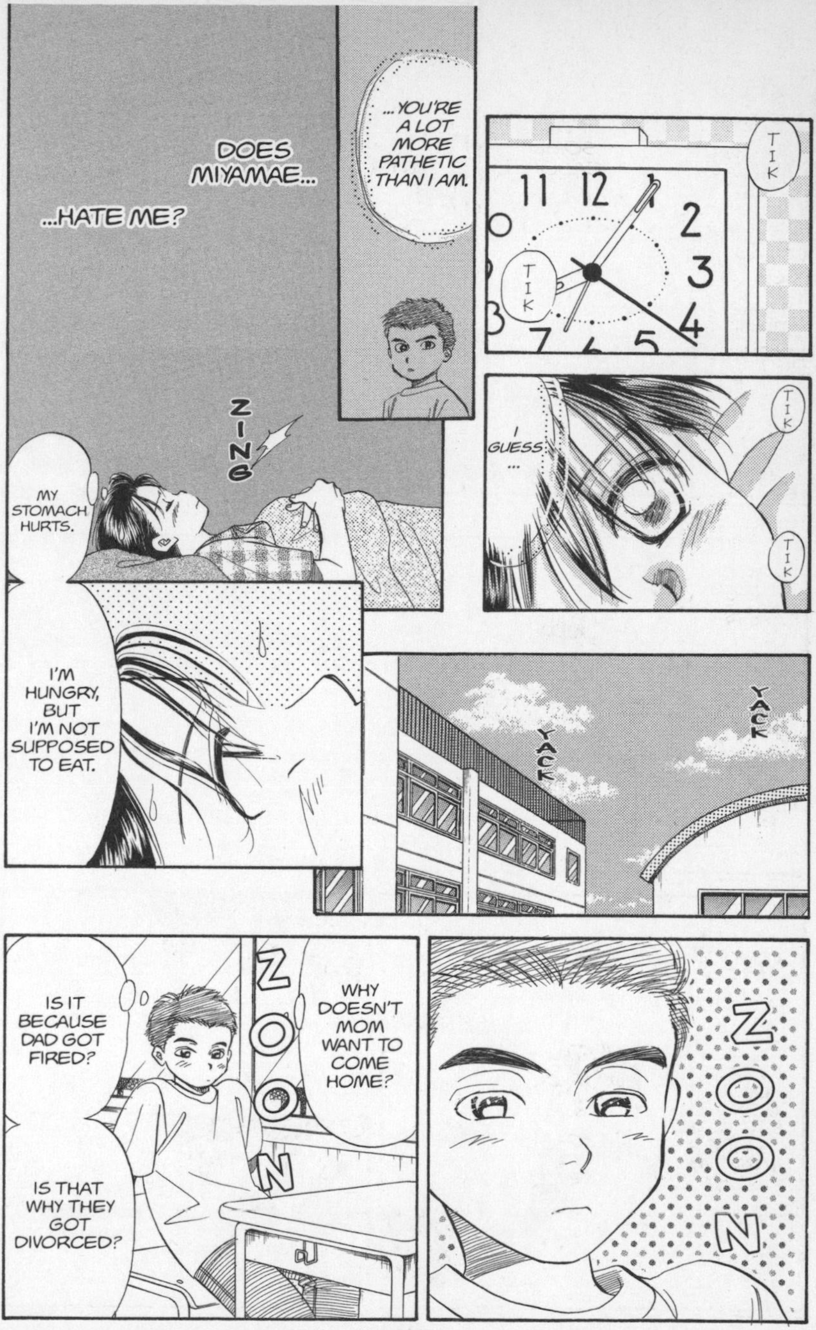
TIK
TIK
TIK
I GUESS...
TIK
...YOU'RE A LOT MORE PATHETIC THAN I AM.
DOES MIYAMAE...
...HATE ME?
ZING
MY STOMACH HURTS.
YACK
YACK
I'M HUNGRY, BUT I'M NOT SUPPOSED TO EAT.
ZOON
WHY DOESN'T MOM WANT TO COME HOME?
ZOON
IS IT BECAUSE DAD GOT FIRED?
IS THAT WHY THEY GOT DIVORCED?

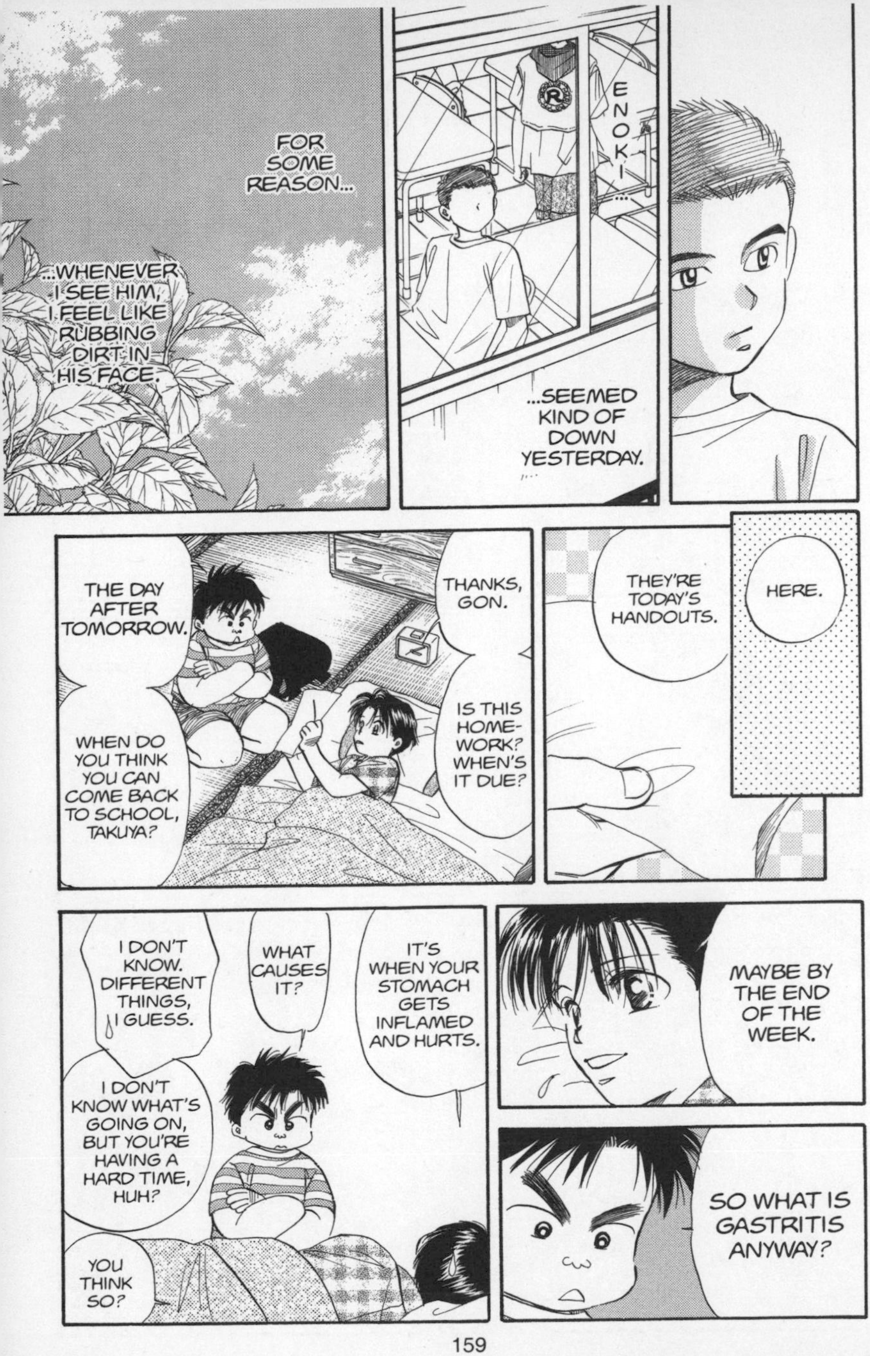
ENOKI...
...SEEMED KIND OF DOWN YESTERDAY.
FOR SOME REASON...
...WHENEVER I SEE HIM, I FEEL LIKE RUBBING DIRT IN HIS FACE.
HERE.
THEY'RE TODAY'S HANDOUTS.
THANKS, GON.
IS THIS HOME-WORK? WHEN'S IT DUE?
THE DAY AFTER TOMORROW.
WHEN DO YOU THINK YOU CAN COME BACK TO SCHOOL, TAKUYA?
MAYBE BY THE END OF THE WEEK.
SO WHAT IS GASTRITIS ANYWAY?
IT'S WHEN YOUR STOMACH GETS INFLAMED AND HURTS.
WHAT CAUSES IT?
I DON'T KNOW. DIFFERENT THINGS, I GUESS.
I DON'T KNOW WHAT'S GOING ON, BUT YOU'RE HAVING A HARD TIME, HUH?
YOU THINK SO?

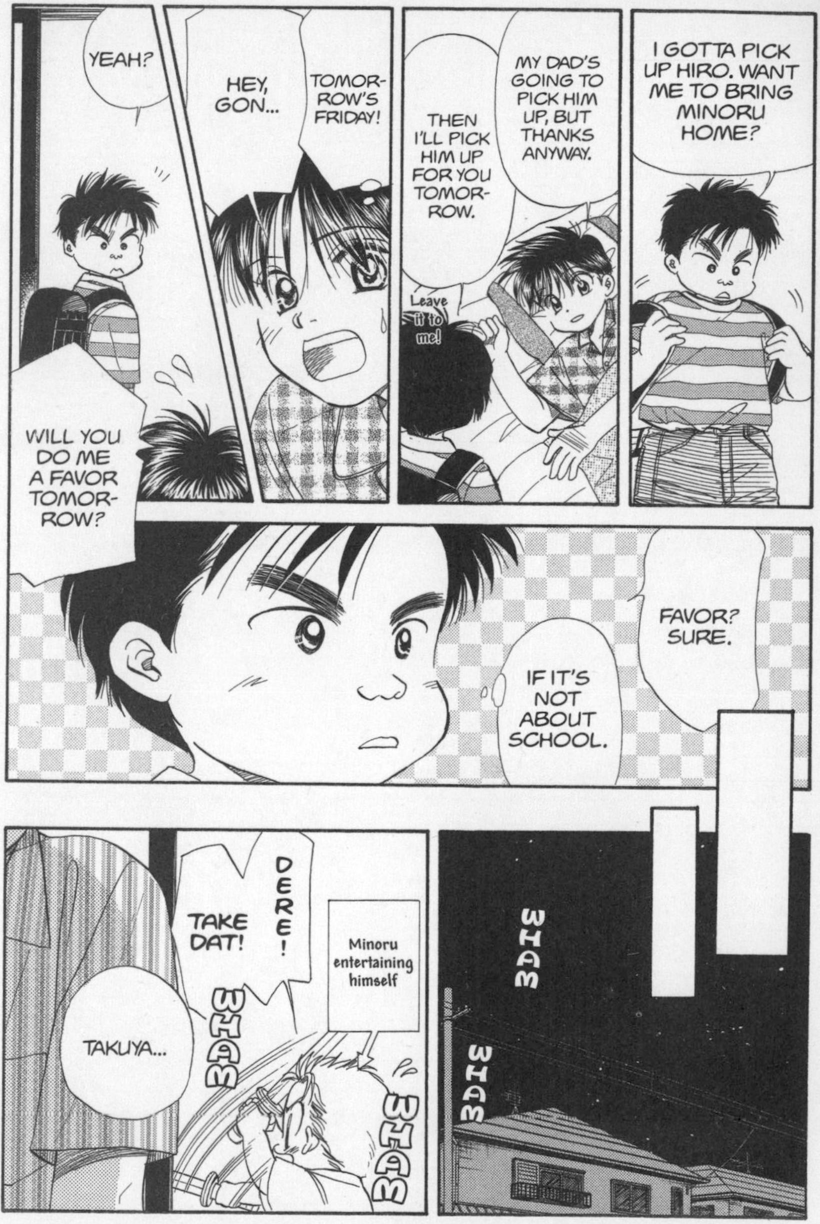

I GOTTA PICK UP HIRO. WANT ME TO BRING MINORU HOME?
MY DAD'S GOING TO PICK HIM UP, BUT THANKS ANYWAY.
THEN I'LL PICK HIM UP FOR YOU TOMORROW.
Leave it to me!
TOMORROW'S FRIDAY!
HEY, GON...
YEAH?
WILL YOU DO ME A FAVOR TOMORROW?
FAVOR? SURE.
IF IT'S NOT ABOUT SCHOOL.
WHAM
WHAM
DERE!
TAKE DAT!
Minoru entertaining himself
WHAM
WHAM
TAKUYA...

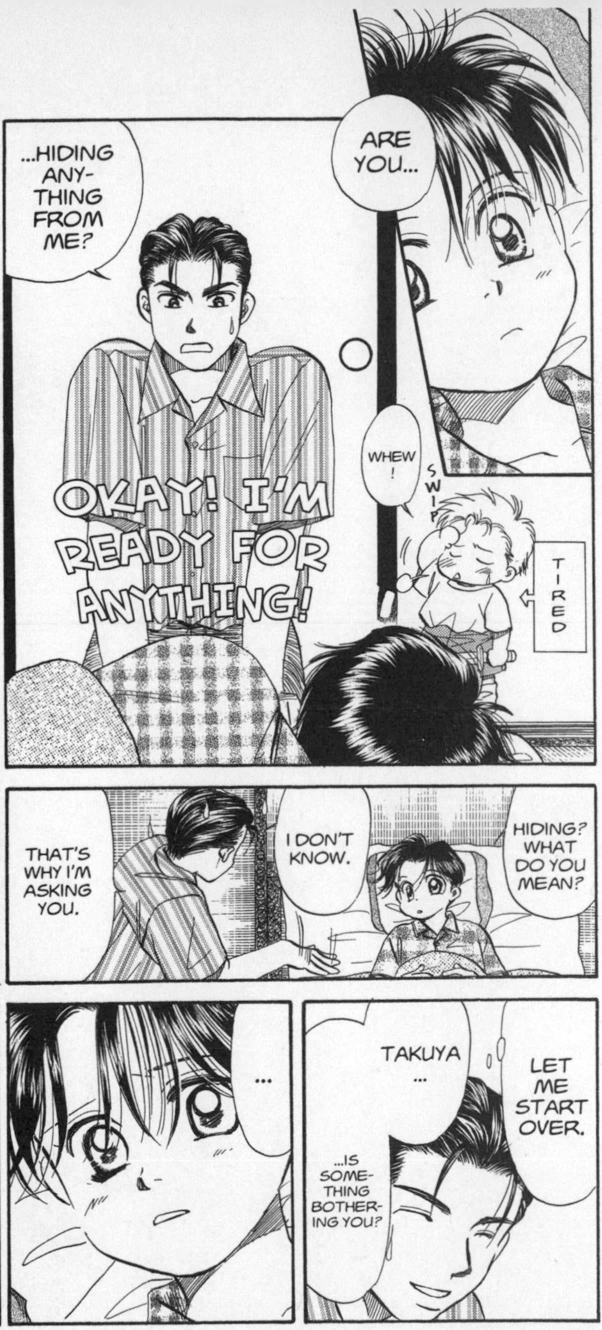
ARE YOU...
WHEW!
SWIP
TIRED
...HIDING ANYTHING FROM ME?
OKAY! I'M READY FOR ANYTHING!
HIDING? WHAT DO YOU MEAN?
I DON'T KNOW.
THAT'S WHY I'M ASKING YOU.
LET ME START OVER.
TAKUYA...
...IS SOMETHING BOTHERING YOU?
...

Author's Note Part 6

The kids we saw were all cute.

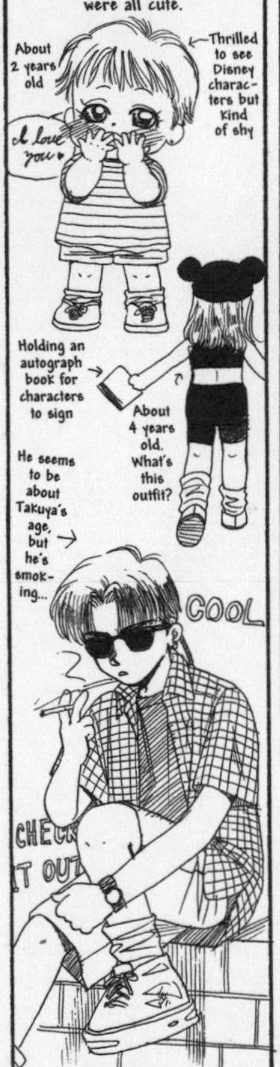
About 2 years old
Thrilled to see Disney characters but kind of shy
I love you♥
Holding an autograph book for characters to sign
About 4 years old. What's this outfit?
He seems to be about Takuya's age, but he's smoking...
COOL
CHECK IT OUT

When his cigarette smoke wafted over to me, somebody said, "Sorry." But it was the father, not the boy, who apologized.

Hey, straighten out your son!

I joined a group of kids and took a lot of photos with the characters. How silly!

☆ Most memorable attraction—*Terminator 2* (It's a 3D movie. That's not a Disney movie, is it? Ha ha!)

Well, bye for now!

February 1997

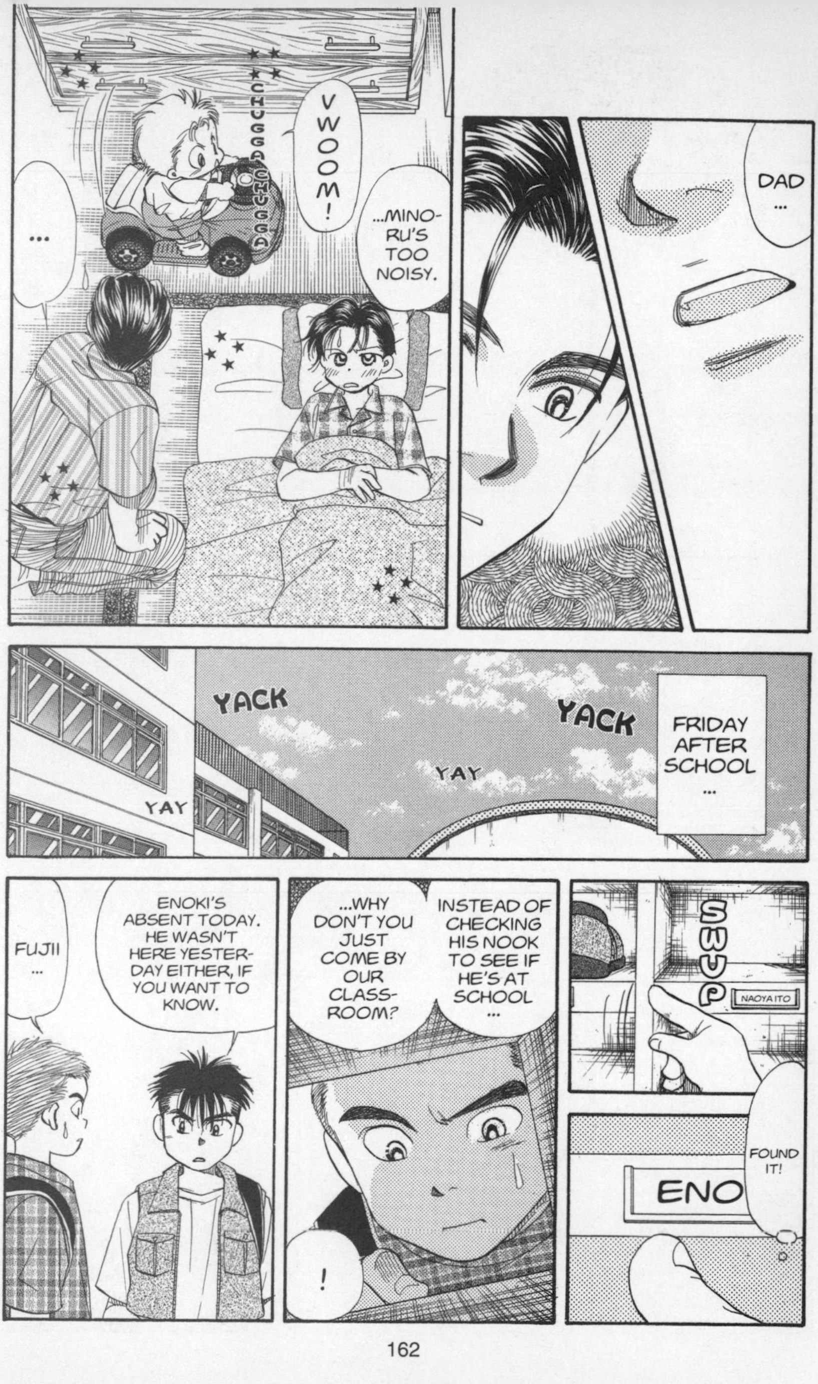
DAD ...
...MINO-RU'S TOO NOISY.
VWOOM!
CHUGGA CHUGGA
...
FRIDAY AFTER SCHOOL ...
YACK
YAY
YACK
YAY
SWUP
NAOYA ITO
FOUND IT!
ENO
INSTEAD OF CHECKING HIS NOOK TO SEE IF HE'S AT SCHOOL ...
...WHY DON'T YOU JUST COME BY OUR CLASS-ROOM?
!
ENOKI'S ABSENT TODAY. HE WASN'T HERE YESTER-DAY EITHER, IF YOU WANT TO KNOW.
FUJII ...

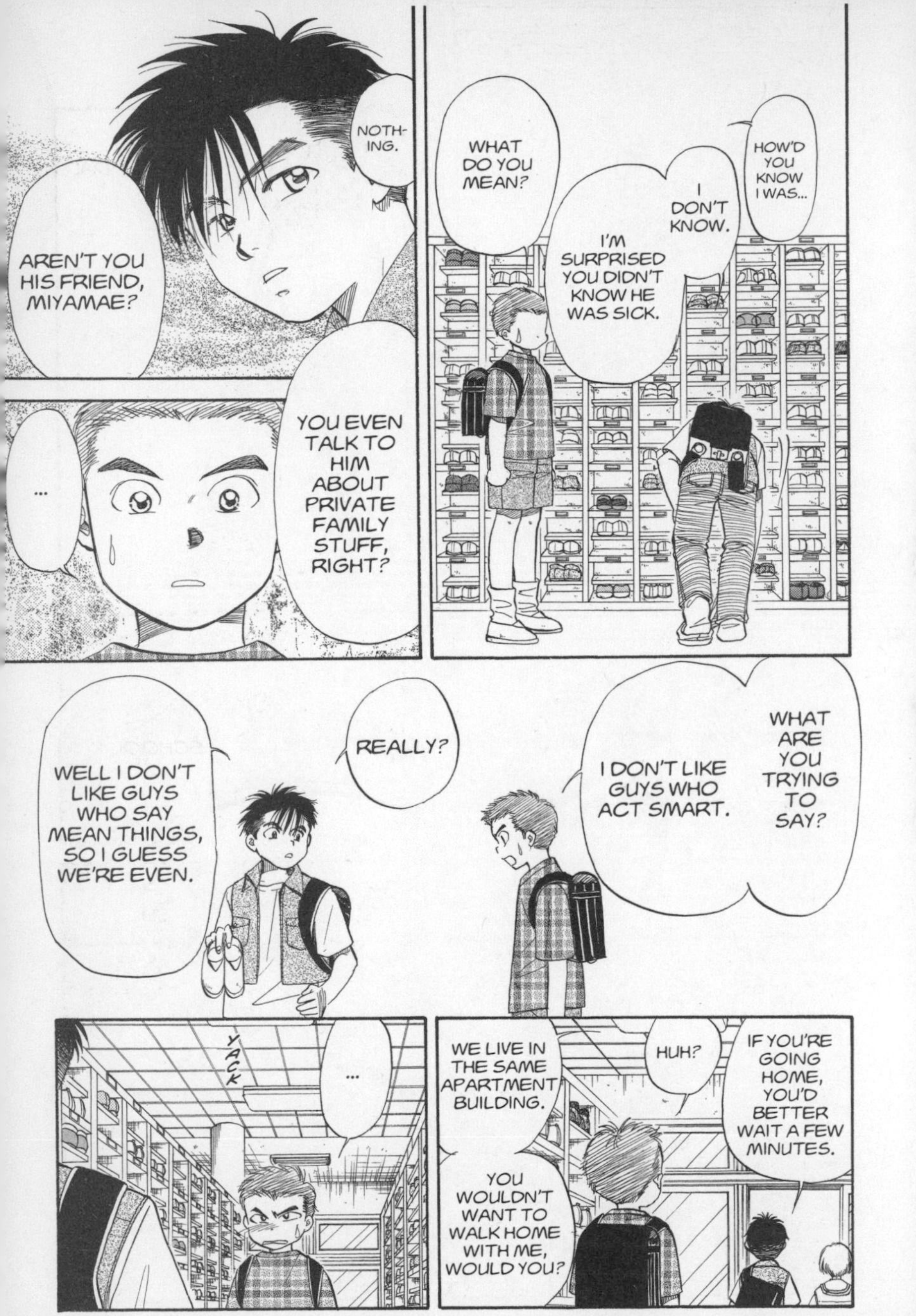
HOW'D YOU KNOW I WAS...
I DON'T KNOW.
WHAT DO YOU MEAN?
I'M SURPRISED YOU DIDN'T KNOW HE WAS SICK.
NOTH-ING.
AREN'T YOU HIS FRIEND, MIYAMAE?
YOU EVEN TALK TO HIM ABOUT PRIVATE FAMILY STUFF, RIGHT?
...
WHAT ARE YOU TRYING TO SAY?
I DON'T LIKE GUYS WHO ACT SMART.
REALLY?
WELL I DON'T LIKE GUYS WHO SAY MEAN THINGS, SO I GUESS WE'RE EVEN.
IF YOU'RE GOING HOME, YOU'D BETTER WAIT A FEW MINUTES.
HUH?
WE LIVE IN THE SAME APARTMENT BUILDING.
YOU WOULDN'T WANT TO WALK HOME WITH ME, WOULD YOU?
...
YACK

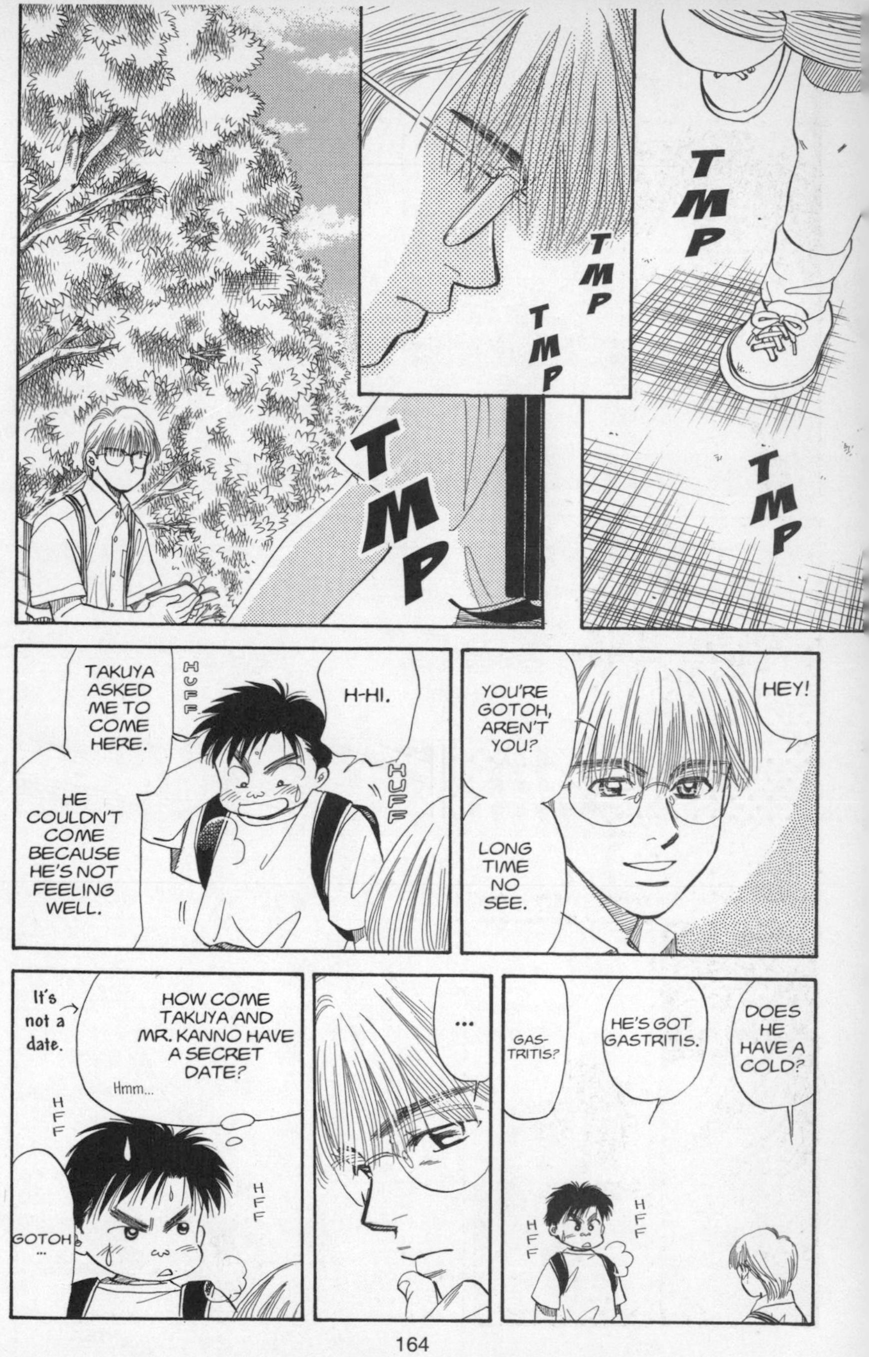
TMP
TMP
TMP
TMP
TMP
TMP
HEY!
YOU'RE GOTOH, AREN'T YOU?
LONG TIME NO SEE.
H-HI.
HUFF
HUFF
TAKUYA ASKED ME TO COME HERE.
HE COULDN'T COME BECAUSE HE'S NOT FEELING WELL.
DOES HE HAVE A COLD?
HE'S GOT GASTRITIS.
GAS-TRITIS?
HFF
HFF
...
HOW COME TAKUYA AND MR. KANNO HAVE A SECRET DATE?
Hmm...
It's not a date.
HFF
HFF
GOTOH ...

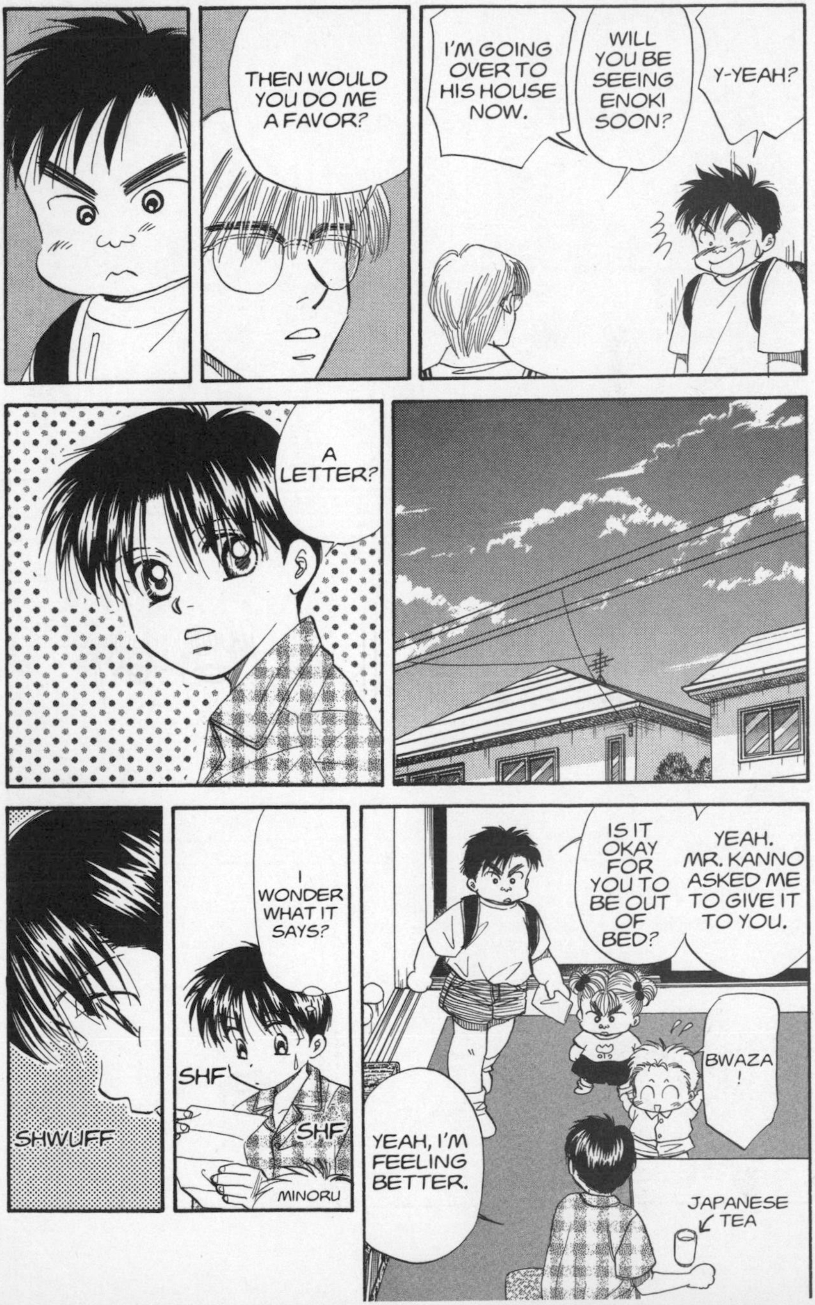
Y-YEAH?
WILL YOU BE SEEING ENOKI SOON?
I'M GOING OVER TO HIS HOUSE NOW.
THEN WOULD YOU DO ME A FAVOR?
A LETTER?
YEAH. MR. KANNO ASKED ME TO GIVE IT TO YOU.
IS IT OKAY FOR YOU TO BE OUT OF BED?
BWAZA!
YEAH, I'M FEELING BETTER.
JAPANESE TEA
I WONDER WHAT IT SAYS?
SHF
SHF
MINORU
SHWUFF

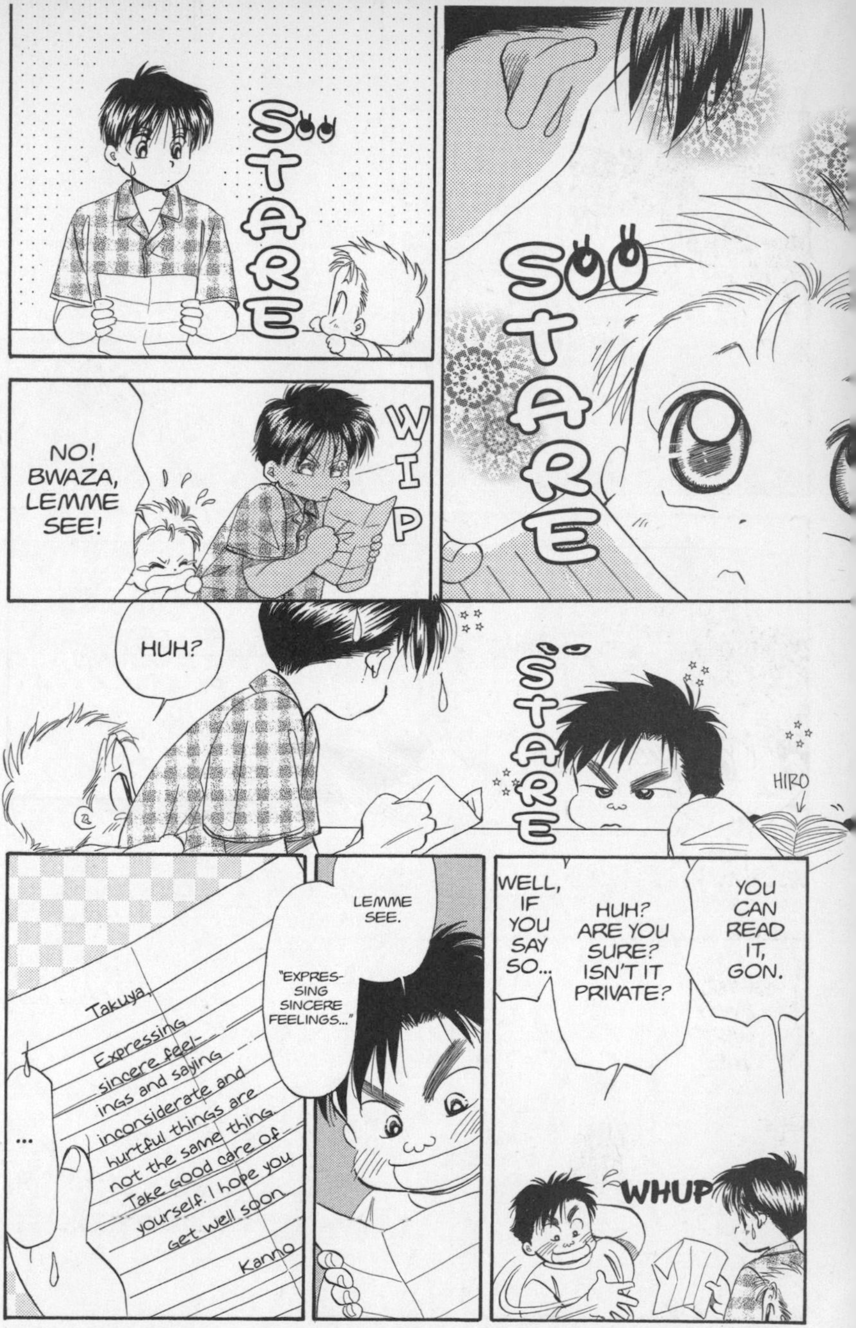
STARE
STARE
NO! BWAZA, LEMME SEE!
WIP
STARE
HIRO
HUH?
YOU CAN READ IT, GON.
HUH? ARE YOU SURE? ISN'T IT PRIVATE?
WELL, IF YOU SAY SO...
WHUP
LEMME SEE.
"EXPRES-SING SINCERE FEELINGS..."
Takuya,
Expressing sincere feel-ings and saying inconsiderate and hurtful things are not the same thing. Take good care of yourself. I hope you get well soon.
Kanno
...

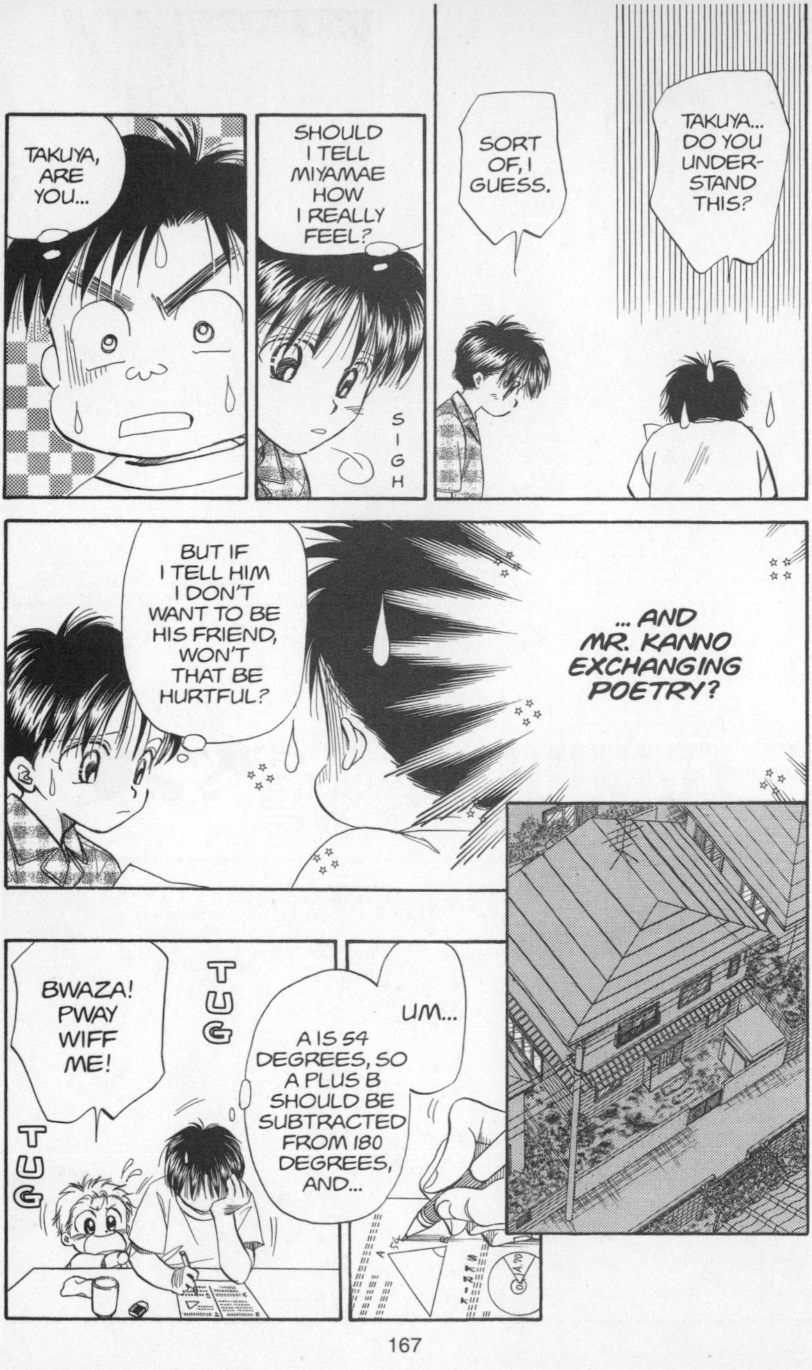
TAKUYA... DO YOU UNDER-STAND THIS?
SORT OF, I GUESS.
SHOULD I TELL MIYAMAE HOW I REALLY FEEL?
SIGH
TAKUYA, ARE YOU...
... AND MR. KANNO EXCHANGING POETRY?
BUT IF I TELL HIM I DON'T WANT TO BE HIS FRIEND, WON'T THAT BE HURTFUL?
UM...
A IS 54 DEGREES, SO A PLUS B SHOULD BE SUBTRACTED FROM 180 DEGREES, AND...
TUG
BWAZA! PWAY WIFF ME!
TUG

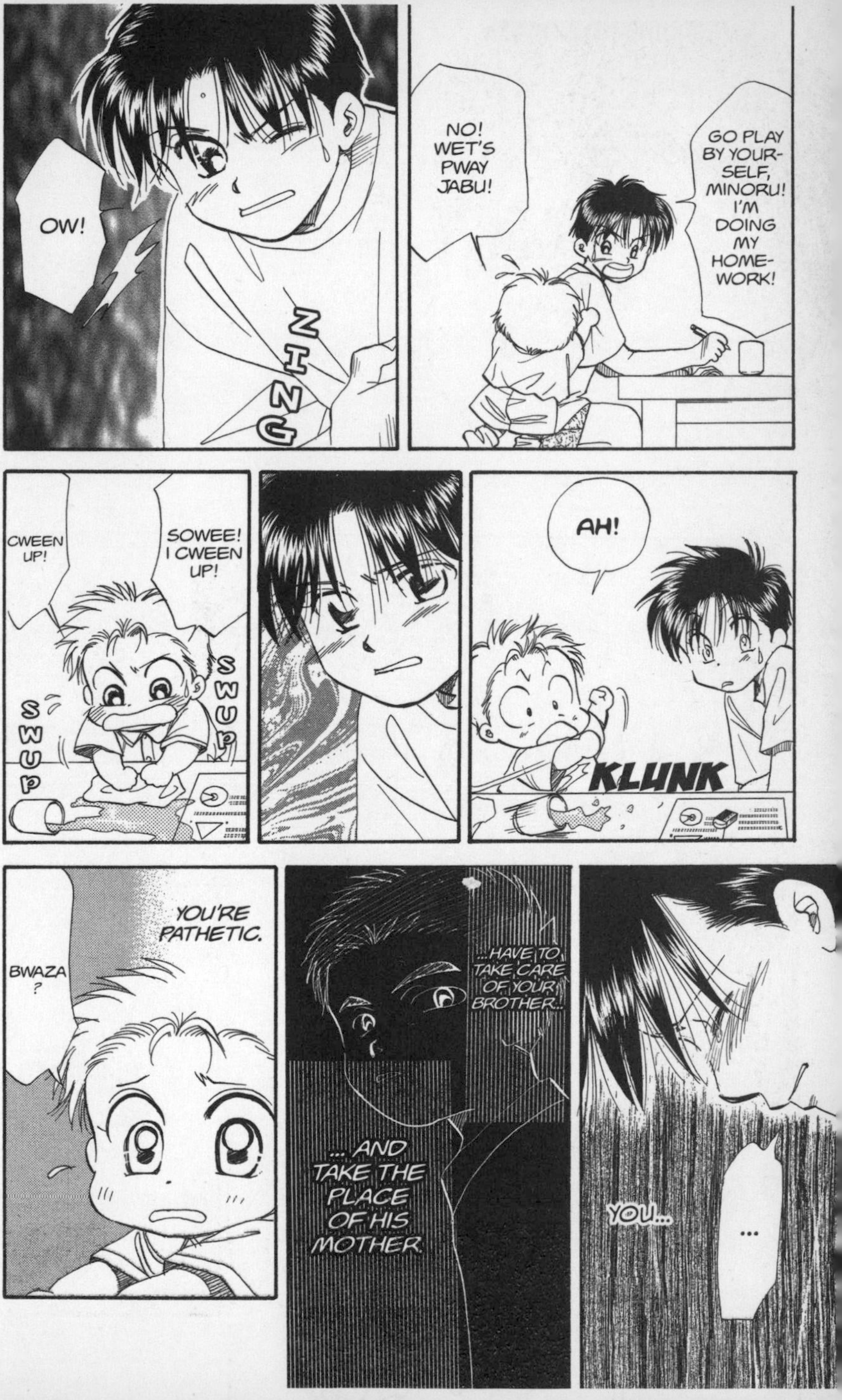
GO PLAY BY YOURSELF, MINORU! I'M DOING MY HOMEWORK!
NO! WET'S PWAY JABU!
ZING
OW!
AH!
KLUNK
SOWEE! I CWEEN UP!
CWEEN UP!
SWUP
SWUP
...
YOU...
...HAVE TO TAKE CARE OF YOUR BROTHER...
...AND TAKE THE PLACE OF HIS MOTHER.
YOU'RE PATHETIC.
BWAZA?

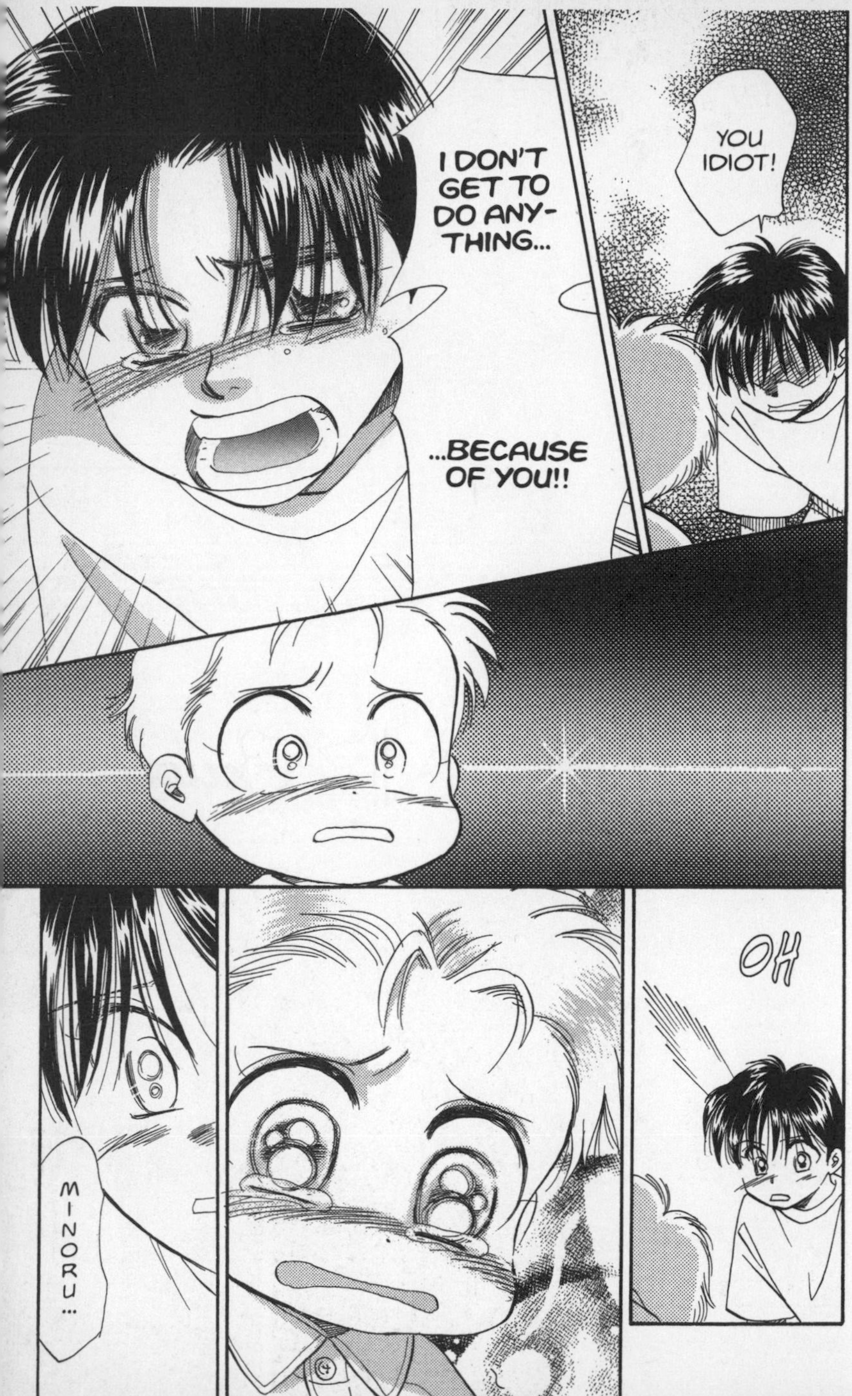
YOU IDIOT!
I DON'T GET TO DO ANY-THING...
...BECAUSE OF YOU!!
OH
MINORU...

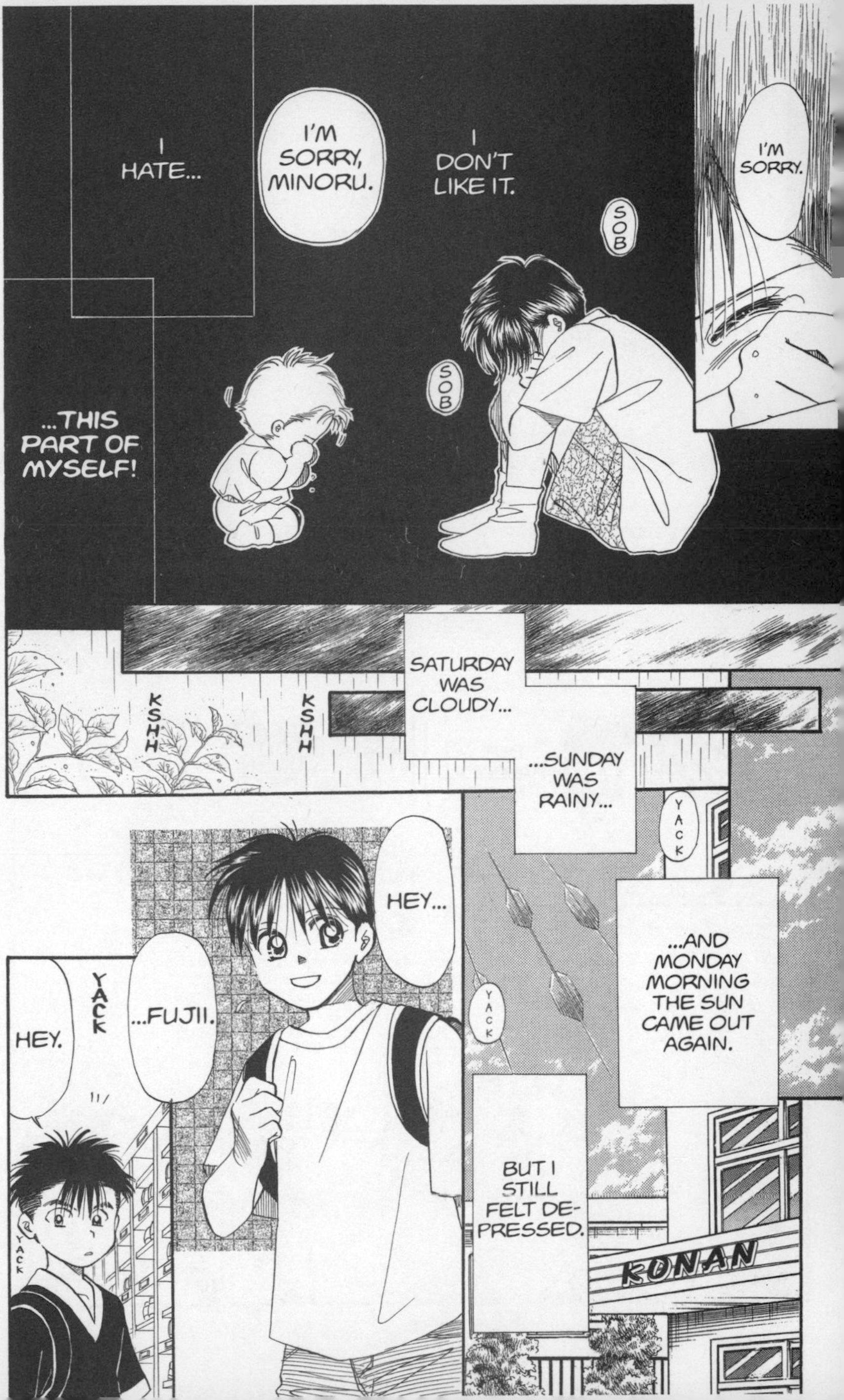
I'M SORRY.
I DON'T LIKE IT.
SOB
I'M SORRY, MINORU.
I HATE...
SOB
...THIS PART OF MYSELF!
SATURDAY WAS CLOUDY...
KSHH
KSHH
...SUNDAY WAS RAINY...
YACK
...AND MONDAY MORNING THE SUN CAME OUT AGAIN.
YACK
BUT I STILL FELT DE-PRESSED.
KONAN
HEY...
...FUJII.
YACK
HEY.
YACK

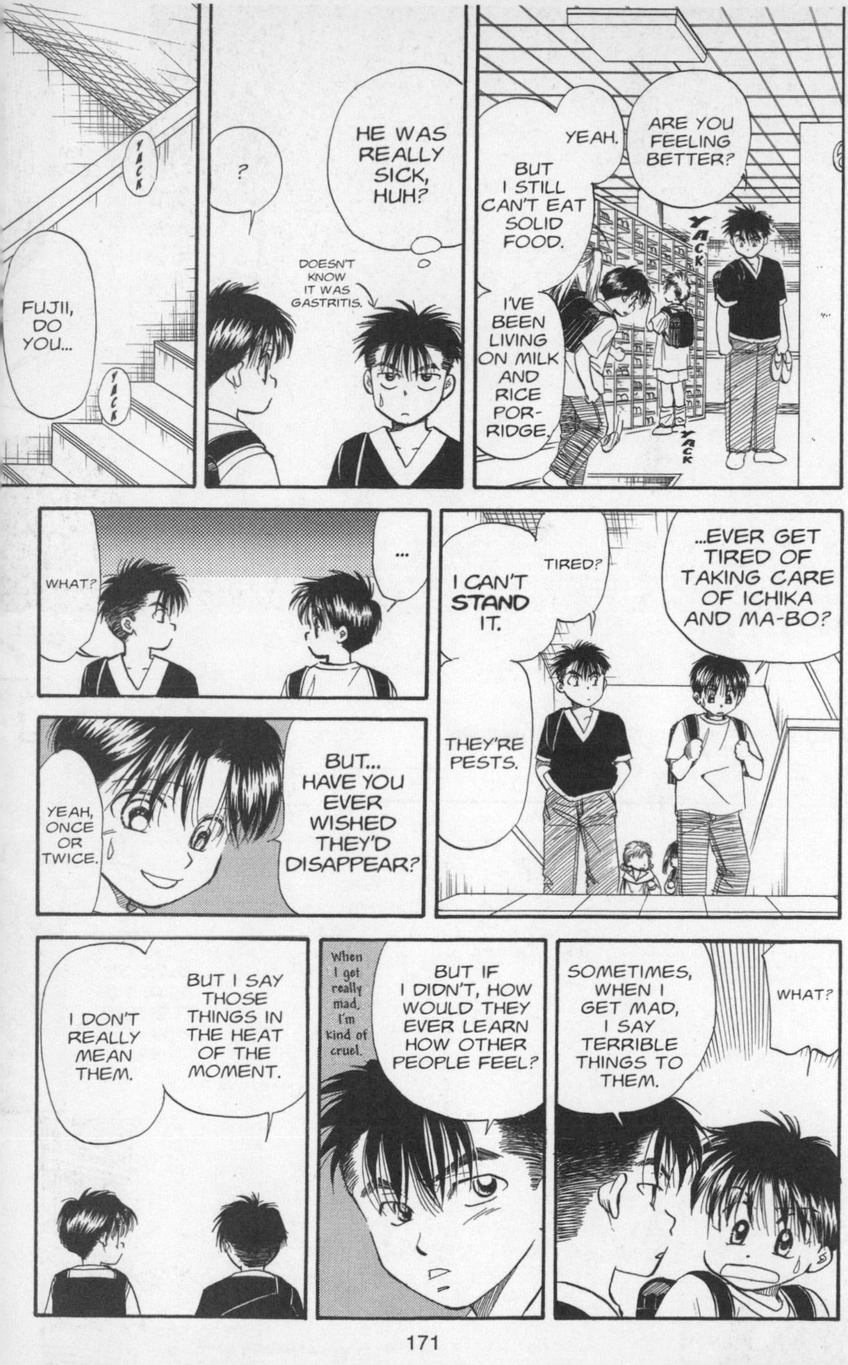
ARE YOU FEELING BETTER?
YEAH.
BUT I STILL CAN'T EAT SOLID FOOD.
I'VE BEEN LIVING ON MILK AND RICE PORRIDGE.
YACK
YACK
HE WAS REALLY SICK, HUH?
?
DOESN'T KNOW IT WAS GASTRITIS.
YACK
FUJII, DO YOU...
YACK
...EVER GET TIRED OF TAKING CARE OF ICHIKA AND MA-BO?
TIRED?
I CAN'T **STAND** IT.
THEY'RE PESTS.
...
WHAT?
BUT... HAVE YOU EVER WISHED THEY'D DISAPPEAR?
YEAH, ONCE OR TWICE.
WHAT?
SOMETIMES, WHEN I GET MAD, I SAY TERRIBLE THINGS TO THEM.
BUT IF I DIDN'T, HOW WOULD THEY EVER LEARN HOW OTHER PEOPLE FEEL?
When I get really mad, I'm kind of cruel.
BUT I SAY THOSE THINGS IN THE HEAT OF THE MOMENT.
I DON'T REALLY MEAN THEM.

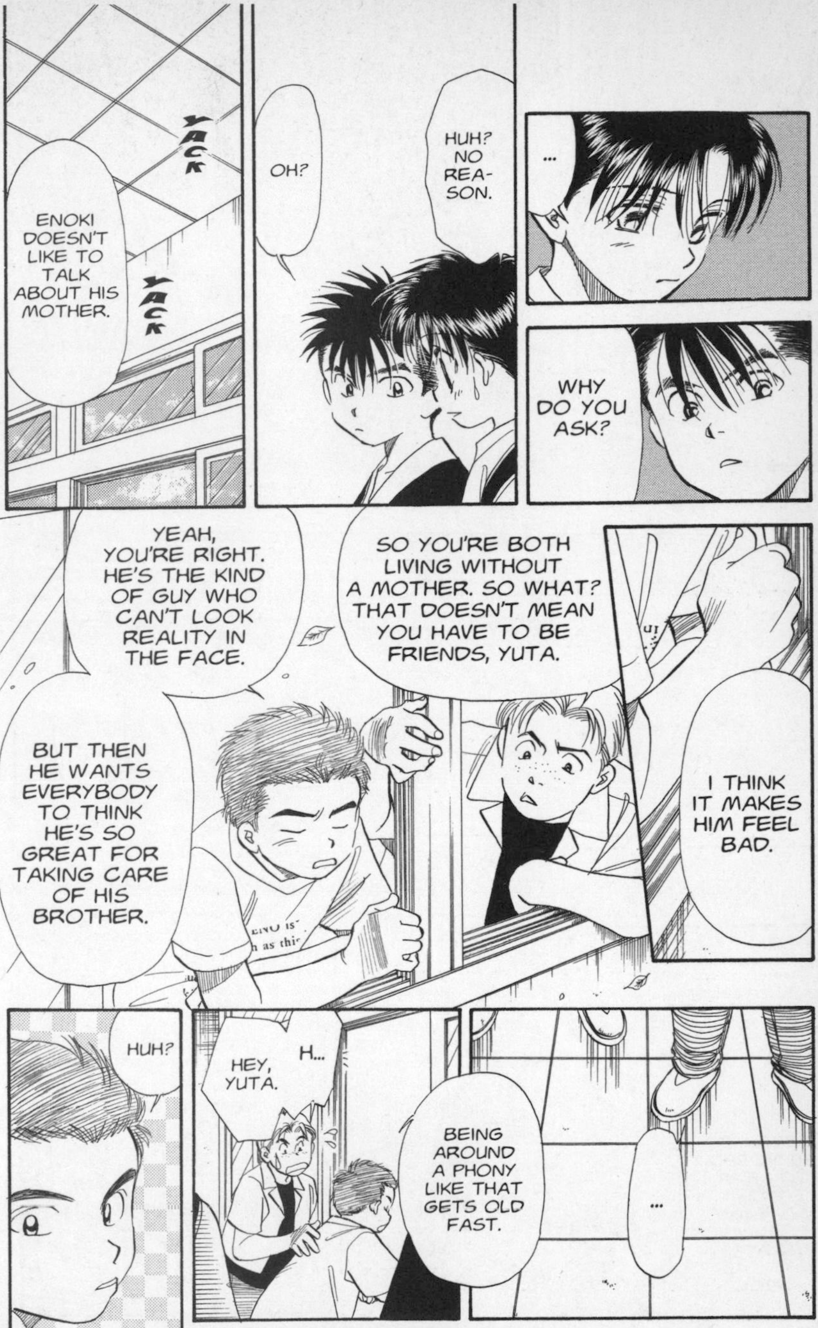
...
WHY DO YOU ASK?
HUH? NO REA-SON.
OH?
YACK
YACK
ENOKI DOESN'T LIKE TO TALK ABOUT HIS MOTHER.
I THINK IT MAKES HIM FEEL BAD.
SO YOU'RE BOTH LIVING WITHOUT A MOTHER. SO WHAT? THAT DOESN'T MEAN YOU HAVE TO BE FRIENDS, YUTA.
YEAH, YOU'RE RIGHT. HE'S THE KIND OF GUY WHO CAN'T LOOK REALITY IN THE FACE.
BUT THEN HE WANTS EVERYBODY TO THINK HE'S SO GREAT FOR TAKING CARE OF HIS BROTHER.
...
BEING AROUND A PHONY LIKE THAT GETS OLD FAST.
H...
HEY, YUTA.
HUH?

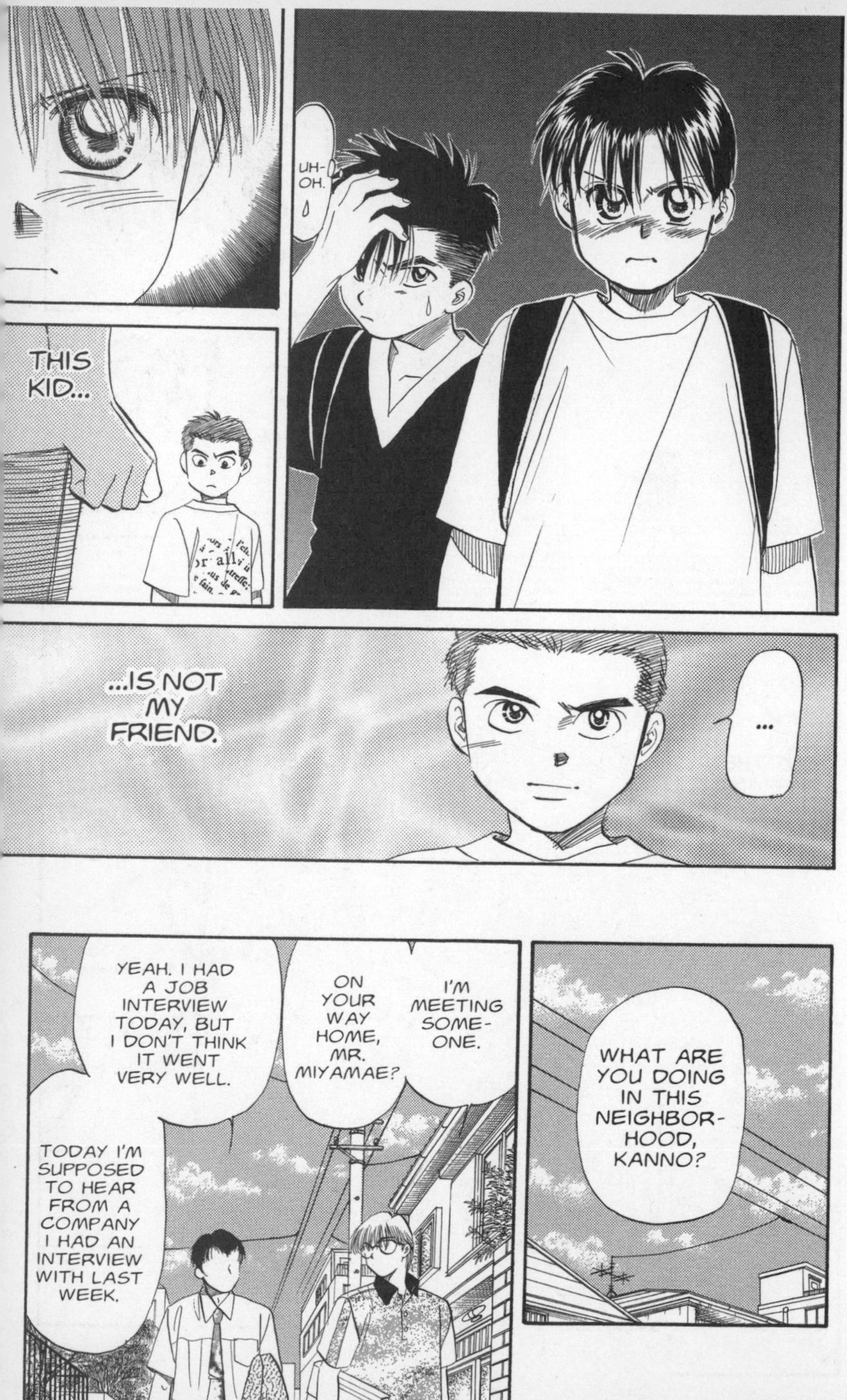
UH-OH.
THIS KID...
...
...IS NOT MY FRIEND.
WHAT ARE YOU DOING IN THIS NEIGHBORHOOD, KANNO?
I'M MEETING SOMEONE.
ON YOUR WAY HOME, MR. MIYAMAE?
YEAH. I HAD A JOB INTERVIEW TODAY, BUT I DON'T THINK IT WENT VERY WELL.
TODAY I'M SUPPOSED TO HEAR FROM A COMPANY I HAD AN INTERVIEW WITH LAST WEEK.

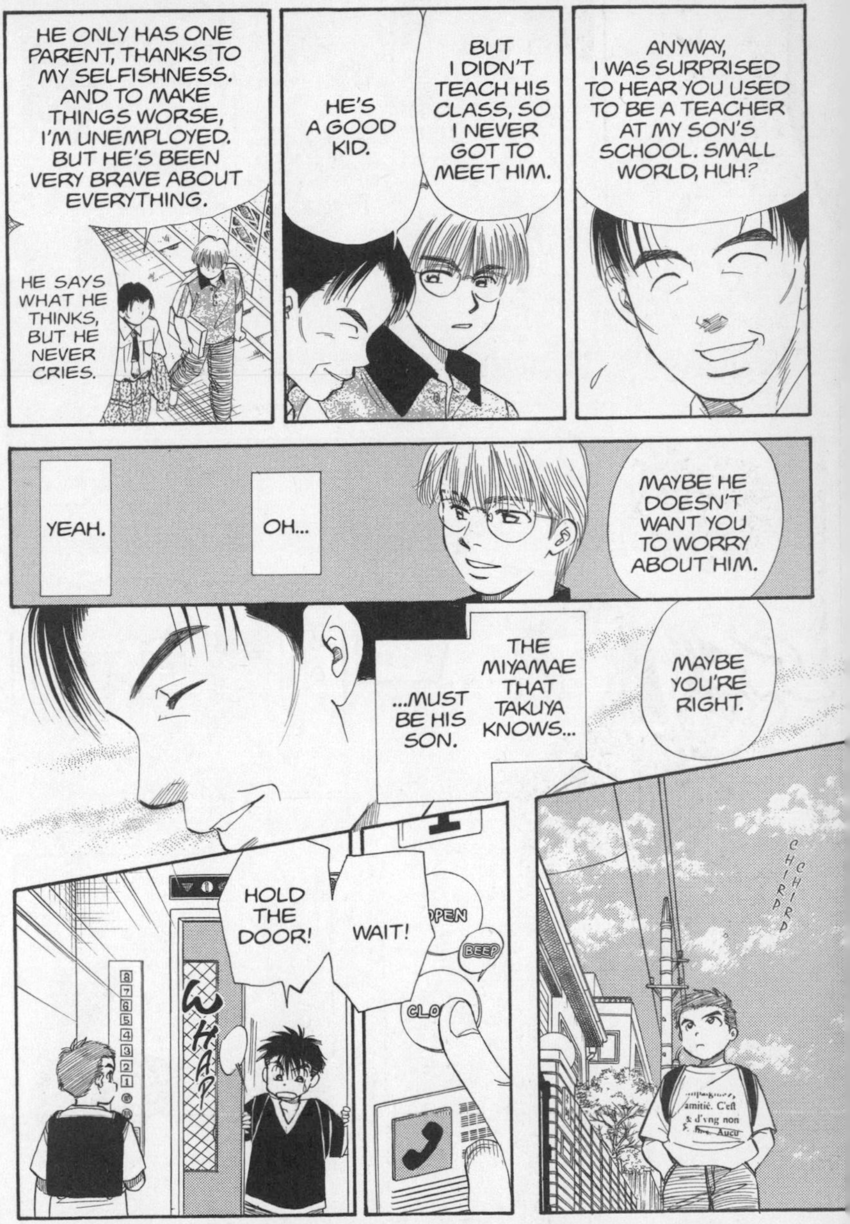
ANYWAY, I WAS SURPRISED TO HEAR YOU USED TO BE A TEACHER AT MY SON'S SCHOOL. SMALL WORLD, HUH?
BUT I DIDN'T TEACH HIS CLASS, SO I NEVER GOT TO MEET HIM.
HE'S A GOOD KID.
HE ONLY HAS ONE PARENT, THANKS TO MY SELFISHNESS. AND TO MAKE THINGS WORSE, I'M UNEMPLOYED. BUT HE'S BEEN VERY BRAVE ABOUT EVERYTHING.
HE SAYS WHAT HE THINKS, BUT HE NEVER CRIES.
MAYBE HE DOESN'T WANT YOU TO WORRY ABOUT HIM.
OH...
YEAH.
MAYBE YOU'RE RIGHT.
THE MIYAMAE THAT TAKUYA KNOWS...
...MUST BE HIS SON.
CHIRP CHIRP
OPEN
BEEP
WAIT!
HOLD THE DOOR!
WHAP

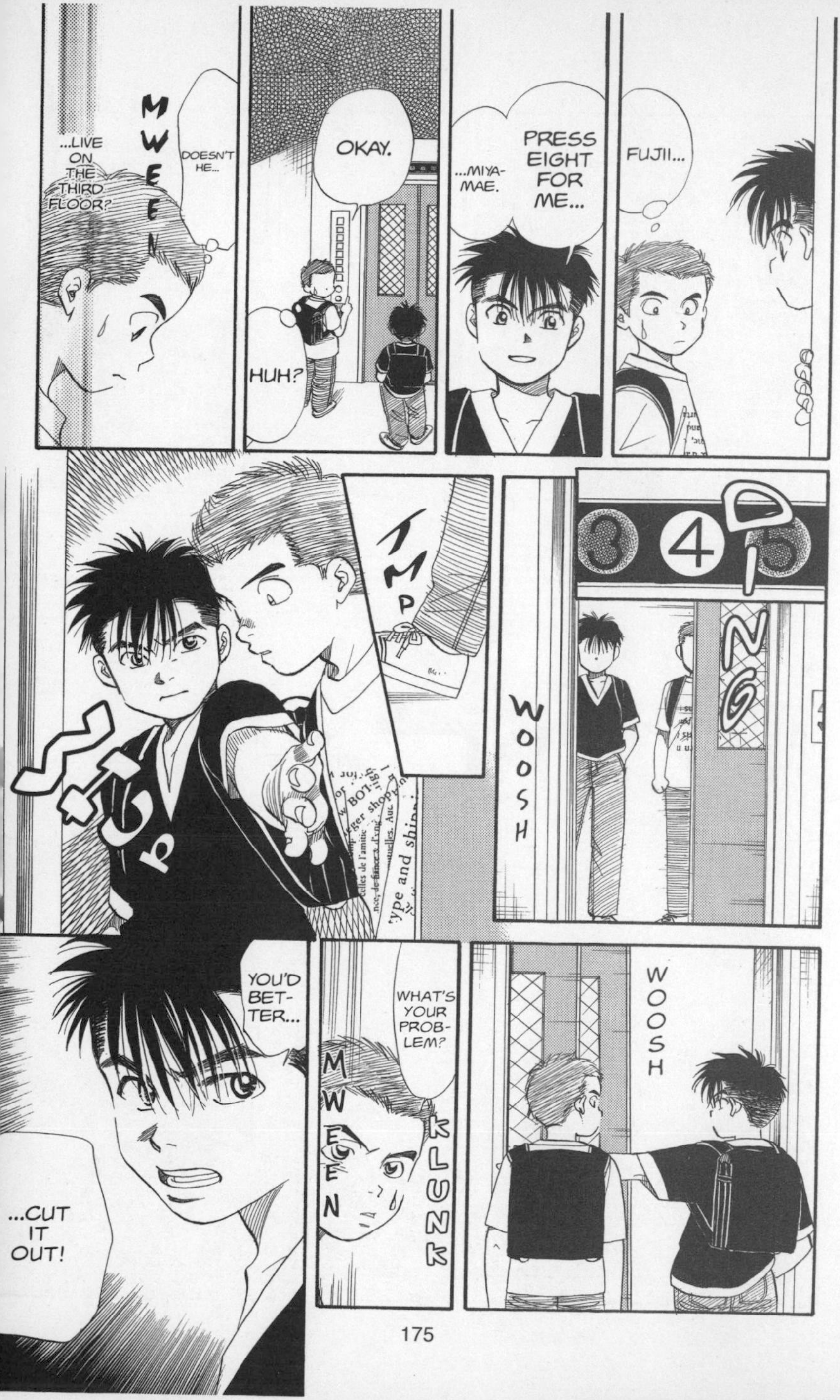

FUJII...
PRESS EIGHT FOR ME...
...MIYA-MAE.
OKAY.
HUH?
DOESN'T HE...
MWEEN
...LIVE ON THE THIRD FLOOR?
DING
WOOSH
TMP
WOOSH
WHAT'S YOUR PROB-LEM?
KLUNK
MWEEN
YOU'D BET-TER...
...CUT IT OUT!

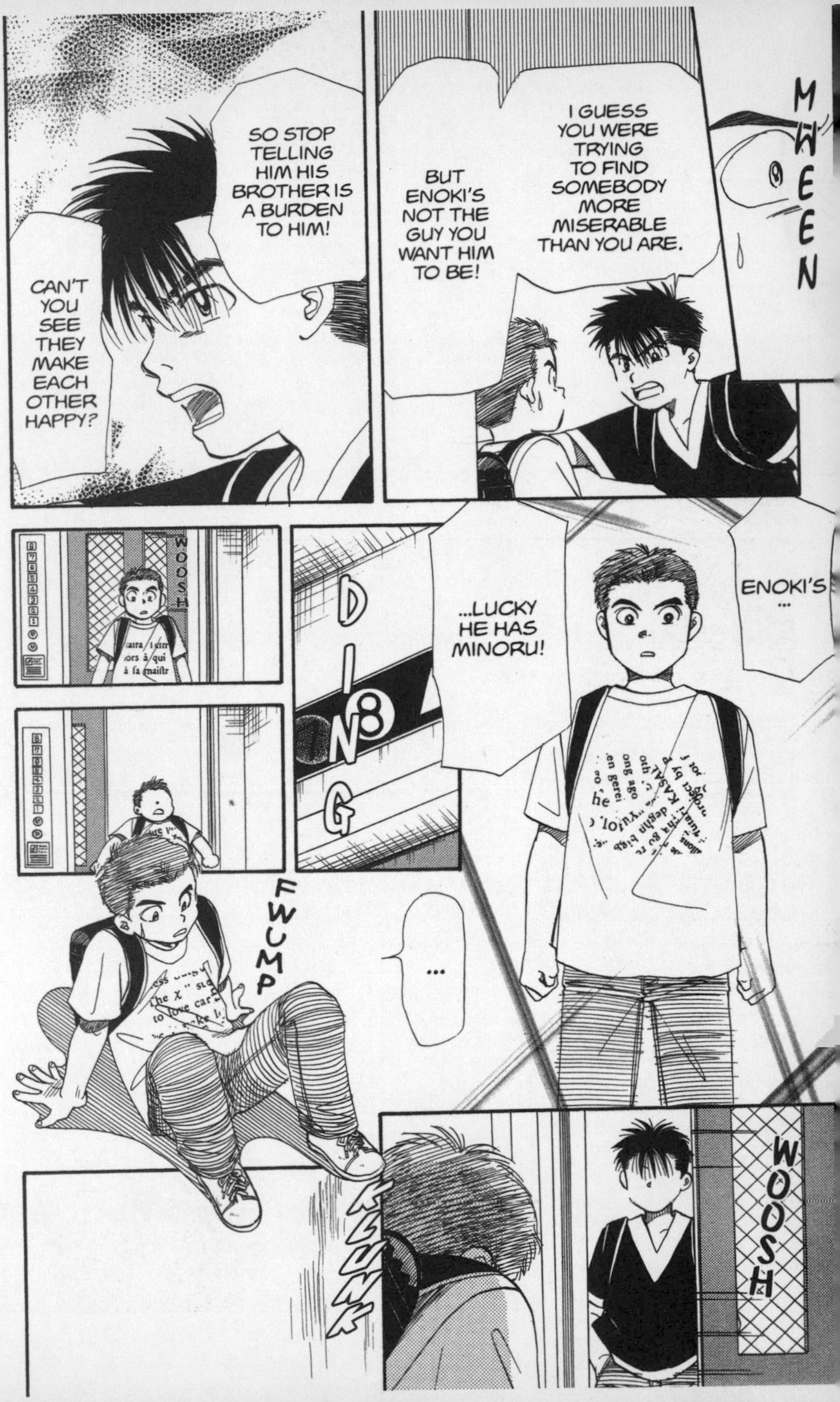
MWEEN
I GUESS YOU WERE TRYING TO FIND SOMEBODY MORE MISERABLE THAN YOU ARE.
BUT ENOKI'S NOT THE GUY YOU WANT HIM TO BE!
SO STOP TELLING HIM HIS BROTHER IS A BURDEN TO HIM!
CAN'T YOU SEE THEY MAKE EACH OTHER HAPPY?
ENOKI'S ...
...LUCKY HE HAS MINORU!
...
DING
8
WOOSH
FWUMP
WOOSH

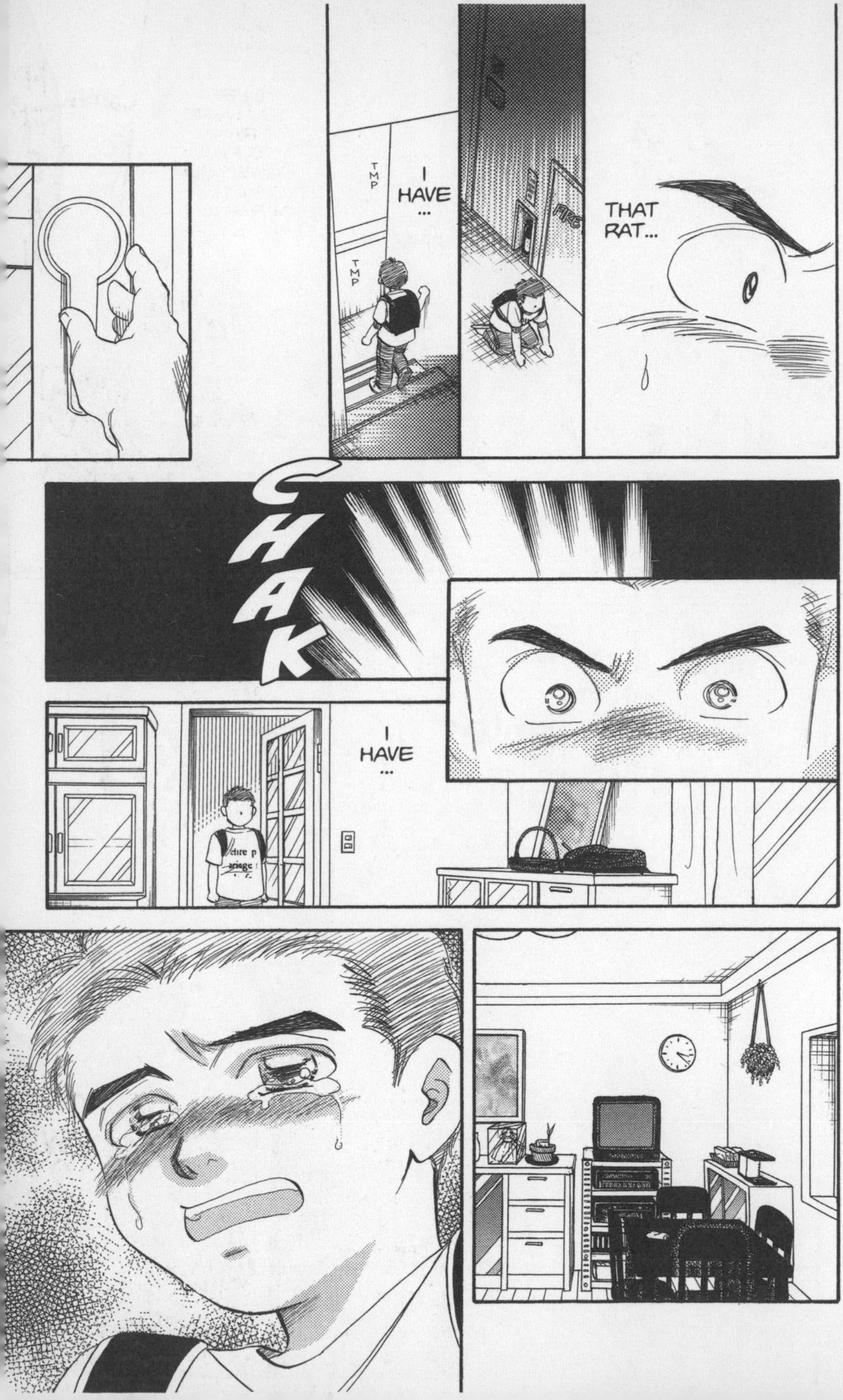
THAT RAT...
I HAVE ...
TMP
TMP
CHAK
I HAVE ...

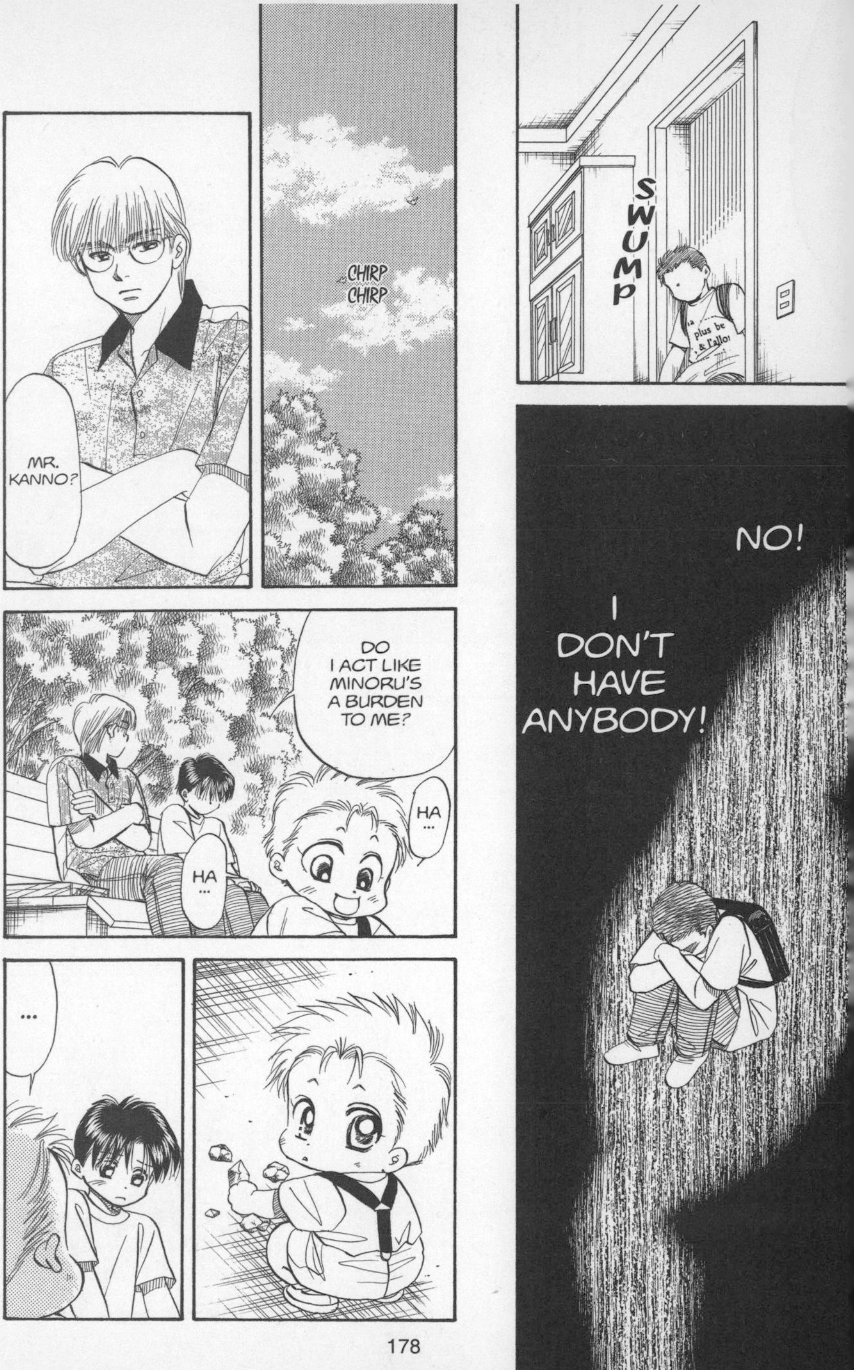
SWUMP
NO!
I DON'T HAVE ANYBODY!
CHIRP CHIRP
MR. KANNO?
DO I ACT LIKE MINORU'S A BURDEN TO ME?
HA...
HA...
...

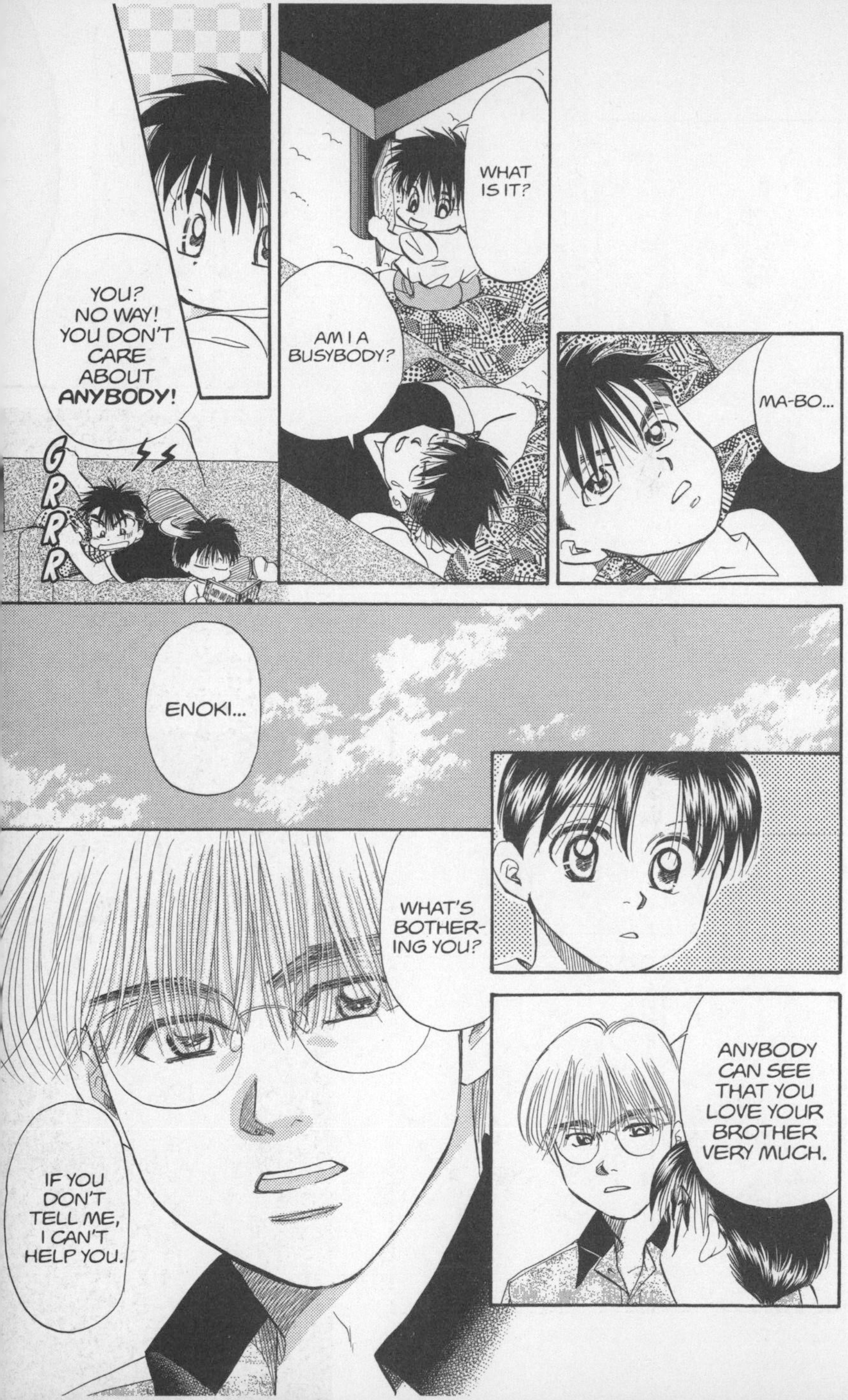
WHAT IS IT?
AM I A BUSYBODY?
YOU? NO WAY! YOU DON'T CARE ABOUT **ANYBODY**!
GRRR
MA-BO...
ENOKI...
WHAT'S BOTHERING YOU?
ANYBODY CAN SEE THAT YOU LOVE YOUR BROTHER VERY MUCH.
IF YOU DON'T TELL ME, I CAN'T HELP YOU.

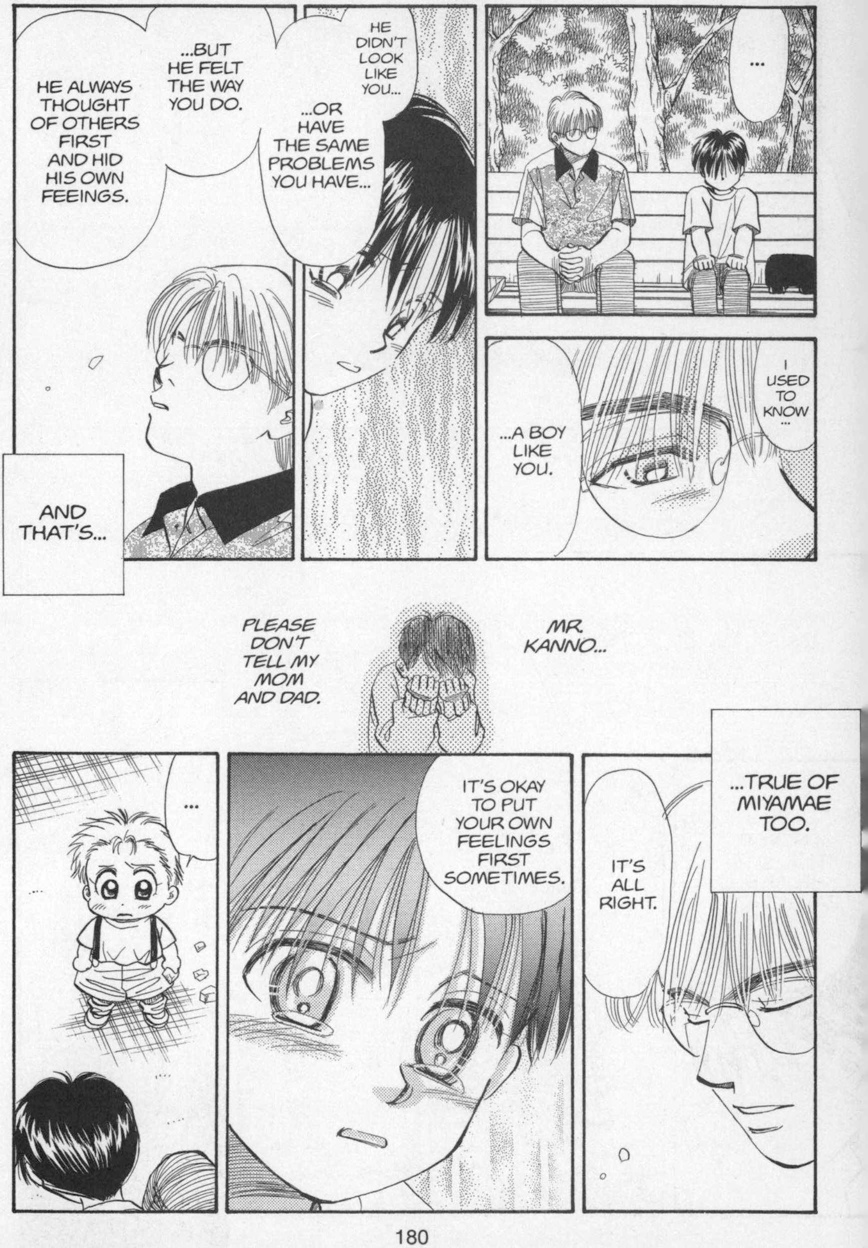
...
I USED TO KNOW...
...A BOY LIKE YOU.
HE DIDN'T LOOK LIKE YOU...
...OR HAVE THE SAME PROBLEMS YOU HAVE...
...BUT HE FELT THE WAY YOU DO.
HE ALWAYS THOUGHT OF OTHERS FIRST AND HID HIS OWN FEEINGS.
AND THAT'S...
MR. KANNO...
PLEASE DON'T TELL MY MOM AND DAD.
...TRUE OF MIYAMAE TOO.
IT'S ALL RIGHT.
IT'S OKAY TO PUT YOUR OWN FEELINGS FIRST SOMETIMES.
...

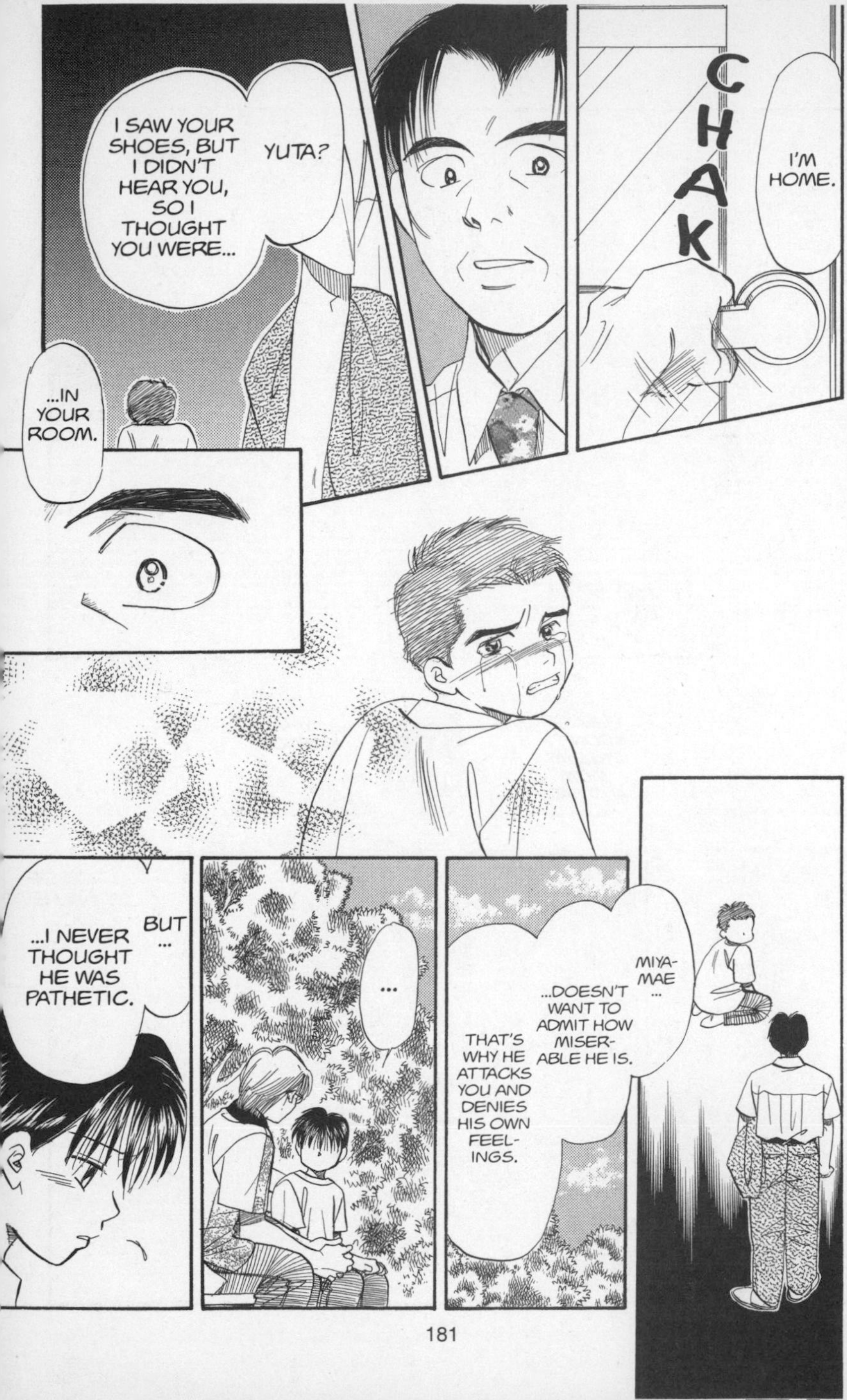
CHAK
I'M HOME.
YUTA?
I SAW YOUR SHOES, BUT I DIDN'T HEAR YOU, SO I THOUGHT YOU WERE...
...IN YOUR ROOM.
MIYA-MAE ...
...DOESN'T WANT TO ADMIT HOW MISER-ABLE HE IS.
THAT'S WHY HE ATTACKS YOU AND DENIES HIS OWN FEEL-INGS.
...
BUT ...
...I NEVER THOUGHT HE WAS PATHETIC.

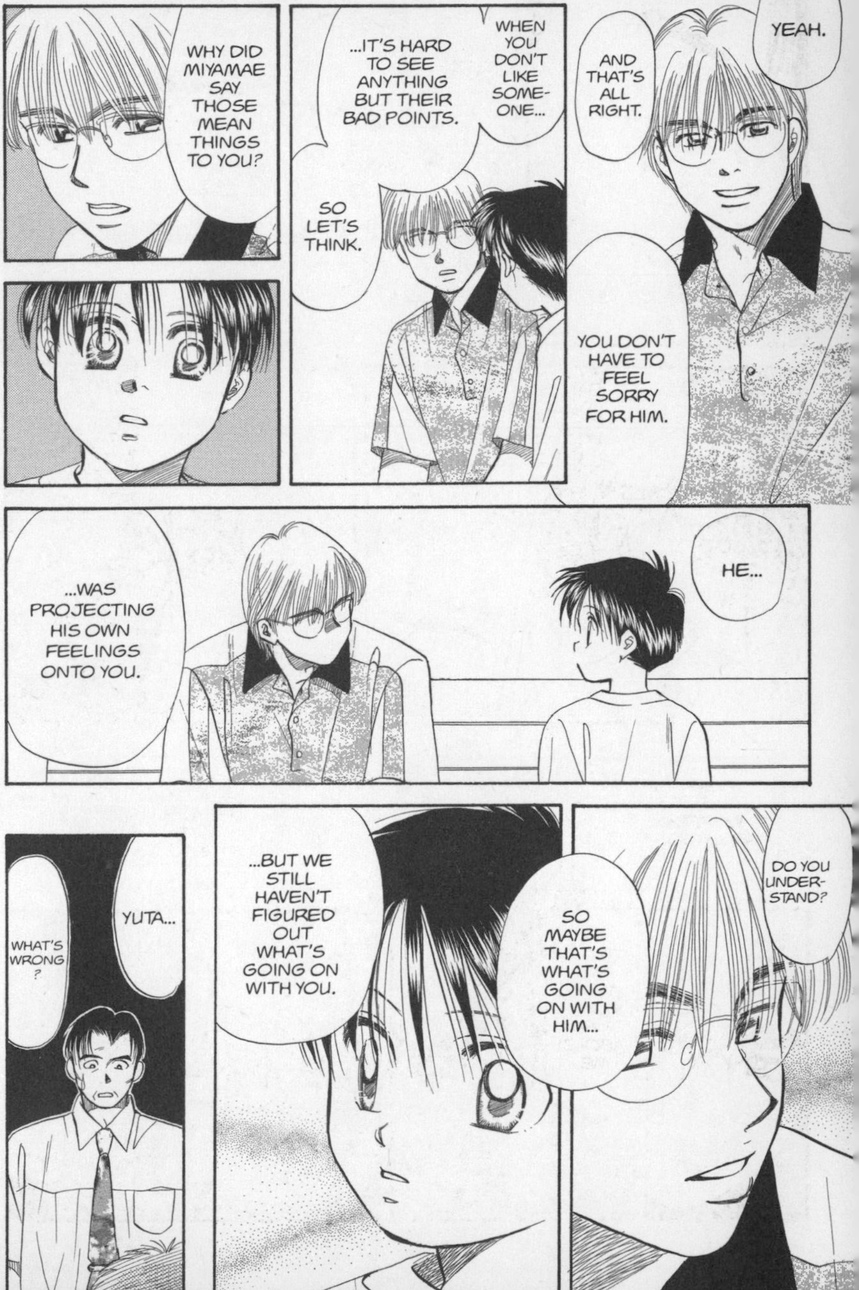
YEAH.
AND THAT'S ALL RIGHT.
YOU DON'T HAVE TO FEEL SORRY FOR HIM.
WHEN YOU DON'T LIKE SOME-ONE...
...IT'S HARD TO SEE ANYTHING BUT THEIR BAD POINTS.
SO LET'S THINK.
WHY DID MIYAMAE SAY THOSE MEAN THINGS TO YOU?
HE...
...WAS PROJECTING HIS OWN FEELINGS ONTO YOU.
DO YOU UNDER-STAND?
SO MAYBE THAT'S WHAT'S GOING ON WITH HIM...
...BUT WE STILL HAVEN'T FIGURED OUT WHAT'S GOING ON WITH YOU.
YUTA...
WHAT'S WRONG?

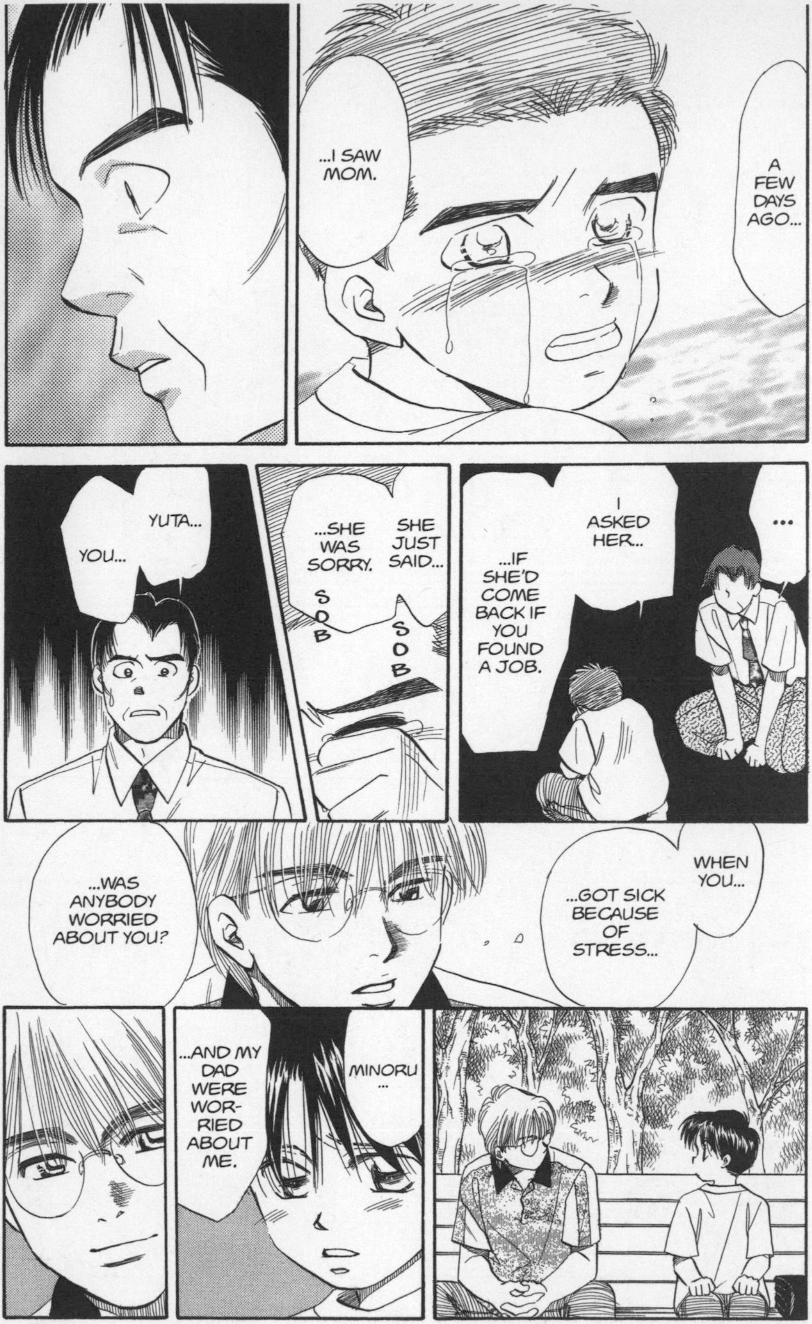
A FEW DAYS AGO...
...I SAW MOM.
...
I ASKED HER...
...IF SHE'D COME BACK IF YOU FOUND A JOB.
SHE JUST SAID...
...SHE WAS SORRY.
SOB
SOB
YUTA...
YOU...
WHEN YOU...
...GOT SICK BECAUSE OF STRESS...
...WAS ANYBODY WORRIED ABOUT YOU?
MINORU...
...AND MY DAD WERE WOR-RIED ABOUT ME.

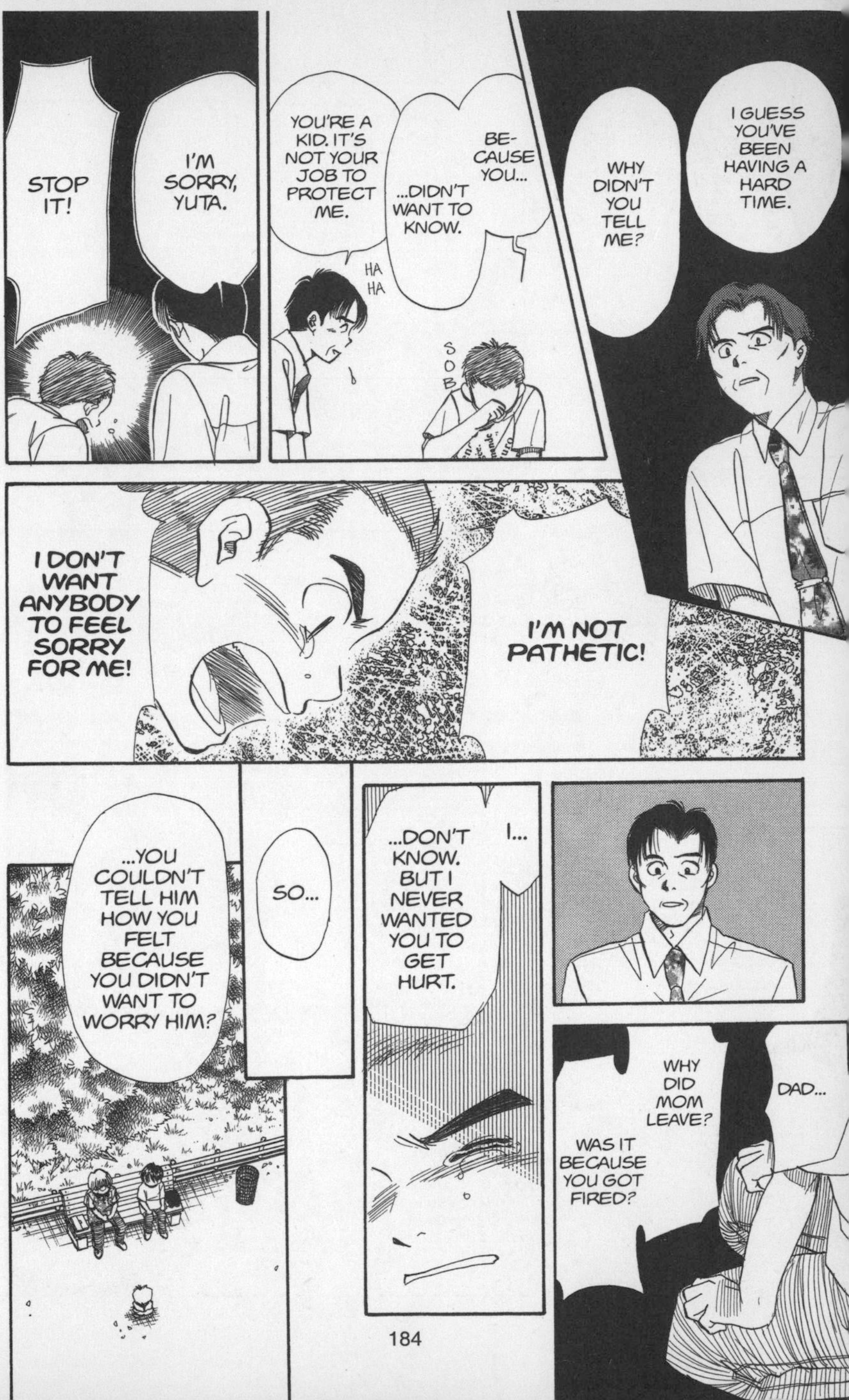
I GUESS YOU'VE BEEN HAVING A HARD TIME.
WHY DIDN'T YOU TELL ME?
BE-CAUSE YOU...
...DIDN'T WANT TO KNOW.
YOU'RE A KID. IT'S NOT YOUR JOB TO PROTECT ME.
HA HA
SOB
I'M SORRY, YUTA.
STOP IT!
I'M NOT PATHETIC!
I DON'T WANT ANYBODY TO FEEL SORRY FOR ME!
DAD...
WHY DID MOM LEAVE?
WAS IT BECAUSE YOU GOT FIRED?
I...
...DON'T KNOW. BUT I NEVER WANTED YOU TO GET HURT.
SO...
...YOU COULDN'T TELL HIM HOW YOU FELT BECAUSE YOU DIDN'T WANT TO WORRY HIM?

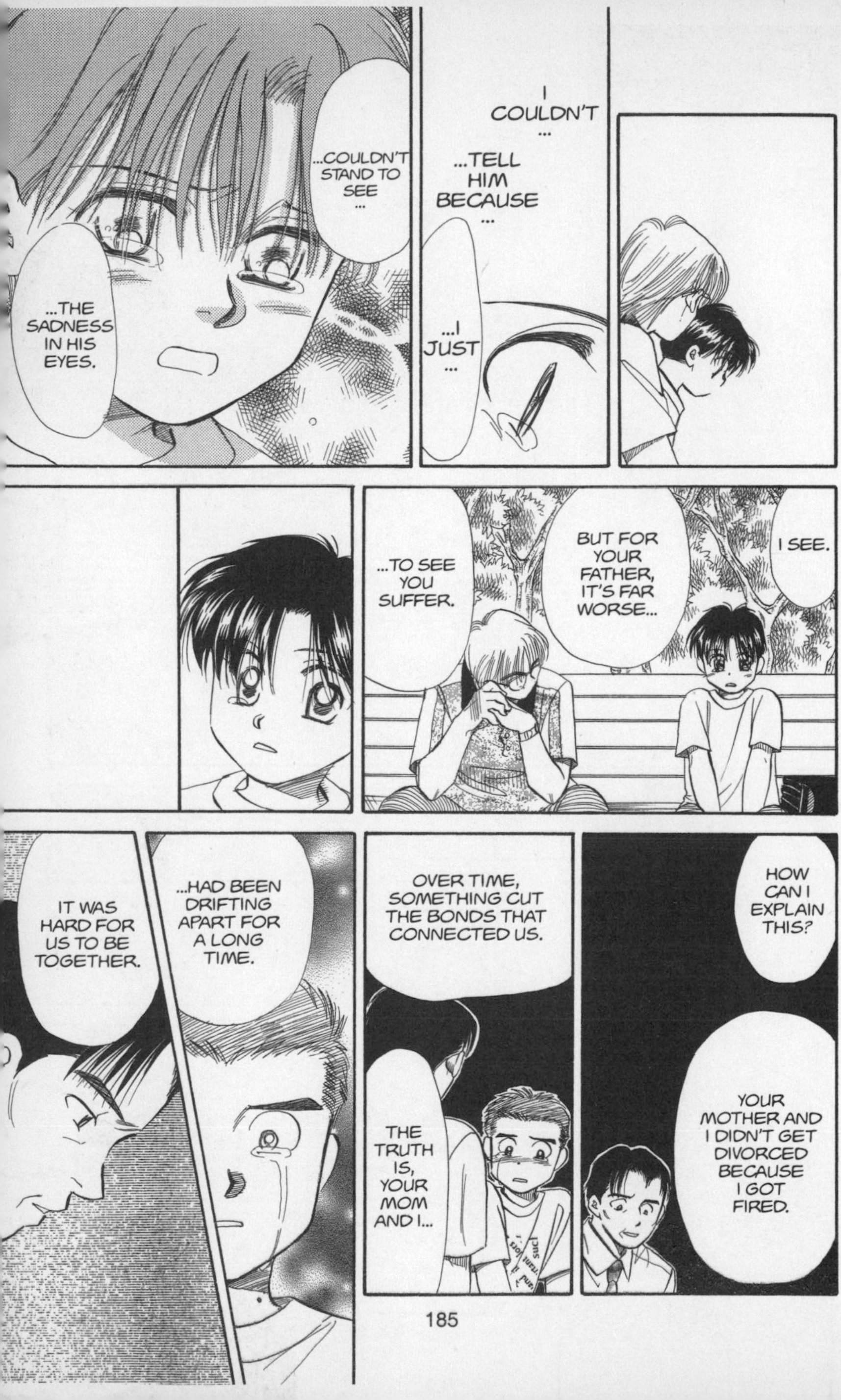
I COULDN'T ...
...TELL HIM BECAUSE ...
...I JUST ...
...COULDN'T STAND TO SEE ...
...THE SADNESS IN HIS EYES.
I SEE.
BUT FOR YOUR FATHER, IT'S FAR WORSE...
...TO SEE YOU SUFFER.
HOW CAN I EXPLAIN THIS?
YOUR MOTHER AND I DIDN'T GET DIVORCED BECAUSE I GOT FIRED.
OVER TIME, SOMETHING CUT THE BONDS THAT CONNECTED US.
THE TRUTH IS, YOUR MOM AND I...
...HAD BEEN DRIFTING APART FOR A LONG TIME.
IT WAS HARD FOR US TO BE TOGETHER.

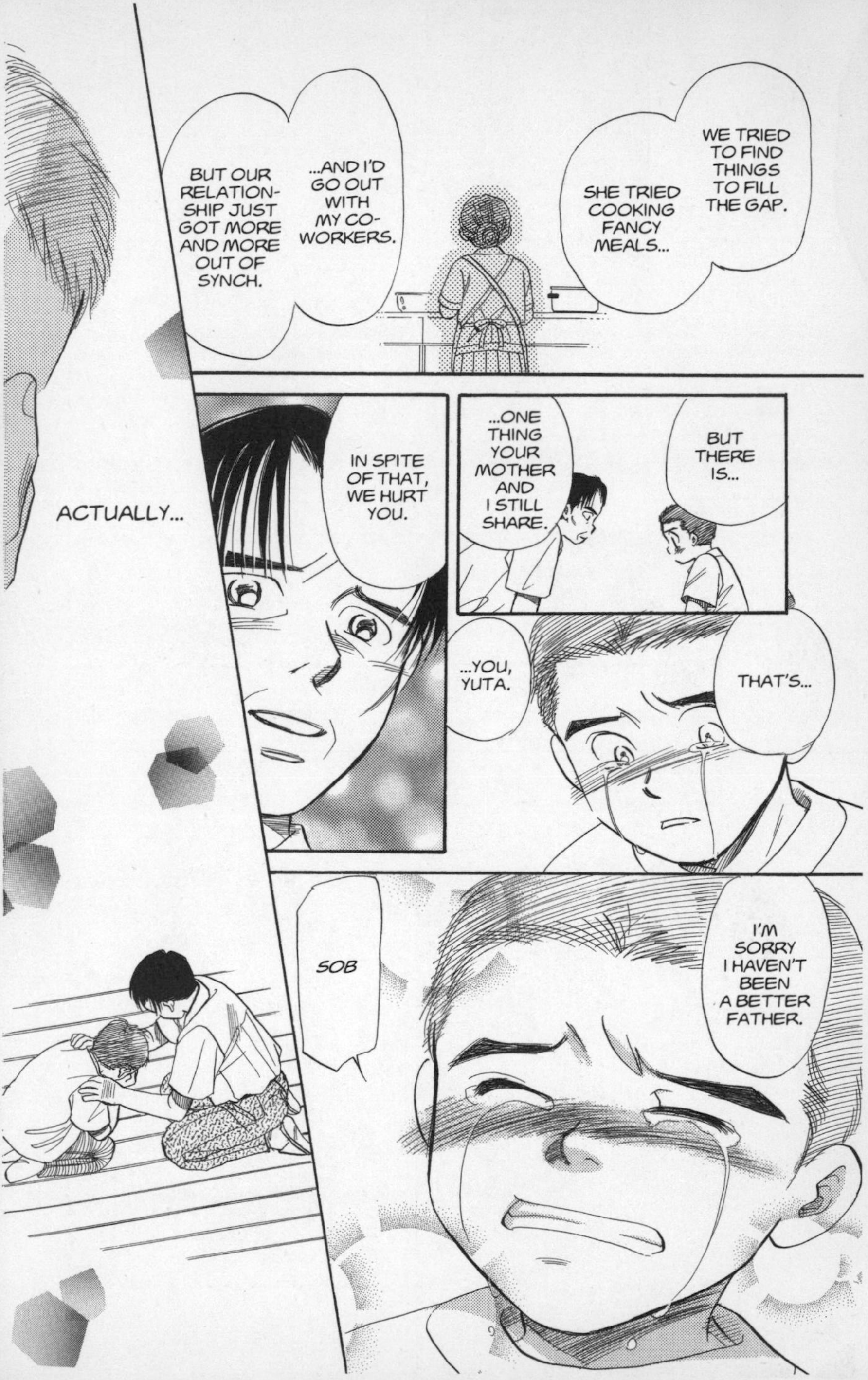
WE TRIED TO FIND THINGS TO FILL THE GAP.
SHE TRIED COOKING FANCY MEALS...
...AND I'D GO OUT WITH MY CO-WORKERS.
BUT OUR RELATION-SHIP JUST GOT MORE AND MORE OUT OF SYNCH.
BUT THERE IS...
...ONE THING YOUR MOTHER AND I STILL SHARE.
THAT'S...
...YOU, YUTA.
IN SPITE OF THAT, WE HURT YOU.
I'M SORRY I HAVEN'T BEEN A BETTER FATHER.
SOB
ACTUALLY...

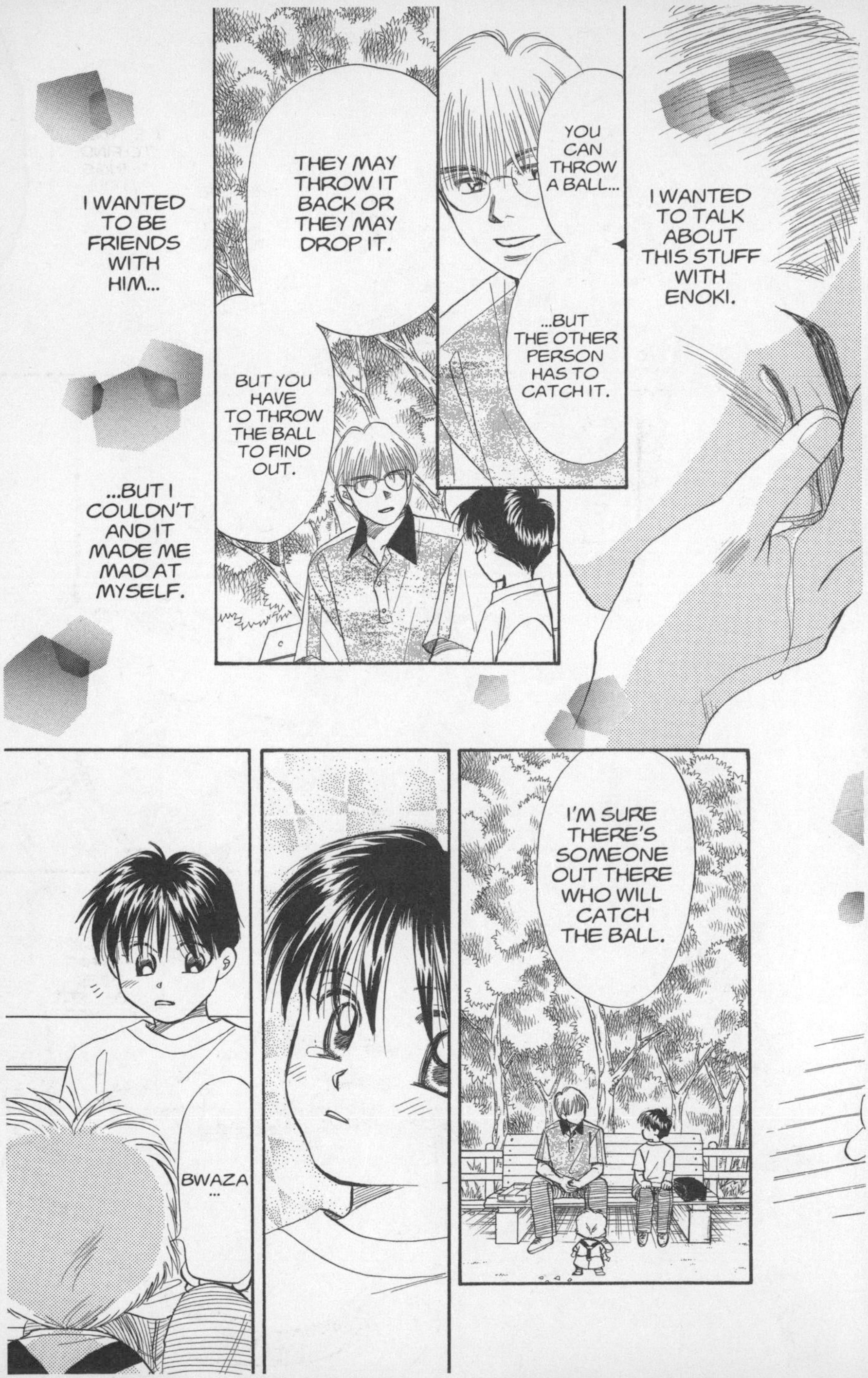
I WANTED TO TALK ABOUT THIS STUFF WITH ENOKI.
YOU CAN THROW A BALL...
...BUT THE OTHER PERSON HAS TO CATCH IT.
THEY MAY THROW IT BACK OR THEY MAY DROP IT.
BUT YOU HAVE TO THROW THE BALL TO FIND OUT.
I WANTED TO BE FRIENDS WITH HIM...
...BUT I COULDN'T AND IT MADE ME MAD AT MYSELF.
I'M SURE THERE'S SOMEONE OUT THERE WHO WILL CATCH THE BALL.
BWAZA ...

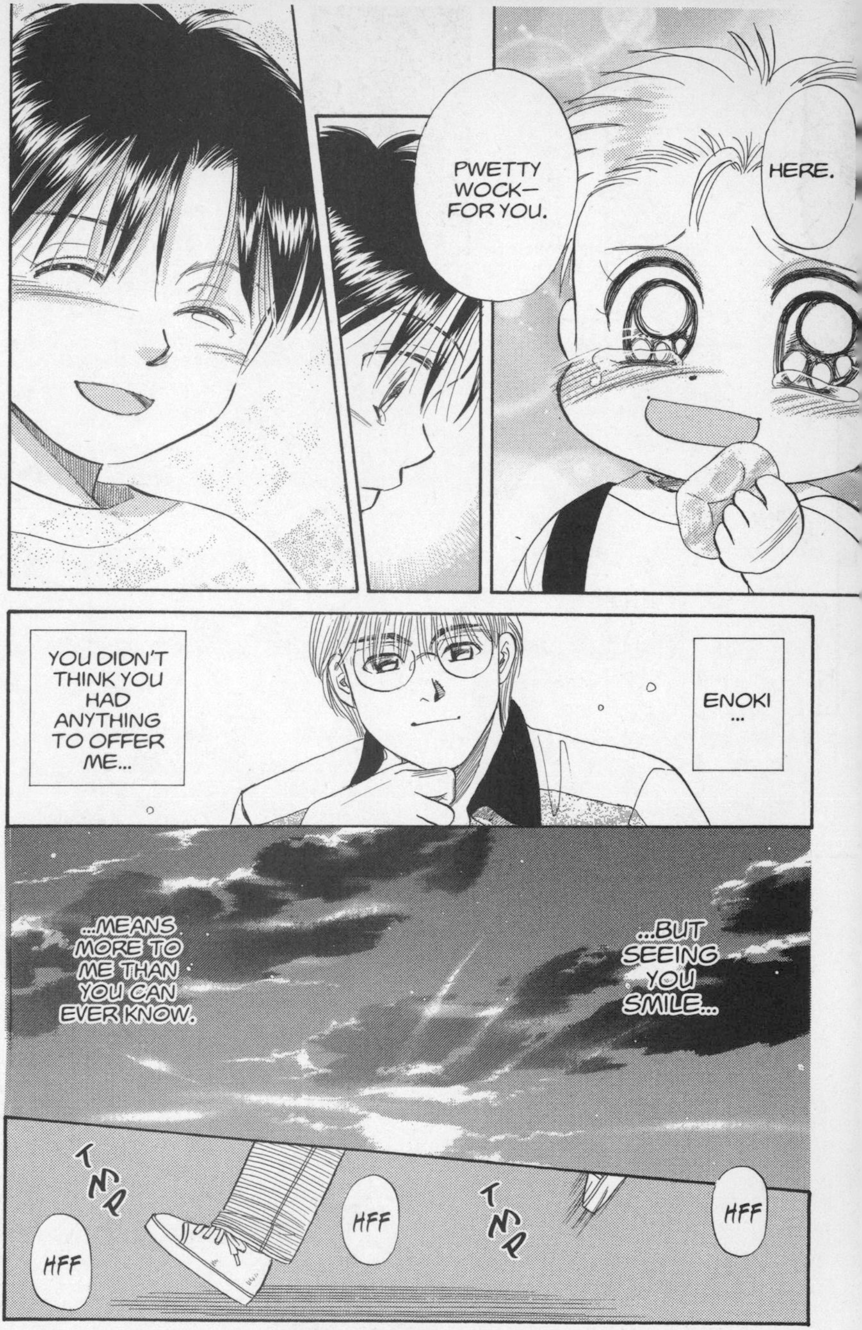
HERE.
PWETTY WOCK— FOR YOU.
ENOKI ...
YOU DIDN'T THINK YOU HAD ANYTHING TO OFFER ME...
...BUT SEEING YOU SMILE...
...MEANS MORE TO ME THAN YOU CAN EVER KNOW.
HFF
TMP
HFF
TMP
HFF

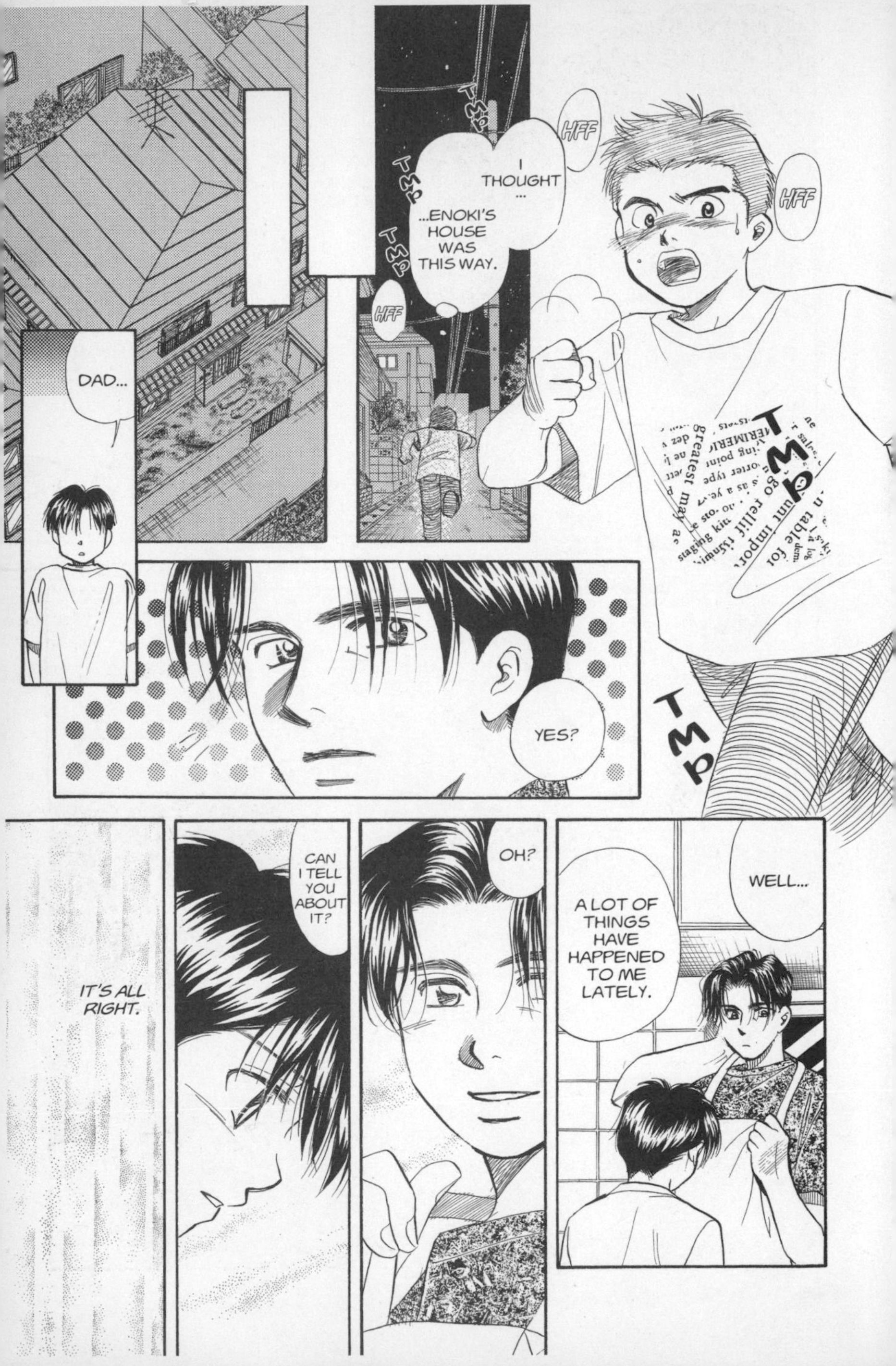
HFF
HFF
TMP
TMP
TMP
I THOUGHT ...
...ENOKI'S HOUSE WAS THIS WAY.
TMP
HFF
DAD...
YES?
WELL...
A LOT OF THINGS HAVE HAPPENED TO ME LATELY.
OH?
CAN I TELL YOU ABOUT IT?
IT'S ALL RIGHT.

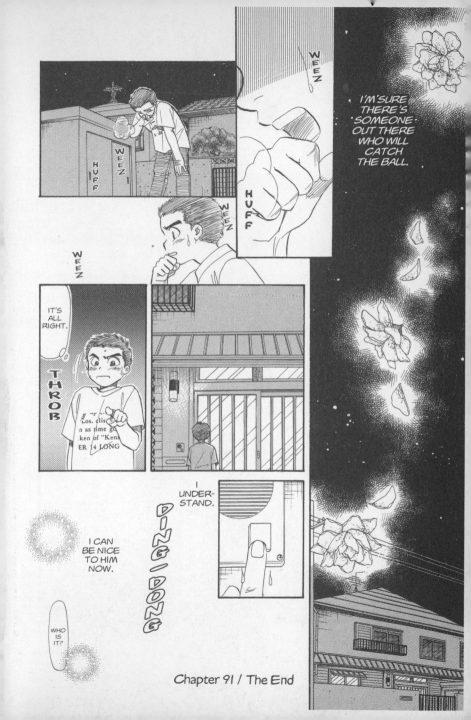

WEEZ

I'M SURE... THERE'S SOMEONE OUT THERE WHO WILL CATCH THE BALL.

WEEZ

HUFF

HUFF

WEEZ

WEEZ

WEEZ

IT'S ALL RIGHT.

THROB

Los, clis... a as time g ken of "Ken ER 4 LONG

I UNDER- STAND.

DING DONG

I CAN BE NICE TO HIM NOW.

WHO IS IT?

Chapter 91 / The End

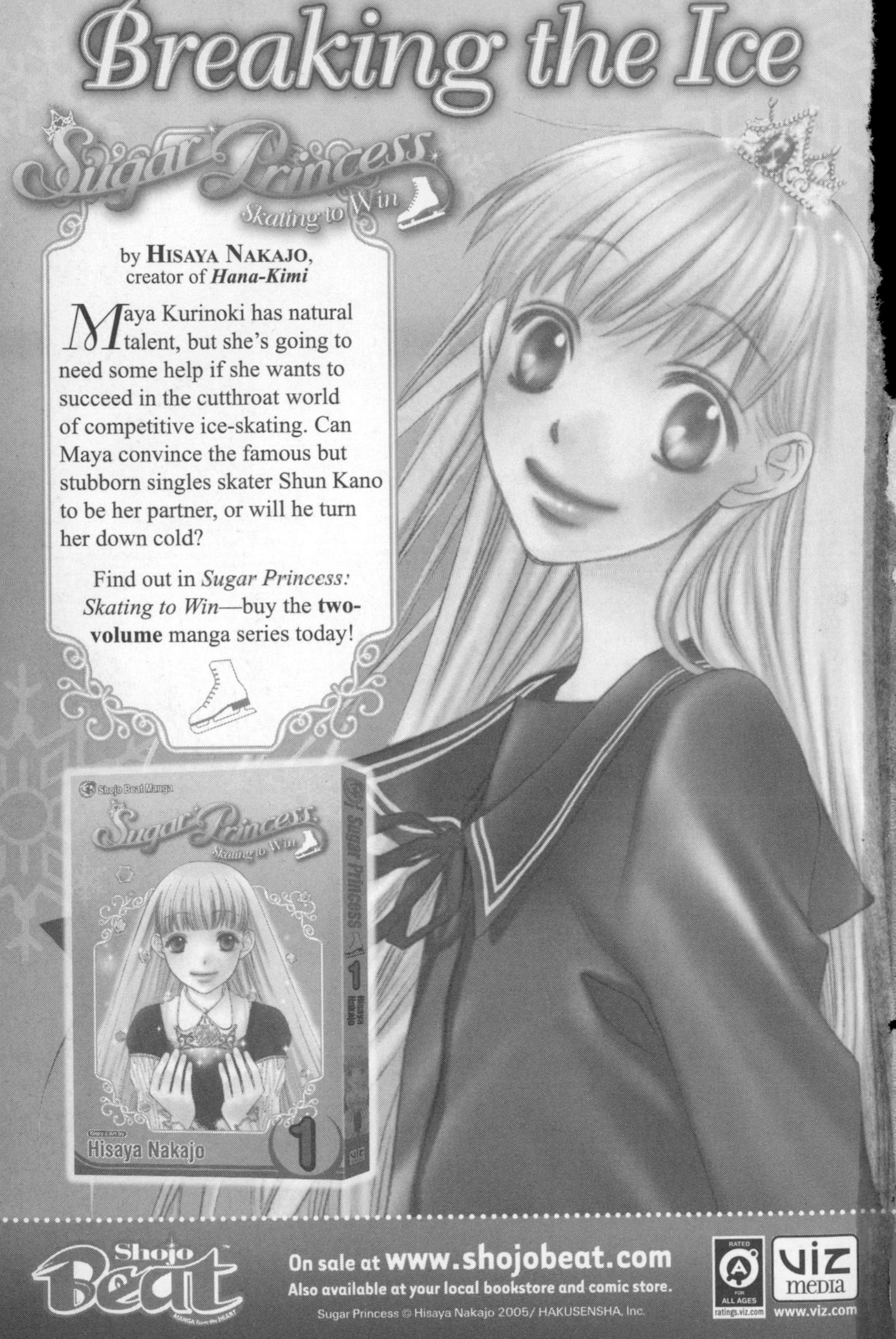
Breaking the Ice
Sugar Princess
Skating to Win
by HISAYA NAKAJO,
creator of Hana-Kimi
Maya Kurinoki has natural talent, but she's going to need some help if she wants to succeed in the cutthroat world of competitive ice-skating. Can Maya convince the famous but stubborn singles skater Shun Kano to be her partner, or will he turn her down cold?
Find out in Sugar Princess: Skating to Win—buy the two-volume manga series today!
Shojo Beat Manga
Sugar Princess
Skating to Win
Hisaya Nakajo
1
Shojo Beat
On sale at www.shojobeat.com
Also available at your local bookstore and comic store.
Sugar Princess © Hisaya Nakajo 2005/ HAKUSENSHA, Inc.
RATED A FOR ALL AGES
ratings.viz.com
VIZ media
www.viz.com